Fernando Wood. Courtesy of the National Archives.

FERNANDO WOOD

FERNANDO WOOD

A Political Biography

JEROME MUSHKAT

THE KENT STATE UNIVERSITY PRESS
Kent, Ohio, and London, England

To Barbara

© 1990 by The Kent State University Press, Kent, Ohio 44242
All rights reserved
Library of Congress Catalog Card Number 90-4486
ISBN 0-87338-413-X
Manufactured in the United States of America

Library of Congress Cataloging-in-Publication Data

Mushkat, Jerome.
    Fernando Wood: a political biography / Jerome Mushkat.
        p.   cm.
    Includes bibliographical references.
    ISBN 0-87338-413-X (alk. paper) ∞
    1. Wood, Fernando, 1812–1881. 2. Mayors–New York (N.Y.)–
Biography. 3. Legislators–United States–Biography. 4. United
States. Congress. House–Biography. 5. New York (N.Y.)–Politics
and government–To 1898. 6. United States–Politics and
government–1865–1900.   I. Title
F128.44.W8713   1990
973.5'092–dc20
[B]

                                                          90-4486
                                                          CIP

British Library Cataloging-in-Publication data are available.

CONTENTS

PREFACE

THE biography of Fernando Wood, a three-time mayor of New York City and a nine-term congressman, is in many ways a microcosm of national life, urban developments, and Democratic party operations during the nineteenth century.

Despite his achievements, Wood seems notable for the wrong reasons. According to the conventional interpretation, he was the model for scores of corrupt machine bosses, beginning with William M. Tweed of Tammany Hall. While mayor, Wood encouraged street gangs and class violence. His notion of making New York a free city republic on the eve of the Civil War was tantamount to treason. During the Civil War and Reconstruction periods, he was a disloyal Peace Democrat and racist whose activities proved that he deserved his notoriety.

This view is debatable at best and obscures Wood's real significance. An understanding of the man begins with the three goals—money, respectability, and power—that obsessed him. After achieving material success at a fairly young age in the best tradition of the self-made man, he turned to politics as a natural extension of his drives. Over the course of a controversial career that electrified generations of Americans for nearly fifty years, Wood followed a consistent ideology rooted in Jacksonianism and the equalitarian politics of the Locofocos that generated his values and policies.

When he began his first mayoral term in 1855, multiple unprecedented crises gripped the city government, its institutions, and its traditional leaders, casting doubt on the ability of people to govern themselves. Wood confronted the situation with bold, innovative reforms, far beyond the scope of previous mayors. In the process, he created several unique advances in the art of governing cities. He was New York's first modern mayor, a prescient city builder whose proposed improvements in the quality of urban life anticipated several of the divergent strands that formed the later and often contradictory Progressive Movement. He championed the interest of the working class and immigrants, and sought to

avoid incipient class conflict by urging businessmen to develop a social conscience that placed human rights over property rights. At the same time, Wood
was a prototypical professional politician, replacing the older elite that had considered public service a temporary civic duty. As a political organizer, he laid the
basis for constructing a political machine, headed by a fresh type of centralized
leader, the city boss. Moreover, Wood was a businessman's mayor. He stimulated a new form of municipal mercantilism to ensure steady economic growth
through capital investments in both physical and human resources and further
protected the city's vital trade links to the cotton-producing South.

Wood was also a key figure on the national scene. In the antebellum period, he
numbered among the most prominent Northern defenders of Southern institutions and slavery. During the Civil War, he stood in the vanguard of the Peace
Democratic movement as an articulate spokesman for reuniting the nation
through negotiation and compromise. His mark on his era became even more
pronounced when the war drew to a close. Although a reactionary during the initial stages of Congressional Reconstruction, Wood's basic quarrel with Republicans centered on the interpretation and application of traditional Democratic
principles.

By 1871, Wood made his peace with these issues. Instrumental in orchestrating the party's adoption of the New Departure, he urged fellow Democrats to
drop racial questions for economic ones. In his mind, Wood believed that the
Democracy had survived the war and its consequences, but faced the new challenge of justifying that survival and facing the future. He pleaded with the
Democracy to restore itself as a positive force in modern American life around
traditional ideological principles, particularly Locofocoism and its stress on equal
rights for all, special privileges to none. In doing so, he redirected the party back
to its traditional free-market policies based on natural laws that regulated the marketplace, flow of money, and international trade.

Although Wood was a Democratic conservative, he was neither a defender of
the status quo nor a politician who spent his time on the petty spoils and partisanship that supposedly typified the Gilded Age. By updating Democratic programs, he spearheaded the ideas that shaped the Bourbon Democracy in the
1880s and beyond.

In offering a fresh assessment of Wood, I believe that he has suffered much in
the verdict of history because of the way historians reconstruct the past. His foes
left behind voluminous and often biased manuscripts and newspapers. In contrast, he was secretive when he wrote and careless in keeping his own correspondence. As for his supporters, most were from the anonymous masses who left
few formal records, or published newspapers with short runs and incomplete
files. Because of these problems, I searched through numerous collections and
newspapers. All the same, Wood's inner life remains what he wished, private and

rather reclusive. I can only speculate about many of his motives and goals. Even the most friendly biographers work against great odds because they know him primarily as his enemies described him. Thus, this biography is a political biography, not a study of the total man. As a result, when I consider the evidence solid, I make conclusions; when I consider the evidence soft, I offer educated guesses; and when I consider the evidence equivocal, I present both sides.

My basic thesis is that Wood was a combination of high ideals and deep moral flaws. I do not deny his shortcomings, but I reject the idea that he was a failure or that his career was insignificant. I realize that the pitfall in any biography is the tendency to lose critical judgment and become an apologist. It is difficult, I admit, to work on such a study without developing some sort of affinity for that person. I have tried not to let sympathy outweigh scholarship. Yet in the final analysis, Wood's total career reveals an extraordinary man who left his stamp on New York and the United States in a variety of unacknowledged ways.

When I began this biography of Fernando Wood, I did not anticipate that the project would require ten years of travel, research, and writing, with much of the time devoted to locating his letters in numerous manuscript depositories scattered throughout the United States. As a result, I owe a debt of gratitude to a large number of librarians, archivists, and historians who helped me find pertinent material. I wish to acknowledge their assistance and specifically thank the following for permission to quote material from their manuscript holdings: Special Collections, The Library, Bowdoin College, Brunswick, Maine; Special Collections, The John Hay Library, Brown University, Providence, Rhode Island; John A. Dix Papers, Rare Book and Manuscript Library, Butler Library, Columbia University, New York City; Department of Manuscripts and University Archives, John A. Olin Library, Cornell University, Ithaca, New York; Courtesy of the Trustees of the Haverhill Public Library, Special Collections Department, Haverhill, Massachusetts; The Historical Society of Pennsylvania, Philadelphia, Pennsylvania; The Houghton Library, Harvard University, Cambridge, Massachusetts; The Henry E. Huntington Library, San Marino, California; Manuscript Division, Courtesy of the Illinois Historical Society Library, Springfield, Illinois; Manuscript Division, The Library of Congress, Washington, D.C.; Anna E. Carroll Papers, Manuscripts Division, Maryland Historical Society Library, Baltimore, Maryland; Samuel J. Tilden Papers, Rare Books and Manuscript Division, The New York Public Library, Astor, Lenox and Tilden Foundations, New York City; Fernando Wood Papers (Personal Miscellaneous), Rare Books and Manuscript Division, The New York Public Library, Astor, Lenox and Tilden Foundations, New York City; Manuscript Division, New-York Historical Society, New York City; Special Collections Department, Van Pelt Library,

University of Pennsylvania, Philadelphia, Pennsylvania; Department of Rare Books and Special Collections, Rush Rhees Library, University of Rochester, Rochester, New York; Manuscript Department, Alderman Library, University of Virginia, Charlottesville, Virginia, and the Department of Archives, Virginia Historical Society, Richmond, Virginia. I also wish to thank the National Archives and Columbia University for permission to reproduce photographs of Fernando Wood. I also owe a special debt of gratitude to the University of Akron for generous interlibrary loan assistance and faculty research grants. Without compromising them, I am indebted to Professors Robert H. Jones and James F. Richardson for their thoughtful criticism and help. Above all, I thank my wife Barbara, my children Linda and Steven, and Ivan, my silent friend and companion, for their special understanding and patience as I made Fernando Wood a part of our family.

ONE

The Beginning

IN 1856, a curious publication appeared on the shelves of New York City bookstores. It was the biography of Fernando Wood, the city's "Model Mayor," in office barely fifteen months, but already the era's most controversial politician. Author Donald MacLeod portrayed Wood as a brilliant descendant of a respectable colonial family, a man with a deep sense of public service, destined for greatness, perhaps the presidency. But MacLeod was hardly objective. What the public did not know was that the "Model Mayor" had not only subsidized MacLeod, but had probably ghost-written substantial sections.[1]

MacLeod's stress on respectability, the idea that the Wood family had progressed until it touched the heroic with Fernando Wood, formed one of the mayor's obsessions. His compulsion revealed more than he realized. The Woods were actually not distinguished. They worked and died as ordinary people. But when a person became famous, his background became fertile ground for imaginary greatness. So it was with Fernando Wood. What he stressed about his heritage, however, reflected deep-seated needs, largely because many New Yorkers questioned his integrity, feared his megalomaniacal tendencies, and suspected he had his hand in the public till. Wood sought a more luminous image. He fabricated an eminent lineage and courted the public as a man of honor deserving of respect for his talents, achievements, and promise as a principled public man.[2]

Part of MacLeod's biography was accurate. The Wood line in America began around 1670 when Henry Wood, a Welsh Quaker and carpenter, arrived at Newport, Rhode Island, with his wife Hannah and four young children. In 1678, they moved to West Jersey, where he purchased seven hundred acres, including part of the future city of Camden, and built a homestead called Peashore fronting on Coopers Creek and the Delaware River. By the time of his death in 1694, Henry Wood numbered among the local gentry.[3]

Over the course of the next three generations, his descendants scattered, sparking a history of family decline that became Fernando Wood's true inheritance, and eventually owned little beyond the original site at Peashore. During those years, Henry Wood's offsprings were remarkable only in that they proved prolific breeders, as twenty-nine children were born by the 1740s, with Henrys, Benjamins, Williams, Zacharias, Isaacs, Hannahs, and Elizabeths appearing regularly with each successive generation.[4]

By the time that the third Henry Wood, Fernando's paternal grandfather, was born in 1758, the Woods were hardly a family of consequence. Yet this Henry Wood was different and fulfilled his grandson's requirements for prominent lineage. Standing over six feet tall and weighing nearly two hundred pounds, he formed his own company during the American Revolution and served as captain. Wounded at both Germantown and Yorktown, he became in his grandson's mind a fit ancestor to justify family eminence. Henry Wood also gave his grandson a less satisfactory heritage. The Society of Friends ousted him for breaking Quaker antimilitarist rules, and the lingering consequences of his wounds took their toll, eventually giving way to consumption. When his third child, Benjamin, Fernando's father, was born in 1784, the Woods had evidently sunk to the bottom of the economic ladder.[5]

Benjamin Wood, the fourth of his line to bear that name, spent his youth at Peashore. There, in 1807, he married Rebecca Lehmann, the strong-willed daughter of Henry Lehmann, a recent emigrant from Hamburg. Very little is known about the Lehmanns beyond Fernando Wood's recollection. He informed MacLeod that they came from a Prussian military background that included at least one general. While his claim was unsubstantiated, Henry Lehmann did serve in the revolutionary army and was also wounded at Yorktown.

Benjamin Wood had scant interest in hardscrabble farming. A year before his marriage, he had moved to the burgeoning city of Philadelphia and opened a small retail tobacco and cigar manufacturing business. Wood was ambitious and hardworking but lacked both the capital and practicality for success. During and after the War of 1812, he went heavily into debt speculating in wholesale dry goods. By the spring of 1819, he went bankrupt when the Second Bank of the United States reversed its easy credit-inflationist paper money policies and contracted currency. The resultant depression, his son later recalled, "swept off the merchants of the day," leaving Benjamin Wood, "one of the unfortunate victims," bankrupt. Details are vague at this point, but he apparently also suffered a nervous breakdown.[6]

So far, the Woods were similar to many other young striving families, long on hope but short on cash. In the accepted tradition of the Woods, Rebecca Wood was frequently pregnant. At regular intervals in her first thirteen years of marriage, she bore seven children, five sons and two daughters. Fernando Wood, her third son, was born on February 14, 1812, in Philadelphia.[7]

Fernando Wood's first conscious memories must have been of grim times. His father was a failure, a man with wrecked hopes. Following his collapse, he searched for new opportunities and health in a restless trek that took his family from Philadelphia to Shelbyville, Kentucky, then to New Orleans, to Havana, Cuba, and next to Charleston, South Carolina. Finally in 1821, his quest ended in New York City. With borrowed funds, he again opened a small tobacconist store.[8]

Little direct evidence exists to assess Benjamin Wood as a parent, or his psychological influence upon his son. Beset as he was by business and physical problems, he probably paid little attention to Fernando during his formative years. But for a few years, his store prospered slightly and he managed to stabilize his family's existence. He became an elder in the Presbyterian Market Street Church, and insisted that his children receive a proper education. This situation was short-lived. The store floundered by 1825 and ended in ruin four years later. Suffering another breakdown, Benjamin Wood moved on while his family remained behind. Impoverished and despondent, he died alone two years later in a Charleston boardinghouse.[9]

One can only guess about Fernando Wood's relationship with his father. If MacLeod can be believed, Fernando admired Benjamin Wood's enterprise, fashioned half-truths about his achievements, and, judging what was left unsaid, spent his life compensating for his father's shortcomings. Wood's hunger to romanticize his origins, his need to prove a history of family respectability, disguised unpalatable truths. From the evidence available, Wood's boyhood was a time of insecurity and tension, marred by a peripatetic father who was a poor provider.

As he matured, Fernando Wood was indeed influenced by Benjamin Wood, both directly and indirectly. Fernando apparently learned that security lay in economic success, that inflation was a fiscal bane, that life was a gamble where only winning counted, and that long odds were against him if he wanted to avoid his father's fate. The elder Wood probably provided his son with another belief, that he could rely only on himself. Also, he had to prove that his father was not a failure to justify his own self-image. In short, Benjamin Wood's legacy was essentially negative. His son's life, in many critical ways, was a direct reaction to everything that his father's was not.

As for his mother, Rebecca Wood remains a shadowy figure. Even in an age when women were rarely remembered beyond their immediate circle, she was remarkably indistinct considering that she survived her husband by thirty-two years and lived with her son until she died in 1863. Despite the paltry evidence, one can surmise that Rebecca was vital in shaping Fernando's personality. She held her family together as long as possible, and gave him the love and attention he must have craved. Evidently a genuinely pious person, she insisted upon his moral and spiritual training.[10] It is difficult to know how she affected his inner development as he matured. She presumably encouraged his single-minded drive for respectability and wealth. The fact that he, of all her children, took care of her for so long was beyond simple duty. She evidently solaced him in bad times, goaded him to press forward, and remained a visible reminder that he ought to become a better man than his father. In pleasing her, Fernando Wood pleased himself.

Throughout Wood's later political career, commentators would laud his organizational skills, clear executive abilities, and sharp native intelligence, backed by a physical force of extreme stamina and energy. Above all, they recognized his total self-reliance. Wood deviated from this pattern in one way. He trusted only one person, his brother Ben—a loyal comrade, a man of absolutes, who never questioned Fernando's greatness. What propelled Fernando Wood, then, was his enormous sense of self and desire to dominate others through what he considered his right to power, an almost dictatorial obsession to control men and events. Such attitudes gave him indomitable mental vitality, a psychological edge over others less secure or more introspective. Wood's psyche was a source of both his strengths and flaws. He simply never doubted himself. When adversaries termed him corrupt or overbearing, he defended his actions as logical extensions of his ego. Yet as events proved, he became his own worst enemy because his soaring ambitions blinded him to the sensibilities of others. Hostility left Wood unaffected. Men under attack, he explained years later to a fellow politician, sometimes "feel compelled to motion & reply to assaults. Before doing so they should take the advice of a cool-headed friend, who is exempt from the excitement of injury."[11]

Wood's physical appearance also worked to his advantage as he loomed large in the life of New York. He was tall for his era, standing slightly over six feet, and had an erect and slender figure. His face was sharply-drawn, with a strong chin, expressive eyes, sandy-brown hair, and a florid complexion. Even his enemies admitted he was "strikingly handsome." Wood took pride in his personal appearance and dressed faultlessly in subdued colors. People meeting him for the first time confessed that he "might be easily mistaken for a preacher." That demeanor carried over into public behavior. Physically, he was "emotionless" and projected "a dignity and reserve of manner that became him," appearing unruffled and "imperturbable as marble." The result was that Wood was not a backslapping, outgoing person, although he had immense charm when it suited his purposes. Instead, he usually seemed "cool," masked by a smile some interpreted as "sardonic." His personal habits were impeccable, probably because of his mother, as he "pursued a rigid course of abstinence from all indulgences to which the flesh is heir." For political reasons, he sometimes broke that rule and hoisted a "lager" among his German constituents. Otherwise, he followed "temperance principles, [and] habits of sobriety and self-control."[12] These traits shaped Wood as a man and as a politician. Above anything else, three drives dominated his life—respectability, money, and power.

Fernando Wood early in his political career. Courtesy of the Kilroe Collection, Rare Book and Manuscript Library, Columbia University.

Although unreliable data and suppositions obscure the first years of Wood's life, the details become more distinct in 1821 when his family arrived in New York City. At a private academy run by James Shea, a well-regarded Columbia College instructor, Wood evidently gained a worthwhile education, learning sufficient grammar and rhetoric to construct sound sentences, present ideas in a logical manner and with an economy in words, especially in public speeches, much different from the contemporary prolix style considered erudite.

Mathematics applied to accounting was the only other subject that apparently sparked his interest. Human experience, more than systematic academics, probably provided his most effective schooling. As an adult, he read a wide variety of newspapers and assimilated a surprising amount of wide-ranging information from public documents and reports.[13]

In 1825 at the age of thirteen, Wood went to work out of economic necessity. For the next six years, he drifted through a variety of low-paying jobs, eventually moving from New York to Richmond to learn the tobacco trade. A flirtation with the stage followed, and he toured the South as a fledgling actor, but it soon paled because he was too ambitious and the theater too disreputable. Somewhere in his travels, he met and fell in love with Anna W. Taylor, the only child of a moderately prosperous Philadelphia merchant. They were married on June 30, 1831. Wood was nineteen; his wife, sixteen.[14]

After seven years of wandering, Wood returned to New York City in 1832, eager to achieve his goals. Little came easy. His wife's small dowry helped, but his father's death left him responsible for his mother's care, along with that of three younger siblings, all under twelve. Wood must have welcomed the challenge. He was now ready to make money and become respectable.

When the young couple, along with his mother and her children, took up residence in an apartment at 140 Greene Street, the city's skyline was dominated by low wood-framed buildings, with an occasional church spire thrusting upward. Few streets were paved and most were no better than primitive lanes littered with garbage and manure. Public services, where they existed, were inadequate for the city's growing population of almost two hundred thousand, especially proper police and fire protection. But everywhere one looked, New Yorkers were in a frenetic quest for wealth. The city was most impressive on its waterfront, where ship upon ship symbolized frenzied commercialism. Such was the city in which Wood sought his fortune, along with thousands of other ambitious Americans and Europeans. Despite their disparate backgrounds, all were determined to maximize New York's material promise.

This growing metropolis rewarded those who had the ambition, ruthlessness, self-assurance, and keen entrepreneurship to grasp success. That promise became a reality for Fernando Wood. Few men, starting with little beyond native talent, eventually succeeded so well.[15]

Wood faced a hard climb. His first job with auctioneer Varnum P. Shattuck as a combination salesman and accountant ended three years later with the firm's bankruptcy. To make ends meet, his wife opened a wine and tobacconist store at 322 Pearl Street, where he labored evenings using skills his father had taught. Late in 1835, Wood's fortunes took an upswing. He became friends with Francis A. Secor, a minor Tammany Hall politician and businessman, and Joseph A. Scoville, a young merchant with good connections. With their aid, he borrowed money to start a chandlery firm. Two years later, Wood went under, a casualty of a general recession, with barely enough profits to pay his debts and start anew.[16]

It was a harsh blow, but fortunately his wife's remaining dowry was enough for a fresh start. In 1838, he opened a "grocery" or grog shop near the waterfront, at 133 Washington Street, under a short-term lease. Decades later, Scoville (writing under the pen name of Walter Barrett), who by then had broken with Wood, would claim that Wood had bilked illiterate longshoremen by overcharging for their drinks and billing them for unpurchased drams. Although these accusations flustered Wood and would become part of the city's folklore, little direct evidence supports Scoville's accusations. He may have made them out of spite or partisanship, and Wood's enemies chose to believe him. Wherever the truth lay, Wood had nothing to show despite his best efforts. At the end of 1839, he confessed to a creditor that heavy losses and disappointments had forced him "into a suspension."[17] Fernando Wood seemed destined to repeat his father's dreary fate.

In the meantime, however, Wood was a far more successful budding politician. While never explicit about his attraction to politics, he probably sought a political career as a natural extension of his inner drives. Moreover, it must have struck him as he looked at the city's power structure and the types of men who were officeholders, that businessmen basically ran New York for their own interests and set public policies which protected the propertied. Another reason, much more subjective, might have come into play. Wood craved public approval, perhaps as a morale booster, considering the streak of failure running deeply in his background.[18]

Wood began as an apprentice Jeffersonian-Jacksonian Democrat. His reasons are again unknown, but evidently he was attracted by the Democracy's ideology in defending traditional republican virtues, which he associated with the interests of small upwardly mobile urban entrepreneurs. Then, too, he despised the Whiggish Second Bank of the United States and its president, Nicholas Biddle, whom he held accountable for his father's plight. These grounds, in turn, dovetailed into his assumption that no man could rise in local politics unless associated with Tammany Hall.

During the mid-1830s, Wood was a journeyman learning his trade. Never impulsive nor impressionable, he cultivated William Leggett, the young Democratic editorial assistant on William Cullen Bryant's influential *New York Evening Post,* and made himself useful as a ward worker. His energy impressed party leaders. In 1836, they lifted him from obscurity by initiating him into the exclusive Tammany Society. The society pictured itself purely as a social and fraternal order with an incidental political association. Yet becoming a brother was highly prized among Democrats because it represented the first rung on the political ladder. While not every "brave" was a politician, the party's entire hierarchy came from its ranks.[19]

Almost immediately, Wood plunged into an intraparty struggle destined to complete his political training and mold his ideological principles. By 1835 President Andrew Jackson's war against Biddle's "Monster Bank," eastern financiers, and their political supporters sparked a national debate over currency and financial policies. Similar strains erupted in Tammany Hall. Conservative Bank Democrats, normally the Hall's dominant faction, supported Jackson but interpreted his program as an opportunity to create their own monied aristocracy through corporate monopolies, easy credit, inflationary money, and protective tariffs. Moderate Tammanyites, including Wood, were generally small-scale businessmen and would-be capitalists. They clamored for a competitive system based on limiting privilege, deflationary hard money, and free trade. Moderates often overlapped a small group of middle-class artisans, intellectuals, and a developing wage-earning class which sought a more extensive antimonopoly program than the moderates. Extolling the values of complete entrepreneurial freedom, they wanted to limit the paper-issuing authority of all banks and favored free trade, the destruction of special privileges, and a militant defense of labor's needs. When Bank Democrats rebuffed their demands, these so-called workies split from Tammany and formed the Equal Rights party, whose nickname, "Locofocoism," became a general pejorative for Democratic radicalism.[20]

Appearances were deceptive. The Equal Righters were intent on changing Tammany Hall's procedures and institutions, but were far from being wild-eyed radicals. They did hurl abuse against Bank Democrats for limiting laboring men and threatening the middle class with diminished opportunities because of chartered monopolies that restricted competition. Moreover, they were convinced that Bank Democrats and moderates had strayed from traditional Jeffersonian principles and were captives of special interests. Picturing society in terms of a class conflict between hardworking "producers" and "non-producing" speculators and monopolists, they called for Tammany's ideological revival around time-tested party principles and orthodox tenets of Jeffersonian political economy. Even their egalitarianism had limits. Clinging to a narrow interpretation of the Constitution, they sympathized with Southern planters who fought against increased federal power. By that belief, most defended slavery out of racism, or because they were convinced Southern markets and cotton benefited the city's economic prosperity.[21]

Knowing a false step as a novice politician could destroy him, Wood initially shunned the Locofocos. Bank Democrats in the Fifth Ward rewarded his apparent loyalty with a slot on the Young Men's Democratic-Republican General Committee, which groomed Tammany's future leaders. By the fall of 1836, Wood served regularly as vice-president of various Young Men's rallies, one of which endorsed the Bank Democrats' stand against Locofocos. He was equally active on the hustings and campaigned for "regular" candidates, generally conservatives. Election eve found him on a Democratic Vigilance Committee, turning out voters and watching the polls for possible frauds. It was not a good year for Tammany, however, despite helping elect Martin Van Buren to the presidency. Locofocos proved the critical difference between local victory and defeat, damaging the Hall in the process, by scorning conservatives, rewarding friendly moderates, backing a few sympathetic Whigs, and voting for their own candidates only if they had a chance to win.[22]

Wood's position became precarious by May of 1837 when economic conditions worsened. Local banks suspended specie payments; a flour riot broke out among the poor; and Bank Democrats shouted for federal assistance. The economic crisis provoked a political crisis, particularly among the members of the Young Men's Committee, whose entire prospects were at stake. In assessing the situation, the Young Men gradually concluded that the Locofocos had proven their key points: they were the true standard-bearers of party principles, and Tammany could not survive without them. Another factor was equally apparent. Ousting the Bank Democrats from Tammany, the Young Men concluded, was a means to purge the Hall's old guard and take its place. In short, Locofocoism was now both an ideological imperative and a useful political expedient.

By June, Wood made a wrenching decision despite the risks of failure. He not only spearheaded the Young Men's dramatic shift to Locofocoism, but became their most visible symbol by accepting the chairmanship of their first anti–Bank Democratic rally. Equally dangerous, he guided the adoption of resolutions that censured "all special banking corporations" as unjust privileges opposed "to the spirit of universal rights," and "a hindrance to the accumulation of property by honest industry." At a subsequent meeting, the Young Men were just as forceful. They endorsed a hard-money currency and reemphasized Wood's call for anti-monopolyism.[23]

Bank Democrats were unimpressed. Accustomed to power, they still controlled Tammany because of their wealth, command of party machinery, and linkage to Van Buren's Albany Regency through Governor William L. Marcy. On September 5, however, a wave of anxiety swept over them. President Van Buren's special message to Congress which attacked paper money and speculative credit, coupled with a call for economic recovery through a proposed Independent Treasury, signalled his acceptance of Locofocoism. While his plan did nothing to halt the nation's drift into a major depression, Van Buren confirmed the party's emerging realignment. Moderates copied the Young Men in scuttling the Bank Democrats and prepared to battle for Tammany Hall.[24]

Wood and the Young Men's Committee guided the moderates' fusion with Locofocos through mutual suspicion. Since neither wanted to deal from a position of weakness, the Young Men took on the task of convincing many skeptical

Locofocos that the moderates were sincere. At the same time, they had to prove to a few hesitant moderates that amalgamation made political sense.[25]

Poised and ambitious, Wood played an integral part in these delicate factional maneuverings through his growing importance in the Young Men's Committee. Now a member of their inner circle, his name appeared in early September on a list calling on Tammany for a major public gathering to sustain the president. Bank Democrats were not ready to surrender. Fighting for a postponement, they lost by a split vote in Tammany's Democratic-Republican General Committee, its executive arm, to stop the Hall from co-sponsoring the meeting. "The decision in this state," former governor Enos P. Throop cautioned Van Buren, "is a struggle for life and death."[26]

On September 21, 1837, during a heat wave, nearly two thousand Tammanyites milled around the Wigwam's Long Room, Tammany's main concourse, crowding it "almost to suffocation." Emotions reached fever pitch when Wood made the motion to begin and read a prepared list of Young Men's resolves. How much he actually wrote is unclear, but taken as a whole his statements revealed a mature political philosophy. "Special banking incorporations" were responsible for current economic woes, he said. Democrats of "our political faith . . . cannot rely on them for recovery." Abusive monopolies stifled competition, credit, individualism, free trade, and equal opportunity. Talent, integrity, and industry must operate free of artificial restraints to the greatest benefit of all people. Sweating profusely, he sat down as thunderous cheers filled the room. When the noise subsided, the moderates adopted his resolutions and ousted Bank Democrats.[27] It was now clear that Tammany had uncovered a new talent.

Wood's meteoric rise continued when the intraparty battle reached its climax. As a Fifth Ward delegate to Tammany's nominating convention, he helped secure candidates most Locofocos accepted on a combined moderate–Equal Rights slate. More honors fell his way when the General Committee chose him as special secretary at the Hall's last rally before the November municipal and state elections. Again, how much he influenced the platform is uncertain. What was important was its ideologic thrust–"equal rights for all," antimonopolyism, limited government, dogmatic individualism, and hard money.[28]

Politically, the Whigs were the chief immediate beneficiaries of Tammany's virulent infighting. They wrestled control of the municipal government from the Hall, and most Bank Democrats deserted Tammany and permanently joined the Whigs. Even the few remaining conservatives, huddled around Marcy, caused trouble. Differing with Van Burenites over fiscal policies, they continued intraparty bickering culminating in the Barnburner-Hunker feuds of the 1840s. Balancing these losses, moderates fused with most Locofocos, won the support of numerous workingmen, and refurbished traditional political principles.[29]

Wood did not waste time assessing pluses and minuses. Everything about his relationship with Locofocoism was critical in shaping his subsequent career. By accepting its main points, he gained a lasting political ideology and social philosophy, along with a clear set of economic commitments. As for practical politics, he learned important lessons in orchestrating mass support and emerged as a polished practitioner. On a personal level, his efficient labor on the Young Men's Committee tested his mettle and proved his leadership capabilities.

Rewards were not far behind. The Young Men selected him as secretary in 1838 and chairman in 1839. These positions had long-range implications. With four years of politicking under his belt, Wood's innate flair and manifest ability had won the admiration of his contemporaries, many of whom remained his staunchest future supporters.[30]

Wood's maturity and confidence flowered with responsibility. The Young Men reelected him chairman in 1840, taking special care to praise "his able discharge of the chair" and "directing energy and enthusiasm." More honors followed. In March, Tammany's General Committee placed him on a special Committee of Safety, which coordinated ward protests against a Whig-sponsored voter registry law. The next month, the party sent him to his first national convention as a Van Buren delegate. Wood's prestige increased in September at the state's Young Men's meeting in Syracuse. "Mr. Fernando Wood," the *New York Evening Post* announced, "was unanimously chosen President." His dazzling rise culminated in October 1840. Tammany nominated him, at the age of twenty-eight, as one of four men running on the general ticket for the House of Representatives. Wood's search for respectability now seemed within reach.[31]

Not all Tammanyites, especially Marcy Democrats, agreed. To them, he symbolized everything wrong with Tammany's new politics, both as a man and as a symbol. William F. Havemeyer, a wealthy sugar merchant and future mayor, for example, warned Van Buren that Wood was "without character or consequence, yet shrewd & subtle, a cunning politician," who had achieved "ephemeral popularity" among the Hall's young men, but "not deserving of confidence either morally or politically." In the future, these conservatives, later known as "swallow-tail" Democrats, were destined to become Wood's bitterest intraparty rivals.[32]

Another problem, much more intimate, marred Wood's glow. The end of the 1830s saw him settle into a daily routine running an unrewarding business and carefully plotting a political course. Something else went with these tasks, something painful and wrong to his wife—long blocks of time when he paid her no attention. Bored and neglected, she committed adultery on several occasions with at least two of his friends. A shocked servant witnessed one of these affairs and tattled to Rebecca Wood, who immediately informed her horrified son. He moved out and instituted divorce proceedings.

The Court of Chancery dissolved the childless marriage on July 29, 1839, decreeing that Anna W. Wood "shall not marry again during the natural life of the complainant." What became of her remains problematic, although one of Wood's later political enemies claimed she became an alcoholic prostitute.[33] Judging from Wood's dogged quest for respectability, the entire episode must have humiliated him. Wood certainly acted that way, never again mentioning Anna W. Wood, nor their marriage. Under those conditions, his race for Congress took on new personal dimensions.

TWO

Foundations

S UDDENLY, Wood stumbled over the Whigs' new political gamesmanship and his own imperfections. In the 1840 elections, Whigs wooed voters using innovative smear and name-calling techniques, evoking emotional symbolism, and avoiding specific issues. Tammanyites countered by registering fresh voters, naturalizing questionable new ones, and seeking evidence of Whig misconduct. Luckily, they uncovered the shocking "Glentworth Affair" that implicated local Whigs in the hiring of illegal voters from Pennsylvania to swell their city count.[1]

Wood was busy on his own. Early in September, he picked up an Anglophobic theme, popular among the Irish, and fumed that "British stockjobbers" had contributed large amounts of "gold" to ensure Whig victories. The *New York American,* edited by Charles King, the son of the eminent Federalist Rufus King, unleashed a splenetic reply. The paper ripped Wood's credibility and snapped that he was a charlatan attacking his betters. The *New York Evening Post* defended Wood. He deserved better, it wrote, than the typically vile Whig tactic of attacking the person while evading the truth. Voters should ignore King's "wretched print" because Wood's nature was "as courteous and generous as his reputation is unspotted."[2]

On Saturday, October 31, four days before the election, the self-righteous King shot back by disclosing a potentially damning incident about Wood's business affairs, one that threatened to destroy him both politically and financially. According to King, Wood had a small account at the Merchants' Exchange Bank from September 1836 through March 1839. His deposits ranged from a low of $96.98 to a high of $349.42. In November 1836, a clerk mistakenly posted a $1,750.62 check to Wood's account. Over the next two years, he withdrew "the whole of that amount" in a series of small checks. In 1838, the chief cashier discovered the error and demanded he return the money. Wood admitted that the check "did not belong to him," but insisted that the bank's bookkeeper must have erred and contended "that he owed the bank nothing." When the cashier sought to inspect his books, Wood answered suspiciously that a recent fire had destroyed them. At that point, the matter went to three referees. They found against Wood and ruled he owed the bank $2,143.90 for the initial error plus interest. Armed with a collaborating statement from Whig Daniel A. Cushman, one of the referees, King concluded that Wood "dishonestly appropriated to his own use monies that he knew did not belong to him."[3] Instead of Congress, Wood belonged in a penitentiary.

Wood faced a monumental crisis, and friends and foes alike awaited his response. They did not wait long. Aware that something was afoot, he had gathered supporting testimony from the other referees, lined up friendly editors, and secretly held a pamphlet in reserve to give the public his version if necessary.[4]

Such careful groundwork was now necessary. Wood decided his best defense lay where he could control, slant, and sift the facts through a long public document published in every Democratic newspaper. After questioning King's basic decency and motives, Wood issued in full the affidavits of the two other referees, John Gilbert and William McMurray, both of whom contradicted Cushman. Gilbert, a Democrat, minced few words. He wrote that Wood did not owe the bank "a dollar." Absent "in the evidence" was anything "derogatory to [Wood] as an honest man, or in the slightest degree affecting [his] character." Whig McMurray was slightly less effusive but just as forceful. Skeptical about Wood's lost ledgers, he nonetheless agreed with Gilbert that Wood had done nothing "to impeach [his] character or standing unless the charge of an overdraft is considered." Next, Wood produced a letter from Thomas G. Tallmadge, the bank's Whig attorney. The entire episode, he wrote, pivoted around a simple overdraft, which Wood had satisfied. As for the clerk's error, Wood honestly believed that his deposits covered the amount. The bank, in short, eager to help the Whig party, had maligned Wood. Finally, Wood played his trump card with a letter from his attorney, Whig William Inglis, a former judge. Inglis, like McMurray, was dubious about the missing ledgers, but admitted that Wood had in all their conversations maintained his ignorance about the original error and "acted like a person who was called upon to pay an amount which he did not know." Furthermore, Wood's probity was incontestable. Although he still "considered the debt not to be due," he had repaid the bank with an amount equal to the clerk's mistake.[5]

Wood ended his brief with a direct appeal to the bar of public opinion. Inviting the community "to judge of the atrocity of this attack," supported by only one partisan referee, he trusted that good sense would pronounce the charges against him "an unjustified calumny." If votes were a litmus test of public opinion, Wood passed. Running fourth among the Democratic congressional candidates and slightly behind Van Buren, he beat his nearest Whig opponent by 886 votes.[6]

The bank scandal opened a sore on Wood's reputation that festered over the years and never healed. Given his shaky business operations, many New Yorkers assumed him guilty. They were probably correct; it seems improbable that he was unaware of the bank's error. As a result, people sensed a troubling contradiction in his character, one that stirred deep passions, positive and negative. A part of him contained praiseworthy innate strength, aspiring to great achievements, geared to ideals. At the same time, he was flawed. To his enemies, this episode became the first link in a chain of suspicious events, turning them first to anger, then to bitter and measured hatred. By contrast, his supporters forgave his shortcomings and judged him by his deeds as a leader who made their times better. The resultant dichotomy left a complex man torn in two, a principled politician and a cheap trickster, a man of great potential and equally great self-devouring habits.[7]

Still, Wood was a congressman, ready to take his place on the stage of national politics. Serving in the Twenty-seventh Congress was important to him, although as a freshman he did not receive any major committee assignments. Yet Wood was productive. His voting behavior, speeches, and self-serving maneuverings foreshadowed certain tendencies when he indeed became a figure of national importance. Above that, he was now The Honorable Fernando Wood, a term by which he insisted people address him. However negative his recent divorce and the bank fiasco, congressional service put new meaning back into his obsessive drives.

The opening of Congress in May 1841 found Wood on the Public Buildings and Grounds Committee. The work was hardly burdensome, and he used his free hours to make important contacts. He sought out and ingratiated himself with Henry Clay, by now a pariah among his fellow Whigs because of his recent break with President John Tyler. Clay's influence was not political but personal. He became a model for Wood in deportment and clothing style. Wood also gravitated toward a tight circle of young Southern Democrats around Senator John C. Calhoun. In a similar way, he courted two other promising Southerners, Henry A. Wise of Virginia and James K. Polk of Tennessee.[8]

Wood's voting behavior indicated his commitment to the South. On seventy-six roll calls affecting proslavery interests, he voted with them fifty-six times, and would have followed the same course in his twenty absences. Out of forty-one New York congressmen, he was easily the most pro-Southern. These votes signalled future problems. Since the Democracy's unity hinged on excluding the slavery question from political debate, Wood's southernism indicated a powerful ingredient in his political nature, but one whose long-range implications were as yet unclear.[9]

Wood's sympathies had a darker side, another amoral characteristic that revealed him at his worst. The situation unfolded with the colliding presidential ambitions of Van Buren and Calhoun. In order to win the 1844 nomination, Calhoun had to dislodge Van Buren's grip over the New York Democracy.

Locally, the brunt of Calhoun's efforts fell upon many young men in Wood's constituency: free traders, states' righters, and racists, along with some workingmen who believed slavery protected them from potential black competitors and prevented Northern businessmen from exploiting white labor. Their immediate aim was to capture Tammany Hall, and through it the state organization.[10]

From every variable ranging through friendship to ideology, Calhoun was Wood's man. Practical politics made things less predictable. Since Van Buren was popular among many Tammanyites, Wood could not go on record for Calhoun without alienating party leaders. He solved the dilemma by double-crossing both sides. To the Calhoun people, Wood posed as a trusted ally, attended secret strategy sessions, and offered advice about how to approach potential delegates. The Calhounites did not know, however, that Wood secretly corresponded with Van Buren and sold them out. "I have been sounded on" various points by your enemies, Wood confided to Van Buren, "and being desirous to learn all things behaved quite *diplomatica diplomatique*."[11]

No documentation exists that Calhounites discovered Wood's duplicity. They probably never did because the senator and Wood stayed friendly. The story was far different with Van Buren. Informed early on by Tammany committeeman Thomas A. Carr that Wood was "only true to you face to face, not behind your back," Van Buren encouraged Wood to undermine Calhoun. In the process, Wood's trickery backfired. Van Buren never trusted him, and his brilliant son, "Prince John" Van Buren, became Wood's implacable enemy for almost the next two decades. As for Wood, although such underhanded shuffling characterized many other politicians of his generation, he often took duplicity to an extreme and made it an integral part of his operations. The upshot was that even when he was principled, many people remained suspicious, and he often ended by hurting more than helping himself.[12]

When Congress began, Whigs set the session's agenda through a wide-ranging financial program to cure the depression's last stages. Democrats marshalled their forces, opposed each Whig program, and baited the growing rupture between President Tyler and his party. Wood proved an orthodox Democrat. Still a neophyte, he listened to debate and awaited the proper time for his maiden speech. His moment arrived on July 9, 1841. The issue centered upon a Whig emergency bill authorizing the president to float a $12-million loan, at 5 percent interest, to fund the depleted Treasury.[13]

With uncharacteristic but becoming modesty, Wood thanked the chair for allowing him to express his views. Beginning in a voice "not distinctly heard" and speaking too rapidly, he thrashed nervously for a few moments before growing more comfortable and finally exhibiting his potential as an effective debater. The bill was wrong, he said, from a constitutional and political standpoint. Since the Constitution had not authorized Congress to commission such bonds, the bill clearly breached states' rights and imperiled economic recovery by needlessly increasing the national debt. The more Wood reviewed the bill, the more partisan he became. Whigs had only one motive in mind, creating patronage slots for a fresh class of "Government [loan] brokers" as a payoff to Wall Street "stock-jobbers." Democrats had a better solution. Evoking Locofocoism, Wood championed a hard-money currency, not a "powerful moneyed engine, backed by a large national debt." When he ended, friendly observers agreed his first address "was a very creditable effort."[14]

A month later, Wood was still apologetic when he took the floor in a debate over rechartering a third national bank. Terming himself neither a lawyer nor a "talking man, either by profession or inclination," he argued that Van Buren's Independent Treasury deserved a "fair trial." Again recalling Locofocoism and perhaps remembering his father, he assailed the entire concept of national banks, maintaining that their record of misadministration dating back to 1791 had cost American taxpayers an "aggregate loss" of nearly "three hundred millions of dollars." His constituents, "solvent and prudent merchants" and small "traders and mechanics," did not need a "Government Bank to regulate exchange." The true test of a viable economy lay in "the immutable laws of nature—by supply and demand."[15]

Wood continued these economic battles with Whigs as a minor but consistent Democratic foot soldier. In outlook and votes, he was a partisan, opposing all Whig attempts to use the federal government to stimulate the economy, change the banking system, or spend funds to improve the National Road and internal waterways. Another pattern emerged. Continuing his Locofocoism, Wood was clearly a fiscal conservative and a deflationist. In a series of roll calls, he indicated his commitments to limiting federal discretionary spending, preventing the linkage of preemptive land sales to the distribution of their proceeds for internal improvements, and cutting the government's size, including the elimination of unneeded federal jobs such as the State Department's despatch agents. To put the matter bluntly, he said Congress's wisest policy lay in taking "a recess of five years" in order to give the public "relief by non-interference."[16]

Wood's fiscal tightness had limits. Just as other congressmen, he was not austere serving constituents. He sought funding for the construction of more efficient facilities in the city's Custom House, appropriations for city fortifications, and money for the United States Coastal Survey to improve the harbor. Then, too, he exploited his position on the Naval Committee during the third session to expand the Brooklyn Navy Yard as a lucrative prize for local contractors and a source of prime Democratic patronage. Nor was he backward in his own interest. He voted against reducing the mileage allowance and lowering salaries for absentees. Moreover, Wood was one of Samuel F. B. Morse's staunchest backers in securing a subsidy for developing his experimental telegraph. In later years, Wood never let anyone forget his foresight.[17]

One particular group of New Yorkers received Wood's special attention. On several occasions, he demanded that the State Department protect and help release Irish political prisoners, some of whom were naturalized Americans, whom the British had forcibly resettled in Tasmania. When John Quincy Adams defended Secretary of State Daniel Webster, Wood gleefully embarrassed the former president and garnered more regard among Southern Democrats. Adams, he taunted, had often spoken against "imaginary slavery and oppression." If sincere, he should speak out against Great Britain's "*real* slavery and oppression."[18]

The eager way Wood thrust himself into the protectionist thicket capped his congressional career and epitomized his growing political maturity. During the second session, Whig Millard Fillmore, chairman of Ways and Means, sent shivers through the city's shipping community and raised Wood's hackles with a bill raising the tariff. While preliminary skirmishes ran their course, Wood studied revenue statistics, carefully followed debate, and sharpened his thoughts. When he finally spoke on February 8, 1842, he was hampered by a severe cold and cut by a time limit. He was therefore forced to insert the bulk of his remarks into the *Congressional Globe's* appendix. Yet even if fellow congressmen did not hear the entire address, his words echoed clear Democratic ideology and set the basis for a position that hardened over the years.

Before the House voted, he began, it needed full information about how government officials would collect the tariff, what groups would benefit, and if its sponsors were free of "prejudice, passions and [private] interests." The appendix found Wood more forceful. In harmony with Locofoco principles, he maintained that protectionism was inherently one-sided. It granted manufacturers "exclusive privileges," forming an indirect government subsidy since they raised prices without worrying about foreign competition, and undercut states' rights. Buttressing his ideas with a mass of statistics, he insisted that tariffs made imported goods too costly for American consumers and encouraged smuggling since ordinary folk could not afford imported commodities. Even more, protectionism injured overseas trade due to higher priced American goods and foreign retaliatory measures. That made American workers double losers. They consumed artificially exorbitant goods and faced unemployment since the tariff restricted production to the "home market." In contrast, only revenue tariffs were justifiable. Anything else betrayed the nation because "the spirit of the age" was "tending toward free trade."[19]

Democrats were impressed. The *Evening Post's* Washington correspondent flatteringly noted: "Mr. Wood seldom speaks, but when he does, it is always to the purpose, and he is heard by the House with respectful attention."[20] Taken as a whole, then, the debate over the tariff marked Wood's congressional coming of age and earned plaudits from both Northern free traders and states rights' Southern Democrats. For a young man of Wood's obvious ambitions, it was a heady time.

The ending of Congress in September 1842 found Wood pleased with himself and anticipating a well-deserved reelection. Just as satisfying, his personal life had stabilized. The previous July, he made a brilliant second marriage. His new wife, the daughter of Common Pleas Judge Joseph L. Richardson of Auburn, proved a remarkable helpmate. Anna D. Wood, who ironically had the same name as his first wife, a lineal descendant of the William Penn family through her mother, was sweet-tempered and intelligent and deeply loved her husband and shared his dreams. While not wealthy, she enjoyed a comfortable inheritance, which he badly needed since he apparently depended upon his meager federal salary. From a political standpoint, she also brought with her critical connections through her father who was on excellent terms with key upstaters, numbering Van Buren, Senator Silas Wright, and Governor William C. Bouck among his closest friends. This network proved invaluable to Wood's ventures outside the city. On all counts, Anna D. Wood fit Fernando Wood's needs for respectability, money, and power.[21]

In such a mood of deepening happiness, Wood turned his thoughts to the fall election. What he had no way of knowing was that over two decades would pass before he reentered the House.

A political ferment brewing within the city greeted Wood in September as he touched base with Tammany. Decennial reapportionment, coupled to a new congressional requirement which mandated elections from specific districts rather than general districts, created a mess. Wood's home district in the new Fifth was the base of another incumbent, John McKeon, an immensely popular Irish attorney. After taking soundings that indicated McKeon would win the primary, Wood established residency in the Sixth District. It was a calculated risk. The Sixth was a Whig bastion, and two equally strong Democrats sought the nomination, James I. Roosevelt, another incumbent, and Ely Moore, longtime champion of labor causes and former congressman. Hoping they would split the vote, Wood gambled he could slip through.[22]

Each passing day challenged Wood's resourcefulness. Roosevelt withdrew and left the contest between Moore and Wood. Both organized committees in the district's sixty precincts, buttonholed uncommitted delegates, and bribed others. The primary was inconclusive. Wood held a one-vote edge over Moore, with a scattering for several minor candidates, but fell short of the required majority. When the stalemate persisted, Moore suggested holding new delegate elections. Wood refused, interpreting the offer as a sign of weakness. Moore was furious. He considered Wood an unscrupulous interloper and pulled out in favor of McKeon, who had paradoxically lost the Fifth District's nomination. The trade worked and McKeon won. Outwardly a good loser, Wood was privately out for revenge. He raised nativistic fears about McKeon among supporters and even suggested that McKeon was a covert abolitionist. In the end, Wood took grim satisfaction when Hamilton Fish, a coming power in the Whig party, gained the seat.[23]

No matter how Wood rationalized his loss, the bleak fact was that his once-promising congressional career had ended with abrupt suddenness. Yet politics was the least of his worries. With his wife pregnant with their first child, he faced a harsher reality, the need to earn a livelihood, which forced him to make a fortuitous move he might have ordinarily avoided. While he could not divine the future, he would be a rich man the next time he ran for public office, campaigning on his own terms. Until then, he poured considerable vigor into rebuilding his chandlery company and announced to friends that he was "entirely out of politics."[24]

Making money during the mid-1840s proved harder than Wood anticipated. Limited by the lack of capital, he borrowed from a variety of creditors and slowly rebuilt his firm. Times were so desperate, however, that he pleaded to Henry Wise for a patronage appointment as the State Department's local despatch agent, despite having tried to abolish the office. In an agonizing confession of despair, he told Wise the agency "would put some 6 or 800 dollars per annum in my pocket, which *God knows I need very much*."[25]

Wise complied and recommended him to Secretary of State Abel P. Upshur, a fellow Virginian. Upshur refused. Satisfied with the present agent, he knew the change would create unneeded turmoil. The script changed when Upshur accidentally died and President Tyler named Calhoun as his replacement. Hearing the news, Wood rushed for pen and ink. "My pecuniary circumstances induces me," he implored Calhoun, to have the position out of "your friendship and generosity."[26]

On May 8, 1844, Calhoun gave Wood the job. Under its terms, Wood sent official despatches overseas "with respectable American citizens" to various consuls and ministers.[27] On returning vessels, he collected the documents and mailed them to Washington. Despite these minimal duties, Wood prized the berth. Its pay subsidized his business, and it kept his name alive politically by reminding Tammany that he had powerful contacts in Washington, as any government job, no matter how minor, was a mark of status.

Wood never forgot Calhoun's favor and became even more pro-Southern. When Calhoun returned to the Senate, Wood supported his states' rights position, kept him informed about local politics, praised his efforts to expand slavery into territories gained from Mexico, and assured him "the *people* are your friends, especially [my] class of businessmen and merchants." As abolitionists grew more vocal in the late 1840s, Wood denounced their "fanaticism" and told him that if such men fomented disunion "our *homes* will be found south of Potomac, where true freedom, chivalry and honour characterizes the people."[28] Wood revealed his Southern bias again later by naming two sons after Calhoun and Wise.

These days may have been the happiest in Wood's life. His chandlery firm, located on the East River waterfront, gradually expanded as he leased ships and engaged in the coastal trade, mainly with Southern markets. His wife was everything his first was not. Between 1842 and 1846, the young couple had three children, Joseph, Rebecca, and Fernando, Jr., spaced at nearly two-year intervals. Still renters, they lived in the somewhat fashionable Nineteenth Ward in upper Manhattan and could afford three Irish servants. While by no means rich, Wood had at least established himself as a rising merchant.[29]

At age thirty-two in the presidential year of 1844, Wood seemed a settled businessman, but his inner political fires still burned. Before the party's convention he backed Van Buren with little warmth. When dark horse James K. Polk unexpectedly became the nominee, Wood quickly renewed their friendship and plunged into electioneering. He formed "an association of talented young men" for Polk in the city, spoke in New Jersey and Brooklyn, canvassed upstate through the Southern Tier, and even lectured Polk about the intricate web of local intraparty factionalism. Regardless of these efforts, Wood denied that he had any ulterior motives. "I am not now, *under any circumstances* a candidate" for office, he told Polk. Election day found Wood in the city, hustling votes. When Polk carried New York on his way to the White House, Wood sent fawning congratulations: "And now with Jefferson, Jackson and Van Buren shall be associated Polk."[30]

Wood struck a less altruistic chord after the election. Based on his efforts, he offered Polk "with the utmost deference and respect" unsolicited suggestions about local patronage. It was a waste of time. Wood was a minor character in a much larger drama. Barnburner-Hunker cleavages had widened, chiefly over the annexation of Texas, and each group expected, but did not receive, Polk's exclusive spoils. None of these developments harmed Wood. Still insisting that he was a full-time merchant, he avoided a premature commitment to either side, despite his hidden dislike of Van Buren and the Barnburners.[31]

In any case, Wood's efforts did have one vital side-effect. He saved his own appointment. Many Tammanyites expected his removal since he held the job under a Whig president, and they bombarded James Buchanan, the new secretary of state, with the names of suitable replacements. Aware that he stood on shaky ground, Wood lined up prominent supporters, including Moore with whom he had reached an accommodation, and wrote directly to Buchanan. Feigning indifference, Wood said the office "had great responsibility and little compensation." As a former congressman and faithful Democrat, however, he had every right to remain. For the moment, Buchanan left well enough alone.[32]

Wood's crisis was not over. By early 1848, the issue of extending slavery in the territories hardened the Barnburner-Hunker split. While both supported slavery where it existed, Hunkers favored the idea of squatter sovereignty, which gave local citizens the option of establishing slavery. By contrast, Barnburners supported the Wilmot Proviso, which contended that Congress had the power to limit slavery's spread. Their crossfire caught Wood in the middle. His

noninvolvement meant each coveted his position and neither defended him.
Wood realized that his firing "by a *democratic administration*" would be a devastating insult even from a job that he was now financially secure enough to call "a
two-penny office." Once more he called on friends for support and wrote Polk
reminding him of past services. Whether Polk interceded with Buchanan was
unclear, but Wood retained the post until Zachary Taylor took over the White
House.[33]

Wood's balancing act worked because of his intransigent assertion that he was
solely a "practical merchant and ship owner." Even when the national Democracy
fragmented in the presidential campaign and Van Buren ran on the Free-Soil
ticket, Wood remained "disconnected," almost passive. The reason, he informed
Polk in a somewhat boastful mood, was that the pro-Administration Hunkers
believed he was a "warm & efficient" friend because Buchanan had not removed
him, while he enjoyed the Barnburners' "regard & confidence" since he did not
oppose them.[34] In this instance, Wood's double-dealing was successful. Yet his
pose was deceptive. He was only apolitical in the sense that he did not seek any
elective office. That distinction made his neutrality plausible.

As the decade neared its end, Wood fretted about not achieving his ultimate
goal, the respectability and power associated with wealth. He found that opportunity in the city's burgeoning real estate market.

During the 1840s, New York City's population swelled by 202,837, mainly
immigrants, to reach a total of 515,547 in 1850. Many settled and worked in the
nine East Side wards below Canal Street, raising density rates, putting a premium
on rentable space, and making future expansion inevitable in the relatively unsettled area above Twenty-sixth Street. Along the East River and the West Side,
various forms of manufacturing developed, further escalating real estate values.
Upper-class New Yorkers began moving and left the lower wards for the Fifteenth, Sixteenth, Eighteenth, and Nineteenth wards below Forty-second
Street. This shift had a dual effect on property values. Within the older wards,
such as the Fourth and Sixth, which had the highest concentration of Irish immigrants, homes became apartments and any type of property became invaluable.
In the newly settled wards, land sold rapidly. The startling climb in assessed real
estate values between 1848 and 1860, which more than doubled from
$256,197,143 to $557,230,656, dramatized this enormous growth.[35]

At the same time, Manhattan's spatial geography changed from a compact
"walking city" to a sprawling metropolis with uneven land usage. Not all wards
were slums, nor preserves of the rich, but were a mixture of rich and poor, commerce, industry, homes, and tenements, often on a block-to-block basis.[36] The
incessant demand for housing, the need for building lots, indicated that a sharp
speculator who appreciated where the city would grow, understood the differen-
tiation of land values on almost a street-to-street basis, and grasped the potential

value of older and newer buildings, could reap a fortune. Fernando Wood was such a man.

Wood stumbled into the real estate market almost as an afterthought. For some time, he and his wife had tired of renting and sought a permanent home. In 1848 their search settled them on a large undeveloped parcel in the Nineteenth Ward's western side. With $3,500 of his wife's money as down payment, he took out a $4,000 mortgage to buy 150 acres of the old Somerindyke estate, along Bloomingdale Road.[37]

The purchase evolved into a spectacular bonanza and laid the basis for Wood's finally achieving great wealth. The estate, which he subsequently enlarged with additional buys of fifty acres, occupied what became 110 city lots, running from the Boulevard (present Broadway) on the east, to Riverside Drive and Eleventh Avenue on the west, and Seventy-sixth Street on the south to Seventy-eighth Street on the north. Included were a small clapboard building with low ceilings, where the Woods lived, and a number of rental units. Within a year, he liquidated the mortgage; within twenty years, his acreage was worth more than $650,000.[38]

In 1849, Wood plunged into a speculative mania lasting a lifetime. Using the rapidly intensifying value of his original acreage as security for a series of brilliant transactions over the next eleven years, he, with his wife as cosigner, bought, built, and sold homes, office buildings, stores, lots, and rental properties in nearly every ward. Among these were twenty-nine separate acquisitions, seventeen involving $48,523 in mortgages, most repaid within two years, leaving a gross indebtedness of only $3,222 by 1861. Wood's profits stemmed from rents, sales, and mortgages on residential and commercial spaces; from the municipal government for properties rented as offices and firehouses; from the selling of lots, which he subdivided; and, above all, from the incredible appreciation of land values. He then pyramided these gains into more real estate, often paying in cash, or investments in a variety of businesses, including banks, insurance companies, and railroads.[39]

Nor was his speculation confined to Manhattan. In 1852, he completed a complicated swap with Mr. and Mrs. Thomas O. Larkin of California. In exchange for forty-one city lots mainly in the lower wards, with homes and furniture, valued at about $90,000, Wood received a comparable amount of commercial buildings in San Francisco, running from the corner of Washington and Montgomery streets for 1,372 feet on Washington and 122 feet on Montgomery. According to a contemporary, Wood earned a total "ground rent" on his San Francisco parcels of slightly more than $100,000 during the next seven years. Moreover, he bought plots in Brooklyn and held a $39,000 mortgage on Stephen A. Douglas's Chicago property.[40]

How wealthy Wood became during those twelve years is difficult to establish. Tax records are often incomplete or misleading. In 1857, William H. Boyd published a tax list based on the city assessor's report of people who had paid real and personal property taxes. Since New Yorkers with assessments below $1,000 were not liable, Boyd listed about thirty thousand resident taxpayers, some one-third of whom were personal property taxpayers. Wood was taxed on $25,140 worth of real property, at a rate of $1.38 per $1,000, and none on personal property. When compared to city liber records of deeds and mortgages, both totals were too low. Others came up with similar inaccurate estimations. In 1855, Moses Y. Beach, the publisher of periodic registers of wealthy New Yorkers, put Wood's fortune at $200,000. Six years later, Reuben Vose, Beach's successor, guessed at $500,000.[41]

None of these figures seems reasonable. The most credible information came from material Wood supplied for the 1860 census. He reported real estate worth $1 million and personal property of $200,000. Whatever the actual total, the overwhelming fact was that he had indeed become the rich man of his dreams. While not in the high extremes of opulence, he stood in the respectable upper niche of real fortunes.[42]

Now, Wood awaited the respect he craved. After all, he had prospered in the best traditions of an era that glorified the rags-to-riches motif. Unfortunately, his breakthrough raised questions about the sources of his investment capital. At a time when women were usually invisible in the business world, society's conventions plus Wood's ego kept his wife's contributions in the background. Even if Wood had acknowledged her vital help, nagging suspicions bothered many people who scrutinized his new affluence. How could a man barely able to support his family in 1842, they wondered, suddenly become so affluent? No better symbol existed of his dubious behavior than memories of the bank scandal. Was he, they wondered, somehow guilty again? Answers came that confirmed the worst when evidence surfaced apparently proving his riches had an unsavory side, a side that diminished all his achievements and negated his quest for respectability.[43]

Like many other New Yorkers, the discovery of gold in California filled Wood with greed. Unlike the hoard of "forty-niners" who rushed impetuously toward "the golden river," Wood believed maximum profits lay in exploiting the miners. With that in mind, he became one of the first city merchants to engage in the gold-rush trade. Along with four partners at the end of October 1848, Wood loaded a barque, the *John C. Cater*, with a full cargo ranging from "a general assortment of staple fancy goods," to farm machinery, mining implements, and mundane but necessary household items. After a 144-day voyage, the *Cater* reached San Francisco on March 15, 1849. Employing local agents, the Wood combine quickly sold its inventory at inflated prices. For the rest of the year, the *Cater* garnered added income in the coastal trade, taking passengers to Oregon and returning with lumber heavily in demand in San Francisco. The amount

Wood and his associates made was undocumented. Scattered reports from news-papers, however, indicated that they received a minimum of $34,383 in specie during 1849 alone.[44]

This lucrative venture set off a chain of events that badly tarnished Wood, starting with the way he had raised the money for the ship and its cargo. Some-time in September 1848, Wood visited his brother-in-law, Edward E. Marvine, a retired merchant. Amid casual conversation, Wood purportedly read a letter, written by a "Thomas O'Larkin," the American consul, navy agent, and naval storekeeper in Monterey, California. "O'Larkin" thanked Wood for helping him secure his posts and suggested that he could make $100,000 on a $10,000 invest-ment by selling merchandise in San Francisco. The letter galvanized Marvine. He not only backed Wood with his own funds, but convinced three others to become partners.

The turning point came when Marvine and the others tracked down mounting expenses and sued Wood for bilking them. Subsequent court records then detailed how Wood allegedly acted as a "confidence man," swindling his partners out of approximately $20,000 before the *Cater* sailed, through forged bills of sale, double-billed invoices, and false vouchers. Wood's deposition offered a weak defense. He denied ever receiving the "O'Larkin" letter, despite contrary testimony from Marvine that he had indeed read it. When the real Thomas O. Larkin testified in another deposi-tion that he was unacquainted with Wood in 1848 and that they had never corresponded, Wood reversed himself and lamely suggested the letter must have come from a different "O'Larkin." As to the other allegations, Wood admitted that "unintentional errors" might have resulted in certain overpriced goods, but he did not produce validating receipts.[45]

In 1851, the Marvine affair shoved Wood on a runaway roller coaster heading for disaster. A grand jury reviewed the case and found cause for a "secret bill of indictment" against him for perjury and "false pretenses." District Attorney Frederick W. Tallmadge and his assistant, A. Oakey Hall, both Whigs, took the findings before the Court of General Sessions. The judges, however, quashed the charges because the statute of limitations for criminal action had expired. Quickly, unsubstantiated rumors swirled through the city which accused Wood of bribing Tallmadge with $700 to ensure the delay.[46]

At any event, Wood was not exonerated. On November 29, 1851, the city's Supreme Court assigned the case to three referees. Five years later, they found against Wood, ordering him to pay the partners $5,635.40 and Marvine "some $8,000 in damages, and nearly the same in costs." These awards meant Wood stood before the legal system and, by extension, the public, as a forger and swin-dler, a man who had apparently escaped prison only with the connivance of a corrupted official. No matter how much he tried, Wood never completely escaped that image.[47]

During these legal developments and before the referees' report, Wood launched a bristling counterattack. Claiming complete innocence, he instituted a libel suit against Moses Beach's *New York Sun* for prematurely printing details of Marvine's deposition and maintained that his erstwhile partners were guilty of "extortion." After the referees' decision, he avoided further comments, but filed an appeal that dragged on for the next six years.[48]

Two unexpected sources helped Wood to salvage some public respect. The influential *New York Herald* and its editor-owner James Gordon Bennett, with whom Wood had a never-ending love-hate relationship, explained that Wall Street operators considered "sharp practice" among "the finest points in the character of a businessman." Wood had been "from the commencement of his career, a sharp practitioner in trade and commerce and politics." Thus, his actions were no different from other successful men. The Republican *Morning Courier and New York Enquirer,* a longtime foe, issued a similar apology. The Marvine episode, it suggested, typified him because "what is usually called 'luck' is really foresight and bold action."[49] Wood represented his era's ethos, then, either in business or politics—success, by any means, was the only thing that counted.

The facts surrounding the Marvine case did not support these rationalizations. Its connection to the bank scandal was hardly a coincidence, and added more details to the picture of a man relentless in whatever he tried. Twisted consistency was Wood's only virtue. Believing in himself and his destiny, he was driven by a desire to leap to the top of the ladder at whatever cost in ethics. At the same time, he had a contrary emotion, the desire for public approval. The result both fascinated and repelled on-lookers.

Out of these conflicting emotions, one point was clear: the judicial system had discredited him. But Wood did not waver. Instead, he was more determined than ever to win public approval. Only his methods changed. Since he could not automatically command respectability, he used his money to buy it. His villa and estate, named "Woodlawn," became a showpiece of quiet but obvious plushness; he and his wife joined the Protestant Episcopal Church; they sent their children to private schools; and they vacationed at the fashionable spa at Saratoga Springs.[50] The next step to vindication lay in political power.

Wood's opening wedge lay in the Democracy's pragmatic realization that the Whigs were the chief beneficiaries of its inability to resolve the slavery extension problem. As a result at the 1849 Syracuse state convention, the Barnburners, including many Free-Soilers, accepted the Hunkers' idea of squatter sovereignty and agreed that the federal government had no right to interfere with slavery where it existed. In return, most Hunkers endorsed the Barnburner idea that Congress could theoretically prevent the establishment of slavery in the territories.

The agreement fell apart in the fall elections, largely because a few Hunkers wanted to punish the Free-Soilers for desertion. Three new factions emerged. Soft Shell Democrats, consisting of many Barnburners and moderate Hunkers under Marcy and Horatio Seymour, endorsed the Syracuse platform, including squatter sovereignty. In contrast, conservative Hunkers or Hard Shell Democrats, led by Senator Daniel S. Dickinson, were firm proextensionists. The remaining Free-Soilers, along with some Barnburners, controlled by John Van Buren, adamantly rejected any extension. A similar split disrupted Tammany. Softs and Hards formed rival general committees, while Free-Soilers were isolated but willing to cooperate with Softs provided they nominated acceptable candidates.

Wood's passivity was a luxury he could no longer afford because a galaxy of equally young and promising Tammanyites jostled for a starring role on the political stage. The Hards had Daniel S. Sickles, an impetuous but brilliant attorney; merchant Henry Western, the popular chairman of their general committee; Mike Walsh, the workingmen's advocate; James T. Brady, a prominent attorney and fund-raiser; Isaac V. Fowler, a skilled organizer; and John McKeon, Polk's federal attorney for the southern district of New York and Wood's long-time nemesis. The Softs numbered just as many bright lights: Lorenzo Shepard, Marcy's close associate and a brilliant tactician, chairman of their General Committee; Isaiah Rynders, a hard-bitten brawler and founder of the notorious Empire Club, whose stature rested on intimidating Whig voters; and banker Elijah Purdy, an influential German Tammanyite. To the side, John Van Buren seemed his father's clone. In the wings, three others awaited their turn, William M. Tweed, Peter B. Sweeny, and Richard Connolly.[51]

Ordinarily, Wood should have joined the Hards since they pandered to slavery extensionists. Practical reasons probably barred the way: the Softs held a working majority within Tammany; he interpreted the Syracuse formula as a defense of slavery; and he harbored such a strong grudge against McKeon that any cooperation was unthinkable. Within this welter of factionalism, however, Wood never lost sight of the main prize. Backing Softs was an expedient step to advancing his own political ambitions.

Wood opened a new era in city politics in December 1849 by announcing to astonished Nineteenth-Ward Soft precinct workers that he was willing to stand for election as their committeeman. Taken back because of his previous stance, they nonetheless chose him. Left unsaid was Wood's larger goal, the rewards that Tammany might lavish on a peacemaker, someone capable of fusing the party and restoring the Hall to its accustomed glitter.

At this juncture, California's request for admission to the Union as a free state became the catalyst for Wood's comeback. As Congress debated various bills that eventually became the Compromise of 1850, Hards sponsored a mid-February meeting at Tammany's main assembly, the Long Room, to discuss the issues, but barred Softs. Rynders responded with muscles, not words. The Empire Club fomented a riot, and he assaulted Sickles to prevent him from taking the rostrum.[52]

The ferocity of the Hall's divisions enhanced Wood's availability as a moderate. Shortly afterward, the Softs organized their General Committee. By common consent, he was the logical chairman. Rich, mature, talented, a former congressman and federal officeholder, his credentials linked them to past Democratic triumphs. Moreover, his years of neutrality made him the only Tammanyite who might forge party reunion, provided that was possible.[53]

Wood played his role energetically. Chairing the first Soft meeting under his leadership, he made a sincere case for accommodation through the Syracuse platform. "The only hope of success," he emphasized, "is union–union without the sacrifice of principle." Upstate, both the party's legislative caucus and the state central committee, sometimes called the New Albany Regency, run by railroad magnate Dean Richmond of Buffalo, endorsed his position and urged an amalgamated fall state convention. The Hards remained obdurate, citing slavery's right to expand as their reason for rejecting Richmond's invitation.[54]

The question spilled over into the Tammany Society. With two general committees claiming exclusive regularity, the Council of Sachems, the society's governing board, faced a hard choice. Under traditional party usages, the council had taken on the right to decide which general committee could meet in the party's sanctuary, Tammany Hall, automatically making its choice the Democracy's sole legitimate arm. Under these conditions, Wood's position hinged on the April election for a new council. Purdy's Soft ticket gained an ostensive majority, but ballot-stuffing by both groups obscured the picture. Surprisingly, the old council refused to dissolve. Holding itself above the battle, it disbanded both committees and called for the election of a citywide convention, based on new population figures, which would then select an entirely fresh-blended, official General Committee.[55]

Wood accepted the council's dictum, confident he could control the convention. Although Shepard became chairman, Wood was president pro tem and set the tone of the convention in a keynote speech. All delegates, he lectured, must show "a conciliatory spirit" for the sake of party "peace and union." The means lay with Congress's new solution to extensionism embedded in the Compromise of 1850, Stephen Douglas's version of squatter sovereignty, now called popular sovereignty, which denationalized the question by making it a matter of local control. Reflecting that spirit, Wood maintained the issue was not germane to Tammany's factionalism because the Constitution did not delegate Congress any power "to establish or prohibit slavery" in the territories. On that basis, Wood proposed a compromise. He endorsed the Hard and Southern position that Congress lacked control over slavery but accepted the Soft idea that local settlers could decide the extensionism issue through popular sovereignty.[56]

Neither side budged. The convention deadlocked, and the council held the elections anyway, resulting in a fusion General Committee, with a slight Hard majority, chaired by merchant Edward C. West. Tammany's strained mating dance fit Richmond's needs. Although many Hards tried to sabotage an agreement, Wood's position became official party doctrine when the state convention endorsed the Hall's "harmonizing" efforts and ran Seymour for governor on that basis.[57]

Tammany now turned to the mayoral race. One towering man, Fernando Wood, the chief mover behind fusion, was the acknowledged front-runner. Leaving nothing to chance, Wood organized primary electors in each ward and discretely assured chairman Edward West of financial support for other nominees. In the convention, some stubborn Hards, who wanted a clear-cut extensionist, termed his candidacy a prescription for disaster. Their opposition repelled more realistic party workers, and he won easily.[58]

Wood was halfway home because victory revolved around a total party effort. In a clear bid to dissident Hards, the *New York Herald* acted as his surrogate and warned them to unify. Wood, it gushed, was a "talented, sensible, active and reliable man," whose impeccable private and public character, along with his proven "capacity for business," suggested an ideal mayor. At least Whigs were impressed. They considered Wood a formidable foe, highly capable of beating their candidate, Ambrose C. Kingsland, a wealthy oil dealer.[59]

Wood had little time to savor these assessments as he had only three weeks to campaign. As hints of things to come, he ran his own race, spent freely from deep pockets, and took special care to court ethnic, working-class, and Hard voters. At the same time, he was not above using dirty tricks. Either he or some supporters planted stories accusing Kingsland of selling overpriced oil to the city government.[60] By the end of October, Wood was sure he had waged a strong campaign and would win.

But Wood was mistaken. Across the state and in the city, a Whig groundswell developed due to the Compromise of 1850, which had passed under President Fillmore's auspices. Nothing better illustrated their strength than the Castle Garden, or Union Committee meeting, held on October 31. Originally conceived by nonpartisan city merchants to endorse the compromise, the gathering attracted "men of wealth and character" from both parties who associated their continued well-being with Whig victories.[61]

Another crucial blow sent Wood reeling. McKeon, now one of Marvine's lawyers, decided to settle old scores and offered Whig editors privileged information about the case. At first, they hesitated, fearing Wood had cause for a suit of libel or invasion of privacy because most of the litigation's particulars had not yet reached court. When the slurs against Kingsland surfaced, however, several Whig newspapers published selective items, again on the Saturday before polling, that covered Wood with guilt. "We do not believe the result [of these revelations] will be flattering to Mr. Wood," the *New York Tribune* sneered, "but each inquirer will judge for himself."[62]

This attack, so clearly similar to the one he faced a decade earlier, found Wood unprepared. He scarcely slept on Saturday and worked frantically all Sunday. By Monday, his lawyers issued a public statement seething with contempt for Marvine and termed the allegations totally "untrue." Wood also published an open letter that urged voters to reserve judgment until the legal system settled the matter and flayed his former associate, the "recipient of my favor and bounty," for such a "base attempt" to injure him at the eleventh hour.[63]

Nothing Wood did or wrote made any difference. Whigs routed Democrats at every level. They won three congressional seats, thirteen out of sixteen assembly races, and the governorship for Fish over Seymour. The Whig romp buried Wood. He lost fifteen of nineteen wards, including his own, and he had the lowest popular percentage, 43.8 percent, of any Tammanyite since direct elections for mayor began in 1834.[64]

One by one, Democratic newspapers surveyed the damage. All agreed that last summer's unity was cosmetic and that Whigs had capitalized on the Compromise of 1850's popularity. They also agreed on another point: Fernando Wood was a dead politician. The *Evening Post* wrote the harshest obituary. Confessing "mortification" about his tawdry business affairs, it took some pride in proclaiming that Wood "encountered the fate which his presumption merited." By overrating the importance of party organization, he "grossly under-rated the importance of unimpeached personal integrity."[65] Only Fernando Wood knew if those words were indeed his political epitaph.

THREE

First Victory

Woods's brutal defeat was a mixed blessing. Whatever the emotional and psychological costs, it did provide invaluable time for his burgeoning business ventures. Over the next three years, he seemed content as a real estate magnate. He immersed himself in consolidating his wealth, spent many hours with his wife refurbishing their home, and welcomed the birth of two more children. The Wood household, with three permanent servants, along with five active children and his aged mother,[1] settled into a stable routine, far different from his parents' disruptive lives.

Wood furthered the impression that his political days were over by leaving the city on April 27, 1852, with Larkin as a traveling companion for a trip to San Francisco to investigate his holdings, some of which suffered through a rash of disastrous fires. Upon landing, Wood signed deeds, viewed his properties, and found a collection agent. By August, he was back home.[2] In short, Wood appeared no different from a host of other failed mayoral nominees, a brief meteor who had burnt out after momentarily lighting the partisan sky.

By 1853, a major political reorganization gripped New York City politics. Both Democrats and Whigs crumbled under the weight of almost similar internal ambiguities involving slavery extension, temperance, class tension, civic reform, and nativism. The Whigs fell first over, many finding a home in the fledgling Know-Nothing party, whose membership was secret. Tammany was in shambles. President Franklin Pierce wielded patronage aimed at making the Democracy a moderate, national force by isolating extremists on the right and left. He failed in New York. The Hards, interpreting Pierce's program as an insult, revived their General Committee. It was chaired by Thomas J. Barr and guided by his nephew, Peter B. Sweeny, and promising Congressman William M. Tweed. They then formed a permanent state party under former Senator Daniel S. Dickinson of Binghamton. In reaction, the Softs organized a second General Committee, run by Lorenzo Shepard and Congressman John Cochrane, which created a second state apparatus that cooperated with the Albany Regency. For the moment, Softs held a tenuous upper hand. They controlled the bulk of federal and state patronage through United States Custom House collector Herman Redfield, Secretary of State Marcy, and Governor Seymour. The few Van Buren Free-Soilers were restive over what they construed as an insulting lack of spoils, resented Pierce's support of the Fugitive Slave Law, and attacked both Soft and Hards for backing slavery.[3]

As for Wood, politics remained his abiding passion even though real estate apparently absorbed his time and energy. Although nominally a Soft, his support was a matter of factional and personal alliances rather than policy differences with Hards because he sympathized with them. As a result, he again played both sides of the issue. Posing as a centrist, he sought unity among all Democrats for his ultimate goal, reconstructing his power base before making another run at the mayoralty.

In November 1853, Wood tested the political waters. Writing to Marcy, he suggested the city Democracy was sound except for Free-Soilers, "and it has been with great difficulty that we have kept them within ranks." Unless Tammany used them as a catalyst to reorganize the Democracy along the Hards' pro-Southern lines, "it will become what our enemies charge it to be now, 'the John Van Buren party,' or what there is left of it."[4] Even though Wood's effort fizzled because Marcy had neither the power nor the inclination to follow his advice, Wood had signalled his desire for a political comeback.

Wood pressed harder with the new year. A member of the floor committee for Tammany's annual January 8 celebration of Andrew Jackson's victory at New Orleans, the highlight of the Democracy's social season, he was instrumental in dedicating festivities to the "Union of the Democratic party." To further that goal, Wood supported the Democratic-sponsored Young America Movement, which sought to unite the sections around free trade penetration of foreign markets and aggressive national expansion in the Caribbean. Keeping his name alive for maximum political exposure, Wood furthermore explained that he was now willing to sacrifice his business career for the party's good. Softs in the Nineteenth Ward responded positively. They elected him a committeeman, and he served as temporary chairman until Shepard emerged as the permanent one. All the same, Shepard shared Wood's concern for party unity but for different reasons. Where Wood sought personal advancement, Shepard wanted to end party divisions. Yet in policy terms, they agreed that most Softs and Hards were "national Democrats," men marching under similar pro-Southern flags, and were only divided by personal animosities.[5] What both realized was that each side lacked a means to make fusion workable.

By late winter of 1854, Senator Stephen Douglas's Kansas-Nebraska bill unwittingly supplied the glue Wood sought. In repealing the Missouri Compromise, Douglas ignited a political explosion. The Whig party shattered to the point where it ceased as a national organization, but its Northern wing gradually fused into the new Republican party, which was based on the containment of slavery. Among Tammanyites, the impact was just as severe. President Pierce made the bill official policy, and Softs wheeled into line. Hards were equally willing to back Douglas, but could not without endorsing the president. Most Free-Soilers were furious at Douglas's betrayal, considering it an elaborate trick to expand slavery, and slowly began shifting toward the Republicans.[6]

Wood was thrilled by those developments and tried to enhance his position through a devious tactic. With Cochrane out of town, he took over a Soft committee, arranging Tammany's first pro-Douglas rally. Wood dictated a series of resolutions against John Van Buren and in favor of popular sovereignty and Southern rights. Wood then planned to stack the Long Room with his men and schedule only Hard speakers. They would then endorse his resolves to create the impression that the Free-Soilers were the only group opposed to Douglas. That done, the Hards and Softs would unite around a common cause, Kansas-Nebraska, while sacrificing a common enemy, the Free-Soil Democrats, on the altar of party unity. Wood's strategy was brilliant but defective. Learning of his plan, Cochrane hastily returned, reconvened the committee, and quashed Wood's agenda because both he and Shepard feared that the Hards would use the opportunity to "censure the Administration." Even so, Wood emerged a winner because he wrote the meeting's major resolutions. He pleased Hards, Softs, and Douglasites by endorsing the bill and the principle of popular sovereignty. With the Hards placated, Wood then added to his laurels by also praising President Pierce and his administration. Only the Free-Soilers gained nothing. Always a realist, Wood understood that their bent toward Democratic political suicide rekindled his chances of using them as a vehicle for party unity.[7]

Shepard tried another means to limit Wood's growing stature. In his official capacity, Shepard opened peace negotiations with his Hard counterpart, merchant Augustus Schell. While each supported Douglas, their accommodation failed when Schell demanded a mutual condemnation of Pierce's patronage appointments as the price for cooperation. At that point, Shepard gave up in disgust, much to Wood's delight.[8]

Wood pressed on, aided by a series of fortunate events beginning in the spring of 1854. His luck began with Governor Seymour's veto of a prohibition bill passed by legislative temperance forces led by Senator Myron H. Clark. Wood sided with Seymour. Assiduously cultivating Democratic "drys," especially immigrants, Wood agreed with party leaders that Softs and Hards had cause for uniting around the Democracy's principle of noninterference in private behavior, whether it involved drinking or maintenance of slavery where it existed.[9]

Wood's stature increased in July when Pierce alienated practically every Tammanyite in selecting John McKeon, a Hard, instead of Shepard, as federal attorney for New York's southern district. Embittered Softs shouted that the president had insulted their local leader; furious Hards cried out that McKeon opposed the Kansas-Nebraska bill. As far as Wood was concerned, his long hostility to McKeon made him more attractive to both factions; Shepard's credentials as a party leader declined, and the Hards were split.[10]

Other factors helped Wood. In July, John Van Buren, physically ill and politically untouchable, left New York for an extended European vacation. Without him, the Free-Soilers were impotent. Then, too, the inept Civic Reform party, a group dedicated to good government, had sponsored a new municipal charter in 1853 that did not measurably improve the quality of urban life. Their failure left a vacuum that Wood intended to fill.[11]

Wood also helped himself, but in a scarcely ethical manner. As the Know-Nothing party grew, its secrecy attracted both nativist Whigs and Democrats. Moreover, while Know-Nothings were duty-bound to vote a straight ticket, nothing prevented them from secretly endorsing other candidates. As a result, several prominent Hards courted the Know-Nothings. In contrast, most Softs prodded by Shepard denounced them. New Yorkers expected nothing less from Wood. Since the 1830s, he had supported immigrant causes, backed Irish independence, contributed money to German and Irish relief agencies, and gained a devoted constituency among the city's so-called adopted citizens.

Wood found Know-Nothing secrecy a temptation too great to resist. He not only became a clandestine Know-Nothing, but accepted a place on their shadowy executive committee. Given his ego, Wood probably never considered the immorality of betraying immigrants, or the latent danger of a public disclosure, even though he knew few things in politics remained secret for long. As Horace Greeley's Republican *New York Tribune* cautioned, the Know-Nothing "conspiracy" was "a cut-throat affair, which ought to be resisted and exposed."[12]

When Democrats began gathering for municipal mayoral primary elections in late September, Wood assumed that he had preempted the field as the party's only symbol of unity. Over the last year, he had earned Soft admiration for supporting Pierce; most Hards endorsed his southernism; workers and immigrants found him a warm champion; and Douglas's backers were pleased when he held a reception for the visiting senator.[13]

Events occurred according to Wood's plans. He easily controlled the Soft convention, outpolling his nearest rival by better than three to one. Some Hards proved harder to sway, although Wood had won the majority of delegates in their primaries. It came as no surprise when he captured their mayoral nomination, 64 to 17, over James S. Libby, a hotel-keeper and president of the Sixth Avenue Railroad Company. Barr and Sweeny, however, wanted one of their own men who had a record of not truckling with anyone connected to Softs. Muddling the entire picture, they formed yet another faction, and eventually settled on Wilson H. Hunt, a former Civic Reformer, who paradoxically had Greeley's blessing.[14]

These moves exhilarated Wood since he was essentially a fusion candidate. He had the support of a majority of Softs, even though a few could not tolerate his alliance with Hards and contended that his nomination was a "gross" insult. Nor was he worried about Hunt. A majority of Hards wheeled into line because the Democracy made a fetish out of regular nominations; the traditional doctrine held that once the party selected a nominee, all opposition ceased. Even better, Wood ran against a divided field. In addition to Hunt, Know-Nothings nominated prohibitionist alderman James W. Barker, while the moribund Whigs, in a last gesture of defiance, selected merchant John J. Herrick.[15]

John Cochrane, a Hard who had little reason to support Wood, revealed how well Wood had changed the political game, but not its rules. Speaking at a Tammany rally, Cochrane endorsed the ticket and announced, "The Wood we adopted was neither Hard nor Soft; [his nomination] was Democratic." The gratified Wood took little for granted. Shunting aside state and national issues since they were too divisive, he concentrated on local reforms. A vote for him, he stressed, was a vote for progressive, honest, and efficient civic government. As for Tammany, he trusted it to hold firm, turn out party workers, and naturalize immigrants in time for the November election.[16]

Suddenly, on October 27, the campaign's texture abruptly changed. Wood's character became the sole issue. Two weeks earlier, the nativist *Morning Courier and New York Enquirer*, edited by the fiery James Watson Webb, had ominously noted that a grave "public rebuke" awaited Wood. At the proper moment, Webb promised in a somewhat mysterious manner, the paper would "exhume" his "antecedents" for public airing. The hour arrived, eleven days before polling.[17]

Wood's misery unfolded when several Know-Nothings filed affidavits disclosing that he was one of them. Forewarned by Webb, Wood denied any impropriety, bluntly called the nativists liars, and threatened to sue any newspaper which repeated their "libels." Webb was not cowed. He not only substantiated the accusations, but reprinted King's bank exposé, and for the first time documented the entire Marvine case. If those disclosures, Webb piously ended, "perfectly annihilate Mr. Wood's chances of an election, it is no fault of ours. We have simply discharged an imperative duty."[18]

There was something sadly amiss in Wood. Showing no sense of remorse, he tried to bluff by refusing to admit that the question was a legitimate campaign issue. His attitude, however, dismayed the stiffly upright Democratic *New York Evening Post*. "This double-dealing is one of the arts of able politicians at the present day," it intoned. Wood had gone beyond the bounds of comparable indecent behavior, and New Yorkers were "waiting with some curiosity to know which one of them he intends to cheat."[19]

Finally realizing the depth of the problem, Wood stiffened with righteousness. He bought advertisements in each Democratic newspaper to announce flatly, "I am not a member of any secret society whatever." When Webb retorted that "a rounder, baser, falsehood has never been perpetrated in Tammany politics," Wood instructed his attorneys to begin libel proceedings. To support that threat, Wood instituted such a suit against Beach's *New York Sun* for an allegedly defamatory editorial, and took satisfaction when Police Justice Michael Welsh ordered Beach's arrest. As for the Marvine case, Wood solicited a letter from former district attorney Tallmadge, who swore that *"no evidence was adduced implicating your integrity in the slightest degree."* When A. Oakey Hall, Tallmadge's assistant and a Whig candidate for that office, and Police Justice Benjamin Osborne corroborated the statement, Webb backed off. Perhaps the premature "publication of our account," he admitted, was "too flimsy." Nonetheless, Webb did not flinch from the key issue, Wood's connection to nativism. Greeley was right behind. How anyone could trust Wood was unfathomable, he jeered. Wood's Know-Nothingism was "terrible, withering." He had defrauded Marvine, despite what Tallmadge and Hall said, and was defrauding the gullible Irish and Germans the same way.[20]

These caustic and personal attacks disrupted the political system beyond any previous election. Strange allies formed. Greeley, a longtime foe of nativism, shifted to Barker as a lesser evil than Wood, and the antiextensionist *Evening Post* endorsed the proslavery Hunt out of his connection to civic reform. Even many Softs had second thoughts. At their last rally, speakers ignored the mayoral race and concentrated upon Governor Seymour's reelection. Only the *New York Irish-American* held firm. Editor Patrick Lynch assailed Hunt as a spoiler, and defended Wood as an enemy to bigots who persecuted people "on account of religion."[21]

Tuesday, November 8, began with an overcast sky, and a chill northwest wind swirled through the city. Wood cast his ballot early, then went home to await results with his anxious family. The returns were slow, and garbled reports indicated that the eventual winner would have the narrowest of margins. On Thursday, election inspectors ended the suspense and declared Wood the victor, and the die-hard Webb snarled, "supported by none but ignorant foreigners, and the most degraded class of Americans."[22]

Wood's triumph was bittersweet. Out of twenty-two wards, he carried a mere nine, and his plurality was paper-thin. He won with only 33.6 percent of the total vote; Barker was second with 31 percent; Hunt had 25.8 percent; Herrick limped in with 9.6 percent. As expected, the key to Wood's victory lay in his coalition based on working-class support, German and Irish ethnicity, and low per capita wealth. He scored best in the most poor and most heavily immigrant and working-class wards located generally on the East Side in lower Manhattan. Even so, in some traditionally strong Tammany East Side wards and newer ones uptown, Democratic defections to Hunt cut Wood's potential pluralities, and Barker eked out narrow wins. As Wood further anticipated, he was weakest among the native-born and the wealthy, people who lived usually on the West Side and above Fourteenth Street.[23]

In other contests, Democrats paid a stiff price for squabbling. A combination of prohibitionists, Know-Nothings, and Whigs, soon metamorphosed into Republicans, controlled the Common Council, the street commission, surrogate, city judge, district attorney, and register. Only one Hard won a city race, James M. Smith, the recorder. Outside of Wood, Softs lost every slot except a single Almshouse governor, Daniel F. Tiemann.[24]

The deflated Wood, his brio gone, soberly assessed what victory meant. Prospects were not pretty. He was a minority mayor, with scant means for effective leadership, heading a split party. Enemies dominated the municipal government's legislative branches and executive departments, and controlled the bulk of city spoils. The situation in Albany was just as bleak. Myron Clark defeated Seymour, largely because of Democratic bickering, and prohibitionists intent on passing a fresh temperance law ruled the state legislature.[25]

Before unraveling this bramble, Wood had to judge himself. He would have been less than human if he chose to ignore how the campaign battered his reputation and humiliated him, or discounted Greeley's harsh judgment, "No man ever went into higher office under a deeper cloud of ignominy than [Wood] will."[26]

Shortly after the election, Wood paid a courtesy call on William Cullen Bryant, the Democracy's self-anointed conscience. Explaining why he had sought the office, Wood told Bryant that he had lived too long with innuendoes questioning his honesty. The victory gave him a chance "to prove that, whatever reproaches he had incurred in times past as a merchant and citizen; in times to come, as their servant and public functionary, he would entitle himself to their esteem and gratitude." Bryant gave him the benefit of the doubt. The next day, the *Evening Post* editorialized that Wood had demonstrable "ability and experience to make a good [chief] magistrate."[27] The rest was up to him.

Ever since he settled permanently in New York, Wood had sought respectability, money, and power. Respectability was now suspect, no matter his riches, leaving only the so-far indefinable pursuit of power. It slowly came into focus for him, now. The mayoralty was his means for personal redemption.

As Wood prepared to take office on January 1, 1855, the municipality faced unprecedented possibilities and problems. The economy was booming. Foreign and domestic trade, particularly with the slave states, along with flourishing shipbuilding, made the harbor the nation's busiest. New York was America's banker, its center for venture capital. Stock speculators, headquartered on Wall Street, along with like-minded men in real estate, heralded a new get-rich-quick mentality. In manufacturing, older industries modernized and new ones sprang up. All these factors combined to create a massive job market, which lured huge numbers of internal native migrants and external immigrants. The swelling

population, which grew from 629,801 in 1855 to 805,358 in 1860, the years overlapping Wood's three terms as mayor, bore testimony to the city's vitality.

New York's surging commercial growth and its consequences, its glory and
shame, remade the urban landscape and set the framework for Wood's tenure.
Beyond all else, he was an astute student of everyday life. New York, he
observed with pride, was "a great empire–great in its extent–great in its
population–great in its wealth; great in its commerce; great in its splendor." Such
greatness had a reverse side. New York was just as "great in the quantity of its
vice, destitution and wretchedness which pervades its streets."[28]

Wood aptly described a city divided against itself. Economic growth triggered
massive social disorders, weakened older ties of family and community, altered
the workplace, and strained the nature of traditional governance. A widening gap
between rich and poor highlighted the city's latent socioeconomic antagonisms.
Rhetoric about equality to the contrary, the class system was becoming more
rigid. At the top, men with inherited wealth and some lucky artisans with capital
reaped the real benefits of economic growth, lived well, and patronized lesser
breeds. In the middle were those of modest prosperity but great aspirations, generally native-born, hoping that with hard work they would join the ranks of this
monied elite. Others among them were less sanguine. Advancing technology and
industry eroded craftsmanship, and skilled wage earners, long the bulwark of the
labor force, lost autonomy and status. Many sought a solution through militant
trade unions and confronted employers and even politicians with increased
demands for more influence in decision-making.

Times were particularly harsh among the semiskilled and unskilled, no matter
their origins, the city's underclass, its largest group. Employment was sporadic,
and unlimited competition for jobs usually lowered wages. With life set in unremitting squalor and poverty, these people needed special care. In an era of
limited government, however, municipal fathers usually ignored them, further
degrading their quality of life. Even worse, many nativists considered the immigrants the causes, not the victims, of these conditions. The upshot was that some
of the poor turned to youth gangs, crime, and prostitution as a means of upward
mobility.

Wood's mayoralty becomes understandable only within the context of
extraordinary economic progress and severe human crises. New York was ready
for a reform-minded, innovative leader, a man with an overarching and compelling vision of a better society, a city builder, a person with the capacity to make
the government respond to needs which other mayors had not acknowledged let
alone addressed. It was here that Fernando Wood established himself as a major
figure in the life of his city and, ultimately, his nation.

Little was assured from the very beginning. In theory, the mayor was the municipality's chief executive; in practice, the recently revised city charter hindered

Wood to the point where he was nearly powerless. His two-year term was far too short for consistent, long-range planning. He did serve on nine city boards, excluding his mayoral department, either as president or an ex officio member, and presided over a mayor's court, but only three contained possible administrative functions: the sinking fund, which controlled $20 million of city property; the board of supervisors, the county's legislative body, consisting of the mayor, recorder, and aldermen; and the three-man police board of mayor, city judge, and recorder. Since he shared decision-making on these boards, leadership rested upon collegial, not executive, methods. Wood's only countervailing strength lay in a presidential-style veto, subject to a legislative override.

Other executive restraints existed. The charter spread administrative duties among the nine departments, each independently elected, and headed by men over whom Wood lacked authority. That meant he had no control of basic municipal operations, ranging from budgets to taxation, from street-cleaning to lighting, and could not coordinate overlapping jurisdictions or contrary management practices.

Limited structural and statutory appointing powers equally stymied Wood. Contrary to the standard political cry that the mayor was a spoils-monger, the charter divided patronage among the nine departments with legislative approval. Wood, heading only the mayoral department, the tenth one, directly named less than thirty people and shared another sixty or so with appropriate divisions. As a would-be strong mayor, Wood needed vast amounts of patronage at his disposal but found little. Hostile department heads were uncooperative, especially "streets" which had the largest number of positions. His alternatives lay in somehow convincing the departments to share patronage, manipulating the boards to choose his people, or forging an alliance with the collector of the Custom House, whose seven hundred or so federal jobs formed the biggest pool of potential local spoils.

The bicameral Common Council equally frustrated Wood. It consisted of a twenty-two-member board of aldermen, elected on a staggered ward basis, serving for two years, and a sixty-member board of councilmen, with the sole right of appropriation, chosen annually from districts equal in population. The system, geared to checks and balances, did not work. Both houses were often more concerned with guarding their parochial interests and prerogatives from the mayor or departments than what was best for the city.

As if these problems were not enough, the state legislature had taken over the process of charter revision. Although the issue was debatable, a spate of recent judicial opinions had stripped the city of its traditional municipal powers of home rule derived from colonial charters. The result left New York a pawn of upstate legislators, many of whom had an antiurban bias against the "wicked city" and anything smacking of Tammany Hall.

Taken as a whole, the city government's structure, with all its fragmentation and competing centers of gravity, conspired against Wood's obsession for an effective administration. No systematic method of delivering public services was available, notably in vital welfare and unemployment aid. Taxation and spending, based on real and personal property rates, were disorganized, often caving under political and business pressures. Any raises in rates or expenditures drew outraged shouts of extravagance, waste, and corruption. While some evidence existed that these charges were valid, the fact remained that more money was necessary to meet even minimal requirements for urgent services.[29]

By every variable, then, the mayoralty was almost an empty honor, perhaps a political dead end. Since 1844, no mayor had been reelected. Totalling all of Wood's predecessors back to 1787, only DeWitt Clinton, nearly forty years earlier, had vaulted beyond the city's petty ward politics to become a state and national figure.

Where others saw a feckless mayor, Wood saw opportunity. Between the November election and his January inauguration, he was invigorated, not awed, by the conditions he inherited. Through administrative daring, personal charisma, and political skill, he prepared a broad program of government action, emphasizing his inborn executive abilities, to serve human ends, promote urban development, and guarantee commercial progress.

In sculpting his executive persona, Wood realized how badly the charter's endemic disorder, its diffusion of power, coupled to the Democracy's ceaseless factionalism, crippled his prospects for positive leadership. As a result, he planned a new departure in running the city. Effective municipal reform, he realized, held the promise of garnering endless support from groups he helped, but would also generate equally strong opposition from other groups he challenged. In order to mobilize support and minimize inevitable political opposition, then, Wood refused to act as a creature of Tammany Hall and strove to create a broad public coalition based on being the nonpartisan mayor of all New Yorkers.

No previous mayor was better equipped and ready to move against the old order than Fernando Wood. Following his own instincts and ego, Wood characteristically took charge of everything—"one-man rule," he called it—and concentrated decision-making in himself. Few mayors better understood the eventual political rewards. While his personal redemption rested in good government, the mayoralty was a political office and Wood was a political animal. Wood dreamed a great dream: a successful mayoralty, the unification of Tammany under his sole leadership, and, perhaps, even greater rewards, maybe the presidency. With these goals before him, Wood confronted his challenge. In the process, he became a unique figure, New York's first modern mayor, a city builder, and the prototype for later municipal leaders, a man who anticipated much of what would become the urban Progressive Movement.

FOUR

The Model Mayor

M AYOR Wood was the very picture of a chief magistrate: tall and erect in bearing; urbane in manner; intelligent, forceful, and personable, with a commanding, authoritative presence. These traits became clear in his opening annual address. Some parts echoed previous mayors—platitudes and promises flowed about construction of modern docks, efficient street cleaning, maintenance of public order, suppression of crime and vice, frugal government, enforcement of ordinances, public accountability of monies spent, and absolute impartiality in administering the law.

Where Wood diverged from predecessors was more important than where he was the same. Going directly to the fundamental issue, he termed the charter an "ill-shaped monster" which prevented any semblance of home rule. In fact, "so far as my duties are defined, I feel some embarrassment." The police department stood out as the worst example. Ostensibly "the head of the Police Department," the mayor lacked "the essential elements of authority, that of controlling the retention or removal of his own subordinates."[1]

Tinkering with the charter was fruitless. A thorough revision was the only remedy, grounded on home rule, structured along federal lines, with departments consolidated into a bureaucratic cabinet, topped by a strong executive who had "one-man power." Until then, Wood pledged bold leadership. "As I understand and comprehend my duties and prerogatives, they leave me no alternative, without dishonor, but to assume a general control over the whole City Government, so far as protecting its municipal interests."[2]

As for human needs, Wood shocked traditionalists by proving that he was unshackled either by the past or by distorted perceptions of the present. In a day when governments were indifferent toward protecting citizens from the hazards of the marketplace, he proposed the radical idea of having the city hire some temporarily unemployed laborers for public works. His quest for social justice ended with Locofocoism. "This is the time to remember the poor," the victims in a two-tiered society of a privileged few and the disadvantaged many. Using words that became his theme song, Wood predicted that capitalism could not survive if "labor, which produces every thing, gets nothing, and dies of hunger in our midst, while capital, which produces nothing, gets every thing and pampers in luxury and plenty."[3]

Wood's tone seemed right for the man and his city. He was a reformer facing staggering problems but determined to stretch the limits of possible power. Once in office, he began to implement his nonpartisan strategy as a consensus mayor, and he revealed an unsuspected talent for finding symbols to win a favorable press for himself and his programs. The image he projected was that of a hard-working, honest, dedicated, almost driven public servant who epitomized the passing of an old passive order to a fresh dynamic leader.

His routine began before dawn at Woodlawn. Prior to breakfast with his family, he read and answered mail, prepared messages, and outlined work schedules for subordinates. Living over five miles from city hall, almost a two-hour ride on omnibus lines, he rented rooms during the winter in residential hotels or stayed overnight in a house he owned in the Fifth Ward.

Wood arrived at his office promptly at nine and wove his way through an awaiting crowd of job applicants, favor-seekers, and sycophants. Shaking hands with some, nodding to others, he walked into an inner room, guarded by a police doorkeeper, and began seeing callers. Interviews often proved tedious, but Wood kept up the pace until the last person departed. Explaining his reasons to a reporter, he remarked that the mayor was "a court of last resort for ordinary people, caught in 'red tape.'" They left with a cordial feeling, convinced "the only friend they have in government is Fernando Wood."[4]

His office closed at four, but ceremonial duties often propelled his hectic schedule far into the night. Performing as the city's first citizen and official master of ceremonies, during only January and February of 1855, for example, he attended or spoke at Tammany's New Orleans Ball, the New York Typographical Society's gala, a police parade, the George Washington Day annual dinner, and a rally for militia units. No matter the demands on his time; each event was vital symbolically and politically because Mayor Wood was the star. As one toaster spontaneous put it to "protracted cheering," Wood "has already ascertained that the true road to popularity is the discharge of duty."[5]

During the first week of August, Wood and his family fled the city's heat for a ten-day holiday at the United States Hotel or Congress Hall in Saratoga. While his wife and children relaxed, he rarely strayed from politics, and touched base with other politicians who vacationed there. Even then, he was never far from city hall. Nativist Isaac O. Barker, the president of the board of aldermen and ex officio acting mayor, often took advantage of his absence to push legislation which he opposed, forcing Wood to make a hasty return.[6]

Wood's image-building touched other matters. Making sure the community appreciated his honesty, he prohibited, with suitable publicity, anyone in his administration, including himself, from accepting gratuities grateful citizens normally heaped on city officials, and dramatized his integrity by ordering the arrest of a newsdealer for distributing a "vile sheet." Beyond all else, the police formed his showcase for efficient one-man rule. Strengthening discipline, insisting "that every requirement is complied with," he tightened efficiency by personally hiring competent physicians and reorganizing the department's medical section to maximize manpower and prevent shirking. To identify individual achievement, he awarded silver medals, cast at his "own expense," to several outstanding men, and lectured others to take pride in their work. Similar aims spilled over to Democratic factionalism. He wrote a nonplussed Marcy: "My mind & time is so completely occupied with municipal affairs, that politics is almost forgotten."[7]

Such was the picture Wood sought to draw. During his first months in office, he was everywhere, nagging, prodding, giving orders. From his desk poured suggestions for building a new city hall, paving streets, separating the dates of local and national elections, pushing harder on the construction of Central Park, taxing foreign property, setting procedures for supervising municipal expenditures, cutting unnecessary spending, strictly regulating public health, and speeding the piping of water to new districts. Cynics scoffed that he proved the old adage about reformers: they found unimportant problems and then solved them. Wood forced nay-sayers into initial shocked silence. The problems he exposed were real; his solutions were innovative; his style mustered public support. Some crusades were not new, but he put his stamp on practically every issue previous reformers had advocated, went far beyond them, and made sure the public appreciated that his administration and civic reform were synonymous.

His assault on the status quo started with a flourish. Early in January 1855, he opened a "complaint book" for ordinary citizens, and promised to remedy "any violation of the ordinances and derelictions of duty upon the part of any person holding office under the City Government." The book became that and more. People "from all parts" of New York, even with the "mercury 16 [degrees] below zero," came to city hall to fill it with a litany of urban woes. They grumbled about intoxicated policemen, indifferent street cleaners, defrauding contractors, hostile omnibus drivers, juvenile gangs, dirty public markets, cheating merchants, pimps preying on young women, and poor sewerage. Even Bennett of the powerful *New York Herald* came to gripe about "the loafers on his block." In almost all cases, Wood took personal charge or delegated solutions. The bemused Republican *New York Times,* speaking for his former critics, was enthralled. "Every day chronicles some new reforms—sees the end of some hoary old abuses." While the book lost its novelty by the close of 1855, Wood made his point. Humble citizens had a friend in "our Hercules" in city hall.[8]

His credentials established, Wood launched an energetic crusade to improve the quality of urban life by enforcing Sunday closing laws, running gamblers out of town, and ending prostitution. None proved easy targets. Police were selective in arresting offenders; influential Democratic aldermen complained that he crippled the heart of their clubs in neighborhood saloons; and party ideologues warned about meddling with personal liberties. The fervor against "harlots" dissipated in unforeseen complications. Judges released most prostitutes because of illegal warrants, and some came out of jail a more professionalized group of street-walkers. Wood's major problem lay in his unwillingness to consider prostitution's economic causes or its place in the city's subculture of poverty. One poor woman, caught in a raid at a "dancing saloon," put the matter straight. Her alternatives were "to dance or starve." Since she "was capable of taking care of herself," the mayor could do nothing to stop her and thousands of others. With little accomplished, then, Wood's misfires made him faintly ridiculous, but he did score an important point. As the *Herald* noted: "People said he was to be the rowdy's man, the rum mayor, the blackguard's friend and many other things. What a blunder was here!"[9]

Despite Bennett's accolade, legislative temperance leaders had their own agenda, and in April 1855 the state adopted an ambitious sumptuary law that compromised Wood's position. Letting emotions override judgment, however, they wrote a defective law that he manipulated to his advantage. To begin with, the law delayed implementation until July 4, essentially voiding previous restrictions between the dates of passage and enforcement. Wood contended that older statutes no longer applied and interpreted the provision as a legitimate excuse to end unpopular Sunday closings. Prohibitionists were furious but impotent because Whig District Attorney Hall filed a concurring brief, justifying Wood on legal as well as nonpartisan grounds. Beyond that, Wood blasted the bill's biases, especially one clause which did not specifically bar the sale of imported liquors to appease wealthier classes and another excluding upstate districts from enforcement. As July 4 neared, he instructed the police that the law was so vague in certain instances that they were liable for false arrests, and the city would not defend them in such suits. In his final shot, he promised to obey the legislature, provided the court of appeals declared the law constitutional.[10]

When the judiciary found against prohibitionists in September 1855, Wood's triumph was complete even if his championship of virtue was tarnished. To drys, he claimed that he still favored a strict standard of public control but chided them for preventing workable regulations. To law and order advocates, he emphasized that Hall and the court had sustained his position. At the same time, Wood retained the loyalty of party saloon keepers and immigrants, who considered him a wet, since he had disassociated himself from the bill. While drys such as Greeley called him a hypocrite, Wood lost minimal political support and emerged as a practical, if thwarted, reformer.[11]

Important as these efforts were, Wood considered them a prelude to his key contribution to making New York a livable city through ensuring public safety. By the 1850s, many New Yorkers linked antisocial behavior and the rise of youth gangs to immigrants. Wood rejected this simplistic interpretation. Within his lifetime, New York had rarely been orderly. Instead, he bent on halting endemic lawlessness through a strong police department, organized along paramilitary lines, under his sole responsibility.

After barely a week in office, Wood ignited a long and bitter battle by sending the Common Council a special message to amend the 1853 police act. The police board, he argued, was unworkable because its two judicial members, Hard Recorder Smith and Whig City Judge Sidney Stuart, had incompatible roles as officers of the court and commissioners, while their elective positions inevitably politicized the department. Having outlined the problem, Wood projected himself as the solution. He forcibly maintained that the aldermen must put him in charge, the one man in city government above petty politicking. Trust him to eradicate "politics from the department," he told New Yorkers.[12]

Cynicism was the order of the day. Supporters believed his posture "as a no-party chief magistrate" was a smoke screen, and clamored for police appointments in the same way previous mayors from both parties had manipulated the department into a political annex. Yet to converts, Wood promised that he was different. That, in turn, raised a conundrum. He had few patronage positions to begin with, and the public wondered how to trust a mayor who professed elevating the public interest and reform to new ethical plateaus but then might use the police force for spoils.[13] Beset on all sides by distrust, then, Wood assumed his popular reforms would silence critics. Amid these contrary expectations, one question remained unclear: Was Wood intent on improving the police, or building a personal political empire? For the moment, no one was sure, and the aldermen ignored his message.

Republican legislators did not wait for his answer, and introduced two bills limiting any possible discretionary power. One proposed the popular election of the chief of police; the second replaced the board with four elected commissioners. Wood met the challenge head-on. Brandishing his immense prestige, he wrote a public letter to Republican Lieutenant Governor Henry Raymond, the *Times*'s owner and editor, threatening to resign. Whether his warning intimidated the legislators was uncertain, but both bills died.[14]

Wood's bold move did not sit well with Raymond and his staff. Since January, the *Times* had been his staunchest booster, and its support strengthened his freedom of action. Approval turned to disillusion over the police. By early spring, the paper began admonishing Wood that although it had "more generously" commended him "for the good that he has done" than any other paper, its support was not automatic. After praising the general thrust of his reforms, it issued a veiled hint wrapped in flattery. "One-man rule" was a dangerous doctrine if the city "lacked the services of a Mayor so free from party biases and predilections as you." As for the police, the *Times* claimed Wood dominated the board and only appointed foreign-born Democrats.[15]

Wood did not retreat under such heavy fire but became more prudent. He intimidated Recorder Smith to back him, indeed becoming the board's actual head. Aware of public concern, however, Wood pledged to form a professional force by personally weeding out incompetents, hiring honest replacements, promoting the efficient, and creating the order the community craved.[16]

On the surface, everything seemed calm, almost tranquil, because Wood's police were "working well." Nothing better illustrated his galloping popularity than the protest meeting against the police bills held on March 21 at the Broadway Tabernacle. Bankers, reformers, merchants, former mayors, even Greeley, the cream of the city's elite, shared the platform and passed a series of resolutions which praised Wood and supported his efforts.[17]

Convinced that he had passed his first test of confidence, Wood moved on to other pressing causes. For years, New Yorkers had been scandalized by haphazard street cleaning, treating it as a dismal joke. Wood resurrected the issue for practical reasons. During the harsh winter of 1855, he echoed longtime, almost obligatory, strictures about nativist Street Commissioner Joseph Ebling's failure to clear snow and remove ice from heavily traveled thoroughfares. Yet Wood had no intention of just repeating trite complaints. In the summer when lackadaisical garbage collection was most acute, he proposed the novel idea of replacing individual street sweepers with more efficient machinery. On his own, he found such devices in Baltimore's Smith, Seckel and Company, and lobbied aldermen and Ebling for an experimental contract. Wood won their reluctant approval and watched with pride as the machines worked better than anyone expected. To his chagrin, the Common Council refused to renew the contract, the *Times* mentioned, because "horses, carts and revolving brushes can't vote." Nonetheless, Wood emerged a winner. A grand jury indicted Ebling, alleging that he had solicited a bribe from the company for his consent. While the trial ended in a hung jury, Wood indirectly wounded a key rival and the entire nativist movement. Wood's obsession with clean streets reaped another dividend during August when city residents braced themselves for the recurrent cholera season. With fear running rampant, Ebling ran out of money due to gross overpayments to nativist cronies and could not carry out his duties. All that proved, Wood preached, the wisdom of charter revision, putting all departments under his control.[18]

The cholera menace led to another of Wood's concerns connected to public health, food distribution for poor consumers. Problems abounded. City-licensed stalls monopolized sales, often at inflated prices, and Ebling paid little attention to sanitary oversight. Outraged, Wood demanded a freer marketing system to widen competition, and upbraided Ebling for mismanaging Washington and Fulton markets, the city's major public distribution points.[19]

The health issue, however, embroiled Wood in a personally damaging dispute. The year before, a merchant ship, the *Joseph Walker,* sank adjacent to a city pier. In January 1855, notices began appearing in the complaint book that its rotting cargo might "breed pestilence." To prove the effectiveness of one-man rule, Wood responded through his statutory seat as head of the Board of Health. He selected Walter H. Jones as the lowest bidder to remove the wreck and accepted his surety for $150,000. Technical snags developed. By August, Jones had raised only the stern out of deep mud, and the stench of decomposing grain fouled the air. Suddenly, work halted in controversy. Alderman Anson J. Herrick, editor of the weekly *New York Atlas,* one of Wood's bitterest foes, published "records of rascality" about the *Walker* episode, and hooted that corruption, not concerns for public health, motivated "Fernando the First." Jones, Herrick swore, was not the lowest bidder, and won the contract only by bribing Wood with $11,000.[20]

Herrick's contention compromised Wood's hard-won glitter and revived doubts about his honesty. This time he was lucky. Herrick destroyed his own credibility when he was among five other aldermen charged with bribery in another matter. His assaults, then, seemed an effort to deflect his own guilt. Still, Wood knew suspicion existed; discretion dictated a swift reply. After sending a dignified message to the Common Council promising a full investigation of Jones's tardiness, Wood forced Jones to issue a public statement denying bribery. Wood closed the case with a haughty challenge. "I am willing to make good any money that the City will lose by any act of mine while Mayor, where I assume the responsibility. I mean this as a general declaration." On that note, Wood seemingly salvaged his reformist credentials.[21]

Wood turned then to the matter of safe and efficient mass transit. The New York & Harlem Railroad, the major Manhattan passenger carrier, drew his special wrath. Acting as a consumer watchdog, he warned directors that they risked loss of contracts if fares increased and services decreased. On a related matter, he warned about excessive speeds in populated areas, and advanced the idea of redesigned cars with front and rear fenders to prevent people from falling under the wheels. Wood's other novel recommendations included new platforms, sturdy iron railings, and clearly marked right-of-way. For Staten Island commuters, he urged the Common Council to take greater care in drawing future ferry contracts, and questioned fare raises.[22]

In the same vein, Wood intensified his commitment to city planning and urban land usage through development of Central Park. While others, notably his immediate predecessor, Mayor Jacob A. Westervelt, had sponsored it, Wood protected the park from greedy speculators who convinced the Common Council to pass an ordinance reducing its size. Anticipating the later "City Beautiful" movement, Wood championed the idea of providing urbanites, mainly the under-class living in tenements without sufficient air and light, with open spaces for relaxation. Perhaps less idealistic reasons were afoot. The park ran along his property in the upper wards, enhancing its value. But the motives that guided his thinking were less important than his actions. In a ringing veto, Wood told alder-men they were "derelict" if they allowed selfish feelings to "deprive the teeming millions yet to inhabit and toil upon this island" of the one place free commercial-ism "to observe and worship nature." As late as 1873, Wood took a paternal interest in the park's evolution by making suggestions to its architects about landscaping.[23]

During this flurry, Wood never lost sight of his basic immigrant constituency. In his official capacity under the charter as a commissioner of emigration, he wel-comed newcomers and praised their arrival as a source of national pride. More-over, he ordered the investigation of ships as they arrived to inspect sanitary conditions and food supplies, barring them from future berths if they failed to meet fundamental standards of decency. Despite this solicitousness, Wood may have also been playing his characteristic double game. In statements easily trans-lated into either a defense of sterling immigrants or support of nativism, Wood blamed European nations for dumping undesirable criminals in the United States and called on the state legislature, Congress, and President Pierce to set up screening procedures which in some cases were tantamount to exclusion.[24]

Halfway through his first term, Wood's personal popularity reached its zenith. His innovative programs garnered massive public support, and he was well on the way to fulfilling his pledge to Bryant. Wood was even a national phenome-non. Newspapers in other cities recorded his accomplishments and pleaded for interviews; strangers wrote for autographs; and throughout the country politi-cians marked him as a man with a larger future stage than New York City. Per-haps most pleasing, American Family Publications, which disseminated didactic literature for young people, crowned his search for respect in issuing his biogra-phy, whose title left no one in doubt about its thesis: *A Model Mayor. Early Life, Congressional Career and Triumphant Municipal Administration of Hon. Fernando Wood, Mayor of the City of New York.*[25]

It was equally clear, however, that while Wood was a leader with vast talents, he had conspicuous personal flaws which he was unable to overcome. The one-man ruler's quest for unlimited power, coupled to police and charter reforms, stirred too many controversies for his own good. In the end, Wood squandered his carefully built assets and made himself seem nothing more than a dangerous demagogue.

However high-minded Wood's goals or the enormous prestige he enjoyed, critics inevitably began scrutinizing his handling of sensitive police personnel matters. A loose-knit group of Know-Nothings, Republicans, Hards, and Whigs interpreted removals as political purges, discipline as partisan punishments, hirings as discrimination against native-born Protestants, and promotions as favoritism. Of these, the *Times* was the most formidable censor because of its earlier support, and now accused him of treachery. Wood, it editorialized, had politicized the force and acted "as a party man," carrying "his partisan sentiments into a department that he promised should be sacred from that approach."[26]

Although preferring silence, Wood tried to clear the air by listing his appointments and renewals. Out of fifty-three men, thirty-one were Whigs and twenty-two Democrats. Among them were fourteen adopted citizens and thirty-nine native-born. The *Times* looked at the same statistics and came up with a different analysis. Many of the so-called Whigs were really Democrats who had hidden their identity to protect their jobs from previous Whig mayors. At least those earlier mayors were not hypocrites, braying about nonpartisanship.[27]

By July 1855, the previously cowed Common Council shifted sails with this breeze. A Know-Nothing and Hard alliance, the majority in both houses, demanded full information, with specific names and dates, about each appointment, renewal, and removal. Wood came up with a disingenuous brush-off. Citing a legal technicality, he noted that both government branches, legislative and executive, had to make the request. Since he did not, the issue was moot.[28]

The *Times* flared with contempt. While the paper harbored few illusions about the Common Council's quality—"not one man in ten doubts that our City Government is a sink of evil"—it wrote, the aldermen were correct about the mayor's false "shower of golden promises." Wood's honeymoon was over. In dirgelike tones, the paper reported that the streets were still filthy, public morals squalid, corruption omnipresent, and thus the fruition of reform was remote. So "much promised," it sadly concluded, "so little has been accomplished." The legislature agreed. In December, it formed a special investigation to study Wood's conduct of the police.[29]

In a major way, these judgments were unfair. Many of Wood's programs languished because the Common Council refused to enact them. Even so, the police situation revealed Wood at his worst. For a politician of his training and instincts, his failure to anticipate that juggling patronage and reform could not work bordered on the ludicrous. On closer inspection, he really had few options, given the paucity of legitimate spoils at his disposal and his obsession with one-man rule. Under those conditions, the police were indeed his showcase, but for the wrong reasons. Beneath Wood's studied veneer of impartial government and public service, a downturn in public opinion was taking place about his relationship to the department. The result destroyed his prospects.

By fall elections, the Model Mayor was a troubled man. Convinced his reforms were still viable, he kept above politics and avoided the continued friction between Hards and Softs. Instead, he broke up a "Freelove Club" in the

Ninth Ward, held public meetings about new omnibus routes in midtown, and reviewed police parades. It was an exercise in self-deception. As a sign of how deeply his popularity had plunged, "hisses" spewed out at a Civic Reform Party rally when a speaker read a resolution praising his administration.[30]

On election day, Wood seemed indifferent, but the returns negated any prospect of forming a nonpartisan government. The Common Council belonged to his opponents. Know-Nothings won the comptroller's office, three local judges, the street commission, and the city inspector. Whig Elisha S. Capron, who thoroughly disliked Wood, replaced Stuart on the police board. Hards gained three departments and one almshouse governor, putting into office Richard B. Connolly and C. Godfrey Gunther, each of whom cut into Wood's Irish and German constituencies respectively. Only one Soft was a victor, Lorenzo Shepard as counsel to the corporation, but he was scarcely Wood's ally. Upstate, Know-Nothingism increased, and Republicans replaced Whigs as the dominant power in many counties.[31]

Surrounded by enemies, Wood must have realized that under existing conditions he could only propose, not execute, his ideas. Bowing to necessity, he laid out a fresh master plan to regain the initiative. As the Model Mayor, he still wanted to end his term with eminent reforms. But while he planned to accentuate his nonpartisanship and forceful administrative daring, he understood he could not rely alone on operating as the consensus mayor of all New Yorkers and needed somehow to gain Tammany's full support. The achievement of these ends could place the 1856 gubernatorial nomination within reach, or perhaps even the vice-presidency if the party nominated a Southerner and needed to balance the ticket. If those efforts failed, a mayoral renomination was still worthwhile, but under his terms, not that of either faction. At the same time, Wood eyed the presidential field, ready to clamber aboard the likely winner's bandwagon before other New York Democrats, thus earning exclusive title to local patronage and using it as a lever to dominate the Democracy.

Still confident, energetic, and iron-willed, Wood assumed his entire future as well as his historic reputation rested on proving that New York was the best governed city in the United States. With that in mind, he spent the next six months proposing visionary solutions to old ills. His goals were nothing less than to revitalize his society and lift ordinary citizens to a better tomorrow. In the process, the Model Mayor restored his luster and forced opponents to debate the issues on his grounds.

Beginning with his annual address in January 1856, Wood advocated a dynamic variety of creative programs dealing with the urban environment: stronger building codes, including requirements that contractors were responsible for laying sidewalks along properties and connecting conduits for sewers; a new sanitary police empowered to enforce hygienic rules; an equally new group of inspectors to supervise food marketing and the construction of modern stalls, either by the city or private businessmen; and a steady supply of fresh water ensured by installing meters on each building to prevent wastage. For pedestrians, he demanded that builders remove equipment piled carelessly on sidewalks and suggested the Common Council use Broadway as an example for the rest of the city to regulate the size of porches, stoops, and advertising signs.[32]

Beyond the present city lay the New York of the future. Continued commercial growth required the erection of permanent stone and brick wharves to replace older, wooden structures; expansion of the Croton Water Works; better means of rapid mass transit; and a new commission to expedite street construction according to the grid plan, but sprinkled with parks and greenswards. If the Common Council played politics with any of these public improvements, he suggested that private entrepreneurs take over the tasks.[33]

A large part of tomorrow's potential rested on tangible human resources, the city's young people, Wood believed. He had no quarrel with the board of education, which had recently replaced the Public School Society and ran semiautonomous ward schools through local trustees. Seemingly, he considered them efficient and a potential patronage resource. He was more concerned with making higher education available to all New Yorkers, both men and women. Borrowing ideas from others, he advocated expanding the current system, capped by forming a "great university. . .to be free and open to all who will partake of its great advantages."[34]

Wood's wish list required large spending. Aware that city budgets were not only about dollars and cents, but votes and political power, he soothed taxpayers with assurances that his programs were cost-effective, resting on fiscal prudence and sound management. Wood had much to prove. During his tenure, municipal taxes and expenditures rose in a heart-stopping spiral. From 1855 to 1856, the tax rate climbed from $1.20 to $1.38 per $100 on the assessed valuation of property; spending increased by $1,231,605; and bonded debt rose from $14,010,737 to $15,587,053. During 1855 alone, the cost of paving streets escalated by $1,250,000; school costs increased $689,000; and the annual outlay for the almshouse ran $800,000 per year. To critics, these figures proved his administration was shot full of fraud.[35]

Wood pleaded for understanding. Such increases, he noted, were inevitable given "the extending area and increasing population of New-York" which "has been so rapid that local legislation has hitherto been unable to keep pace with progress." Even so, Wood observed that he was blameless for higher taxes and costs because the charter put finances beyond his control. If citizens sought culprits, they should fault irresponsible aldermen and department heads, who never stayed within budgets and authorized "profligate" payments for unapproved projects that breached conservative fiscal policies. "The same haste to get rid of every dollar appropriated and, if possible, to create the necessity for additional appropriations, has been apparent in every bureau, with but one or three highly creditable exceptions." By contrast, he proudly asserted, the police department had a flawless record. It protected the lives and property of more than six hundred thousand residents and thousands of visitors; arrests were up; discipline improved; and it carried on all its complex duties within its budget. These facts indicated to his satisfaction the validity of one-man rule.[36]

As a city planner, Wood urged new businesslike management techniques for more productive government. He again called for an up-to-date structure to replace the old and inefficient city hall. The municipality also owned property which did not generate revenues. Those should be sold to the highest bidder. As for handling public monies, he called on the comptroller to assure taxpayers that the city was indeed frugal by opening his books for public inspection. Then, too, nuisance suits bogged down the law department. Levying a small fee on plaintiffs and collecting costs if they lost would dissuade capricious litigants.[37]

Then there was the charter, the source of all of New York's troubles. "The object of government is simple," he asserted, "it is to govern in the public interest, for aiding the many without threatening the few." Since the legislature was uninterested in such aims, Wood advocated a grassroots movement to secure home rule. The example lay in the past when public-spirited people had revised outdated charters and submitted them for voter approval. Wood's trust in participatory democracy, however, was limited. Determined to guide the public, he had no intention of accepting anything less than one-man rule which gave the mayor "ample power" to correct "every municipal wrong."[38]

The sum total of all these proposals, Wood concluded, would guarantee a greater municipality than the city his generation had inherited. Because of his efforts, he predicted, New Yorkers would be rightfully proud of their "citizenship in this metropolis," for they could "say with Paul of Tarsus, 'I am a citizen of no mean city.'"[39]

It was a virtuoso performance. His addresses sparked enthusiasm from all sides of the partisan press, and dispelled notions that he had lost initiative. In a representative editorial, the *Times* counseled the Common Council to give his programs "respectful consideration." Response from the city's commercial and banking communities was just as gratifying when the legislature's special investigation found irregularities in police appointments, citing in particular Wood's alleged favoritism toward the Irish. In April their endorsement of Wood proved instrumental in convincing the legislature to adjourn without taking action on two bills to reorganize the force and revise the charter. Still, signs of trouble abounded. One Republican legislator told a reporter, Wood "must be put down; and as we have the power here now, we will do it."[40]

At first, the reaction within the Common Council ranged from lukewarm support to outright hostility, then sharply veered to confrontational, almost petty, politics. Several nativist aldermen tried to fire Wood's police chief, George Matsell, who had held the office since 1845, on the dubious grounds that he had lied about his purported English birth and had never become a citizen. Other Hard and Soft aldermen rescinded an emergency contract that Wood had personally granted to several private companies for snow removal on the grounds that he had not consulted them.[41]

None of these actions harmed Wood's rebounding popularity. Most voters backed his recommendations, praised his snow cleaning as the work of a conscientious mayor protecting the property and health of the citizens, and generally sympathized with Matsell as an honest if abrasive chief, the butt of nativist hostility. Growing desperate in March, the Common Council called on Wood to revoke the notorious contract Jacob Sharp had made with the city four years earlier for the construction of a railroad along Broadway. There was little morality here. Knowing the contract was legal, even though Sharp was presently under indictment for bribing several city officials, the aldermen reasoned that Wood's veto would arouse suspicions that he was implicated. Wood saw easily through this transparent dodge. He jeered at the Common Council's "belated" ethics, and called attention to the sad fact that a grand jury was considering indicting several sitting aldermen for accepting Sharp's bribes. The proper course, he lectured, was to wait until the Court of Appeals decided the contract's legality.[42] Measured against the Common Council's standards, Wood emerged from this sorry affair with honor.

Defeated at every turn, the Common Council lapsed into sullen negativism. In April, Robert Kelly, the city chamberlain and Wood's close ally, died. His death left vacant a political and financial bonanza. Under the charter, the chamberlain or county treasurer, the custodian of public monies, pocketed substantial personal income on interest the deposits gathered. Wood had the right to select Kelly's successor, with the Common Council's approval. At once, an uproar developed. Wood grasped that the council would reject any appointment as a reflex action. For that reason, he shrewdly named Andrew V. Stout, a highly respected banker, much admired in the city's commercial establishment, and announced that Stout was willing to forego the customary fees, the interest going to the city. As Wood guessed, the Common Council tabled the appointment without giving the public sufficient reasons. The upshot was that Wood had again increased his commitment to municipal purity and made the council seem mean by comparison.[43]

In this heady atmosphere, Wood shifted to his next goal, dominating Tammany Hall. During the Soft's New Orleans ball, a reveler made his evening, shouting that the city was fortunate to have a mayor whose administration entitled him to "the respect of all whose interests demand good Municipal Government." Wood used such leverage to assert leadership over the fractured Democracy. Speaking at the Young Men's Democratic Union Club, an organization striving for factional harmony, he promised to "advance the Democratic party, and so far as I have influence to, to bring it together."[44]

These sentiments indicated that Wood was on the threshold of a new and even more critical phase in his career. As a potential kingmaker, he meant to unite Tammanyites around the most available presidential nominee and had already chosen him, James Buchanan, currently the minister to the Court of St. James. The decision was simple. Pierce had too many enemies; Marcy was too old; Douglas was too divisive; and Virginia Governor Henry A. Wise, a longtime friend, was too young. In terms of sectional balance, however, it pained Wood to admit that the Pennsylvanian would probably pick a Southern running mate, dashing his vice-presidential dreams. Wood's disappointment was somewhat eased by his admiration for Buchanan's Young America expansionist designs on Cuba and the brute fact that Hards wanted anyone but him. Thus, Wood emerged as the first prominent New York official to cast his lot for Buchanan. As early as November 1855, State Senator Daniel Sickles, Buchanan's unofficial campaign manager, wrote him, "One of your best friends in NY is the Mayor — (Wood) — and he has made himself one of the strongest men in the State."[45]

With Buchanan in London, Wood sought to convince Sickles that the nomination was impossible without his aid. The aborted police bill, which Sickles had opposed, handed Wood an opening. In May 1856, he presided at a testimonial for Sickles and presented him with a dinner service for eight, valued at more than $1,000, for protecting municipal rights. Duly flattered, Sickles fired off another letter informing Buchanan that Wood supported him on a broad range of issues. On the evening of Buchanan's arrival in New York, Wood and his wife held a private six-hour party at Woodlawn and introduced Buchanan to the city's major Democratic moneymen. By the eve of the July convention, Wood was certain that he had entered Buchanan's select inner circle.[46]

News of Buchanan's nomination galvanized party unity and stimulated Wood's ambitions. Scribbling a letter of congratulations, Wood observed that as a "prudent man" he had "prayed for this result," and flattered himself as a representative of "a large class of the people of the middle states." What Wood did not mention was that he expected Buchanan to reciprocate by supporting his bid for governor.[47]

As Wood awaited a response, his candidacy repelled many Democrats. Wood expected Hard opposition, but he was unprepared for the cold-blooded reaction among Softs, especially state chairman Dean Richmond and former governor Horatio Seymour. Intent on maximizing party unity, they favored either Addison Gardiner, who had just retired from the Court of Appeals, or

Judge Amasa J. Parker of Albany. Each was a moderate, acceptable to both Hards and Softs. In contrast, Wood's selection would alienate Hards and cost the Democracy both the governorship and the White House.[48]

Richmond and Seymour needed a legitimate reason, however, to block Wood, and found it in the nettlesome chamberlain affair. The Common Council finally accepted Stout, but the choice spawned further wrangling. The Hard *Daily News,* noting that Stout was a former Know-Nothing, insinuated that Wood was again wooing nativists and blared that he was not a reliable "Democratic Mayor." Other Hards picked up the theme, agreeing with Richmond and Seymour that Wood's candidacy would cause an explosion in party ranks and put the presidential ticket in jeopardy.[49]

During the hectic month of July, New York Democratic harmony held firm on Buchanan, but remained uncertain over local and state candidates. Sickles was worried. The "imperfect union of Hards & Softs," he complained to Buchanan, caused party "lethargy" and harmed fund-raising. Consequently, the party desperately needed Wood's "vigor, courage, tact, and genius for organization and *electioneering*" at the head of the state ticket. Even more, the party needed Wood's money. "It will cost 30 to 40 thousand dollars to organize N.Y. for the next election. Wood will, if we get him into the *canvas,* and thoroughly *aroused,* spend fifty thousand to carry the state." Ending on a plaintive note, Sickles asked, "Can you aid us?"[50] Buchanan did nothing, indicating a lack of decisiveness that boded ill for Wood in particular and all Democrats in general during the days ahead.

Still in the dark about Buchanan's intentions but now expecting the worst, Wood played coy and told reporters he would "not seek the nomination." Behind the scenes, he was remarkably active for a noncandidate. Dashing off a series of letters to Buchanan, he spelled out the intricacies of factional maneuverings, warned that voters were "tired of the bickerings & intrigues of the old leaders in this State," and implied the time was ripe for younger men, meaning himself, to "abolish both of the present organizations & have one formed from the people." When Buchanan stayed silent, Wood moderated his pitch. Now as a selfless party worker, "I advise peace & preparation for the great combat of November." Toward the Regency, Wood was more candid. "The feeling is strong for Union—unanimous on that," he informed Seymour. "The Soft delegation from this county will be 16 for myself on first choice, if my name is presented and the Hard delegation will be for myself—balance scattered"[51]

As Softs and Hards gathered in Syracuse for their separate conventions, Sickles and John Kelly, Tammany's future leader, scurried through the halls buttonholing potential Wood delegates. Nothing worked. At the Softs' convention, Kelly put Wood's name in nomination with an impassioned speech and pointed out that the party had not honored the city with a gubernatorial nominee since the 1820s. History aside, he deserved the nomination since "no Democrat has ever done more for New York City than Fernando Wood." Regency delegates sat on their hands. Wood trained badly through four ballots, ultimately withdrawing in favor of Parker, the eventual winner. That done, the Hards' convention endorsed Parker; they joined Softs in a single state committee; and both formed a united Union General Committee in the city.[52]

Losing was bad enough, but Wood feared that he had forfeited Buchanan's respect as New York's "strong man." To rebuild his image, Wood cynically disowned Sickles. He again wrote Buchanan, telling him that Sickles's lobbying was an "imprudent interference" in local party affairs. All the same, Wood indicated that his days of nonpartisanship were over and that he now intended to create factional unity around Buchanan's candidacy. Wood promised, "Though contrary to my views of propriety," to "speak [for you] in several of the interior counties next month."[53]

Clogging Wood's avenue to state power opened a new phase in his career. No doubt now existed that he lusted for reelection, unlike previous mayors, men generally also from the commercial class, who had served a single term out of civic duty and then retired. As a result, Wood was becoming a prototypical modern municipal leader, a professional politician seeking to get, keep, maintain, and expand power. In even a larger sense, Wood verged on being the forerunner of a more important development. Since his inauguration, he had combined in himself divergent and often conflicting strands of urban life as the one man capable of creating a coordinated and cohesive society out of the chaos that was New York City. By sort of a natural progression, Wood was unwittingly laying the basis for a new mechanism in city politics, a political machine under a single "Boss."

Immediately after the convention, Wood executed schemes worthy of his political reputation. Protesting that a seat on Tammany's new Union General Committee was beneath a mayor's dignity, he nevertheless secured one. Asked why he had stooped to such a lowly position, Wood cited a letter purportedly from Buchanan requesting that he not only join the committee, but to again "run for the office of Mayor."[54] Although he did not produce the letter for public inspection, probably because it existed only in his imagination, Wood's invoking of Buchanan's blessing, no matter how suspect, made his reelection a test of party loyalty.

On September 3, 1856, Wood's ingenuity reached new heights. Conscious that his nomination was still precarious, he fabricated his own groundswell. In an open letter to the public, he said his frustration with the charter was so intense that he intended to retire. Attached to it was a list signed by nearly one hundred prominent businessmen who begged him to reconsider for the city's sake. His cynical reply followed. Claiming that such a voluntary gesture "consoles me for past sacrifices," he agreed to undertake "fresh exertions in the path of duty."[55]

It was unclear whether Wood bullied the signers, or if they were sincere. In a way, he did threaten the commercial community. A word in the ears of tax assessors could raise or lower personal and property rates; he could steer contracts through the police department; and Stout had the power to reward or punish bankers by depositing or withdrawing funds. Perhaps these people needed no compulsion. As a city builder, Wood was a businessman's mayor. His proposals for new municipal construction, including improvements in urban transportation, provided a stimulus to industrialists, the construction trade; and uptown developers. Moreover, his known support for slavery strengthened vital Southern trade for the city's merchant class. Motivation proved less important than effect. In previous campaigns he was a Tammany politician; now he appeared a self-effacing public servant with an acute sense of civic obligation, drafted by the city's most respectable element, anointed by no less a man than Buchanan.

Better than that, Wood's incredible streak of luck, or maybe foresight, again intervened. Lorenzo Shepard died and left a political vacuum on the Union General Committee, which he had headed as chairman and leader of a robust bloc of anti-Wood Softs and Hards. Wood's decision to become a committeeman now changed the Hall's entire complexion. Without anyone of Shepard's comparable ability as a viable challenger, Wood held the advantage ground as Tammany's titular leader, and named his clerk, Wilson C. Small, as the new chairman. Then, with Small's consent, Wood established a special subcommittee to screen primary vote inspectors and ballot counters. By controlling the mechanics of electing delegates, Wood held a majority at the mayoral convention and was easily renominated despite frustrated cries of police harassment, voting fraud, and outright deceit. "It is true we have some local dissensions as to municipal office," he smugly told Buchanan, but blamed the press for magnifying the situation.[56]

Wood underestimated the fears he raised as the one-man ruler, both in city hall and Tammany Hall. A dissident group of Hards, led by Sweeny, coalesced with some Softs under Cochrane, and selected James Libby to run for mayor as an independent Democrat. The field was now complete. Know-Nothings ran Isaac O. Barker, with the backing of a few remaining Whigs; Republicans pushed auctioneer Anthony J. Bleeker; and the Civic Reform party chose Supreme Court Judge James R. Whiting.[57]

The campaign quickly degenerated into an ill-tempered ordeal with Wood the center of the storm. Charges and countercharges plunged the election into gutter politics. Perhaps the most vicious mudslinging came in a pamphlet, published under the pseudonym of "Abijah Ingraham," *A Biography of Fernando Wood. A History of the Forgeries, Perjuries, and other Crimes of our 'Model Mayor,'* which reduced every aspect of his business career to a study in chicanery. McKeon attacked Wood among immigrants as a fraudulent nativist. Even Whiting shared Wood's odium. Libbyites, noting that he had been Wood's attorney in the Marvine case, circulated rumors that he was on the mayor's payroll as a spoiler. Greeley was just as active. After inspecting the list of men who had signed Wood's public letter, the *New York Tribune* claimed that some of those men had never seen the correspondence until it was published.[58]

Violence flared on all sides. Gangs of roving toughs broke up meetings; riots interrupted rallies; street orators were stoned and hospitalized by brickbats; and demonstrators hooted down speakers. In one instance, this savagery had gallows humor. Tammany hung a "costly" banner from the Wigwam's second story, decorated with "an eagle and American flag," embossed with the words, "Democratic Republican Regular Nominee–The Choice of the Democracy–For Mayor, Fernando Wood." During the night, someone cut out his name, leaving a gash nine feet wide.[59]

It was left to Greeley to put the contest into perspective. Answering the *Herald*'s endorsement that Wood's executive qualities more than compensated for his "shortcomings," the *Tribune* retorted, "It is not the *ability* but the *integrity* of Wood that is in question."[60]

Wood knew he was fighting for his political life, and his campaign underscored the basic contradictions in his character. On the positive side, he ran an ethical campaign by emphasizing his impressive mayoral record, his standing as a regularly nominated Tammanyite, and his linkage to Buchanan. But Wood was Wood. Egotistically assuming that his reelection was necessary for personal ends as well as civic reform, he adapted and refined Tammany's traditional but shady electoral practices, breaking new ground as the most flawed, crafty, and unscrupulous political operator of his day.

Starting during the campaign and running for the next nine months, Republicans unearthed a grim story beginning with how Wood picked candidates. According to their exposés, he auctioned off Shepard's vacant corporation counsel, worth $10,000 in salary and fees, plus a number of patronage jobs, for control over its spoils. Sickles felt he deserved the slot for services rendered, and rejected Wood's demand. Unabashed, Wood named the more compliant Richard Busteed, a popular Irish attorney. His choice made tangled sense. Choosing Busteed shored up Wood's immigrant base, and he placated Sickles with a congressional nomination. The moves backfired when Sickles joined the Libbyites. Wood continued to insist that other municipal candidates, no matter how minor, such as the collector of arrears on taxation, must surrender all appointments. His mania even extended into the judiciary where he supported Abraham Russell for city judge against Elisha Capron because Russell was related to James Gordon Bennett.[61]

Wood's trickery with the police was another dirty piece of business. He demoted uncooperative captains and assessed vulnerable policemen a portion of their salaries, on a graduated scale, raising a campaign chest estimated at nearly

$10,000. Prior to the election, Wood released some patrolmen from their normal duties for his campaign, and furloughed others on election day so his hoodlums had a free hand to menace voters and filch return. When fellow commissioners objected, Wood illegally suspended the board.[62]

Republicans and anti-Woodites could not and did not let these "shames" go unnoticed and swore that Wood was a "wicked" man who showered his office with "infamy." Instead of a reply, Wood held his tongue. Years later, in a somewhat analogous situation, he explained why he considered such allegations the occupational hazards of any politician and how to treat them: "To be silent will allow the thing to die still-born." Interpreting the charges, then, as partisan claptrap, his supporters rejected them and continued to back him as a leader with almost a prophetic ability to anticipate the needs of his city. With that in mind, Wood wrote Buchanan that "the dissatisfaction toward myself has almost entirely subsided."[63]

Wood's confidence was not as unrealistic as it appeared. His defenders took heart that critics such as Capron, who was easily the most vocal of these attackers, did not say where or how they gained their information; they used anonymous sources; they treated gossip as truth; they depended upon after-the-fact evidence; and thus their partisanship tainted their perspective. Moreover, many of Wood's purported transgressions, his supporters reasoned, were actually part of the city's political culture tracing back to the 1790s. At least that was what a grand jury concluded. Convened at the behest of John McKeon and Sidney Smith, it uncovered familiar testimony about fictitious voters, high-speed naturalization mills, multiple voting, more actual voters than registered ones, and delayed counts in 72 out of 157 electoral districts. Every faction, however, was implicated. Consequently, the grand jury did not indict Wood, and implied that each instance could have applied to almost any election in the city's checkered political history.[64]

What Wood and the grand jury could not rationalize was his manipulation of the police, activities which made him appear less a public servant and more a dark destroyer of the democratic process. Then, too, the totality of these frauds, whether provable or not, fit into a pattern, reviving images of an older disreputable Fernando Wood, and eventually paving the way for massive alterations in city government. Perhaps Wood's efforts were no more than normal politicking carried to excess, but in terms of ethics and honesty his reputation was now forever damaged beyond redemption.

Wood won the election whether his means were fair or foul. Out of twenty-two wards, he carried fourteen and won with 44.6 percent of the total votes cast. Barker, his closest competitor, trailed with 32.2 percent. Bleeker ran a weak third with 12.3 percent, and Whiting managed only 4.6 percent. The Libbyites suffered the worst setback with merely 6.2 percent.[65] In short, Wood's totals reflected basic Democratic expectations.

Wood's victory also indicated that his 1854 coalition was still viable, particularly among immigrants. The electorate had increased by 18,490 over the last two years, mainly newly naturalized citizens. Wood increased his totals among them. He carried the heavily German and Irish East Side and four of six wards above Fourteenth Street. Another pattern persisted with native-born West Siders. Barker won the five wards in that area, and Wood's percentages were even lower than in 1854.

Despite Wood's triumph, his victory was only a partial vote of confidence. Cochrane, Sickles, Busteed, and Russell won, largely because of Buchanan's coattails. Even more disheartening, Wood ran 8.5 percent behind Buchanan's plurality of 53.1 percent, and a combination of anti-Wood Democrats, Know-Nothings, and Republicans dominated the Common Council. Just as threatening, Republican John A. King became governor, and his party held a commanding edge in the legislature. Even Libby's poor showing was deceptive. In a year when Democratic defections harmed the entire party, many Tammanyites voted a straight party ticket to help Buchanan, not Wood.

The election left Wood teetering on a delicate political balance. After two years in office as the Model Mayor, he had recommended major plans to improve the entire quality of municipal life. Measured in terms of specific gains and losses, however, he had failed as a broker politician and leader. While it was true that his aldermanic foes had effectively stymied his programs, many of his problems stemmed from his ego and style. His dictatorial nature alienated far too many potential allies; his politicization of the police ruptured community goodwill; and his campaign tactics threatened to become a cause of further disarray. At this point, Wood's only hope to carry out his aims lay in convincing the new Democratic council to cooperate. Even that was a problem. The majority of Softs and Hards distrusted his ambitions, especially when they realized he meant to control Tammany as the first step to implement city improvements.

Wood's predicament, then, stemmed from his peculiar combination of good and evil. Over the next two months, he settled back into his comfortable routine as the Model Mayor to establish continuity between his old and new administrations. Holding lame duck aldermen at bay, he vetoed a street-cleaning contract and another for repairing the Tompkins Street Market on the grounds that each was "fraudulent." Imagery again came into play. He scolded Street Commissioner Joseph Ebling for authorizing work on the "sacred Sabbath," and still commuted to work on the omnibus line, speaking with fellow passengers, listening to their complaints, and keeping tabs on bad service. As for the continuing problem of taxation, he promised relief to some property-owners, who protested that street assessments were "outrageously high."[66]

Politically, Wood pictured himself the logical successor to such giants as DeWitt Clinton, Martin Van Buren, and Thurlow Weed. Since these men had made control of patronage the first axiom of New York politics, Wood cultivated Buchanan, intent on mastering the flow of federal spoils.

As soon as it became apparent that he had won, Wood brashly wrote Buchanan, "My own election I know will be gratifying to you." Seeking a more intimate relationship, Wood added that his wife also "begs to send her congratulations to Miss Lane," Buchanan's favorite niece. Warming to the subject, Wood capitalized on the president-elect's assumption that his coming administration needed Bennett's support and indicated his willingness to act as an intermediary. "Fortunately, my own relations with Mr. B & his really kind feelings towards you personally places matters in good shape." Yet according to Wood, a complication existed. Bennett was worried that Wood's enemies might "obtain your confidence & get controul [*sic*] of the patronage of this city." But Wood insidiously ended that he could handle Bennett. "I have assured him that there can be no probability of this," since "you will not select" those "who have taken action at the last election with the small minority of the party which opposed me." Buchanan was not a political innocent and held Wood at arm's length until he took his own soundings. "In regard to the N Y appointments I can say nothing, but that I shall hear all sides & hope for the best," he replied.[67]

Unknown to Wood, Buchanan dispatched Henry Wikoff, an old friend from their days in London, to conduct the delicate negotiations with the touchy Bennett and to test Wood's standing with him. Wikoff discovered that Wood was a cheat. To Buchanan, he had falsely asserted "close intimacy" with the editor; to Bennett, Wood had lied that he was Buchanan's confidant. Wikoff considered himself a man of the world, but he was thoroughly shocked. He ripped off a letter to Buchanan that Wood's "vaulting ambitions" was solely for "his profit." The truth was that Wood, in attempting "to impress you," had forfeited all future confidence and must not be "allowed to 'grind his axe' to the exclusion of all other axes."[68] Once more, Wood's deceit had failed.

In late December and early January, however, Wood demonstrated his flair for organizing Tammany, although his methods were scarcely subtle. Using handpicked vote counters in his special subcommittee, he screened the selection of disputed primary delegates. Wood then weeded out Libbyites and ordered Small's reappointment as chairman over violent but ineffectual objections raised by John Savage, a defeated Fifth Ward committeeman.[69]

Wood's strong-armed tactics seemingly had far-reaching consequences. By the first week of January 1857, he was ostensibly impregnable. Practicing DeWitt Clinton's personal style of politics, he had abandoned the Hall's normal collective leadership to become the first man to serve simultaneously as mayor and apparently the head of Tammany Hall. As a would-be Boss, he was evidently in an ideal position to dominate lines of authority from city hall through

the General Committee to neighborhood precincts. All that remained was control of federal patronage in the Custom House.

While Wood played out his role in the city, Albany prospects grew ominous.
In December 1856, the Court of Appeals dismissed his contention that local
voters had authority to draw up a new charter or vote on one the legislature
might pass. A section in Governor King's inaugural address menaced Wood
more directly. "Experience renders it quite certain that the Legislature will hesi-
tate to entrust the management of that [municipal] system to the Mayor alone."
Threats became real by mid-January. Republicans introduced a variety of bills,
the *New York Sun* reported, directed toward taking "the control of our City government out of the hands of the persons elected by the people."[70]

To defend himself, Wood sought help from the Regency by tying his fate to
the party's best interests. Republicans, he forecast to Erastus Corning, were con-
templating measures "which will materially affect the municipal interests of this
city—not only the public but the Democratic party is to be made the victim." Picturing himself as a martyr, he predicted: "Several of their schemes are intended to
cripple me, & to take away the little power this office now has left to it."[71]

To further strengthen his position, Wood managed his inaugural into a display of public approval. Standing in a receiving line for over two hours, he shook
the "hand of each that presented himself." Although some thirsty well-wishers
were disappointed that he "furnished no refreshments," they "poured in an
unbroken stream during the continuance of the reception."[72]

Wood delivered his 1857 annual address in that spirit of firmness and challenge. With every variable indicating the legislature would change the charter, he
snapped that Republicans were robbing citizens of New York of their legitimate
rights, "vigorous Government and vigorous men to administrate it." Promising to
resign if that happened, Wood peevishly declared, "If the ship must go down, let
those who drive her on the rocks take the helm and command—I will not."[73]

When his rhetoric ended, it was clear that Wood's nascent machine rested on
insecure foundations. Two facts were clear. Despite his grasp over the General
Committee, many Democrats believed his leadership put enormous strains on a
party which rejected the direction he felt best. More dangerously, Republicans,
banking on a series of judicial opinions which treated the city as a creature of the
state, were not going to make charter reform a negotiable item. His fate rested
in their hands.

FIVE

The Political Mayor

O N January 8, 1857, a gloating Fernando Wood wrote James Buchanan: "There is no other general committee [than Wilson Small's] in this city and no body of men assuming to be so. We have *one* organization for the first time since 1848." Armed as the master of the city and encouraging the belief that he was a "personal friend of the President-elect," Wood was unaware that Henry Wikoff had discovered his deception, and never doubted that he was Buchanan's chief patronage agent.[1]

Wood's self-promotion signified a general intensification of political activity in the city among his Democratic antagonists. Hards and Softs—men such as Sickles, Fowler, Purdy, Cochrane, Sweeny, Tweed, and Samuel J. Tilden, who were normally enemies—coalesced behind their mutual hostility to Wood. Quite simply, the distinction between local Hards and Softs over differing versions of slavery extensionism was now meaningless. The result split Tammany in new directions. City politics became less issue-orientated and more personal, directed against the one-man ruler. The party would have few days of peace until it accepted Wood's will or laid him to rest.

The showdown between the Democracy's new alignments began when the anti-Woodites, now called the New York Hotel Committee, used the one variable Wood did not control, the Tammany Society, as a protective cover to launch their attack. Warning signs surfaced the previous November. By a two-vote majority, the Council of Sachems had foiled Wood's attempt to name Small grand sachem, and started a systematic program of enrolling new brothers, none Woodites. In January, shortly after Wood formed Small's committee, seven out of twelve sachems, huddled around Isaac Fowler, swung their weight by authorizing an investigation of the suspicious circumstances surrounding the General Committee's construction and barred Small from holding meetings in the party's tabernacle, the Wigwam. Mobilizing further support, Fowler, Purdy, and Sweeny used Savage as a figurehead chairman and created a second

General Committee, which petitioned the sachems to accept them as the party's official organization.[2]

The council's sudden concern for political morality held deep implications. Its self-appointed role as an impartial umpire and guardian of party legitimacy was an article of faith among Tammanyites. By refusing Small the use of the building, the council denied Wood the trappings of party regularity and cast doubt whether his committee represented the rank and file.[3]

Wood had expected something of this sort because he was a seasoned Tammany Society brave. He tried to finesse the sachems by bribing John Howard, the building's lessee, into allowing Small to hold meetings as if nothing had changed. Things had changed. The council, again seven to five, dissolved both committees and called for a new election, but under fresh rules. In order to block Wood's subcommittee's dominance of the ward primary system, the sachems substituted a new table of organization based upon enrolling Democrats into "a permanent association" housed in larger electoral districts, and set primaries under "the district association."[4]

With one blow, the Tammany Society had undermined Wood's entire position. Although preoccupied with federal spoils, he tried to escape the predicament. Appealing over the council to party workers, he emphasized the Locofoco principle that Small's power came from the people, not a self-aggrandizing group of sachems. Moreover, he cited technicalities in the lease to deny that the sachems had any legal hold over Howard. The council was just as conscious of public opinion. It published an elaborate pamphlet and explained that the district plan gave all Democrats, rather than a dictator, a chance to influence policy. As for the lease, they hired a team of four lawyers which predictably sustained their contention.[5]

Outnumbered and outmaneuvered by the council, Wood struck back with a deceptively easy gimmick. With fresh council elections scheduled in April, he sponsored a ticket to oust the old sachems. Fowler and Purdy were ready. Packing the Long Room early in the evening, they locked the doors before Wood's main force arrived. After winning handily, their reorganization machinery hummed along. They put together a new Union General Committee, including Cochrane and Sickles, under one of their own, Sachem Edward Cooper, the nephew of ironmonger Peter Cooper.[6]

The implications were enormous. It was Cooper's unionists, not Small nor Wood, who had established legitimacy as the guardians of the Democratic organization, as "regular" Tammanyites with traditional "usages." The result left Wood outside the fold as a renegade if he did not accept the verdict. Reacting to these developments, Wood vented his anger at the enemy at hand, the Council of Sachems. Calling on the rank and file's sense of Democratic fair play, he asked, do the "sachems rule the people, or shall the people rule themselves?"

Cochrane, answering for the council, termed Wood's statements misleading. The sachems were the sole disinterested force laboring for the Hall's common good, which was "of more importance than the advance of personal ends." Wood was too vulnerable to back down. He rejected the council's order to disband the Small committee. In self-defense, Savage followed the same course by refusing a similar command to dissolve.[7]

In this new factional situation—personal, political, and maybe principled—Wood was clearly the loser. The sachems' ideological thrust against one-man rule, putting the onus for fracturing the party on him, had worked. Yet, the result was symptomatic of Wood's personal style. Unable or unwilling to delegate authority, his embryonic machine ran only if he took personal charge of each detail. It faltered when other issues distracted him. As it turned out, the reasons for his defeat lay not in New York City, but in Washington and Albany.

Things began unravelling for Wood as early as the week after the presidential election with Buchanan's careful search for the collector of the New York Custom House. The post was a heady prize. The collector controlled the largest patronage pool in the city and state. Even better, he had almost unlimited resources to finance a wide range of political operations by assessing appointees and from the moiety system under which he shared all fines and forfeitures. For these reasons, the proper collector was crucial to Wood in building and running his machine.

Pondering the choice, Buchanan searched for a reliable, trustworthy Democrat, one with an impeccable business reputation to assure the commercial community that the Custom House was not purely partisan. Those considerations meant the president was about to make a calculated gamble. Whomever he selected from the lengthy lists various New York Democrats circulated would surely alienate the others.[8]

Wood was just one in a prestigious field pestering Buchanan. Of these men and the groups they represented, Wood feared three rival power brokers: state chairman Dean Richmond intent on retaining incumbent Herman Redfield; Congressman John Cochrane, the leading anti-Wood Tammanyite, pushing Royal Phelps, a respectable businessman who had previously backed Wood; and Sickles, a lame duck state senator before taking his congressional seat. Wood considered Sickles his only real challenger because of his close friendship with Buchanan. Sickles certainly thought so. He confidentially told reporters that Superintendent of the Mint Samuel F. Butterworth had the job.[9]

Under optimum conditions, Wood wanted Small. If Small proved unacceptable, Wood sought the right to veto any choice he found objectionable. Presuming much, then, Wood plunged into intensive lobbying. During the five months following Buchanan's election, Wood made three trips to Washington and also tried unsuccessfully to visit the president-elect at his Lancaster, Pennsylvania home. On March 14, Wood was back in Washington where money did his talking. Taking a suite at Willard's Hotel, he stocked the rooms with good food and expensive liquor, and employed his considerable personal charm to impress congressmen that he was indeed New York's preeminent Democrat.[10]

Richmond and Cochrane were equally busy angling for the office, and both denigrated Wood's pretensions to anyone who would listen. Sickles worked alone, confident he could manage the "old man." As jockeying continued, the claimants awaited their interviews with Buchanan and rehearsed plausible arguments to guide his choice.[11]

When Wood's turn arrived, he found Buchanan in a distracted, choleric mood. Cabinet-making, caterwauling about spoils, and angry cries from Republicans against the Supreme Court's recent Dred Scott opinion had visibly strained the elderly president. Entering his office, Wood was startled when Buchanan did not recognize him. His annoyance increased when Buchanan mistakenly called him "Alderman Wood." When corrected, the president became cooler. Maybe Buchanan wanted to create that atmosphere. Perhaps smarting over Wood's double-dealing in the Bennett affair and prejudiced by Sickles, he refused any commitment. Whatever the reason, the bewildered Wood walked out of the White House understanding that he had somehow lost Buchanan's confidence.[12]

The president handled Sickles with more grace, but with the same end. Buchanan said that he had already decided upon national committeeman Augustus Schell, a Hard anti-Woodite, whom none of the others had considered a viable candidate. From Buchanan's standpoint, the choice made sense. Schell was a close friend and had a sound reputation among fellow businessmen. Sickles was not reasonable. Although he and Schell were once allies, they had fallen out the previous November when Schell refused to back his race for Congress. Stunned, Sickles walked out of the White House refusing to answer reporters who wanted to know what had happened.[13]

The next day, Sickles revisited Buchanan and "energetically protested" against Schell. Wood was far more flexible. He, too, disliked the appointment. But once he saw "that it would be made," however, Wood left Washington without exercising his "dreaded veto" and promised to cooperate with Schell.[14]

All told, Wood had spent two unproductive weeks in Washington. During this period the sachems had exploited his absence to begin their takeover of Tammany. Worse, he just had to read the balance of Buchanan's local appointments to realize how badly he wasted his time. To placate Sickles, the president gave the bulk of federal spoils to the New York Hotel Committee. Buchanan did not name any of Wood's supporters and effectively endorsed the sachems by naming Fowler as city postmaster, second only to the collector in the number of jobs he controlled. Wood's only solace was that Buchanan replaced John McKeon with Thomas Sedgwick as federal attorney.[15]

Once Wood returned, the gossipy Wikoff noted that the "dissatisfied" mayor had for some strange reason recovered "his temper" and was, in fact, rather cheerful. What might have been eccentric to Wikoff was Wood's flexibility. Adopting the adage that whomever my enemy opposed was my friend, Wood shocked the less resilient sachems by sounding out Schell about an alliance against Sickles.[16]

Wood had scarcely moments to read his mail or digest local political news when developments in Albany demanded his presence. Since January, Republican legislators had been busy preparing a series of mortal blows against him and the entire city Democracy. As they neared completion of their onslaught by the end of March, Wood had to leave the city once more, accompanied by unverified rumors that his pockets bulged with $100,000 for bribery. Even if true, he did not depend on corrupting the corruptible. From all indications, Republicans were divided into two conflicting but overlapping sections: partisans out to destroy Wood and establish a toehold for their party in the city; and sincere reformers convinced that state-imposed controls were the lone means to foster sound government. Going upstate, Wood sought to steady Democratic ranks and widen Republican divisions. Despite this necessity, he paid a costly price. Without him on the scene, the sachems finalized their hold over Tammany Hall and the Tammany Society.[17]

As any good politician, Wood had planned ahead. Back in January 1857, he had begun marshalling the forces of municipal home rule for a counterattack under the banners of the Model Mayor. To implement his blueprint for a greater New York, Wood repeated calls for more efficient street cleaning and proposed higher salaries for government officials to lure quality civil servants. To end traffic congestion and growing gridlock, he urged a ban on Broadway of certain types of vehicles, and suggested new street construction and improvements on older ones. Turning toward spending, he requested restraint from Comptroller Azariah C. Flagg on all disbursements. Following his own advice, Wood avoided new police appointments and cooperated with fellow commissioners.[18]

More than anything else, Wood tried to turn the tables on the Republicans. With Common Council approval, he sent the legislature an innovative charter revision which incorporated all the specifics he had recommended for the past three years, starting with a strong mayor, weak legislative-federated system to end diffusion of authority. The mayor, chosen for two years, was a true chief executive. His sweeping powers included the right to appoint a bureaucratic cabinet from current departments, including the police, subject to aldermanic concurrence and mayoral removal for cause. The bicameral Common Council, reduced in numbers and elected from the wards on a staggered basis, surrendered most prerogatives to the mayor. As for expenditures, Wood proposed that a three-quarters majority approve all expenses over $250. Contracts would be

advertised in city newspapers and awarded to the lowest bidder. Any city official accepting a bribe, in either the letting or functioning of contracts, was subject to impeachment.[19]

Republicans scorned any suggestion coming from Wood, the emblem in
their eyes of everything wrong in the city, and his charter died. Instead, they
kept the pressure on legislative hearings by inviting friendly officials to testify,
such as District Attorney Hall about the police, but studiously avoided Wood or
others committed to home rule.

By the time Wood trekked to Albany, most party workers believed that lobbying was futile. The independent but generally pro-Democratic *New York Sun*
aptly observed that Republican measures were "partial, defective and oppressive," based on partisan prejudices against "the *persons* who hold office at
present in this City." On April 15, Republicans completed their work. Governor
King signed multiple bills fated to create vast changes in the city's municipal
institutions and the types of men who would administer them.[20]

The new Municipal Charter of 1857 ostensibly strengthened the mayor, as
Wood forcibly suggested. Five independent agencies were consolidated into
three "executive departments"–street, city inspector, and Croton Aqueduct–
each headed by a single appointee chosen by the mayor with aldermanic
approval. The mayor, with the aldermen, named ten clerks in his office, the
chamberlain, two health commissioners, the superintendent of buildings, and
one Harlem Bridge keeper. He remained either a full or ex officio member of
various municipal and county boards, and served along with the recorder, chief
justice of superior court, and the first judge of common pleas, as a commissioner selecting the grand jury. As for vetoes, the mayor could reject legislation
subject to a two-thirds override.

What the charter gave in executive control was less important than what it
denied. Instead of forming a bureaucratic structure answerable to the mayor,
Republicans went in a contrary direction by institutionalizing fragmentation
through the popular election of key city administrators: corporation counsel,
recorder, register, comptroller, surrogate, and eighteen judges of various courts.
They also stripped the mayor of authority over the almshouse, fire and health
departments, and the board of education. Lastly, the mayor had no say over
contracts. He could make suggestions, but the departments and bureaus let
them under whatever regulations the Common Council imposed.

Nothing better illustrated Republican partisanship than in contrasting the
mayoralty with the reorganized Department of Finance. The charter left
Comptroller Flagg's term intact because Republicans trusted him, but slashed
Wood's in half and ordered a new election in December 1857. In that way, the
charter denied Wood any coattail effect by separating the mayoral election from
state and national ones and scheduling elections in off-presidential years. At the

same time, they divested the mayor of any supervision over the city budget, specifically by denying him the right to oversee the comptroller's spending, bonding, tax collection, auditing, and guarding of municipal property.

In an all-out attack on Wood, Republicans specified that mayoral appointive powers were inoperative until January 1, 1858. To further impede Wood's chances for strong leadership, they whittled mayoral prerogatives by establishing unprecedented state commissions, appointed by the governor, for the Harlem Bridge, construction of Central Park and a new city hall, and supervision over harbor pilots, wharves, and piers.

In terms of patronage in general, the charter created an administrative nightmare. Total city jobs numbered 4,644. Of these, the mayor shared authority to appoint 29, who in turn selected 223 subordinates. The school system and the police were the two largest employers with 1,729 and 1,837. That left 1,078 for all other departments and bureaus. Assessing the situation in another way, the city population nearly doubled from 1840 to 1860, but the number of jobs increased by slightly over two thousand. In other words, Republicans might have prevented elected city officials, the mayor especially, from building a vast honeycomb of cronyism through their inability to reward and punish or to add new civil servants. Yet by scattering appointments, Republicans blocked effective policymaking by denying administrators the ability to coordinate consistent policies.

The Common Council's structure blended politics and reform. For efficiency and costs, the charter trimmed the number of aldermen and councilmen, and reapportioned them from wards to state assembly and senatorial districts respectively. Both the council and mayor lost a key function. In a related bill, the legislature replaced the old county board of supervisors of mayor, recorder, and aldermen, with a new, popularly elected bipartisan board, which by fiat consisted of six Republicans and six Democrats. Among their duties, the supervisors, acting as a county legislature, levied taxes, subject to the city supreme court's review and possible correction, and determined the number of policemen.[21]

The Metropolitan Police Act, passed on the same day, exploded with even more anti-Wood political dynamite. In a single stroke, Republicans replaced the entire existing force with a totally fresh, consolidated metropolitan unit consisting of New York, Kings, Richmond, and Westchester counties. Members of the superseded police remained in place until the board's first meeting when they became part of the new department. A five-man, state-appointed board, three members of which came from New York City, administered the new Metropolitans. Wood, along with Brooklyn's mayor, was merely an ex officio member.

The police bill destroyed not only Wood's authority, but home rule as well. Ignoring high-sounding phrases about nonpartisanship, King did not name one Democratic commissioner. Considering their moralistic fervor against Wood, Republicans ironically then turned the Metropolitans into their own partisan instrument. Local control was nonexistent. The police board was free of all elective municipal officers, ordinances, and restrictions. It had unchecked discretion over department operations, including the regulation of elections, public health, and Sunday closings. The city government furnished the Metropolitans with the bulk of their operating funds, but neither the mayor nor Common Council supervised spending.[22]

From the standpoint of reform, Republicans did in many ways make good on their promises of enlightened government. If one accepted the premise that the city was incapable of running itself, they took practical steps to implement state control and did set forces in motion that led toward the eventual 1898 formation of "Greater New York." Giving Republicans their due, they also split politics from taxation through the new board of supervisors, and laid the basis for the possibilities of nonpartisan municipal and county governments. State commissions conjecturally operated free of politics; taxation and spending were theoretically independent of party; and they had dispersed patronage apparently to protect competent civil servants.[23]

To satisfy their political wing, however, Republicans perverted their accomplishments. They circumvented the electoral process by guaranteeing themselves equal membership on the board of supervisors regardless of their local minority status. Having the governor choose commissioners, as King graphically illustrated, was hardly the stuff of impartial government. Furthermore, folding the city under state jurisdiction negated municipal home rule and was undemocratic and antiurban in nature. Moreover, state control was inherently nativist; it insulated the boards from any checks by immigrant voters. Even governmental structure was deficient. Taken as a whole, the laws hedged executive power with multiple state appointive boards and autonomous elective officials, continuing structural decentralization and fragmentation under a new guise. Far more seriously, the Republicans' vendetta against Wood distorted their reform impulse, and treated every future mayor as a cipher. Never before had the legislature or any political agency bludgeoned any previous mayor so extensively or so personally.[24]

In perspective, Republicans were bunglers. Their efforts, both reformist and political, spurred rather than hindered the formation of a political machine. Taking patronage as an example, Republicans may have limited municipal spoilsmongering, but they could not actually eliminate the discretionary power departments and bureaus, or a mayor working in tandem with them, had over the awarding of contracts. Nor could they guide the enforcement of contracts, often involving the illegal but customary practice of kickbacks to officials. Above that, dispersing power and responsibility left unresolved problems in the city's teeming slums and among its mix of contentious ethnic and religious groups. With increasing numbers of people desperate for help, political machines, by working around the system, could end this constitutional disorder by centralizing decision-making in itself and becoming the major cohesive force in city life.

In short, the times more than ever demanded a strong man, a person or his system that could concentrate both responsibility and authority, deliver municipal services, and make New York City work in the process. Fernando Wood still fit the bill. True, the spate of Republican bills augured his executive emasculation and a third term was by no means assured. But Wood was resilient. His qualities and political skills were still operative. Republicans had not totally blocked him from finishing what he started.

By chance, Republicans handed Wood a reprieve. The timing of yet another bill, the Excise Law of April 16, seemed part of the Republican package attacking him specifically and Democrats in general. As a remodeling of the earlier attempt at temperance, the law was clearly antiurban and nativist, and settled the prohibitionists' grudge against the obstructionist, although legal, obstacles Wood had raised against their 1855 measure. It set up a board of excise for each county consisting of three freeholders (landowners with an absolute ownership of an estate), with the sole power to grant liquor licenses, the cost of which ranged from $50 to $300 on a sliding scale based on size. Getting one was expensive and cumbersome. Applicants had to submit vouchers of good conduct signed by thirty resident freeholders and post a $250 bond, subject to forfeiture if not granted. Each saloon was required to have boarding facilities for travelers and stables for horses. Sales were barred on Sunday, election day, and in grocery and cigar stores, such as those Wood had operated. The *New York Herald* had no illusions about its effectiveness and surmised that because the municipality contained only about five thousand freeholders, thirteen out of fourteen saloons would shut citywide, and ninety-nine out of one hundred in the lower wards where few freeholders lived.[25]

Although many Tammanyites were secretly pleased at how the charter and police bills wounded Wood, the Excise Law affected all Democrats and required a different response. The party valued saloons as political cells, and the liquor lobby routinely bankrolled Democratic candidates. Here, then, rested Wood's opportunity to revive his standing.[26]

Clouds of indecision hung around city hall when Wood returned from Albany empty-handed. He had three options, none palatable: resignation, which he had threatened; acquiescence and the end of his career; or fighting back and risking worse retaliation. His fierce pride and combative temperament, along with cries from the Democratic press against the Excise Law, made the decision easy. As his poise returned and proved contagious to his followers, Wood girded for the political fight of his life.

Most New Yorkers respected Wood's enormous political skills, but few took him seriously as a theorist. In the strictest sense, they were correct; his ideas were not original. Nonetheless, he had an unsuspected talent for enunciating coherent party principles in clear and compelling terms, drawing inspiration from his Loco-foco apprenticeship, the creed for a principled defense of home rule.

Wood staked his challenge to state control during the next four months as a powerful Jacksonian ideologue defending "the sovereign people" and majority rule. Under the federal compact, he emphasized, independent voters had the natural right to determine government power. Their means lay in the ballot box and home rule, the tools of self-government, through which they foiled "judicial, executive, or legislative tyrants and unjust laws." Only the mayor represented this entire electorate. Any infringement of his autonomy destroyed popular rights as well as executive leadership. "Insolent" state centralism, the antithesis of true republicanism, turned New York into a "subjugated" city, robbed voters of their constitutional guarantees by passing "outrageous" laws, and plunged citizens into "such a feeble state of vassalage as to be bereft of any voice in the selection of our own masters."[27]

These were Wood's first shots in such an audacious war against the state government as New Yorkers had never witnessed before. Backed by the Common Council and skirting a fine line between defending home rule and disturbing public order, Wood told Federal Attorney Thomas Sedgwick: "I am determined to test the Police Bill, & to take *offensive* action." True to his words, Wood sponsored an aldermanic resolution that it was unconstitutional, directed the old board not to obey its provisions, and placed the former police under his direct command. All of these actions contradicted his stance in the 1855 prohibitionist question when he stressed citizens must obey the law until either the court ruled or the legislature revoked it. With scant regard for Wood's lack of consistency, the Common Council provided him with $10,000 for a legal challenge. Purportedly using an additional $20,000 of his own, Wood first sought a permanent injunction, and, when that failed, filed a suit in the state Court of Appeals to test the police act's constitutionality. On other grounds, he asserted that the city retained the option under the colonial Dongan and Montgomerie charters to create a separate and independent Bureau of Day and Night Watch or Municipal Police, and the aldermen reconstituted the old police under him. In a final blast of defiance, he called for a popular convention to express "the voice of the people against the charter." Wood galvanized the Democracy, and the sachems buckled. Reluctantly co-sponsoring his anticentralism rally, they listened with mounting distress as Cochrane echoed Wood, perhaps in even a more reckless manner: "The only remedy for oppressive law is Revolution! Revolution at the ballot box, it may be—at all events Revolution—peaceful, violent, unarmed or armed!"[28]

The next few weeks left the city in confusion over the police. Some New Yorkers were willing to await the court's decision, but many more worried that the rivalry between the two forces might spawn a crime wave. Apparently, they had good reason for alarm. Newspapers reported the antagonists were at logger-heads about who controlled particular station houses, served writs, and had authority to arrest criminals, often resulting in one group freeing perpetrators the other apprehended. Not the least worried were the police themselves. Remaining loyal to Wood meant that the commissioners would fire them from the Metropolitans; if not, Wood did the firing.[29]

As anxiety increased, anti-Wood Tammanyites realized that Wood had trapped them, and they drew a line separating Wood the martyred mayor from Wood the politician. The more they looked, the more they were dismayed. Small, heartened by Wood's understanding with Schell, attacked the sachems' overhaul of Tammany, calling it "deceptive and anti-democratic" and a haven for the men "who bolted regular nominations last November." Another cause for alarm lay in Wood's connection to the growing radicalism of some supporters who suggested that the city secede from the state to guarantee home rule. Although he advised them to obey the law "as long as it is the law," Tammanyites wondered with Cochrane's words ringing in their ears if Wood's caution-ary counsel was a screen to make himself appear a moderate at their expense. Even the normally nonpartisan Comptroller Flagg forced Wood's police to rethink their positions. He refused to pay them any salaries. With his decision, a number of Municipals began joining the Metropolitans.[30]

The *New York Times* settled matters for most Tammanyites. Its anonymous pundit, "A Bird in the Bush," revived the story of Wood's blighted ethical record, artfully adding that the tyranny he claimed Albany exerted against the city shrouded his own thirst for a dictatorship. More pointedly, the "Bird" told Tam-manyites that the mayor was manipulating them. Burlesquing how he operated, the "Bird" imagined him saying "*never* pay a political debt, or any other debt." The "true course is to quarrel with the man you owe all to, and destroy him by all means within your power." With the mask torn from Wood's pretense, no doubt now existed that Wood had fully lost any chance of regaining the Hall. The one-man ruler was a political lone wolf.[31]

Wood's controlled demeanor did not indicate the inner turmoil he felt at Tam-many's rejection. Yet his grinding physical schedule indicated enormous strain. No longer having time to go home evenings, he worked late at night, often sleeping in his office, plotting stratagems to "checkmate" the "Albany Dictation."[32] Despite his best effort, nothing worked. He did not control events; events controlled him.

The month of June 1857 ushered in the cruelest period in Wood's life. It began with Know-Nothing Street Commissioner Joseph S. Taylor's unexpected death. His department was a spoils-monger's dream since it dispensed jobs and contracts estimated at $2 million. Wood and Governor King elbowed each other to grab this plum. King, citing the new charter, claimed that he had exclusive appointive rights and named Daniel D. Conover, an omnibus proprietor and longtime ally. Wood did not knuckle under. He selected contractor Charles Devlin, and characterized King's move as one of many "unjustifiable, illegal and tyrannical encroachments" against the city.[33]

The affair raised a host of tangled legal and political issues, and quickly degenerated into a ludicrous situation. Even more, the problem again raised the pervasive suspicion about Wood's lack of integrity, particularly when Republicans charged that Develin had bribed him $50,000 for the job and that he split the graft with aldermen to gain their approval.[34]

On June 16, the question of who controlled the appointment reached a boiling point as Conover arrived at city hall to take possession of his office. Wood refused to honor his bond and had the Municipals physically remove him. Conover turned to Superior Court Justice Murray Hoffman and Recorder James Smith for redress. A flurry of writs and warrants followed, backed by the Metropolitans, calling for Wood's arrest for blocking the appointment, for assault, and for inciting a riot. When the Metropolitans attempted to serve him at city hall, the Municipals put a protective shield around the building and an unruly crowd of onlookers barred the way. Pushing forward, the Metropolitans became entangled in bloody clubbings and fisticuffs. Amid the mauling, shouts arose in broken English for "Fernandy Wood" and "Down with the Black Republicans." This police riot was more than Smith could stomach. He issued more warrants, and called for assistance from the Seventh Regiment, which by chance was marching on Broadway en route to Boston.[35]

The farce ended on an astonishing note. Wood choreographed his own arrest by the sheriff for contempt of court and produced a new writ placing the case before his confederate, City Judge Russell, who had prearranged $50,000 bail. Faced by a writ of habeas corpus, however, Russell yielded jurisdiction to Hoffman, who accepted Wood's plea that he was a "law-abiding and order-loving citizen," totally unaware of Smith's various warrants. On that incredible note, Hoffman dismissed the case. As for the rival street commissioners, the Court of Appeals in April 1858 ruled in Wood's favor.[36]

The decision came too late. Depending on the point of view, Wood had either manfully protected home rule or shamed the city. Properly indignant in defending himself and the Municipals, he denounced Republican "usurpers" for their reckless attempt to "take life in an effort to degrade [the city] through my person." Thoughtful citizens were not so sure. His pretensions as the Model Mayor did not square with the Wood who bent the law, abetted violence, defied the court, went out on bail like a common criminal, and then escaped justice through judicial connivance.[37]

The coming days brought Wood more disgrace. On July 2, Democratic Chief Justice Hiram Denio of the Court of Appeals, an upstate Hard with an austere personality but a reputation for probity, wrote the majority opinion which sustained the Police Law and ordered the Municipals to disband. Wood accepted the judgment, and took his seat on the Metropolitan board, leaving many Municipals unemployed and unpaid. A few of them, incensed that Wood had placed them in this predicament, hired attorneys to sue him personally for lost wages.[38]

The end was yet to come. Near anarchy struck the city and Wood two days later. The Dead Rabbits, a fighting gang of Irish youths who often campaigned for Wood, fired by too much bad liquor, touched off a riot against the Metropolitans and a rival gang, the Bowery Boys, in the "Bloody ould Sixth Ward," long a scene of violence. While no one was killed, each gang fought with clubs, iron bars, stones, and finally guns. The riot engaged nearly one thousand people at its height and caused extensive property damage. For the next week, minor scuffles flared in different wards between Metropolitans and "unruly" citizens. It was difficult to assess to what extent, if any, the disgruntled Municipals were involved, but ugly innuendoes circulated that they had encouraged the melees to prove that the new force was incapable of maintaining order.[39]

Although the problems of urban lawlessness and crime were the special consequence of slum life, these violent eruptions cast new doubt on Wood's dedication to public safety and the authority of the law. Giving credence to fears of a nervous public that more rioting was imminent, the *Times* spoke for many New Yorkers in its judgment that he had created the climate for mobocracy by his "disorganizing and reckless opposition to the laws of the State."[40] Once more, the Model Mayor was synonymous with civic disorder.

These were harsh judgments, but during July and August, Wood tempered them with a skillful public relations campaign to restore his battered image. Speaking at several ward meetings, he stressed that the final verdict about his conduct in office lay with voters, and he set the bounds for the fall campaign around the general themes of home rule, his devotion to law and order, and the election of all Democrats. With those ideas in mind, Wood designated five committeemen to negotiate a single state convention delegation with the Union General Committee, based on their collective need to defend the city from the Republicans' "unscrupulous central regency."[41]

Tammanyites responded in a grudging manner, largely at Buchanan's insistence that the party unite prior to the fall elections. Prodded by Wikoff, a meeting did take place. Although Schell and Sickles barely spoke to each other, Wikoff notified the president that Wood's "zeal & alacrity" laid the basis for an "adjustment of all differences."[42]

Wikoff failed to understand that Tammany would not accept an accommodation. In the city, Schell prevented fusion by redrawing the Democracy's political lines by hanging out a sign on the Custom House that none but Woodites were acceptable. Upstate, Wood was just as dangerous seeking to isolate the Hall. He wrote Daniel Dickinson, the Hard's spiritual leader and Schell's ally, that a "prompt & compact reorganization" was the only means to "secure a covenant of action for future movements." Fearful of these developments, the Union Committee ended any chance for compromise on Wood's terms. Sickles warned Buchanan that the party could not survive unless he halted "the complete subjugation of Mr. Schell to Mr. Wood." When the president did nothing, Tammany formed a separate delegation. Small and Savage followed suit.[43]

At the convention, the Credentials Committee took up the three contested delegations as the first order of business. Wood arrived early and struck reporters with his quiet confidence. By contrast, Sickles was uneasy, despite convincing Savage to merge. As hearings began, Wood was adamant. He admitted that the committee could rule on individual challenges, but denied its right to "enter into a discussion or attempted settlement of local differences." Committeemen faced a cruel choice. Both groups represented genuine Democrats; each had intimate ties to Buchanan. John Kelly, nominally a Unionist, proposed a compromise by splitting the seats between them. Wood agreed since the arrangement guaranteed his position as a regular Democrat. Sickles, sensing he could get no more, accepted with a public display of "unhappiness."[44]

That settled, Wood controlled the convention because of his link to Schell, and through him, Buchanan. Placed on the Resolutions Committee, Wood largely wrote the platform and carefully crafted it to please the entire party. Among his planks were praise for adopted citizens, censure of Republicans for attempting to secure equal manhood suffrage for blacks, backing of the Dred Scott decision, criticism of prohibition as an invasion of private rights, endorsement of home rule, and support for Buchanan's efforts to halt "slavery agitation in Kansas." As a final touch, the delegates put Wood, along with Sweeny, on the state committee from the first district. Wood struck only one sour note. Delegates rejected his attempt to prevent Denio's renomination.[45]

With state and county elections coming, implausible solidarity spread throughout the embattled city Democracy. The Small and Union committees consolidated into yet another General Committee, evenly apportioned, including Wood. Cooper and Small served as rotating chairmen. The love feast continued at a series of meetings where "a spirit of fairness and harmony" prevailed; rallies drew large crowds; and even Sickles seemed cooperative. Nominations for county offices went placidly and climaxed with Wood's perfunctory renomination. He received 95 out of 106 votes on the first ballot, far outdistancing fur dealer C. Godfrey Gunther, a German Democrat.[46]

Wood's easy selection seemed proof that he dominated the Democracy. According to the *Sun*, his choice represented "a practical protest against" Republican state control, "and as such will be supported by the whole strength of the party in this city." Yet one major question remained. Many New Yorkers wondered why, after months of dogged opposition, had Tammany given in? The *Times* supplied the answer. It predicted that the Hall's cooperation would end with the November elections. The reason had nothing to do with Wood's "executive ability" which far exceeded those of "any man who has held that office for many years." The real trouble was that he used those qualities "not for the public welfare, but recklessly and unscrupulously for the promotion of his own selfish and partisan purposes."[47]

In the interim, an unforseen economic shock made all political forecasts problematic. By early October, a grinding financial panic gripped the city: banks contracted credit and suspended specie payments, and many businesses plummeted into bankruptcy. As hard times deepened, working-class poor became the chief victims. Observers estimated that by the middle of the month a minimum of thirty thousand workers were unemployed, and the rate was rising by about one thousand per day. Shocked by this "destitution," the *Sun* pleaded for immediate "measures" to "lessen the amount of suffering."[48]

Vigor and imagination were needed. Instead, orthodox beliefs about the proper functions of government held that the municipality was not responsible for aiding the unfortunate. But Wood was cast in a different mold. On October 22, even as fruitless arguments raged among some sympathetic citizens about the merits of private relief versus direct public works projects as the means for helping the unemployed, Wood startled New Yorkers with an extraordinary special message to the Common Council. He proposed an unprecedented public works project for needed municipal projects such as improving Central Park, opening new streets, and improving the Croton Water Works' reservoir, funded by city bonds at 7 percent interest, redeemable in fifty years. Part of the money was for direct relief by having the municipal government bypass middlemen and purchase fifty thousand barrels of flour and a corresponding amount of cornmeal and potatoes. The city would then hire laborers, and pay them one-quarter in cash, three-quarters in foodstuffs. Failure to act, he warned, might stimulate a fresh rash of savage class conflict. As a Locofoco he warned: "In the days of general depression," workers "are the first to feel the changes, without the means to avoid or endure reverses. Truly it may be said that in New York those who produce every thing get nothing, and those who produce nothing get every thing."[49]

Wood's sharp thrust against his era's economic and social pieties dovetailed into his ideological perception of politics, a perception forged in the heat of Locofocoism. When he invoked fears of potential warfare between stratified classes, Wood underscored the Locofoco idea that class divisions endangered individual liberty and equality. By dramatically departing from traditional limited, almost static, government, Wood pioneered the idea of government intervention to alleviate human injustice and set a major precedent for future urban leaders.

It was his finest hour, but Wood could not escape the widespread conservative perception that his gesture was a cynical campaign tool that "endangered the community" and the free-enterprise system, especially among merchants who hoped to profit from his suggestion. Hidebound Democrats and Republicans were in a quandary. Each considered Wood an enemy, but it was difficult for them to drop past hostilities and unite without damaging their own parties. By any measure, however, the danger of his reelection was so great that both groups approached Edward Cooper about fusing in the mayoral election. For the moment, Tammanyites withheld any commitment, but privately began searching for a suitable candidate.[50]

Wood reaped a similar disappointing harvest among the poor. The Common Council rejected his plan with the excuse that the charter denied any direct relief. As a weak substitute, the Committee on Finance suggested that Flagg help the unemployed by the release of funds from a $250,000 bond levy already issued for Central Park. The committee further proposed an additional $50,000 in taxes for street construction but delayed implementation until 1858. While Flagg complied about Central Park, the number of men hired scarcely numbered eleven hundred, far less than Wood intended, and payment was never made in the foodstuffs that the despairing unemployed sought.[51]

At that point, workers vented their fury in a series of protest rallies, gradually whipping themselves into a frenzy of radicalism. After one such meeting, about three hundred defiant people confronted Wood at city hall demanding "work." Barely heard amid the uproar and looking uneasy, he blamed the council for inaction and offered only sympathy. Wood's prophesy came home. Fearful of imminent violence after some sullen workers seized bakers' wagons, he disillusioned additional jobless men by calling on the hated Metropolitans to guard city hall. Many workers were now so furious that they no longer saw him as "the poor man's friend," but a "cynical manipulator" who "had humbugged them."[52]

Wood was now so busy defending himself from the right and left that no political trade-off was possible. In even a larger sense, the relief proposal ended his quest for respectability. Haunted by too many scandals, evidences of misconduct, complicity in rioting, and denial of law and order, he took on a far more dangerous attribute, a man who stooped to demagoguery.

Sweeping Democratic victories in the November elections flushed Tammanyites out of hiding. Sickles set the pace and contradicted the idea that Wood's reelection was necessary to protest the "invasion of municipal rights" because he had forfeited public confidence by sowing class conflict for political gain. Plainly, Sickles jabbed at Wood, Tammany must find a faultless civic-minded candidate acceptable to all New Yorkers. Sickles made the same point to Buchanan. "There is a very strong desire among the best men in our party to get rid of Wood, as mayor, provided a better Democrat and a [more] reliable man can be got in his place."[53]

The pace of fusion quickened. On November 15, hardly three weeks before the election, Tammanyites held a joint session with Republicans and Know-Nothings at the Merchants' Exchange. Out of these deliberations emerged a nonpartisan, ten-man nominating committee from all elements of the commercial class. After former mayor and sugar merchant William F. Havemeyer proved unavailable, these men selected Democratic almshouse governor Daniel F. Tiemann, a wealthy German-American paint manufacturer, under the new People's party label.[54]

Tiemann was formidable. A former Free-Soiler, he attracted conservatives and reformers from both parties, along with what remained of the Know-Nothings, German immigrants, and merchants disillusioned with Wood. More threatening to Wood, Tiemann was a tough campaigner. Brusque in manner, he justified his insurgency to Buchanan by letting him know that "mere organization must yield to principle, and corruption and depravity must be rebuked."[55]

The contest was shaped in an atmosphere of complex political adjustments, along the familiar lines of Wood's mayoral record and personal character. Sickles and McKeon led the charge. It was Wood and Wood alone, they asserted, who had saddled the city with fiscal mismanagement, handed Republicans an excuse to change the charter because of his megalomania, and fomented the recent riots. Wherever they pried, they found a rascal. Raising near criminal charges without documented proof, they said Wood had rigged bids for personal payoffs in the sale of city property, demanded kickbacks in the stalled raising of the *Joseph Walker,* and, along with brother Ben, forced election boards to purchase new glass ballot boxes from a dummy firm they controlled. All those proved, Sickles thundered, that "no Democrat was required by party obligation" to vote for Wood.[56]

Wood struck back by structuring his campaign along traditional lines as a regularly nominated Democrat. He contended that Tammanyites who supported Tiemann were apostates for rejecting "established [party] usages." Wood's contention forced some Tammanyites, who were habituated to the sanctity of those rules, to reconsider. Men such as Cochrane and Tweed, who was running for supervisor, deserted the "rebels." Cochrane was particularly forceful. Democrats must back Fernando Wood, "the regular nominee of Tammany Hall." Even if he were "proclaimed the devil incarnate," the Democracy had willingly selected him and therefore he was "a worthy standard-bearer of our principles."[57]

After hearing Cochrane, a group of exuberant Woodites streamed toward St. Nicholas Hotel, where the mayor briefly addressed them from the balcony. For a short moment, Wood reverted to his old nonpartisan guise. He announced that it was unseemly for a mayor to ask for votes but promised to defend his conduct in office. Yet in the next breath before going back into his apartment, he had a few words for party regulars. Their latent sense of fair play was a far more trustworthy barometer of public opinion than any blustering from "discarded politicians."[58]

Organizationally, Wood's underlings detonated a bristling attack on Tiemann. At ward meetings and street rallies, they castigated him as a bogus Democrat, a covert Republican and Know-Nothing without shame or principles. Wood, intent on proving his integrity, asked the electorate to judge "me on that basis and my principles." Still, he was cautious, and had his attorney present a public affidavit denying any connection to the alleged "swindles."[59]

Wood capped his campaign at the Academy of Music where he turned the election into a civics lesson. Take municipal spending, he began. Admittedly, expenditures had risen, but neither he, the Common Council, nor the Finance Department were corrupt. High spending came from state commissions over which he lacked executive oversight. No mayor "could regulate the monstrous and irresponsible government" Republicans had created. His reelection hinged, then, on the Democratic principle of home rule against Republican scorn of freedom. Having defended his position, Wood left his lofty plateau and attacked Tiemann's administration of the almshouse, pointing out that its costs had escalated more rapidly than in comparable departments. As for Tammany fusionists, the moment "Democratic politicians listen to the siren song" of Republicanism, they were "forever lost to the Democratic party."[60]

The speech came too late. Given Wood's bad press for the past year, many voters paid more attention to his style than his message. Summing up that attitude, the *Times* conceded a "great deal of truth" existed in his speech. But it still denigrated him as a "champion of license and misrule."[61] Wood could not blunt this mindset, nor could he incriminate anyone else. After years of emphasizing one-man rule, voters took him at face value. Whatever ills haunted the city lay at his door. He was its product, beneficiary, and victim.

On election day, Wood left home early in the morning and went with his wife to his voting precinct in the Twenty-second Ward. Later, he took a leisurely carriage ride to city hall, exuding confidence and stopping at several polls to see friends. By early evening, his office teemed with activity. Messengers scurried in with news about the turnout, reporting partial returns, and checking on Metropolitans who were purportedly intimidating voters. Fragmentary results did not indicate any trend, but gradually the tide turned against him. Slowly, the tumult quieted. Head high, Wood shook hands with his brother, and moved out of city hall.[62]

The final tally was closer than anyone anticipated. Tiemann carried twelve wards and won by 2,317 votes, or 51.4 percent to Wood's 48.6 percent. In analyzing Wood's loss, his coalition of ethnicity, labor support, and low per capita wealth was still strong but had begun to decline. The key to his defeat lay in a marginal decrease in his immigrant base. Voters had turned out in record numbers, up 5,972 over 1856 and by 34 percent since 1854. Because most of these new voters were naturalized citizens, previous trends indicated that as the electorate increased so did Wood's strength among them. Tiemann, however, cut into the ethnic vote, particularly among Germans. The resultant drop-off was significant considering that he had inherited the bulk of the nativists, attracted the majority of Republicans, and picked up some Tammanyites. As a result, Tiemann carried all six West Side wards by the substantial average majority of 65.6 percent. Wood somewhat neutralized this loss by winning six Irish and German wards on the East Side, but lost the German Tenth, which was Purdy's home. In the six wards above Fourteenth Street, which were becoming more Irish and German, Wood won only two.[63]

Two facts were clear, Fernando Wood was shorn of power, and members of his own party had worked "assiduously for his defeat." Writing Wood's obituary for Tammanyites, financier August Belmont wanted a third. "Wood is a d–d man, and no action of the executive [Buchanan] can galvanize him into political life again."[64]

The Southern Candidate

W OOD proved a lively cadaver. In the immediate aftermath of defeat, he lashed at voter ingratitude toward the $40,000 he claimed he personally paid for everyday city expenses, rebuffed Tiemann's overtures for a smooth transition of power, and berated the majority of police commissioners for condoning what he termed "grand scale [electoral] frauds." His rage reached epic proportions at the December 1857 General Committee meeting. Branding Sickles and Gunther, Tiemann's campaign manager, as party renegades, Wood demanded their expulsion for disregarding party usages. In the "stormy" debate that followed, Wood lost all restraint. He "resolved to carry the war," a report rather colorfully put it, "to the knife, and should he fail in the struggle, with his hands on the throats of the traitors, he would drag them down with him." Wood drew first blood. The committee voted 63 to 34 for ejecting Sickles and Gunther as "traitors."[1]

Wood was too vindictive. The committee, dreading an even more drastic purge, rescinded the expulsion, 51 to 43, and authorized a new election for the 1858 General Committee based on the Association System. Anti-Wood Tammanyites won a working majority and named Peter Sweeny chairman, but Wood refused to yield. Mocking the system as a travesty of the democratic process because it did not represent individual voters, he sponsored a separate election under the old ward method and formed his own General Committee. Responding quickly, the council repeated its earlier scenario and voted to direct Charles Brown, the building's new lessee, from allowing Wood its use.[2]

Tammany pressed its advantage. In December, Buchanan put all Democrats on notice that he expected them to endorse his position of admitting Kansas to the Union under the dubious proslavery Lecompton Constitution, and ordered them to ostracize Stephen Douglas who disdained it. Wood jumped at the chance to dramatize support for the president and became the first local politician to schedule a public rally. The Tammany Society, however, locked the Long Room, and authorized a "regular" pro-Lecompton meeting. Forced into City Park, the Woodites praised Buchanan, but then shifted to a general denunciation of both Tammany Hall and the Tammany Society, ending with resolutions that condemned each for supporting Tiemann. When Tammany met, raucous Woodites shouted down John Van Buren, the main speaker, and fistfights erupted. "On all sides men were knocking down the next man to them," the *New York Tribune* jibed. "Similar scenes are not uncommon at Tammany Hall, but rarely has Tammany seen such a scene as this."[3]

This episode, though minor in scope, spoke volumes about the changing complexion of city politics. During the past decade, localism, the idea that national issues were secondary to parochial interests, characterized New York politics. Now, temperance, nativism, and civic reform paled as slavery extensionism and its relationship to the future of the nation dominated the spotlight. Whenever the South needed a champion, Wood stepped forward. Why this affinity existed was never clear. Perhaps the cause lay in his formative years spent in Kentucky, South Carolina, and Virginia. Maybe it was gratitude toward Wise and Calhoun, who had helped him at the bleakest point in his business career. Or, it could have been his assumption that Southern trade and slavery were the foundations of the city's booming economy. Then again, Wood's ideology coincided with the South's strict constructionism and states' rights stance. Racism might have been the answer. Whatever the reason, Wood was the South's most reliable friend in New York City, and defended its institutions with all the fire of his personality and the ingenuity of his political skills.

Once Tiemann took office, Wood began putting his life back into shape. Finally calm, he rented an office on Wall Street and busied himself with real estate investments. This indifference masked a tactical withdrawal. With only brother Ben as an adviser, he plotted to regain the initiative.

In January 1858, Wood swung into action, going first to Washington to test his standing with Buchanan. What worried Wood in particular was that the president might replace Schell because the New York congressional delegation resented the collector's working agreement with him. Satisfied that Buchanan would retain Schell, Wood instructed his lieutenants to back the president's Kansas policy, no matter the circumstances. At the same time, Wood knew that Buchanan was too old to run for reelection. Eager to find an early replacement, he moved on to Richmond and settled on Governor Wise as a likely nominee, even though he understood that Wise was less popular with party workers than Douglas. Wood's choice was strictly pragmatic. Since Douglas did not back the Lecompton Constitution, Wood rejected him to appease Buchanan and safeguard Schell. Wood reckoned also that the Democracy's selection of a Southerner could lead to his choice as a Northern vice-presidential candidate to balance the ticket.[4]

Back in New York by the end of January, Wood purchased a controlling inter-est in the struggling pro-Tammany *New York Daily News* for $5,600, eventually installing his brother as editor. Up to this point, Wood had labored at a crucial disadvantage in presenting his side of the political story. He had no quarrel with the prevailing system that with only a few exceptions journalists were little bet-ter than paid political assassins. The problem was that most were on the payrolls of enemies. By owning the *Daily News,* he communicated his position on every major political issue, instructed the faithful, attracted a powerful following among the underclass, the object of its social concerns, and no longer had to rely on the erratic Bennett or Beach.[5]

Wood spent the next two months laying the groundwork for his ultimate April showdown with the Tammany Society over the election of a new Council of Sachems. Once again, he realized, the society held the key solution to the equation of Democratic politics. At this point, Wood's only hope to dominate the party rested on controlling the council and its crucial role in determining the regularity of competing general committees.[6]

Primarily, Wood pitched his appeal to Tammany Society brothers as a tradi-tional Locofoco. He sought their backing by arguing that a small, self-constituted elite had undermined the principle of majority rule in denying the people the "right to settle or determine questions" pertinent to their own inter-ests. On a practical level, he formed a "Forester" slate headed by Schell. Few missed Wood's meaning. Any Tammany Society brave who expected Custom House patronage must support his ticket.[7]

The sachems were less ideological, and exploited their control of the socie-ty's membership mechanism. During March and April, they prepared to stuff the ballot box by initiating new brothers and convincing older ones to vote who rarely bothered with fraternal matters. On election night, carriages clogged the streets near the building, bringing men, some "with white locks and feeble frames," from "places in and out of the State." When balloting began, 378 attended, the largest turnout in recent memory. The result was preordained. Wood lost by better than two to one. Streaming out of the Wigwam, his bitter supporters told watchful reporters that Fowler had corrupted the society by enrolling secret "Black Republicans." John Dix, a longtime party stalwart, who had voted for the first time since his initiation in 1830, supplied Buchanan with a less emotional reason. "I think Mr. Schell committed a fatal error in attempting, through his own influence & that of the Customhouse, to throw the Tammany Society into the arms of Mayor Wood."[8]

Dix was correct. Many of the men Schell axed were staunch Tammanyites, loyal to Buchanan. They complained to local party leaders about the collector's support of Wood, and found Congressman Sickles sympathetic. He relayed their unhappiness to Secretary of the Treasury Howell Cobb, Schell's direct superior. In turn, Cobb began pressing Buchanan to discipline the collector. "The simple question is whether your policy or that of Fernando Wood is to be carried out." Buchanan had already concluded that Schell was a bitter disappointment but feared a peremptory removal might further weaken the Democracy in the coming fall elections. For the moment, the president did nothing, but allowed events to take their natural course.[9]

Wood faced a monumental crisis. Regardless of the hazards involved, he could no longer wait. Losing the Tammany Society meant that remaining in Tammany Hall as the loyal opposition was political suicide since he was a pariah. Well aware that defensive politicians lose, Wood touched off a rebellion against the cradle of his birth, Tammany Hall.

Wood's revolt had been imminent for some time, but few Democrats were prepared for his brashness in building a fresh third-party organization, one which radically altered the fabric of local politics. The bolt demanded great skill, and Wood poured his considerable executive energies into the task. At the start, he labeled his insurrection the "Democratic Society of Regulars," and formed twenty-two subsocieties, one for each ward. Although similar to Tammany's structure, the Regulars were unique because Wood based the apparatus on the idea of making it directly accessible to ordinary citizens. As an exercise in participatory self-government, he explained that the Regulars welcomed every Democrat, the only requisite of membership "being consistent profession and practice of Democratic principles." These groups then elected delegates, based on the number of Democratic voters in the city's 175 electoral precincts, and formed a central governing board, or General Committee.[10]

Despite the different men who served as chairman over the years, one man was in charge, Fernando Wood. This party was his personal party, funded by his wealth and guided by his political cunning. While Wood was still of the Democracy, the one-man ruler now wanted to be the Democratic party.

Wood justified his mutiny in pure Locofoco terms, partly out of principle, partly to neutralize the inevitable charge that he was simply vengeful. The Regulars, or Mozart Hall Democrats, as they became known because of the hotel near the corner of Bond Street and Broadway where they met, represented "the free and fearless will of the Democracy of this City." In contrast, Tammany was the haunt of "Black Republican spies and Democratic traitors," run by a selfish oligarchy through "secret back door dictum." The true issue before the Democracy was "if the people and the people alone, shall govern." Repeatedly, Wood maintained that he was a loyal Democrat, "a party man" with an unblemished quarter-century record of fidelity to traditional principles. Thus, "this is not a contest of to-day waged for personal malignity. I belong to the people."[11] As the conscience of the Democratic party, he had not deserted Tammany Hall. It had betrayed him.

Encouraged by the number of immigrants, workers, and the poor flocking to Mozart, Wood prepared for his first test at the fall state convention. Yet even as Wood struck idealistic notes in forming Mozart, he was characteristically opportunistic at the August 1858 state committee meeting. Seemingly, he bowed to Richmond's directive to seek a compromise delegation with Tammany. Wood, however, betrayed his pledge. He swapped support with Douglasites who were laboring to gain the party's endorsement for the senator, and made a contrary deal with Dickinson, who sought favorite-son status for the national convention. To both, Wood pledged full support if each, unknown to the other, voted to admit only Mozart.[12] While Wood hoped his tactics would force the convention to recognize Mozart, he had another equally important goal. Playing Dickinson against Douglas might lead to a deadlocked national convention in 1860 that would nominate a Southerner, perhaps Wise.

Since Buchanan had the power to spoil Wood's high-level scheming, Wood needed his support, or at worst, his neutrality. For that reason, Wood dispatched a series of letters, one almost autobiographic, stressing the ideology which had shaped his career and place in city politics. As for Tammany, it was full of "folly & wickedness," so much so that "I find it necessary for me to become a member of & to take part with those opposed." Arrogantly, Wood announced the masses will "support me, & my organization when the issue comes, as it soon will." For all his harsh words, Wood backed off and hinted that if the president appointed him governor of the Nebraska Territory, "my absence [might] restore peace." Actually, Wood had no intention of accepting, but wanted the offer to accentuate the administration's backing. Buchanan with good reason shrugged him off. In reply, Wood indicated his willingness to accept a lesser prize, Buchanan's support in exchange for Mozart's attack on any politician "suspected of affiliation with Douglas."[13]

Fowler, Cochrane, and Sickles were just as busy burdening the mails to the White House. All agreed that Wood and Schell were the prime causes of Democratic disunity and Buchanan must fire the collector. "It seems hard to me," Sickles reflected angrily, "that I am obliged to submit to the opposition of the chief officers of an administration which I aided to place in power and which I have faithfully supported."[14] Buchanan was consistent. He followed the course of least resistance and did nothing.

Deliberations at the state convention during the second week of September proved that Wood was far better at criticism than in replacing Tammany. The reason lay in his own fatal deception. Shortly before, the *New York Times* had alerted Democrats to his dealings with Buchanan, Richmond, Dickinson, and the Douglasites. Sickles tightened the noose. After the August committee meeting, he told the president that Wood had introduced resolutions sympathetic to "Wise, Douglas & their friends & condemning" the administration. In a sea of

disorder, then, delegates accepted Tammany. Wood refused to accept the verdict. The issue of which organization represented the city Democracy, he said
before entraining, was far from settled. Voters in the coming November congressional races would decide.[15]

When he arrived home, Wood reopened correspondence with the president,
but in far more hostile tones. Baiting Buchanan's passion against "Douglasism,"
Wood said Mozart would oppose Sickles's reelection because Tammany supported the senator. "My friends," have "suffered so much from the managers of
Tammany Hall that it is like choking a bulldog off of his prey to make them let
go." At last, Buchanan's patience snapped. After reprimanding Wood in sharp
terms, he underscored his "strong desire" to have Sickles back in Congress and
ended with a straightforward threat that his administration would not tolerate
any divisions leading to Black Republican triumphs. Wood did not flinch. In a
fiery speech on election eve, he shouted: "Every vote against Daniel Sickles is a
vote cast for Fernando Wood."[16]

Wood's efforts were wasted. Sickles won over a split field and, as Buchanan
feared, Republicans made strong statewide gains, carrying their momentum into
the December municipal races. Running against both Tammany and Mozart,
they astounded outsiders by cracking the Democracy's once invincible bastion
in electing the corporation attorney, comptroller, and a number of aldermen.[17]

Wood lost more than the elections. Still ostensibly supporting Buchanan's
Kansas policy, Wood nonetheless secretly furnished Douglas with funds he
mysteriously raised to finance his senatorial race against Abraham Lincoln.[18] To
Wood, the deal was sound. Douglas's valuable Chicago real estate secured the
investment, and Wood increased the senator's chances of deadlocking the presidential convention. With everything to win, it was of slight moment to Wood
that he was fooling Richmond, Dickinson, Douglas, and, most risky of all,
Buchanan.

Wood's secret had a short lifespan. Albert Ramsey, a *New York Herald* correspondent, leaking information from Bennett who was angered about Wood's
takeover of the *Daily News,* informed the president that Wood was responsible
for Douglas's sudden raising of $39,000. That information ended Wood's hold
over the Custom House. In December Buchanan summoned Schell and other
city Democrats to a White House meeting. Fowler, Purdy, Cochrane, Sickles,
and Kelly, who had just broken with Wood, were among those who came.
Wood, suspecting a trap, stayed at home. When the men entered his office,
Buchanan forced them to sign an agreement whereby Schell siphoned all
patronage through Tammany Hall. In effect, this so-called Treaty of Washington isolated Wood even more.[19]

Although Tammany was elated by Schell's capitulation, Fowler and Sweeny
were sobered by Republican triumphs and presumed that Wood was ready to

capitulate. They offered to readmit him to the 1859 General Committee and sweetened the deal by promising him one-third of the seats if he dissolved Mozart. Because the Hall supported Douglas, Wood refused, certain that such an arrangement would destroy his credibility and harm Wise. The only compromise, he informed Fowler, was in Tammany's dissolution.[20]

Wood could not so easily dismiss losing the Custom House. Back to Washington he went, intent on having the president either reverse himself or, ironically, replace Schell. Wood was not alone. Fowler was registered in the same hotel, and he sought to cap Tammany's stranglehold over federal spoils by removing the last important Custom House Woodite, naval officer Ausburn M. Birdsall, a Hard, and Dickinson's son-in-law. Buchanan shut the door. He did not speak to Wood, and refused to see Fowler.[21]

Yet something bizarre happened in Washington. Wood astonished Tammany by making peace overtures to Sickles as a preliminary move to a permanent rapprochement with the Hards. On reflection, Wood had logic on his side. Schell had frozen Hards out and most blamed him, rather than Wood. Sickles, who knew better, was nevertheless willing to bargain out of hatred toward Schell. In one way, the alliance died when Sickles killed his wife's lover and fell into personal and political disgrace. The bargain, however, had a life of its own. Dickinson found the trade an expedient way to protect Birdsall and perhaps gain the state's presidential delegates under Mozart's Southern banner. While Wood had no intention of such an eventuality, he welcomed Dickinson as a way to ensure a bartered nominating convention.[22]

In the interim, Wood's family life suffered in direct proportion to the time he poured into politics. Anna D. Wood was the one constant in his life, a symbol of love and stability. Yet heartaches loomed for both. Two more children were born in the mid-1850s, sapping her health and leaving her physically weak. Pregnant again in the spring of 1859 and bedridden for nearly six months, her condition alarmed Wood. Other family cares were less worrisome. His two eldest sons, Joseph L. R. Wood and Fernando Wood, Jr., though uninterested in politics, found careers in commerce and managed his real estate interests. Four younger children were at home, pampered by house servants. Rebecca Wood still lived with him, but his youngest sister Elizabeth had married and rented a home he owned in the Seventh Ward. His two closest brothers were settled. Ben Wood ran a thriving lottery business, in addition to the *Daily News*. An effusive man, he made friends easily, and became increasingly interested in his own political prospects. Henry Wood was equally secure. Already a partner in the flourishing Christy and Wood minstrel company, he was building a theater and had considerable stature in the city's thriving entertainment business.[23]

In the midst of these developments during the spring of 1859, Wood faced several financial problems that stemmed from his last mayoralty. He sought

$20,000 from the state for personal expenses incurred litigating the Police Law, over and above the $10,000 the Common Council had appropriated, and feared that the Court of Appeals might hold him liable in a pending case for the Municipals' back pay. Another problem rested in superior court. A contractor, who had replaced Walter Jones in raising the *Walker*, sought to hold Wood personally responsible for vetoing a warrant authorizing payment although the ship remained stuck. To ease his financial crunch, Wood and brother Ben tried to deal with state Republican leader Thurlow Weed. In exchange for Weed's lobbying the legislature and Court of Appeals, they promised to contact several pliable municipal officials about endorsing Weed's bid to build a lucrative city railroad.[24]

Wood's efforts ended with mixed results. The legislature did not repay him, nor grant the railroad franchise. To balance those setbacks, a superior court jury found for him in the *Walker* case. Even more pleasing, the presiding judge, Charles Bosworth, no particular friend of Wood, said that if he had approved the warrant "he would not have performed his duty." The Court of Appeals was less effusive but equally gentle. It did hold Wood liable for back pay, but only in the cases of fifteen Municipals who had not found jobs on the new force, amounting to $3,750. Yet the judges sustained his contention that commissioners had erred by not reappointing other eligible Municipals and maintained the city, not Wood, should reimburse them. Wood was deeply pleased with this apparent vindication, and maintained that the courts had substantiated his basic honesty and opposition to state interference. Even promising to pay the Municipals and losing his $20,000 claim became a mark of honor. Wood, the *Daily News* intoned, "never hesitated in taking responsibility when the public good required it."[25]

By the late spring of 1859, Wood turned to the state Democratic convention and the making of a new president. Two key imponderables blocked his way: the state committee's method to select New York's thirty-five presidential delegates, and the uncertain outcome of his feud with Tammany. With these questions so imprecisely defined, he invited Dickinson and 350 Hards, or "National Democrats" as they called themselves, to a May meeting in the Astor House. They readily accepted Wood's agenda: petitions asking the state committee to delay naming delegates until after the November elections, and having voters directly elect those delegates in congressional district. Such "popular rights," the *Daily News* spelled out, formed the "corner stone of the Democratic party." On that basis and with National Democratic support, Wood expected Mozart's sole acceptance at the convention. State chairman Richmond was noncommittal and reserved comments until the full August 4 committee meeting.[26]

During the next four months, Wood gave the impression of working for Wise, but his contradictory activities raised questions about his ultimate position. In the city, Mozart actively organized ward clubs for the governor. Yet during his Saratoga holiday, Wood advised upstate Hards to back Dickinson. Then, Wood complicated the confusion by maintaining ties to Douglas. Despite the state committee's uncertainty over where Wood stood precisely, his deviousness did have an internal logic. He sought to divide Wise's opponents as the first step to a deadlocked state delegation.[27]

All of Wood's scheming came to nothing. As one of Wise's "earliest and con-sistent friends," he had continually urged the governor "to avoid too much letter writing." Wise ignored the warnings. In July, he wrote a fool-hardy "private and confidential" letter to a local supporter, which Bennett bought for $20 and turned over to Richmond. In it, Wise scoffingly called Douglas's candidacy "preposterous," sneered at Dickinson "as the leader of a divided faction," cast doubt on Wood's influence upstate but backed his congressional district plan, and, if that misfired, urged "a double state delegation," one pledged to him. On the day of the meeting, Richmond showed Dickinson the letter, and then had it published in William Cassidy's *Albany Argus,* the Soft's official party organ. Dickinson, outraged at Wise's interference in New York politics and Wood's connection to him, reacted by cutting a bargain with Richmond, subject to the convention's certain approval, splitting the delegates between Hards and Softs, giving Wood nothing.[28]

This agreement left three losers. Dickinson was one because Richmond favored Douglas and under the state's unit rule became the senator's potential kingmaker. Wise was next. He failed to unite New York behind his candidacy. That left Wood. Momentarily nonplussed when Richmond flourished the letter, Wood branded it a forgery, and asked Cassidy, to whom he had lent funds to buy an interest in the *Argus,* for the money back. Nothing availed. Wise ad-mitted the letter's authenticity, leaving Wood sputtering about the immorality of reading private mail. Richmond succinctly summed up these developments. "The letter of Wise," he told a Douglasite, "killed Wood and Wise."[29]

Richmond was partially correct. Wise's candidacy was dead, but Richmond underestimated Wood. Little had essentially changed. Although now lacking a specific Southerner, Wood was still committed to seeing one selected in a brok-ered convention, and, through him, securing a possible vice-presidential nomi-nation. Wood's goal was not as farfetched as it seemed. Many upstate and city National Democrats, more hardheaded than Dickinson, realized Richmond would control the New York delegation for Douglas. They continued, therefore, to support Wood's Southernism. All that convinced Wood that the time was ripe to announce his mayoral candidacy. Under those circumstances, he laid out vig-orous plans to manage the Syracuse convention and to set the pace for both the state and national organizations. Once committed, Wood gave the Democracy new lessons in his peculiar flair for ruthlessness and opportunism.[30]

As usual, Wood traveled to Syracuse in a private car, but did not lack for companions. A boisterous group of tough "shoulder-hitters," headed by Californian John C. Heenan, a professional pugilist, fondly nicknamed the "Benicia Boy," was on the same train with the Mozart delegation.

These toughs quickly made their presence felt. A half hour before the meeting formally opened, they used a traditional Tammany stratagem to storm the floor and preemptively began proceedings. When incensed Regency Softs arrived, fistfights broke out and some delegates drew knives and pistols. Near the rostrum, someone, reputedly Heenan, struck John Stryker, the dignified Soft temporary chairman, forcing him to retire and seek medical attention. Crying "shame," the routed Softs retreated. Wood and the National Democrats hastily took charge. They recognized Mozart exclusively, forged a new state committee including Wood, adopted the congressional district plan, named a ticket for the November elections, and scheduled a February 1860 date to elect delegates-at-large and plot further strategy. After they adjourned, the Softs slowly returned. Fearing a dual slate would benefit Republicans, they endorsed Wood's ticket, but the Regency revived the old state committee, minus Wood, accepted Tammany, and chose delegates according to the deal Richmond and Dickinson had arranged.[31]

This brutal display of naked force left Democrats sickened, demoralized, and in disarray. Each side blamed the other for instigating the violence, and both promised vengeance. Wood's prominence and long history of rash acts, however, marked him as the special villain. Softs and Richmond filled the air with a crescendo of accusations at his "outrages" against civilized behavior. Newspapers reported he received "several threatening letters from some of the Tammany fighting men." Jabbing back, Wood blamed Tammany for the savagery; accused Isaiah Rynders as the man who hit Stryker; and encouraged Heenan to file an affidavit swearing that it was actually Tammany which had imported his gang. As for the convention, Wood said the party never authorized it to name presidential delegates. Thus, National Democrats had sustained "one of the fundamental principles of the Democratic party," that "all powers not delegated are reserved to the people" through congressional districts.[32]

Wood was not convincing. The evidence against him was too incontrovertible. Amid this freewheeling fury, his plans for controlling the state Democracy prior to the national convention lay in shambles. His name in New York and the nation was now forever a synonym for brutality, not reasoned civility. By contrast, Tammany was delighted, and anticipated thrashing him easily in the mayoral election.

The situation was too fluid for such an easy resolution. What Tammany overlooked was its own deterioration, a process that began in late summer 1859. The previous spring, Secretary of the Treasury Cobb had proposed a series of cost-cutting measures for the Custom House. As part of his retrenchment in the city, he planned to replace bonded warehouses, where imported goods were stored, with private contractors. Usually, the collector had selected the warehouses, and hired extra guards until buyers arrived. Over the years, this system evolved into a major source of patronage. When Cobb implemented his economies in September, he eliminated nearly three hundred men, reducing Schell's political clout and cutting the number of party workers Tammany leaders ordinarily assessed for operating funds. Cobb's action had a worse dimension on the Hall's rank and file. Neighborhoods were full of unhappy Democrats, convinced the administration had abandoned them. Many turned for relief to Buchanan's foes in Mozart.[33]

The Hall's woes accelerated. Wealthy Democrats, notably August Belmont, corporation attorneys Samuel L. M. Barlow and Samuel J. Tilden, along with William Havemeyer, formed the Fifth Avenue Democrats, also known as the Democratic Vigilant Association, the forerunner of the 1860s "swallow-tail Democracy." Highly conservative, they abhorred Wood, opposed all Black Republicans, and withheld any funding of Tammany unless it nominated one of them for mayor.[34]

Although the General Committee considered these men meddling amateurs, it bowed to their will. Under normal conditions, the Hall wanted William D. Kennedy, an Irish sachem and merchant, for mayor, but the Fifth Avenue Democrats objected. Tammany capitulated to their demands. It selected Havemeyer and ran Tilden for corporation counsel. At no time did the Hall consider renominating Tiemann, whose blunt personality and fusionist policies worked as a candidate but not in a mayor.[35]

Wood was the chief beneficiary of these moves because the nominations, while satisfying upper-class Democrats, estranged many others, particularly immigrants. The *New York Irish-American* bitterly remarked that the ticket "may suit the role of Tammany managers, but it will not stand before the people." Republicans also played into Wood's hands because of Thurlow Weed. Although he had ignored city politics for some time, Weed suddenly broached a swap with Fowler and suggested that Republicans would back Havemeyer in exchange for corporation counsel. The bargain died with Tilden's nomination. Republicans then selected George P. Opdyke, a banker and former Free-Soiler, for mayor, and Solomon L. Hull, a young attorney with minimal political credentials, for corporation counsel. Many Republicans were furious at Weed's ulterior reasons for his interference. He was a lobbyist and stockholder in the proposed Third Avenue Railroad, along with a number of wealthy Democrats and Republicans, and sought to control corporation counsel as a means to secure a charter. More was at stake. If Weed was successful, he intended to assess fellow investors to up "four to six hundred thousands of dollars" as a slush fund for William Seward's presidential bid. Besides splitting Wood's field, then, Weed had forfeited Republican moral integrity.[36]

Throughout his career, Wood had the knack of turning political adversity into personal advancement. The upshot was that the *Daily News* blasted the Fifth Avenue movement "as a kid-glove, scented, silk stocking, poodle-headed, degenerate aristocracy" whose exclusiveness negated Democratic principles. Such men proved Wood correct in protecting popular rights by forming Mozart Hall since they sneered at honest workingmen as "outside barbarians." Havemeyer and Tilden were not real Democrats, the paper continued. Each had supported Free-Soilism and were silent about Republican centralism. It was ludicrous for them, and even Opdyke, to run against the "Champion of Municipal Rights." Wood struck another way. In a brilliant tactical move, he convinced Greene C. Bronson, a former collector and the 1854 Hard gubernatorial candidate, to stand for corporation counsel. His nomination forced Dickinson to back away from Tammany and strengthened Wood's National Democratic base.[37]

The spirited attacks of the brothers Wood sharply contrasted with Tammany's lagging spirits. Havemeyer was listless, knowing full well that Tammanyites had, in the *New York Evening Post*'s estimation, "chosen a man whom they do not want to a position which he does not want, simply to save themselves." Many Fifth Avenue Democrats grimaced over this observation, but grudgingly shared it and stopped bankrolling Havemeyer, convinced he could not win.[38]

Wood's campaign grew even stronger with startling news from Harper's Ferry. John Brown's frontal attack on slavery sent shock waves throughout the nation, raising Southern racial fears and giving many city Democrats direct evidence of what they interpreted as the evil consequences of Republican extremism. Because of Wood's obvious connection to slavery, his campaign took on a new guise. He was the Southern candidate. The result, one Virginian wrote, meant that Wood's "success or defeat will have a national effect."[39]

The campaign started on well-known themes. Republicans and Tammanyites dredged up all the raw political and personal sewage which fouled Wood and made his name odious. The *Times* even found a fresh stench. Editor Henry Raymond, perhaps in the most intelligent contemporary assessment of Wood, acknowledged his undoubted "executive abilities," vigor, energy, and "familiarity with the wants of the city." As "a man of wealth," his fortune further shielded him from the personal avarice that characterized so many politicians of his generation. Yet Wood's "besetting sin" was ambition, the misuse of power for personal ends. Wood's real corruption was not in the misuse of public monies, but his desire for "an imperial crown" to become "Our Municipal Emperor."[40]

Wood's response initially also followed customary lines. Busy running Mozart, he spent freely, chided Tammany for deserting party principles, and set up his own naturalization committees. As usual, he blistered Republicans for interfering with home rule, defended his mayoral record, and promised a sound fiscal administration.

Class and ethnic issues, as in the past, proved infinitely serviceable. Fifth Avenue "aristocrats," he announced, duped "the hardworking, bone and sinew, hard-fisted, noble, laboring-men of New York." Unfair taxation practices were a case in point. Recalling Locofocoism, he said the "rich have been getting richer while the poor are no better off," because wealthy New Yorkers evaded real and personal taxes. Hence, "the producing class" bore "the burden of taxation" through excessive rents upper-class owners charged poor people. Who better than himself represented "the sons of toil"? As for Raymond's assessment, Wood retorted: "Better have an iron rule than no rule at all, as is now." Finally, Wood used an imaginative ruse. He lithographed thousands of personally signed letters, "flattering" the voter into thinking "that he held the recipient in such high esteem as to send him a letter in his own hand writing, asking as a favor, his vote."[41]

Wood departed from normal politicking, however, in a set of proslavery speeches he delivered at several ward rallies, turning passions to white heat about John Brown's "fanaticism" and its threat to the Union. New York, Wood said, was financially dependent upon Southern trade; any agitation over Southern rights harmed the entire community. "The South is our best customer. She pays the best prices, and pays promptly." Let "us, therefore, do nothing to estrange the South." The inevitable result of "Sewardism" was a bloody sectional "carnal-house." People "of the North have no legal or moral right to take exception to anything at the South." That was the lesson John Brown, the "fiend," taught New Yorkers. Brown was the "bastard of a demagogue" Black Republicans had fathered. Thus, all Democrats must rally against "the followers of the Abolition party." That case was particularly true for the Irish. Wood warned that Brown was Seward's tool in an Anglophile plot to antagonize the South, thereby fostering disunion and disrupting Great Britain's chief economic rival. For New York's safety, the *Daily News* lectured, "Let the national candidate for the Mayoralty be elected, and the State is safe against Seward and his revolutionary designs."[42]

Yet, Wood's proslavery formula had the potential for setting off a Northern backlash. While many Tammanyites were appalled at Brown's tactics and defected to Mozart, Wood fretted that Governor Wise might overact by authorizing Brown's hanging. "No northern man could go further than myself in behalf of Southern rights," Wood wrote Wise. But executing Brown was counterproductive and might stir sympathy for abolitionists, perhaps even among the most "ultra friends of the South." By commuting his sentence to life imprisonment, Wood advised, "the South will gain by showing that it can be magnanimous to a fanaticism in its power."[43]

Both men were caught in a dilemma of their own making. Reliance on the South ensnared Wood, and inflamed Southern opinion trapped Wise. Wood, however, had the most to lose. Wise had forfeited his race for the presidency and had little to gain by mollifying Northerners. Wood's failure to alter Wise's approval of Brown's subsequent hanging showed his impotence in shaping Southern policy.[44] Wood was the South's candidate, but also its captive.

In contrast to all the harsh crosscurrents that washed through the campaign, Wood concluded on a high, statesmanlike level, one that his notoriety prevented from being recognized as a preeminent approach to the art of administrating municipalities. The audience at his last rally expected a rousing political address. Instead, they heard a didactic, practical discourse he prepared from the textbook of experience.

New York City, he began, encompassed "an immense aggregate of antagonistic and opposing elements composing a heterogeneous but yet compact social hive, in which all are mingled, but yet separated, as denizens of this little island." With so many "discordant elements" packed so densely, mutual "antipathies" were commonplace. Although theorists stressed the role of public opinion in policy-making, harsh reality indicated, "There is no such thing as *one* public mind; where there is not *one*, a *single* public mind, it is almost impossible that the decrees or wishes of government can be generally understood or made acceptable." Worse, most citizens were "careless about the ordinary events that occur daily in their midst," headlong as they were pursuing individual, not group, goals. "Now, my friends, how best to govern all this?" Since voters did not, and could not, give leaders direction, Wood answered himself, effective government was almost a nullity. In that impasse, the city begged for a positive, progressive figure—the mayor—who had the "integrity, will, courage, and capacity," augmented with "abundant authority of law," to "conduct public affairs in a wise manner."[45]

In advancing the proposition that the city was ungovernable without a strong mayor, Wood knew firsthand that New York's multiple interest groups, coupled to the charter's institutionalized fragmentation, limited innovative policy-making and its implementation. Building on earlier suggestions and far ahead of contemporaries, his solution was a modern one. Like many twentieth-century Progressives, Wood sought to concentrate power in a forceful activist, working for the public good. Only a mayor with centralized authority chosen by all voters could define problems, shape results, and use the political system to build the popular consensus needed to resolve New York's complex religious, ethnic, economic, and cultural frictions. Identifying these problems was not enough. Wood, in his own mind, was the key. His immediate problem rested on whether New Yorkers trusted him to provide such leadership.

The electorate ignored the threat of snow, and intense voter participation reached 88.1 percent of those registered. Wood pulled off a stunning personal victory considering Tammany's normal role in city politics. Carrying fourteen wards, he gained 38.3 percent of the total votes cast. Havemeyer was second with five wards and 34.6 percent. Opdyke trailed with 27.4 percent and just three wards.

Despite the triumph, Wood's normal coalition continued to decline although it was still the basis of his victory. Voting patterns had begun to change. He scored marginally more among slightly better-off voters and marginally worse with poorer ones. As immigrants increased in wealth, it seemed that they continued to back Wood for favors rendered. Since Mozart did not match Tammany's organization in the neighborhoods, however, it also looked that newer and poorer immigrants backed the Hall as the traditional champion of the lower class. Moreover, Wood's appeal to the commercial vote on the basis of defending the South appeared to have made some inroads among merchants and workers dependent on them. Then, too, since Wood was an insurgent who shared the same basic constituency as Tammany, his coalition's weakening indicated divided Democratic loyalties.[46]

As a result, Wood ran strongly in the nine wards of lower Manhattan and on the East Side which contained a number of shipbuilding, commercial, and related industries tied to the Southern trade. He carried six of these with substantial majorities over both Havemeyer and Opdyke. Even in the three wards he lost, Wood's vote—except for Tammany's Irish stronghold in the Sixth—was close to his competitors. On the West Side, Wood picked up the commercial Fifth, the home of concerns with extensive Southern ties, but Havemeyer and Opdyke split the rest. In the six wards above Fourteenth Street, Wood retained sufficient support to win four.[47]

Elsewhere, his coattails helped Bronson beat Tilden and elect eleven school commissioners. All the same, voters denied Wood a mandate. Mozart failed to gain a working majority in the Common Council, leaving Tammanyites and Republicans in charge. The result left mayor-elect Wood still a broker politician, not the powerful executive he had proposed.[48]

Once the returns were in, propaganda mills began to spin out explanations. Republicans snarled that Wood would again make a mockery of the municipal government he claimed to revere, downplayed the significance of his southernism, and concluded his victory was nothing more than "a signal personal triumph." Tammany published a lengthy statement through the General Committee which apologized for overconfidence and savaged Republicans, who, they growled, voted for Wood in order to further disrupt the Democracy. The bigoted Bennett gloated that Wood was truly a national leader, having defended the South against the assaults of Republican "fanaticism." As for Tammany, it merited its "death-blow" because it had identified with "Negro worshipers" by running Havemeyer and Tilden. The *Irish-American* hailed Wood as the people's champion, the immigrant's hero. Upstate National Democrats assumed his victory made their admittance to the presidential convention auto-matic. Douglasites saw the same omens, and urged the senator to open lines to Wood. From the South, the *Richmond Examiner* cheered the defeat of "repro-bate republicanism" in all its "vicious" guises. Even the *London Times* took notice. It lauded Wood as the one person with the courage to "stem the tide of corruption" that tested the American capacity for urban self-government.[49]

Wood never doubted his destiny. At a frenzied Mozart Hall celebration, he told cheering supporters that New Yorkers had sustained "the principles main-tained by me"—municipal rights, Southern justice, and "the Constitution and the Union." The intoxication of success made him magnanimous. "Avoid arro-gance" and "practice no oppression" toward Tammanyites, he urged. Since the Hall's "prestige" meant nothing to "aroused" voters, its day had passed. Mozart now ruled the Democracy and, with "a spirit of toleration and liberality," wel-comed all "fellow citizens" regardless of past differences. The future glowed with optimism. National Democrats would protect "every section of the coun-try" from Republicans and malcontent Democrats, in the process preserving "the integrity of the party." On that basis, Wood promised to mold the Democ-racy "preparatory to the great national contest of 1860."[50]

When the tumult quieted, Wood hurried home to a hushed house. Anna D. Wood had endured a difficult pregnancy, and delivered a frail daughter the Fri-day before the election. Over the weekend, she developed internal bleeding and became delirious. Her spirit rallied momentarily with news of victory, but not her body. On Thursday, December 10, two days after Wood's triumph, she died at the age of thirty-seven, leaving behind seven children, the youngest barely alive, and a somber husband. Ceremonies were held at St. George's Church, where the Reverend Dr. William Tyng eulogized her as "a model wife and mother." Her funeral procession was impressive. A line of six hearses and nearly five hundred carriages moved uptown toward Trinity Cemetery, the *Times* noted, forming "probably the largest concourse of prominent citizens ever assembled at the funeral of a lady in this City."[51]

Though he had every reason to expect this tragedy, Wood was unprepared. How much her loss meant to him was impossible to learn; he left no record of his inner feelings. After a week of mourning, he plunged back into work with a greater frenzy than ever. Almost daily until he took office, he sparred with Tiemann over the transition of power and lunged into almost never-ending rounds of meetings with other city officials and National Democrats.[52] Evi-dently, work became his means of adjustment to a life without the one person who had given him both the chance to become wealthy and the political encour-agement to forge ahead.

SEVEN

The Southern Mayor

NEW Yorkers knew what to expect as Wood strode into office. Based on his last campaign speech, they anticipated mature initiatives to govern the city and ensure its prosperity. Despite these expectations, Wood faced two major limitations: his inability to separate his political liabilities from his vaunted executive leadership, and the difficulties of working with a hostile Common Council.

Wood was predictable. His annual address was a manifesto of grievances against state control, wrapped in dreams for a better tomorrow. "Responsibility and power should go hand in hand," he reiterated. Until a new charter changed "the corrupt element in New York," the Model Mayor promised firm action "within the limited sphere assigned me."[1]

As before, Wood set a demanding schedule. Leaving his children under the care of his aged mother and four servants, he rented rooms near city hall and conducted official business from nine in the morning until three in the afternoon. Wood then retired to a private chamber, often working late into the night. Out of this labor, he produced another blizzard of announcements, proposals, recommendations, and appointments.[2]

Starting with fiscal matters, Wood tried to fix his limited stamp on spending measures, and criticized items he considered extravagant, such as the Common Council's $250 grant for a portrait of former Mayor Tiemann and a resolution to insert a $150,000 item in the tax levy for a new county courthouse. Contracts already let must be enforced, he insisted. As to various municipal agencies, he criticized Commissioner Charles Devlin and the Croton Water Department for falling behind in street cleaning, snow removal, and laying uptown pipelines. Turning toward the board of supervisors, Wood charged that it combined "both executive and legislative powers to an extraordinary degree" without marked improvement in the quality of metropolitan life.[3]

Wood was too forceful to rest with negativism. As he told a supporter, if his fiscal improvements were unimplemented, the fault "will not lie in this office, but in the decentralization of our municipal system." To that end, he sought a Common Council ordinance to publish in selected newspapers notices for open bidding, full disclosure of each contract the aldermen approved over $250, and the right to negate any warrant, "unless accompanied by the necessary vouchers," where he suspected "collusion, fraud or unfair dealing" harmed the public interest.[4]

Then came the police. Although one of seven on the board, Wood still wanted to rekindle one-man rule. Republican General Superintendent Amos Pilsbury thoughtlessly gave Wood a slight opening by allowing him the courtesy of naming the city hall's precinct captain. That selection handed Wood a vital executive lever because his appointee enforced corporation ordinances. Spurred by Pilsbury's acquiescence, Wood then demanded the right to select all policemen in the district. When Pilsbury refused, Wood exploited the factionalism among several Republican commissioners to strip him of all administrative controls. Wood then convinced his colleagues to shift those functions to a subcommittee which he controlled. At that point, Pilsbury resigned, leaving Wood with an apparent lock on the Metropolitans.[5]

Wood then shifted his grasp to municipal patronage. From his outlook, the entire situation pinpointed executive weakness, not strength, and indicated the despicable nature of the 1857 charter and commission system. Measured against these conditions, his selection of two department heads whose terms had expired, president of the Croton and a health commissioner, plus naming a new chamberlain, became critical for practical and symbolic reasons.[6]

Partisan realities crushed Wood's hopes. Adversarial majorities on the Common Council and the board of supervisors were uncooperative. Aldermen refused to consider his contract stipulations with the excuse that it was a ploy to reward pet editors. Proposals over taxation, spoils, and administering budgets went unheeded. By March, the deadlock grew so grave that the *New York Daily News* complained, "The appointees of Mr. Tiemann yet retain their places." None of these developments, according to the *New York Times,* were surprising because Wood was reaping the harvest of past misdeeds. He had alienated the "moral and tax-paying portion of the community," who knew his ideas were solely calculated "to promote his own political ambitions" and ignored real "city wants."[7] Exactly what the city needed his enemies failed to cite.

The Republican majority in the legislature ended Wood's executive dreams. Dismissing any charter revisions, Republicans used the Pilsbury affair to reduce the commissioners from seven to three, cutting out Wood and the mayor of Brooklyn. Even when Republican Governor Edwin D. Morgan appointed three men from his own party, who selected John A. Kennedy, a former Barnburner turned Republican, as general superintendent, public reaction fizzled. Memories of the police riots of 1857 were too fresh. Most New Yorkers simply did not consider the city safe under a Wood police force.[8]

The spring of 1860 was a time of painful losses for Wood. Virtually a cipher as mayor, he turned to the presidential nomination to restore his sagging fortunes. Uncovering the winning candidate, however, taxed Wood's ingenuity, particularly since he had committed himself to a Southerner. At first glance, Wood could not support Vice-President John C. Breckinridge of Kentucky, the main alternative to Wise, because Tammany Buchananites were his key local supporters. There were other potential choices: Howell Cobb of Georgia, Jefferson Davis of Mississippi, James Guthrie of Kentucky, and John Slidell of Louisiana. Wood dismissed each, considering them favorite sons who would neutralize each other.

In that impasse, Wood reassessed his attitude toward Breckinridge. Sometime in late January and then in mid-February, Wood went to Washington and met with Breckinridge. Now deeply impressed, Wood wrote a friend that the vice-president "is a live & ambitious man, with a *clear excellent & geographic status*." My relations "with him," Wood added, are "*good*."[9]

Wood had found his man, then, and still pursued a brokered convention. To that end, he continued to court Douglas, who was abhorrent to the South. Wood's gambit seemed promising. Richmond and most Tammanyites nominally backed Douglas, but they hoped delegates would turn to Seymour, not Dickinson, provided a stalemate developed. Wood had another scenario in mind. If Richmond deserted Douglas and the convention became a standoff, Wood intended to throw National Democrats to Breckinridge at the right moment, stampeding the delegates, earning his gratitude, and thus gaining control of Breckinridge's New York federal spoils. In the final analysis, however, all of Wood's plans hinged on one factor. He had to win recognition for his delegation at the coming Charleston convention. For the moment, he bent all his efforts to achieve that goal.[10]

When National Democrats met in February for their strategy session, Wood took personal charge as the personification of proslavery Northerners. Imminent sectional strife, he said, made it "appear an eternal separation is about to take place." The only way "to save the country" was through the formation of "a thoroughly National party" to "extinguish the followers of the anti-slavery fiend stalking the country." Black Republicans had one aim, "the forcible abolition of slavery" by "the fagot and the sword." Such a war would impoverish both sections and lead to "the annihilation of the black race" which could not fend for itself. Only the admittance of his National Democrats and adhering to their "wise counsel" could unite the Democracy and save the United States.[11]

Southern response proved all Wood wished. Newspapers reprinted his entire speech, accompanied by editorials counseling "the entire South" to champion his delegation because, unlike the Regency, he came to the convention with "clean hands" and a "record unsullied by Free-Soilism." Meantime, the Regency and Tammany prepared their own tactics. Cultivating their image as regular

Democrats, they planned to force the convention to accept them or be saddled with party renegades.[12]

Prior to leaving for Charleston, Wood stumbled on a brilliant opportunity to enhance further his pretensions as the state's leading Democrat and to make his name a byword for southernism. In late March, Connecticut Democrats asked the Regency for help in their hotly contested spring state elections. Wood volunteered. He journeyed to Norwalk on March 20 and spent two weeks stumping the state before ending at a monster rally in Hartford. Speaking before constantly growing and enthusiastic crowds, Wood slashed at Republican "disunionists," defended states' rights, and raised racist fears that abolition would "degrade" white Northern workers by increasing the labor pool and depressing wages. Wood ended hoarse and fatigued, but satisfied. It was beside the point that Connecticut Democrats lost, because he achieved his major aim. He had "fought and suffered for the rights of the South," the *Daily News* blared. "The Southern feeling is with him, from Maryland to Texas." On that note, Wood packed his bags for a great adventure.[13]

Wood went to Charleston in a style befitting his wealth and importance. Ostentatiously flashing his money, he subsidized delegate traveling costs and took care of their "creature comforts" with a "quantity of baskets and mysterious packages." On landing, the men roomed at his expense in St. Andrew's Hall—a hotel, the *Daily News* assured readers—located in the city's "most fashionable" part. Wood lodged at the prestigious Mills House, where a steady stream of politicians or the merely curious came to see him. Feted at several private dinners, he created a favorable sensation, chiefly among those who expected some sort of "New York rowdy" rather than a "pleasant gentleman" in "manner and deportment" who looked "more like an influential clergyman than ever." Almost hourly, his energy and charm wove a net of enchantment among impressionable Southerners. Before deliberations began, the *Times* sourly wrote that his "name is strong and high on the list of candidates for Vice-President, and in case of trouble, it may yet be found a peg higher."[14]

Wood tumbled from these dazzling heights as delegates took their seats. Douglasite executive committee chairman David T. Smalley began his downfall by giving the Regency de facto recognition in ruling that they could sit but not participate in procedural matters until the Credentials Committee decided regularity. Deep South delegates shouted disapproval and tried to introduce Wood's protest, which he had prepared for such a contingency. Douglasites, led by Cochrane, blocked the move. In a series of parliamentary maneuvers, they shifted the question to the Credentials Committee, 256 to 47.

Wood was frantic. Every political sign indicated that he did not have enough votes, and he spent the next day in frenetic lobbying. When the Credentials Committee met, Cochrane led off. Shrewdly emphasizing traditional party

usages, he stressed that Wood's "violence and fraud" at Syracuse had stigma-
tized the National Democrats as apostates who had deserted the New York
Democracy for Wood's selfish ends. Wood, rather than answer Cochrane on
those dangerous grounds, resorted to name-calling. He linked the Regency to
Free-Soilism and maintained that Smalley's "unfair course" had anguished New
York's "true and stead-fast" men. Excluding such Democrats, he warned, would
guarantee Republicans the White House.[15]

As he finished, Wood's confidence soared when a number of Southerners sitting in the audience clapped and rushed to shake his hand. But the votes were
not there. The committee went 27 to 7 against him. Deep South committeemen tried a counter move. They filed a minority report to admit both sets of
New Yorkers and split the votes between them. This effort, too, crumpled.
The full convention adopted the majority report, 210 to 56. Even as the tally
proceeded, Tammany delegate Nelson Waterbury sent a telegraph ordering the
Hall "to have 100 guns fired on account of Fernando Wood's defeat."[16]

Wood's pain was excruciating for a man so keenly ambitious. Part of his
humiliation was self-inflicted. He had lost by magnifying the strength of a narrow base of obdurate Deep South delegates, and minimizing most of the
remaining delegates' commitment to regular, official usages.[17] In that sense, they
made a judgment less on him than in the future. Party moderates, plus potential
Wood allies in the Border States and Upper South, feared that Deep South
"Ultras" might use his example to vindicate a separate ticket if they did not get a
satisfactory platform and candidate. Beyond that, Wood was damaged badly by
his notorious political record, his flirtation with Douglas, and Cochrane's stress
on his strong-armed tactics. In short, many Southerners were willing to use, not
trust, him. Lastly, some of them, despite their gratitude for his support, probably sacrificed the National Democrats in the hope that the Douglasites would
reciprocate in a pro-Southern platform.

While staggered by defeat, Wood appeared unruffled. On the evening after
the convention voted, a band serenaded him at the Mills House and a gathering
crowd called for a speech. When he appeared, Wood was surprisingly gracious,
and called on delegates to act with "harmony and calm deliberation." The
"present struggle was designed by Providence to test the system of government." Yet, he added, he had "no doubt that the worst had passed." Democrats
would heal party divisions for the country's sake.[18]

Wood was too optimistic. Delegates spent a week hammering out a platform. Ultimately the Douglasites rejected the majority report, with Richmond's
aid, that included the Ultras' plank for federal protection of slavery in the territories, in favor of their minority one which diluted popular sovereignty by implicitly accepting Dred Scott and leaving the issue of territorial slavery to the
Supreme Court. This vote did not appease eight Deep South Ultra delegations,

which staged a walkout. Before nominations, Richmond made another fateful move. Casting New York's unit vote, he backed a floor motion that the nominee must have two-thirds of the original number, essentially preventing Douglas, Dickinson, Seymour, or anyone from reaching that total. After fifty-seven fruitless ballots, the convention adjourned to Baltimore in six weeks. Democrats had indeed deadlocked, as Wood schemed, but the result was far different from the one he wished.[19]

In the midst of these distressing developments, Wood reasserted himself in a new role as a voice of moderation and unity. Before leaving Charleston, he said to a crowd outside his hotel that, "No man, no class of men, no faction, no State, is justified, in a national crisis of this character, in permitting any disappointments to interfere with the great principles and interests at issue." Glancing backward, he continued that his delegation "would have saved the Southern Platform" embodied in the majority report. Yet, Wood gave the "seceding delegates" little comfort. Invited to join them, he excused himself to William L. Yancey, one of their leaders, with the explanation that while he accepted their principles and would have used them to preserve party "unity and success," his delegation was not privy to the factors behind the withdrawal and could not properly participate in their insurgency. Wood flung a final word toward his erstwhile Southern friends. Delegates committed "a great and disgraceful error" when they voted against his National Democrats, "and, I am sorry to say, [they were] assisted by some Southern members."[20]

Wood was begging the question. That was, supposing his delegation was admitted, what could he have done to prevent the Democracy's disruption? Considering his characteristic expediency, his mania to beat Republicans, his fear of sectionalizing the party, and even his wooing of Douglas, it seems probable that he would have been more pragmatic than Richmond over the platform and the two-thirds rule. Moreover, considering how much the Douglasites diluted popular sovereignty, Wood was one of the few Northerners with the stature to convince Ultra Southerners to adopt the minority report as a party-saving accommodation and perhaps as a chance to select Breckinridge or some other man like him.

Contemporary observers agreed that Richmond's actions indeed hurt the party and that Wood could have made the critical difference. The *New York Herald* contended, "The Regency made all the trouble at Charleston." Had "the convention admitted half of the delegation chosen by the State convention and half of the Wood delegation, we should have had no such thing as secession at Charleston." Three years later, no less an anti-Woodite than James Buchanan made a similar assessment. "It would be curious to speculate what might have been the present condition, had Fernando Wood, instead of Dean Richmond delegates, been admitted at Charleston."[21]

When Wood returned to city hall, Republicans greeted him with a sarcastic welcome as a wandering mayor who had neglected his municipal duties. In response, Wood left no doubt that he still aimed at one-man rule. Patronage and money were the issues at hand. After months of bickering, the aldermen had finally approved his Croton and health nominees. Wood now went after larger game, Chamberlain Andrew V. Stout, once his former ally, but who had since defected to Tiemann and Sickles. Since the chamberlain was also the county treasurer, Wood wanted to deposit the money in the Artisan's Bank, in which Ben Wood not coincidentally was a large stockholder, to finance Mozart Hall. Stout refused and continued to place the funds in his own bank.

At that point, Wood used his untested power to fire Stout and name a successor. As an excuse, he charged that Stout had illegally spent city monies for Republican causes, was not paying legitimate bills, and put the bulk of funds in noninterest-bearing accounts. On that basis, Wood convinced a majority of Democratic aldermen to replace Stout with Nathan C. Platt, president of the Artisan's Bank. Robert T. Haws, the Republican comptroller, did not accept Platt's bond, and Stout refused to surrender his office. Wood then sought a peremptory mandamus from the city supreme court. In order to run the city, Wood explained, the mayor must "have the power to name and remove department heads." Under present conditions, however, officials such as Haws and Stout treated him with "contempt" or complied "in such a manner as to bring disrepute upon the mayor."[22]

On June 15, the supreme court ruled in Wood's favor. According to the decision, the mayor had the power to remove, with aldermanic consent, all nonelective department heads, and "that they alone are the judges of the sufficiency of the cause." Leaving the courtroom, Stout muttered about seeking redress in the Court of Appeals but finally decided to accept the verdict. The *Times* was furious, and tried to stir up Tammanyites by warning them that Wood's removal powers were now so broad that no city official was safe. If Wood accomplished his goals, it reckoned, he would be "supreme over the City Government."[23]

Wood proved the paper correct. Probing the limits of his newfound power, he dismissed two Croton officers because of "serious disagreements and insubordination." At that point, the board of aldermen's latent hostility erupted. Pushed by council leader Henry W. Genet, they launched an official inquiry purportedly to study if Wood had breached the charter. While the investigation predictably found him at fault and refused to back any more removals, Wood was unconcerned because he had reasserted his executive and political importance. National and state Democrats, he believed, could not ignore him.[24]

Wood illustrated that he was not a part-time mayor in other ways. One was to emphasize his official function as the municipality's chief master of ceremonies. In that role, he made several speeches, most notably at the Old Dominion

Society's annual dinner. There, as the city's first citizen, he proclaimed himself the living symbol of "metropolitan" pride. Another part of his activities lay in greeting visiting dignitaries. Again, Wood excelled, and took personal charge of the Prince of Wales' impending visit.[25]

About the same time, Wood's fabled luck again struck. At the moment Tammany needed steady leadership, it suffered a severe blow when city Postmaster Isaac Fowler, chairman of the General Committee and the Tammany Society's grand sachem, fled to Cuba, a fugitive pursued by federal agents for an alleged $155,000 defalcation. His disgrace stunned Tammany and elated Wood. In Fowler, the Hall lost an irreplaceable tactician while Wood gained added leverage at its expense. Tammany also reeled from another setback. John Dix, the man Buchanan appointed to decontaminate the post office mess, was determined to cleanse corruption by "striking from the Payroll" a host of minor hacks, the majority of them Fowler's appointees. With Tammany disabled, Wood was apparently the only local Democrat capable of leading the party.[26]

Wood did not challenge Richmond at the Baltimore convention. Rather, Wood continued as a nationalistic party unifier and issued a carefully worded public letter which warned both Democratic extremes that a compromise was more important than "individual preferences." In that vein, he pledged full support for the convention's "preferences," even "if not in harmony" with National Democrats, as "the duty of every lover of his country."[27]

Since April, all the Southern states except South Carolina had reconsidered their earlier exits and postponed a separate meeting. Several went to Baltimore with dual delegations, the original ones and other fresh pro-Douglasites. At that point, the *Herald* lamented that the Regency again "permanently hurt the Democratic party." Richmond voted to seat the majority of new delegates, once more sparking Southern flight. Richmond harmed the party a second way. In a last convulsive effort at unity, Douglas secretly wrote Richmond and William A. Richardson, his floor manager, that he was willing to step aside in favor of a "reliable, Non Intervention, and Union loving Democrat." Richmond opposed the move. He realized that Seymour lacked Dickinson's support, and that only Douglas's candidacy held the delegation together. If Douglas dropped out, New Yorkers would split at Baltimore and probably in the fall elections, thus almost certainly giving victory to the Republicans, who were already hatching plans for higher taxes on his New York Central Railroad. Fortunately for Richmond, Richardson refused Douglas's sacrifice and made the matter moot. Matters took their natural course. Regular Democrats nominated Douglas, and the dissidents eventually selected Breckinridge.[28]

With Wood the head of his delegation, the end might have been different. Like Douglas, and far more than Richardson and Richmond, Wood appreciated the consequences of Democratic disorganization. As a moderate who now put the Democracy's needs first, he was ready to forfeit self-interest to save the party and perhaps the nation. Acting as an intermediary between the senator and the South, and assuming that Douglas was sincere, Wood could have used his withdrawal as a bargaining chip for retaining the original delegations. By thus appeasing the South and emphasizing Douglas's sacrifice, Wood might have found the middle ground in a candidate satisfactory to both.

What Wood could not accomplish either at Charleston or Baltimore became his chief priority immediately afterward. Before any other local Democrat, he proposed the unique idea of creating a fusion ticket among Democrats to carry the state's electoral votes. Writing as his spokesman, the *Daily News* announced that the party must form a "union against the common foe on the basis of opposition to the tenets of Republicanism." Left unsaid about this startling proposal was Wood's willingness to drop all past differences and merge with his enemies in Tammany Hall and the Regency.[29]

Wood's astute idea rested on persuading fractious Democrats to cooperate or see a Black Republican president. Working from the top down, he went to Washington to seek approval from Buchanan, Breckinridge, and Douglas. None agreed, but Wood persisted. Returning home, he published an open letter to John V. Van Allen, a Schuyler County National Democrat, outlining his strategy.

In the opening paragraphs, Wood analyzed party problems and took pains to show how he, as a National Democrat, had worked for Southern interests. Having emphasized his credibility as a friend of the South, Wood switched to the future. Since neither Douglas nor Breckinridge could carry the other's section, the "demoralized" Democracy should "let each man run singly where he has the most strength." Between them, they would jointly hold an electoral college majority and defeat Lincoln by using those electors to "concentrate upon either" or "some other person." Even if no agreement could be reached, the party could throw the election into the House of Representatives and choose a Democrat.[30]

Given Democratic disarray, Wood's plan was as unprecedented as it was clever. Yet, in the final analysis, his authorship proved a fatal flaw. Considering his recent twists and turns, from a thorough-going pro-Southerner to a moderate, the majority of Democrats simply found good reason not to trust him. For the next month, then, it was politics as usual, and Wood lost any chance to exert leadership.

As the campaign began, most National Democrats under Dickinson rallied behind Breckinridge. Regarding Wood, Dickinson dismissed his advice as "shallow conceits and blind ambition." The upshot was, a National Democrat assured Buchanan, "Mr. Wood does not carry his State Committee with him." Locally, Wood ran into more trouble with the National Democrats. Schell, encouraged by Buchanan, used federal patronage for Breckinridge. Even Bennett was skeptical about Wood's scheme, and insisted that Breckinridge could carry New York with administration aid. Just as discouraging to Wood, a rebellion flared within Mozart. As a hint of trouble ahead, a small but vocal group supported Schell and Breckinridge. The Regency, too, which supported Douglas, had no patience with Wood's fusion. Some Douglasites believed Wood was still a National Democrat whose plan was a ruse to give the senator's electors to Breckinridge. Others viewed as ludicrous the whole concept of running dual candidates with contradictory stands on slavery extension. In the city, Tammany's Douglasites rejected anything that enhanced Wood, whatever the consequences.[31]

When all these factors were sorted out, Republicans pronounced fusion dead. "With characteristic contempt of consistency, alike of principles and logic," the *Times* scoffed, Wood had proposed "too narrow, too dishonest, too baldly the scheme of spoils-hunters and political gamblers, ever to receive the support of the American Democracy."[32]

Despite these obstacles, many practical Democrats slowly realized that winning the presidency demanded an extraordinary political reorientation. Small signs began appearing. National Democratic federal marshal Rynders risked his job by agreeing with Wood. The Irish, bulwarks of the city's National Democrats, also shifted because of resentment about the influx of Know-Nothings into the Republican camp and racist fears of a flooding black labor market. A squirming Tammany committeeman, André Froment, rejected the Hall's official endorsement of Douglas and spoke for many sober Tammanyites, reasoning the best thing the party could do "is to adopt the course of Mayor Wood." Upstate, the Regency reached the same conclusion. The real threat of losing both the state and presidential elections convinced Richmond to patch up differences with Wood and unite around a blended convention and electoral ticket.[33]

As momentum slowly shifted toward Wood's new conception, a similar process occurred among conservative merchants and businessmen. Those men, the backbone of the Fifth Avenue Democrats, now had a higher priority than blocking Wood, the need to protect their economic ties with the South. Led by August Belmont, the national party chairman, Wood's old enemies met on July 15 at the home of Watts Sherman, Erastus Corning's close associate. Belmont was blunt. To the politicians, he endorsed fusion. To the financiers, he demanded an outpouring of funds. Although these men avoided a commitment, the meeting did, Sherman told Corning, produce the chance for "greater good hereafter."[34]

A similar process occurred among other conservatives, mainly old Whigs who supported the Constitutional Union party's John Bell, the fourth presidential candidate. "Some of the leading Douglas men" promised former Whig governor Washington Hunt that for a combined state Bell-Douglas ticket, they would back Bell in the electoral college if that became the only way to stop Lincoln. Even a few National Democrats were infected. Dix, for one, informed the president that he had concluded Lincoln could not be beaten "unless all the elements of opposition to him can be combined."[35]

Fusion was working. Wood carried that message to a Maryland rally, to the Young Men's state convention in Saratoga Springs, and in Mozart Hall. He restated that "when the Union is threatened, every Democrat should sustain the party organization."[36]

Wood's pragmatism still did not sway Dickinson. The bulk of the National Democrats rejected this emerging consensus, formed a state Breckinridge electoral ticket, and nominated an Irish attorney, Tammanyite James T. Brady, for governor. By contrast, Richmond put his reputation on the line. The Regency admitted Tammany and Mozart on an equal footing at the state convention to symbolize fusion, and ran moderate William Kelly of Dutchess County for governor. In another compromise, the Regency gave Bell ten of the state's thirty-five electoral votes and formed a special three-man committee, including Ben Wood, to explore a merger with National Democrats.[37]

Tammanyites were outraged, but impotent. The leaderless Hall was nearly helpless as Wood's sponsorship of fusion made Mozart its equal, or maybe superior, in both the local and state party. The *Daily News* was on the mark when it exulted that Mozart "represents the voting Democracy of the City of New York, and that, as far as Tammany is concerned, there may be a thing as organization without constituency." The *Herald,* which had finally succumbed to fusion, made a similar diagnosis: "Tammany Hall no longer wields any political influence in New York."[38]

Under these conditions, Tammany made a dangerous decision not to hinder fusion, but to shun its mechanics. Essentially, the Hall gambled that Wood's absorption with national politics weakened Mozart in the city. Integral to Tammany's strategy was an elaborate charade about forming a joint congressional ticket, but separate ones in municipal and county contests. Yet in comparison to Wood, Tammany risked making him stronger if fusion succeeded. For the moment, it did alienate many fusionists. As Supreme Court Justice James J. Roosevelt wrote Buchanan, Democrats were less intent on defeating "the enemy" than on "conquering ourselves."[39]

Meantime, Wood was strangely absent. "Where is Mayor Wood?" the *Times* asked, noting that he had missed the state convention, assigned brother Ben as his surrogate on the bargaining committee, and was out of the city for over a month. Even when he returned without explanation, Wood was oddly distracted from politics, devoting all his time to the Prince of Wales' visit. Perhaps he was merely cultivating New York's best civic image, people imagined. He was clearly engrossed, organizing the welcome, scheduling meetings, and involving himself in every minute detail from instructing Commissioner Devlin to ensure clean streets along the prince's route to having the police jail potential troublemakers. Wood even spent $4,500 of his own money to make the prince's stay in New York the highlight of his trip to the United States, and laid out even more funds hosting a private dinner in his home.[40]

For a man of Wood's towering ambitions and charged personality, this single-mindedness was totally out of character. Before, he had juggled demanding, often conflicting, tasks without missing a beat. What, then, New Yorkers wondered, could be more important than Fernando Wood's political career? The answer lay in an affair of the heart.

During early 1860, exactly when was uncertain because he was an intensely private person, Wood had fallen in love with Alice Fenner Mills, the sixteen-year-old daughter of C. Drake Mills, a retired Republican financier and railroad executive, whose wealth the press estimated at "over half a million of dollars." In contrast to Wood, she was highly educated, having spent twelve years overseas in a Paris school, and spoke five languages. Their courtship, conducted with discretion in the city and at Saratoga, was rocky. The Millses objected to his reputation, the thirty-two year disparity in their ages, and the problems that such a young woman would face as a stepmother in a large family that included two sons older than herself. Even her friends did not understand "how she became so infatuated." Somehow, Wood prevailed; he was a wealthy man in his own right and an attractive catch. The gossipy Joseph Scoville came up with a less flattering reason. According to his account, Wood secured Drake Mills's consent only after he placed "$100,000 in good Croton Water stock" in her name, "where the income, $5,500, can go for pin money." In case of her death, Wood further agreed, "the principle reverts to the parents of the aforesaid lady." During early September, arrangements were complete. The wedding was scheduled for December 25, 1860.[41]

With those matters settled, Wood plunged back into the political arena. Talks had not gone well during August. Conferees disagreed on a formula to share electors, a merged state ticket, and centralized fund-raising. Nor had Douglas agreed on amalgamating with Breckinridge. But the hour was growing too late for waffling. "The election of a broom-stick would be preferable to the success of the Republican ticket," the *Herald* prompted. On September 17, the business community increased the pressure for fusion with a huge unity rally at Cooper Union. Wood was one of the principal speakers. His words were familiar, but carried new urgency. The South would secede if Lincoln won, bringing economic ruin to New York City. The paramount need to protect "the prosperity, if not the perpetuity of the Union" was more "important than any local question." Democrats had an obligatory duty to drop "past partisan prejudices" and support the United States through fusion.[42]

This meeting finally electrified negotiations. Over the next three weeks, the bargainers modified Wood's plan and ironed out an electoral ticket with eighteen

Douglas, ten Bell, and seven Breckinridge electors. Mutual suspicions, however, remained. Serious and unresolved questions lingered about key issues, ranging from the position of slavery in the territories to Mozart's and Tammany's status, to Brandy's refusal to drop out of the gubernatorial race.[43]

For Wood, there was no turning back. As the father of fusion, he sought to guarantee its success, utilizing vague mayoral powers to deny Republican parade permits and warning the Republican-dominated police to stop intimidating voters. More work was needed. He placated the Irish, furious that Mozart did not back Brady, by nominating one of them, James Lynch, for register, a post worth $75,000 in salary and fees. Wood concluded the campaign on a rainy night in the Third Congressional District where his brother was a candidate. Pulling out all stops, Wood repeated that the nation faced the most critical election "since the establishment of our government," nothing less than the "continuance of our Federal compact."[44]

Rather curiously despite the immense issues involved, election day came and went quietly. Missing were the almost customary fisticuffs and gang violence which had marred previous contests. Then the cataclysm broke around the fusionists. They carried the city by 62,611 to Lincoln's 23,311, but watched with foreboding as a Republican tide swept the North, washing away any chance of casting the contest into the House.

Wood read the returns with a combination of relief and sorrow. Local voters had proven his wisdom about fusion, but wherever Democrats had dual candidates, Republicans won, starting with governor and sliding down the scale to legislative and local offices. Even worse, the sobering reality of a growing Southern secessionist fervor failed to halt local feuding. When Mozart snarled, "The men who deserted us" would be consigned into deserved "obscurity," Tammany shot back that the Democracy had no room for the brothers Wood.[45]

With the nation teetering on the edge of disunion, normal politics played out in the December municipal election of nine aldermen in the odd-numbered districts. Gone was any reference to national issues as the Model Mayor pleaded with voters to rid the city of aldermanic "swindlers," the major cause behind municipal "mal-government." Without his magnetic vote-getting ability as a candidate, Mozart proved an empty shell. Voters gave Wood a terrible drubbing by electing only two Mozarters. The result left Wood's authority even more impotent. The *Daily News* fumed that Genet's "Aldermanic Ring" thwarted his attempts to create good government, but the fact remained that Wood was New York's chief executive in name alone.[46]

The Genet-led Common Council pounded that point home. For several months, the old council and supervisors had raised ethical questions about Chamberlain Platt's financial practices, especially heavy depositing of city revenue in his Artisan's Bank. Wood defended Platt, but both were vulnerable to rumors that the bank neared default because it illegally lent large, unsecured amounts to Mozart.[47]

Aldermen then struck when Wood was completely off-guard. The day after Wood left the city on his honeymoon, council president and acting mayor William Peck quickly got aldermanic approval to remove Platt and replace him with Daniel Devlin, a director of the Broadway Bank. Friends called Wood home. Giving his bride an inkling of what came first in his life, Wood unceremoniously dumped her at Woodlawn and called the council into a heated session. Barely containing his chagrin, Wood raised memories of the recent street commissioner mess by overturning Devlin's appointment and leaving the city with two chamberlains. Each side sought a judicial opinion to no avail. Wood's crony, Supreme Court Judge George C. Barnard found for him, but on appeal Common Pleas Judge Henry Hilton, a friend of Sweeny and Tweed, denied that Barnard had any jurisdiction in the case and left Devlin in office.[48]

With things so undecided, the issue went to Albany. After two months of battle, a combination of Tammany and Republican legislators beat Mozart forces, and passed a bill that settled the matter. Devlin retained the post, the term of office was set at four years, and in the future only the governor could remove the chamberlain for cause.[49]

Wood was badly bruised. He had lost a major source of political and financial spoils; aldermen accentuated his lack of executive authority; and Republicans had again interfered in home rule. Against this background, Wood entered the next stage of his mayoral career, one which further blackened his reputation.

New Yorkers long remembered Wood's annual address of January 7, 1861, as the most controversial one ever delivered by any mayor because of his proposal to make New York a "free city." Behind his idea lurked one contentious issue: the Republican threat to local self-government, the link Wood believed existed between Lincoln's menacing of Southern institutions, the reality of secession, and the dismantling of home rule by the state judiciary and legislature.

The drama began on a theme familiar to New Yorkers. Wood had already voiced shrill warnings that secession was inevitable unless Republicans obeyed the Constitution, honored the South's fundamental states' rights, and sought a sectional compromise. In his Thanksgiving Day address, Wood reiterated those points. The holiday presented "no features for which we should be thankful." Citizens should instead pray that Republicans stopped violating "the federal compact."[50]

What, then, Wood pondered, was best for New York City? The idea of an independent municipality did not originate with him, nor was it novel. In the past, various groups had advanced the idea whenever the state hurt local interests, such as during the debate over ratifying the Constitution, or after the flurry of Republican bills in 1857, Many businessmen, as much alarmed as Wood over losing Southern trade, had discussed the idea both in private and in public following Lincoln's election. Moreover, while Wood was a nationalist, he was a New Yorker first. Throughout his career, he took inordinate pride in his city. As he told the United Cartmen's Protective Association in the spring of 1860, "We are citizens of New York—the City of New York—an empire within itself—the metropolitan city of the Western Hemisphere and third city in the world."[51]

Taking these factors into consideration, Wood articulated a preexisting idea, one with its own history and imperatives. In that context, his struggle was not only against Republicans, but in the drifting realm of public opinion where Unionist forces grappled with secessionists, as the nation's fate hung in the balance.[52]

Just as in previous messages, Wood spelled out well-worn, by now almost trite, criticisms of the relationship he saw between New York City and New York State. In particular, he detailed each state incursion against home rule and forcibly maintained Republicans had violated the city's inherent rights it still retained as a corporate autonomous entity under the Dongan and Montgomerie charters. Over the years, the legislature and the judiciary had illegally despoiled the city of those rights, leaving the municipality and its mayor creatures of the state unable to promote their own welfare because they lacked the power to govern themselves. This "foreign power" in Albany "plundered" the city through unfair taxes, and sent dependents "to destroy our liberties by subverting the political system."[53]

Wood then made a subtle shift. New York had no quarrel with the South, he said. Local citizens did their best to keep friendly relations and commercial ties with "our aggrieved brethren of the slave states," and did not question Southern "constitutional rights" nor its "domestic institutions." Yet events indicated "that a dissolution of the Federal Union is inevitable." In that case, "our government cannot be preserved by coercion or held together by force." But by any measure, New York still had vital trade interests with "every port" in the old "American Union" and wished to retain "uninterrupted intercourse with every section."[54]

While the bonds between the city and the South were tightly bound, the reverse was true for the state. As things stood, the city faced more danger from continual Albany "abuses" than from secessionists. If the South left the Union, Wood thought other sections would follow and create multiple independent nations. Probably national disruption, then, might become a blessing in disguise for New Yorkers. It paved the way for the city to rethink prior allegiances, not only to the United States, but to New York State. The logical extension of such a reassessment lay in *perhaps* making New York a "free city," but only if it could be accomplished by nonviolent means.[55]

Wood, in unemotional hindsight, had essentially articulated the consistent ideas and issues that had guided his years as mayor, with all their hopes and frustrations. As a political document, his message further reflected his devotion to localism, states' rights, the South, free trade, anticoercion, an unchanging Constitution, and a refusal to make any distinctions between slavery's immorality and its commercial importance to New York City. In addition, he was in step with many of his contemporaries who treated peaceful secession as a passing stage of Southern anger, provided Republicans compromised with the seceders. Given Wood's serpentine methods, the specter of a free city might also have been an elaborate ploy to frighten Republicans into making such a compromise. After all, since he considered Southern grievances justifiable, he believed only Republican intransigence prevented a sectional readjustment.

And, yet, it was a blunder of the first magnitude. Although he did not urge immediate independence, as critics charged, but merely weighed its possibilities, Wood miscalculated on a growing Northern determination to save the Union, even at the price of war. How badly Wood erred became clear in a few short days. No matter how justified or logical his position, he placed sympathizers in the uncomfortable position of making choices most were unwilling to make, and handed his enemies a club to question his loyalty. Outside of the *Daily News* and a few Breckinridgeites, Wood ran into a stone wall of contempt. Summing up the public mood, the *New York Sun* was particularly rough. "Mayor Wood's secessionist Message has sounded the bathos of absurdity."[56]

Over the next two months, any hope of a national compromise collapsed, and by February 1861 the South had formed the Confederate States of America. Wood found nothing but grief in his foresight because his visibility as the Southern Mayor magnified his steadily mounting image as a traitor. He did enjoy momentary relief at a special Democratic state convention in January that Richmond called to discuss the national crisis. The delegates accepted Mozart's equality with Tammany and endorsed Wood's noncoercionism. On the other hand, the Grand Jury of General Sessions investigated his apparent pro-Confederate sympathies and labeled him "a notorious person who ought to be suppressed." Equally distressing, few Democrats responded to his criticism of the protectionist Morrill Tariff as proof of how Republican "anti-commercial" policies hurt New York.[57]

Ben Wood's editorials as a Confederate apologist kept the derision rolling. Although the *Daily News* asserted "positively and unequivocally that Mayor Wood has no interest" in the paper, people considered it his "personal organ." Connecting the two Woods as one mind, patriots were infuriated by the paper's ranting calls for peaceable secession and attacks on Republican "fanaticism."[58]

Even when Wood took a legitimate position, the results backfired. On January 23, the police, acting under Superintendent Kennedy's order, seized the steamer *Monticello* and its cargo, mainly thirty-eight boxes containing muskets and ammunition bound for Savannah. Wood criticized Kennedy for lacking a proper search warrant, apologized to Georgia Senator Robert A. Toombs for the "illegal and unjustifiable seizure of public property," and cited the incident as yet another example of his executive "helplessness." Few New Yorkers changed their minds. They believed that Wood furnished "to traitors arms to be used in destroying the unity and peace of the Republic."[59]

On February 21, 1861, Wood again became the focus of controversy when President-elect Lincoln stopped in the city en route to his inauguration. Wood was the proper host. He attended an informal reception at the Astor House before holding a civic ceremony in the Governor's Room of city hall. The opportunity to lecture Lincoln about the emergency was too tempting to pass. Wood appeared relaxed and amiable during the opening greetings, but proceeded to prod Lincoln in a combative manner about the need to compromise and avoid war. "Present political divisions," Wood emphasized, "sorely afflicted" the city and endangered its "commercial greatness." New York looked to Lincoln, he said, "for a restoration of fraternal relations between the states—only to be accomplished by peaceful and conciliatory means—aided by the wisdom of God." A murmur went around the room at Wood's audacity, yet Lincoln handled the moment with grace. Thanking Wood for his hospitality, he surprised the crowd in agreeing "on the sentiment expressed by the Mayor," and promised a policy which would not harm the city or nation, provided the Union "can be preserved."[60]

Despite what the public considered Wood's bad manners, something positive developed out of this exchange. As Lincoln was about to step into his carriage, the *Times* observed that he shook "Mr. Wood warmly by the hand, and leaning forward, audibly thanked the Mayor" for his "pleasant attentions."[61] What the paper did not know was that these ceremonies marked the first step in a future working relationship between them.

By April 12, tensions intensified as news spread through the city of the Confederate bombardment on Fort Sumter. Mobs of aroused New Yorkers, with emotions bordering on hysteria, harassed suspected Confederate fellow-travelers, forcing the police to guard Wood's home and detail men around the *Daily News* office. The nation's tragedy became Wood's conundrum. "What will Fernando Wood do?" asked Tammany's official sheet, the *New York Leader*. To this rhetorical question, editor and sachem John Clancy wrote a seemingly logical answer based on Wood's southernism. He "stands solely and alone among the Municipal chiefs of the North as having taken sides with the conspirators against the Union."[62]

Clancy appeared correct. Wood's traitorous position was apparently predetermined because he was a captive of his own word, policies, and principles. On March 4, he had refused to dip city hall's American flag as a mark of respect after Lincoln's inauguration. Mozart, as late as a week prior to the Confederate attack, had condemned "the anti-slavery forces of the North," and called on

"Union men" to urge "conciliatory measures and concessions" to the misunderstood "members of the Confederacy."[63] Even if Wood's position as a crypto-Confederate appeared fixed, however, Clancy should have posed a different question: Did Wood have a legitimate position, or was he simply what people thought, a traitor? Only Wood had the answer.

EIGHT

The Politics of Loyalty

Nᴇᴡ Yorkers swept Wood along as they flocked to defend the Union. On April 15, he issued a proclamation summoning citizens "irrespective of all other considerations or prejudices" to obey the law, preserve order, and protect property. The next day, he literally draped the flag around his shoulders at the city's first Union rally. Speaking rapidly, he exhorted "every man, whatever had been his sympathies, to make one great phalanx in this controversy, to proceed to conquer a peace. I am with you in this contest. We know no party now."[1]

Wood's martial spirit soared. After proposing a special $1-million tax levy to raise troops and defray costs, he told aldermen, "Let us vote the required funds and trust to the patriotism of the people to sustain us." When it came to finding those troops, Wood sponsored his own "Mozart Regiment." He took a paternal interest in its training at Camp Wood near Yonkers, inspected rations and equipment, and, after a review, presented it "with a handsome strand of colors" that he had bought. Tammany formed its own regiment, the Jackson Guards, under Sachem William D. Kennedy, setting off a race full of bravado over which would be first in the state's quota of seventeen regiments. Wood once more swung into action, and pulled strings with the military for "an early opportunity" to show Mozart's "zeal in the defense of [its] country." By June, his men, the 40th New York Volunteer Infantry, won and entrained for Washington.[2]

During these turbulent days, Wood was everywhere. He became an ex officio member and active participant of the Union Defense Committee. When Colonel Robert Anderson, the "hero of Ft. Sumpter," visited the city, Wood clutched his coattails. He commissioned Anderson's portrait and purchased a gold snuffbox, presenting them with maximum publicity. Wood even volunteered. He sent Lincoln a public letter offering "my services in any military capacity consistent with my position as Mayor of New York City."[3]

Wood's transformation from a noncoercionist to a warhawk puzzled many New Yorkers who assumed that he had reverted to his old tricks. One critic growled, "The cunning scoundrel sees which way the cat is jumping, and put himself right on the record in a vague general way, giving the least offense to his allies of the Southern Democracy." On closer inspection, Wood's motives were far more complex, although an element of truth existed in the charge. In the same message where he had urged public calm, he muttered an aside which straddled the issue. Whether the Union would be restored "by fratricidal warfare or by concession, conciliation and sacrifice" was still unanswered.[4]

Wood had compelling reasons for equivocation. Foremost a politician, his chief priorities were self-preservation and the maintenance of power. Yet the war had shattered traditional partisanship and its rules to such an extent that the entire Democracy was hounded by uncertainty. It was split over tactics, had feeble leadership, and lacked a united sense of purpose dealing with the war and its consequences.

For Wood, the man of answers, the situation was intolerable. Many of his constituents, notably his brother, rejected the war's legitimacy. Known as Peace Democrats, they considered it a plot to free slaves, blamed Republicans for fomenting the crisis, and believed an alternative policy based on conciliating the Confederacy was the sole means to reunite the nation. Only an officeholder bent on political suicide, however, could oppose the war considering New York's bursting pugnacity.

Another party faction, Union Democrats such as Dickinson, Cochrane, and Brady, placed country over party and joined the Republicans in seeking consensus politics, based on suspending partisanship for the duration of the war. As a politician steeped in the traditions of a loyal opposition, Wood rejected them more for their sins against the Democracy than their nationalism.

Tammany and the Regency compounded Wood's problems. They were War Democrats who supported military victory but rejected Republican partisan legislation and Lincoln's erosion of civil rights. Wood knew that they also agonized over how much to aid Lincoln without surrendering partisan identities and were far from united. Very often, their devotion to the Union was in direct proportion to military success. As a result, they often overlapped the Peace Democrats, particularly in opposing Lincoln's tampering with constitutional liberties.

As a final complication, Wood anguished over running the city and rewarding Mozart. The Custom House was in Republican hands, making his control over city patronage imperative. But the Genet-led aldermen treated him with contempt, blocked his leadership, and ignored his appointments.

In common with other Democrats, Wood had no way of estimating what policies would work. During the war's early stages, he saw no inherent contradiction between being a loyal American and a loyal Democrat. Out of these considerations, Wood formed the politics of loyalty; his formula was based on endorsing the war to maintain the Union, but questioning Lincoln's wisdom in seeking only a military solution.

In that sense, Wood was not a Confederate collaborator, despite his sympathy with the men who formed the Confederacy, nor did he accept its permanence. He wanted to restore the United States of America, but the nation he envisioned was a slaveholding nation, with unchanged prewar institutions and values. As an extension of his formula, Wood would not support Lincoln if he thought Republicans intended to destroy Southern society and its rights, basically slavery.

Under those conditions, Wood sought the precarious middle, avoiding the extremes of coalition politics and Peace Democratic defeatism, cooperating with War Democrats as far as they agreed with him, but above all, trying to legitimize his own brand of loyalism. To carry out this risky formula, Wood needed all the vast political skills which had made him famous or, perhaps infamous, because the public could easily misinterpret his reservations as opposition to the Union itself.[5]

The strains resulting from Wood's politics of loyalty were intense, both inside and outside the Democracy. No better example existed than the political consequences of the first Battle of Bull Run. Tammany draped the Wigwam in black in memory of Colonel Kennedy's death. Wood called on the aldermen to arrange church services, and issued a special message lauding the "brave spirits in whose loss we now mourn." The *New York Daily News,* which New Yorkers still considered his mouthpiece, differed. It responded to the battle with a harsh editorial assailing "this insane strife" and the "fanatical Abolitionists" who dominated the Lincoln administration. Republicans answered in kind. They characterized all Peace Democrats as subversives, and for proof accused several Mozart soldiers, led by James Lynch, of desertion on the eve of battle. According to Republicans, these men had used the lame excuse that their enlistments had expired to avoid combat, and came home at Ben Wood's expense.[6] Whether Republicans were correct or not was beside the point. By implication, Fernando Wood shared Peace Democratic odium.

Wood was disturbed by his brother's hard line and the widespread assumption that both of them were disloyal. To ease doubt, Wood launched a welfare program for hard-pressed families of volunteers, and convinced his brother to cosponsor a subscription drive to raise funds for their living expenses. Along the same lines, he asked council approval for a system whereby troops selected allotment trustees to send wages home, and asked the aldermen to issue bonds for additional monies. Soldiers from other states were impressed, particularly one Massachusetts regiment that gave Wood a commemorative medal. In accepting, he promised New York would continue "with every power at our command" to preserve "the glorious union."[7]

Among the public, anger and resentment intensified against the *Daily News.* Some hotheads menaced the editorial staff; readers cancelled subscriptions; advertisers dropped orders; and a grand jury under Tammany Recorder John T. Hoffman surveyed its apparent treason. As the attacks increased in number and venom, the aldermen tried to trap Wood as the paper's accomplice by voting to discontinue it as an official corporation newspaper on the grounds that brother Ben gave the enemy aid and comfort.[8]

Wood braved this storm under his loyalist umbrella. In a vain veto, he defended freedom of the press and reproached the Common Council for punishing the paper because of "its opinions on political questions." As for the issues the *Daily News* raised, he wrote that while he did not endorse all its sentiments, Peace Democrats were correct in that Lincoln should seek "a just and honorable compromise." The intrinsic tensions in Wood's formula now became manifest. A federal grand jury through Postmaster General Montgomery Blair denied the *Daily News* mailing privileges, forcing the paper to suspend in mid-September and increasing Wood's traitorous image.[9]

Wood stubbornly held the middle and sought other means to make his loyalism plausible. Part of that effort rested on being indispensable to the Democracy. Since factional lines were fluid, he cooperated with Regency War Democrats in supporting the state committee's rejection of Republican overtures for a nonpartisan Union party, and helped convince remaining Breckinridgeites to merge in the fall elections. Wood's second way was more self-serving. He secretly sounded out Isaac Sherman, Weed's confidant, to silence Republicans. Wood promised that Mozart would repudiate Peace Democrats, adopt resolution based on the politics of loyalism, and advocate "the most vigorous prosecution of the war." For a payoff, Wood was purposely vague about what he expected, but implied "some alliance" with Unionists to symbolize his patriotism in the coming December mayoral election.[10]

The Democracy's first wartime state convention continued its confusion and took away from Wood as much as it gave. At first, delegates admitted both halls on an equal footing. Such waffling was too much for Sweeny, who pictured the issue as one between prowar Tammany and antiwar Mozart. Cast in that light, delegates stunned Wood by reversing the ruling and accepted only Tammany. The Democracy's commitment to the war, however, was cosmetic. Instead of consistency, the platform hammered contradictory planks that put the party on either side of the war or peace issue.[11]

Wood left the convention uneasy because the vote to exclude Mozart made it clear how much his formula's crossfires had reduced his standing and elevated Tammany. He called Mozart into special session to repair the damage, and convinced committeemen that they need not "back the [state] ticket because it repudiated our delegation." Even so, Wood refurbished his tarnished patriotism. He denied Tammany's charge that Mozart was "tainted with disloyalty." We "are for the country, the whole country and nothing but the country," he said, "peacefully if we can, but forcibly if we must."[12]

The profound ambiguities in Wood's loyalism satisfied neither War nor Peace Democrats. While he understood Tammany's reflexive opposition, brother Ben was most disappointing. A few days before its suspension, the *Daily News* scolded Mozart's war platform, and maintained "friends of Peace" were the only true Democrats. "The issue is between a useless and destructive war and a prosperous enduring peace."[13]

Sharper disillusionment with Wood rumbled through Confederate circles. The *Richmond Enquirer* was especially bitter. Such "Northern men with Southern principles" as Wood had encouraged secession, it observed, but "can deceive us no more." Regardless of their prewar support, they were now arming themselves against the Confederacy and "at present they are our foremost enemies."[14]

Democratic drift accelerated prior to the November elections. Under Purdy, Tammany and the *New York Leader* sought prowar pledges from each candidate. Tweed, running for sheriff, was noncommittal to curry Peace Democrats. Mozart defied Wood and accepted brother Ben's position, essentially making the organization Peace Democratic. Wood worked his own side of the street, and walked the tight middle line his formula demanded.

In the end, confusion reigned. Tammany and Mozart informally agreed to cooperate on minor candidates, but haggled about two key offices. Republican Abraham Oakey Hall, the "Elegant Oakey," ran on a combined Unionist and Mozart slate against incumbent District Attorney Nelson J. Waterbury, a sachem and War Democrat. The sheriff's race generated the most heat. After Tweed did not garner Peace Democratic support in his contest with Mozart's James Lynch, he courted War Democrats by attacking Lynch's questionable conduct at the Battle of Bull Run.[15]

Wood was strategically silent during these developments, but now made his presence felt. Recognizing a timely chance to reinforce his standing among the Irish and dampen Mozart's factionalism, Wood defended Lynch on the basis that "he belongs to a race which never produces cowards." Wood impatiently brushed aside national issues, and claimed that the election was purely local in nature, not "dependent upon a party, much less upon any number of miserable factions," nor irresponsible "tricksters" who raised false questions about patriotism for the "selfish purpose of obtaining local political power."[16]

Voters decided little. In state races, a trend developed toward Weed's Union party, but city and county races were inconclusive. Lynch won, as did Hall, who soon jumped to Tammany. These were personal triumphs based on the vagaries of local politics. Only one factor was distinct. In his coming reelection bid, Wood's wisest course lay in shunning divisive national problems and concentrating solely on time-tested municipal reforms.[17]

Wood's strategy hinged on his recurring corruptionist image. Earlier in the year, he had cooperated with Genet's heretofore unfriendly aldermen in granting Andrew V. Hackley a five-year, $279,000 street-cleaning contract. The deal reeked of graft. Everyone involved was guilty of some unethical behavior. Wood breached city ordinances by closed bidding; twenty-three other contractors underbid Hackley, the lowest by $84,000; he purportedly bribed the aldermen $40,000, and bought Wood off by giving brother Ben one-fourth of the contract.[18]

Such unscrupulous behavior was too blatant to go unnoticed. It reached from corrupt public officials to the noxious odors fouling the air when Hackley and his subcontractors failed to clean the streets. By summer, public indignation peaked. Daniel Delevan, the city inspector, who had jurisdiction over enforcing the contract, stopped payments. A few low bidders sued Wood for disregarding regulations. At the subsequent trial, the presiding judge jailed Hackley for contempt when he did not appear.[19]

Several aldermen grew frightened. They self-righteously tried to rescind the contract, and blamed Wood and Genet for the entire muck. Those aldermen were hardly angels. Spearheaded by Genet, they were already known as a venal "Ring," ready and eager to raid the treasury, shameless as practitioners of job-selling and kickbacks. The Hackley contract was one strand in their larger design.[20]

As for Wood, his involvement was difficult to assess mainly because after lengthy litigation the courts absolved him of being a party to bribery. Nevertheless, the bar of public opinion was justified in considering him guilty, even if he did not personally profit. He had betrayed ethical and moral standards which citizens had every right to expect from their chief executive; he accepted institutionalized plunder as a form of governance; and he cynically gave his brother a piece of the action since the aldermen would have overridden his veto in any event.[21]

Wood risked all these considerations for personal political gain. Despite the Ring's gamy reputation, its support was vital to run the city and win reelection. Having made one epic blunder with Genet, Wood then made another.

In September, they struck another deal. Wood promised that Mozart would nominate Genet for county clerk and agreed to absent himself from city hall so that Genet, in his capacity as president of the board of aldermen and acting mayor, could name a crony, Shepherd Knapp, street commissioner. Genet swore to use those multiple jobs and the patronage connected to them for Wood's reelection. Genet further pledged that he would convince Tammany through Tweed to run an innocuous mayoral candidate, guaranteeing Wood a split vote. As Havemeyer admitted, "If each of the opposing parties places its own Candidate in the field, he [Wood] will have an easy victory."[22]

Wood underestimated Genet's political guile. Once Genet was elected and Knapp was safely in office, they reneged and threw all their considerable influence into beating Wood. On that basis, Tammanyites conveniently dropped their pro-war rhetoric and reached out to "all honest men who are against Wood." Although this potential fusion failed because Tammany insisted that the candidate must

come from its ranks, Wood had little reason for confidence. Unionists and Republicans renominated the avowed prowar George C. Opdyke, and Tammany found
an equally impressive man in C. Godfrey Gunther, the influential German Democrat.[23] Wood indeed ran against a divided field as he wished, but one far more
powerful than he counted on.

Graft, more than any other factor, initially dominated the campaign. Outraged
reformers criticized Wood's relationship to the Hackley contract; newspapers
documented its sordid details; and lame duck District Attorney Waterbury con-
vened a grand jury investigation. Several Mozarters added another old wrinkle.
Without supporting proof, they accused Wood of selling nominations and backing out once he had the money. Even the normally supportive *New York Sun*
backed away from Wood. In its judgment, he was "one of the boldest and most
unscrupulous politicians in this or any other country."[24]

The cumulative impact of these jarring accusations forced Wood to reconsider
the nature of his campaign. Every variable indicated that the corruption-in-
government issue was dragging him down to defeat. As he mulled his options,
Wood also assumed that Opdyke and Gunther were vulnerable. Both were totally
obsessed with corruption and slighted national issues. As a result, Wood shifted
toward the politics of loyalism.

As usual, Wood had a contingency plan. Before his formal Mozart nomination, he had employed customary teasing to create the impression of a public
groundswell. In his acceptance speech, he protested that the need to educate his
children and the beckoning "comforts of private life" made him wonder why anyone wanted the office since its duties "at present are merely clerical." Supporters
had prevailed, however, against his personal inclinations, because they believed
the city needed his advice "to quiet the conflicting interests of the country" and
"restore harmony." If "peace was to be restored," such "restoration must be com-
menced here . . . giving no aid to either the South or North by electing any other
than a national and conservative man."[25] Thus, he stepped forward as the spokesman for a statesmanlike loyal opposition rather than a mere local hack politico.

On November 27, Wood wrapped loyalism around his new tactics in a major
address at Volks Garten, a popular social hall for German Democrats. "I have
come here," he began, to say a "few plain words" as a free American citizen, with
"the right to scrutinize the conduct of public affairs and to criticise its rulers."
Republicans had been wrong on every issue from their birth, he claimed. During
the 1850s, they interfered with private choice through temperance, ignored civility in supporting nativism, and negated democracy by depriving the city of home
rule. Wood then drew a parallel between the past and present. Today, he continued, they scorned nonviolent reunion and used similar unconscionable tactics to
destroy the nation's constitutionally guaranteed rights, North and South. "I tell
you that so long as this party rules the country there is no peace for the country."[26]

With the crowd shouting approval, Wood turned toward War Democrats and raised a host of issues revolving around class, race, and internal party politics. Elitist Republicans impressed Irish and German as troops while they "themselves remain at home," intent on freeing slaves to undermine the dignity of white labor. How War Democrats could cooperate with such frauds was unfathomable. In fact, as long as they aided Republicans to stay in power "there will be no peace while there is a dollar to be wrung from the people, or a drop of Southern blood to shed."[27]

Delighted with the "vociferous cheering" filling the air, Wood ended that only his type of loyalty could save the country. On that note, he asked "the lion-hearted democracy of New York" to reelect him so that he might function as its "humble instrument in bringing about a restoration of national unity and national peace!"[28]

Three days later, Wood again stressed loyalism at another rally at Cooper Union, and shrewdly counterpointed Lincoln's desire to preserve the Union with the more radical Republican idea of instituting fundamental changes in the South. The issue that agitated the Union was "between conservative nationalism against abolitionism." The real disunionists, the "Abolitionist faction," wanted the forcible ending of slavery "and the destruction of the South." They believed "not only in the prosecution of the war for this main purpose, but also its prolongation." I do not think "that the American people are ready to sustain this war, founded upon principles of this character." The only alternative lay in his type of loyalty, "a return of the rebellious states to their duty and allegiance" by carrying "the sword" in "one hand, the olive branch . . . in the other."[29]

Both speeches stirred deep passions. Speaking for enraged Tammanyites, the *Leader* shot back: "Fernando Wood is in heart and soul with the armed traitors of the South." Republicans demanded concrete action. Superintendent of Police Kennedy and United States Marshal Robert Murray asked Secretary of State Seward's permission to arrest Wood for treason. Wood held firm. Writing Seward to reiterate his loyalty, Wood again tried to widen the gap among Republicans by asking the administration to defend him against charges of subversion. When Seward's son wrote a neutral, rather sarcastic reply, Wood grasped for other straws. He found a credible means in the so-called *Trent* affair. Captain Charles Wilkes, a native New Yorker and a friend of Dean Richmond, had tapped national pride by perhaps illegally seizing the British mail packet, the *Trent,* and removing Europe-bound Confederate diplomats. Wood contacted Caleb Cushing, the noted Democratic constitutional lawyer, for an opinion defending Wilkes's debatable action. With it, Wood planned a public rally to show Mozart's patriotism. Cushing was no fool. Knowing full well the intense emotions involved in city politics, he delayed an answer until the election was over.[30]

Election day was the wildest in memory. Fraudulent voters were common for all three candidates: each organization supplied men fictitious names and addresses as repeaters; toughs intimidated voters; premature naturalizations reached epic proportions; and inspectors delayed counts for several days in a score of precincts in order to pad the totals. In the end, Wood lost by a razor-thin margin. Opdyke, the winner, carried nine wards and had 34.3 percent. Gunther won seven wards and gained 33.3 percent. Wood trailed with 32.4 percent, although he won six wards. In terms of the 74,314 total voters, Opdyke beat Gunther by 613 and Wood by 1,213.

Wood's defeat lay in multiple causes. Just as in his earlier race with Tiemann, Gunther cut into his immigrant base by winning four German wards. With Tammany's aid, Gunther furthermore won the majority of poorer, Irish wards on the East Side. By contrast, Opdyke beat both Wood and Gunther because he was strongest in the Republican Fifteenth, among former Know-Nothings, and ran well throughout the city. Most embarrassing to Wood was the loss of his home ward to Opdyke by 1 percent.[31]

As a seasoned politician, Wood practiced the rule that things must get worse before they got better. Taking his defeat in stride after his usual grumbling about electoral frauds, he praised Opdyke's personal qualities and merely faulted him for being a Republican whose beliefs Wood thought were "at variance with the true interests of the nation." In a valedictory, Wood doubted that Opdyke, whatever his abilities, could govern the city, and recommended the legislature expand mayoral powers. With his term numbered in minutes, Wood stayed civil and courteous. Unlike his chilly attitude toward Tiemann, Wood invited the mayor-elect to city hall and cooperated in a smooth transfer of power.[32]

Public reaction was discouraging. Tammany jeered at his humble tone, pronounced Mozart dead, and Clancy proposed a party reunion based on absorbing Mozart minus Wood. Republicans and Unionists concurred that his defeat gave all New Yorkers "universal satisfaction." At the same time they feared a contrary development. "The Tycoon never says die, and means to reign in Manhattan once more."[33]

Many signs pointed to such an outcome. Following his defeat, Wood seemed to take an unemotional reading of political developments and visualized a logical sequence of events leading to a comeback. New York's manpower, manufacturing, and finance were indispensable to the Union. Opdyke had won with barely more than one-third of the vote, proving that the Democracy, if united, was still the city's majority party. The man, therefore, who united the Democracy would become indispensable to Lincoln, automatically emerging as the state's key player and strong enough to help put a Democrat in the White House in 1864.

Whatever one thought of this reasoning, it provided Wood with a plausible line of action about the problems facing both parties. Tammany was in a transitional stage, confused by a mounting leadership battle unrelated to wartime issues, between Genet and older sachems led by Purdy, while Tweed awaited his

moment. Upstate, the Regency was in shambles, incapable of mediating factionalism. Among Republicans, the quarrel over war aims divided them into radical
and conservative wings, and Unionism was an untested policy guide.

Since Wood hypothesized that both parties lacked enough unity to cope
with the wartime political crisis, he presumed that his prospects were unlimited, provided he could fuse the entire Democracy. The means were clear.
Neither Democratic faction had by itself the numbers to assure steady victories. Each needed him because Mozart held the local balance of power and
both acknowledged his skill in mobilizing voters, building coalitions, raising
funds, and inspiring the faithful. Wood also probably thought that each faction,
despite their apparent differences on the war, were tired of losing and were
ready to bargain on issues connected to the conservative consequences of war,
chiefly erosions of civil liberties and attacks on slavery. Under those conditions, Wood's loyalism was still viable. It remained a middle course, faithful to
party principles and practices, capable of forging an internal party accommodation. Moreover, Wood banked that his prewar southernism made him invaluable as a potential mediator between Lincoln and Davis. The *Richmond
Examiner* strengthened his case when it observed that Wood's efforts "will
some day bring forth some serious offerings."[34]

Wood took it for granted, then, that normal politics, which he believed had
started the war, could end it. As his final bit of reasoning, he searched for a way
to widen the gap among Republicans. With that in mind, he wrote Lincoln with
praise on December 12, 1862, for revoking General John C. Frémont's premature emancipation order in Missouri and reshuffling the cabinet by removing
Simon Cameron, who had cooperated with the radicals, in favor of Edwin M.
Stanton, a former Breckinridge Democrat. "Your highly patriotic and conservative course," Wood stressed, "meets with the hearty concurrence of the Democratic masses in this state. We will sustain you fully, and you may rely upon my
best exertions in behalf of the administration."[35]

Meanwhile, Wood's private life settled into domestic bliss. His vivacious
young wife enjoyed high society, and he indulged her passion for buying diamonds. They began a second family with the birth of their first son in 1863, and
she bore three more children over the next six years. Just as gratifying, Wood's
father-in-law appreciated and used his political connections, although Mrs. Mills
still had reservations. His younger children were flourishing, apparently content
with their stepmother, and the others were thriving in business. His siblings also
prospered. Ben Wood, now a congressman, balanced the money he lost when
the *Daily News* suspended with a lottery in Kentucky, and he had just published
a Peace Democratic novel to public acclaim. Henry Wood held a political sine-
cure in the street department when his theater fell on hard times. Only one dark
cloud marred Wood's joy; in early 1863, his mother died.[36]

In his free time, Wood reentered the real estate market, but seemingly lost his golden touch. His properties had depreciated, and he cautiously sold off some lots, awaiting an upturn. Not everything turned sour; one investment paid off. In July 1861, Manton Marble, a young intellectual with a sure grasp of party principles, tapped wealthy investors to gain control of the struggling *New York World*, which had recently merged with the *Morning Courier and New York Enquirer*. Samuel Barlow spearheaded the drive, and approached Wood. Marble distrusted him, but needed his money. The upshot was that Wood bought a one-quarter share, partly for speculation, partly in the expectation that Marble would provide Mozart with a political forum. Although Marble's independence eventually dashed Wood's hopes, he profited by selling when the *World* became one of the city's premier newspapers.[37]

A variety of recurring problems kept Wood from testing his political theories to unite the Democracy until the late spring of 1862. Several lawsuits lingered from his mayoralty concerning his refusal to pay contractors for uncollected garbage, and his suit over the Marvine judgment was still bogged down in the Court of Appeals. A brewing uprising among several Mozart committeemen, encouraged by Genet, was similarly time-consuming but potentially more dangerous. Counting on Genet as the coming power, insurgents bolted Mozart and formed an independent organization, with decided Peace Democratic leanings, headed by John McKeon, Wood's adversary.[38]

In a twisted bit of irony, Tammany rescued him. The Purdy sachems, reinforced by Tweed and Sweeny, had ruled the Hall too long to succumb to Genet, and sought Wood's aid in the coming Tammany Society election. Under the banners of organizational reform, they routed Genet's ticket, and Wood watched approvingly as Tweed and Sweeny excommunicated Genetites from the General Committee. Wood then set in motion further peace overtures with Tammany by sounding out Mayor Opdyke and friendly aldermen about firing Street Commissioner Knapp.[39]

During this jockeying, conservative swallow-tail Democrats, headed by Belmont, Barlow, and Sam Ward, a Washington influence peddler, scouted for a possible presidential candidate, preferably a general with a winning military record, who refused to accept any type of emancipation. They already had in mind General George B. McClellan, commander of the Army of the Potomac and a former Breckinridge Democrat with close ties to Barlow and Marble.[40]

What surprised the swallow-tails was that Wood had reached the same conclusion. Sometime in May 1862, he visited McClellan in his camp near Washington to size him up as a potential candidate. Wood liked what he found. McClellan fit his definition of loyalism, someone openly contemptuous of Radical Republicans, a man who wanted to restore the Union on a conservative basis and was sympathetic to slavery. The general was attractive also because his ties to the swallow-tails gave Wood a chance to coalesce with wealthy city and upstate business leaders who had opposed him in the past. Like Wood, they supported the war but spurned any fundamental changes in Confederate society that might disrupt cherished Southern commercial ties.[41]

Wood returned to New York in May just in time for a sensational event. General David Hunter's unauthorized freeing of slaves in his military district, which fit into a spate of recent congressional bills eroding slavery, had just set off a political explosion among War and Peace Democrats, Constitutional Unionists, and even some conservative Republicans. Furthermore, the imminent passage of conscription alarmed many racist city workers, immigrants, and the poor who resented the prospect of being drafted into a war now apparently an abolitionist crusade. Wood was elated. The furor unwittingly gave him a potentially golden opportunity to bond the party around antiemancipation. No less important, Lincoln alienated Radical Republicans when he revoked Hunter's order. Quickly seizing the initiative, Wood worked with Barlow and other conservatives to organize a protest rally against Hunter in specific and Radical Republicans in general.[42]

When the "assembled thousands" gathered at Cooper Union on July 1, shouts for "Fernandy" filled the room. Wood indeed was the "great gun." Even as Confederates mauled McClellan near Richmond, Wood questioned the very foundations of the Union's military efforts. Such doubts, he said, were legitimate because "ours is a Government of *opinion*." For what ends did the North fight, if not to preserve the best of American principles? Emphasizing his distinctive loyalism, Wood asserted that Democrats were hostile "to every form of treason wherever it may appear or in whatever guise it may assume, whether by armed rebellion in the South, or the no less dangerous treason taught by abolition traitors in the North." Patriotism was not the issue; a nation's moral strength, as during the American Revolution, lay in a free public, which created armies and "then made them invincible."[43]

The central question was if "man is capable of self-government." Drawing a familiar distinction between Lincoln and Radical Republicans, Wood argued that Congress used the war as a ploy to destroy freedom by "odious and unconstitutional enactments." In the end, all loyal Americans came "back to the central question of popular rights." Amid deafening cheering, Wood stressed that "without liberty we have no country, and without freedom of speech and action we have no liberty." On that basis, Democrats must unify for the fall campaign against the "Abolitionist traitors" intent on destroying the nation we "inherited from our fathers. Death to all who oppose the Constitution as it is, and the restoration of the Union as it was."[44]

Resolutions that followed indicated how well Wood articulated conservative, antiemancipationist values. One in particular pleased him. It urged that all Americans preserve the Union by backing generals such as McClellan who scorned any expedient which eroded the Constitution, specifically slavery. Another resolution endorsed Wood's racism. This "is a government of white men, and was established exclusively for the white race; [and] the negro race is not entitled to be admitted to political or social equality with white men."[45]

The momentum Wood created proved irresistible when the state committee met in Albany two weeks later. Although not a member, he spoke at Richmond's invitation, repeated his loyalist formula as the means for party unity, and carried the day. In issuing a call for the coming state convention, the committee called for a coalition of conservative, "patriotic citizens, without reference to party combinations," who believed "in sustaining the Government in the prosecution of the war" and "restoring the Union as it was and the Constitution as it was."[46]

The same intense harmony gripped the city Democracy. In July, Tammany and Mozart formed a joint delegation "in view of the exigencies of the hour." When the convention began, a new day in city politics seemed dawning. Purdy and Wood strode down the aisle arm in arm, sat together, and Purdy proudly said he was "much gratified to announce that New-York presented a united front for the first time in many years."[47]

Wood basked in this warm glow of Democratic brotherhood. Delegates treated him royally, chanting his name over and over. "When order was once more restored," he made "a brief, spirited, eloquent and patriotic speech." What followed was somewhat less satisfying. Wood hoped secretly for the gubernatorial spot on the ticket, but the Regency secured Horatio Seymour's unanimous nomination. Richmond, however, mollified Wood with assurances that he was the Regency's choice in the January 1863 naming of a new United States senator. Since a joint legislative caucus made the appointment, Wood redoubled his commitment to party solidarity. He did so in good conscience. The party platform and Seymour's acceptance speech basically reflected his ideas. On that basis, Wood "pledged that the City of New-York would give a thirty thousand majority for Horatio Seymour."[48]

Wood's cocksure manner sparked Republican-Unionist fury. Even conservatives such as Weed, unhappy that they had selected Radical Republican James S. Wadsworth for governor, backed the ticket. With one voice, Republicans castigated Democrats as subversives, intent on hampering the Union and aiding Confederates. Greeley wrote that Democrats "lie—consciously, wickedly lie," when they said that to "support Seymour, Wood and Co., [was] the true way to invigorate the prosecution of the war." Abolitionist Cassius M. Clay of Kentucky added that, "The hanging of such men as Seymour and Wood would [save] thousands of honest lives." The *New York Times* culminated the attack, reserving its bitterest words for Wood. He was "a declared enemy of the Administration," an "avowed opponent of the war," and "a known sympathizer with the rebels, ready to make terms with them on the first opportunity."[49]

Desperation settled over the Democrats, and they mounted a frantic effort to prove their patriotism. Party orators toured the state defending Seymour and vilifying Republican-Unionists as the real disunionists, unable to govern the nation or run the war, directly responsible for corrupting the Constitution and looting the federal treasury. Wadsworth's nomination, they further charged, indicated that his party was only engrossed in freeing slaves in order to undermine white labor, and they used Lincoln's preliminary issuance of the Emancipation Proclamation as evidence. An even larger part of Democratic efforts lay in distancing Seymour from Wood. In unsaid but apparent agreement, the Regency decided that Wood was a liability. As Richmond pictured the situation, the need to ensure a Democratic legislature trapped Wood. He was only valuable in the sense that he contributed to party unity by not disrupting the organization and making Seymour appear a moderate by comparison. Thus, when Greeley ran a headline calling Wood a "Catiline" who was hatching "A Conspiracy to Overthrow the Government," Regency presses were silent.[50]

This situation was inevitable. In every contest in which Wood was involved, the opposition, the Republican-Unionists in this case, simplified the election's complexity into a personality question where he was the chief issue. Wood was ready. He knew that he needed endorsements from conservative and moderate Republicans based on his loyalism to prove that he was indeed a patriotic American. First came Weed. "Since the beginning of this dreadful civil war," Wood wrote, "I have held but one position, and that is of warm support of the government – and at no time either by word or act have I aided or abetted those in hostility to it." Lincoln was next. Wood restated his loyalism, and blamed all his troubles on "the ultra radical abolitionists who persistently represent me as hostile to your administration, and in sympathy with the states in rebellion." In doing so, those men ignored "my early tender of services to you." Out of either malice or pretended patriotism, newspapers compounded the error by trying to "prejudice" him in Lincoln's estimation. The truth was that his "attachment to the glorious cause . . . has not faltered for a moment."[51]

When neither man responded, Wood decided that he needed a fallback position to keep his name alive since he was dubious about the Regency's support for the Senate. For that reason, he became the first former mayor to seek an elected position outside of city government and sought a nomination in the recently reapportioned Fifth Congressional District, which included a bloc of wards along the western waterfront and in upper Manhattan, long his bastions. Complications existed. Although Purdy favored Wood, Clancy joined Genet in an anyone-but-him movement. Wood, the *Leader* warned, "is very smooth, oily, affable and yielding at present." Yet Tammany could not trust him because his only goal was "usurping" control "of the Democratic party."[52]

Wood got Purdy to put a tight leash on Clancy, gained a dual Mozart-Tammany nomination by acclamation, and then campaigned through blatant class and racial appeals to the many Irish and German laborers making up the district. One particular speech, this one before a large crowd in the Nineteenth Ward, was typical in the way that Wood redefined classic Locofocoism for new ends.

"Society was now and ever divided into two classes—the producers and non-producers," he said. The former were the poor; the latter the rich who "amassed their wealth from the products of the other classes." The war fell disproportionately upon the sons of the laboring class. The rich made few sacrifices and further exploited white workers by backing the preliminary Emancipation Proclamation in order to "flood the North" with inexpensive blacks, "many of them mechanics," rather than paying whites "at customary wages." Courting raw racist fears for all they were worth, Wood predicted that the rich intended to integrate the school system, "sustained by taxes which the white laborer largely paid," while their children escaped to private ones. The hypocritical rich, who were largely Republicans, would then demand not only social equality between poor whites and blacks, but favored "the African" being actually "superior to the poor white." The sole way to halt such dire developments rested in defeating abolitionists and electing him to Congress.[53]

Wood joined his brother and three old enemies, Elijah Ward, Nelson Waterbury, and Anson Herrick, on the ticket. Despite a brief uproar in the Eight District when Tweed insisted on replacing Waterbury with former Breckinridgeite James Brooks to complete their merger, the *Times* conceded: "The two Woods running in strong Democratic districts" would win "in spite of their open, avowed, blatant sympathy with the rebellion."[54]

Wood did crush his opponent, Republican-Unionist John Duffy, carrying every precinct, winning by a 69.9 percent landslide. As it became clear that Seymour and the entire congressional slate had also won, Mozart held a "huge, boisterous celebration." Hardly pausing to digest the fact that Democratic legislative gains, although large, did not give them certain control of the joint caucus, Wood shouted that the people had begun a political revolution, one that meant "that this Union is to be restored *only* by a conservative, constitutional course." Victory meant "that if we are to prosecute the war, we are to carry the olive branch in one hand, while we carry the sword in the other" so that New Yorkers could proclaim once again that "we are citizens of the United States of America."[55]

Even so, Wood covered his options by further mending fences with Tammany in order to secure his senatorial bid. During October, he and Purdy, along with Tweed and Sweeny, had used Genet as the catalyst to split the November ticket between Tammany and Mozart. The deal succeeded, and it held in

December. Both evenly split aldermen; Tammany got the coveted comptroller; and Mozart received the offices of surrogate and corporation counsel. Something, however, was puzzling. Wood handpicked several lesser men in certain key races and ignored the claims of stronger Mozart vote-getters. For the moment, few questioned his choices.[56]

After the elections, which the fused ticket won, Purdy, Tweed, and Sweeny demanded a fused, single General Committee as the price for future cooperation. Wood was willing to talk, considering what he stood to gain. Negotiations did not proceed easily, the *Leader* confessed, because Mozart and Tammany had different tables of organization. Nonetheless, Clancy announced that upstaters had not given city politicians a fair share of national offices. The upshot was that "Fernando Wood will be united on from this section of the State as the candidate of the United Democracy for United States Senator."[57]

By December of 1862, Wood assumed that he stood on the threshold of a new, brilliant phase in his career. Events soon indicated, however, that the elections of 1862 marked the watershed of his loyalism and proved the last Democratic successes during the Civil War years.

In retrospect, Wood was mired in unsuspected trouble largely of his own making. Although the fact was not yet clear, his concentration on national issues and the coming senatorial contest opened the way locally to a far more serious rival than he had ever faced. Tweed had studied his tactics, refined them, and profited by his mistakes in ways Wood never anticipated. Upstate, Wood underestimated the Regency's determination to jettison him to enhance Seymour. Just as damaging, Wood's loyalism was becoming obsolete because neither side sanctioned negotiations. In a bitter blow to his hopes, the *Richmond Examiner*, after lauding Democratic triumphs, warned Northerners such as Wood that they must "understand fully and perfectly that separate independence is our irrevocable determination."[58]

Wood ran into the same stone wall in Lincoln. In December 1862, he prodded the president with information he just had received from a Southern authority, whom he believed "reliable and truthful," which indicated that a few Confederate states were willing to reenter Congress based on a "full and general amnesty." Even if the information proved "groundless," it was worth a try. Lincoln was skeptical and put the burden for peace on Confederates. Wood tried again. How could the Confederacy compromise, he impatiently wrote, when the Union shouted "our intention to destroy their local institutions"? Frustrated by this exchange, Wood ended, "I feel that military operations so bloody and so exhaustive as ours must sooner or later be suspended—The day of suspension must come!"[59]

Quite simply, this exchange illustrated Wood's failure to grasp that Northern sacrifices had outmoded his loyalism. As the war's bitterness increased and the

Union army finally won several key victories, many Northerners concluded that Wood's reservations about Republicans weakened the military in ways which went beyond legitimate dissent. In their eyes, he was not only a political obstructionist, but, maybe as Republican-Unionists imputed, a traitor.[60]

Lastly, the dynamics of how Republicans waged that war created consequences that fundamentally negated Wood's conservative vision of a static Constitution and an unchanging United States. On January 1, 1863, Lincoln made the Emancipation Proclamation official. In Congress, Republicans mobilized the Union with a display of unprecedented centralized powers, far worse to Wood than anything the state legislature had attempted. A checklist of congressional programs set his teeth grinding—conscription, high protective tariffs, a national banking system, issuance of legal tender unsecured by specie, vast bond sales which pushed the national debt to astronomic levels, and the authorization of black troops.

Each one devastated Wood's revered principles and every issue on which he had staked his political career. As a man who personified Locofocoism, this new, emerging America was not his America. The longer the war continued, the more it dissolved the republic of his allegiances. When he realized that, he had no option but to live on the edge, taking a step toward the danger zone of the Peace Democrats.

NINE

The Peace Democrat

B Y late 1862, unaccustomed financial pressures lay more heavily on Wood's mind than politics. He had underwritten Mozart, spent his own funds in administrating the mayoralty beyond its yearly salary of $5,000, and subsidized his congressional campaign. Ordinarily, Wood could afford such outlays, but not in an era of wartime inflation which cut into even his considerable wealth. Chancy investments escalated his woes. Wood carried $57,475 in new mortgages, mainly $45,000 on a just-purchased office building at 115 and 117 Nassau Street near city hall for which he found few renters. Legal reverses compounded his troubles. The supreme court ordered him to pay several policemen injured in the 1857 riots, and the court of appeals finally sustained the referees' finding in the Marvine case. While he had originally repaid Marvine $5,000, the court ordered an additional $17,000 consisting of the remainder, plus interest and costs. For the moment, Wood evaded the verdict. His friend and former attorney, Supreme Court Justice George C. Barnard, was in charge of disbursements, and Wood trusted him to schedule payments in depreciated greenbacks instead of gold. In this emergency, Wood sold his San Francisco property, but the proceeds apparently were not enough. A soft city real estate market made further selling unfeasible. On top of everything else, Alice Wood had expensive habits. Little is known of the figures involved, but her grandiose spending for finery and jewels came at a time when he had little disposable income.[1]

As his large debts became larger, Wood worried that some creditors might transfer his notes to unfriendly Republican bankers. In desperation, Wood reverted to tawdry habits. For years, his image as a grafter who sold appointments and then resold them to the highest bidder had grown commonplace. Since proof did not exist, maybe because the men involved never complained fearing arrest for bribery, the Hackley contract served as a handy substitute. During the spring of 1862, New Yorkers read a daily diet of court testimony linking him and brother Ben to a $40,000 payoff for signing the contract.[2]

On January 24, 1863, New Yorkers opened the *New York Times* to read a jolting report which lay bare Wood's sleazy operations. The story had its roots in the previous fall. John K. Hackett, a one-time San Francisco lawyer and actor, had become a confidant of Judge Barnard, and secured his blessing for Mozart's corporation counsel nomination. The position was quite lucrative. In addition to naming the corporation attorney, the corporation council set conditions for city contracts and often received kickbacks for favorable terms. Wood agreed initially but reneged, selling the slot to John E. Develin, the paper explained, for $15,000. After Hackett squawked to Barnard, he saw Wood and told Hackett the "Great Mogul" would have Develin name him as corporation attorney. The grateful Hackett met Wood and was astonished when he demanded $7,500. While Hackett scurried to find a bankroll, Wood bartered the job between George C. Genet and N. Hill Fowler, the eventual choice.[3]

The incensed Hackett forced his way into Wood's home, and drew a pistol when Wood called a servant to throw him out. In the best traditions of melodrama, the *Times* reported Hackett as saying: "If that man comes between us, I shall blow out his brains, and cut off your ears; so you may as well listen: On a certain night at a room in the Astor House, were four gentlemen: Mr. D., Mr. ——, Mr. —— and yourself. One of the four is a scoundrel, a rascal, a perjured villain and a hound. It is not Mr. D., or Mr. ——, nor Mr. ——. Who he is I leave to you to imagine."[4]

This disclosure solved the mystery surrounding Mozart's 1862 nominations. The *Times* editorialized that Wood had disappointed "political allies and [forfeited] the solemnest promises with brazen assurances solely that his personal pockets may be filled." The most intriguing part of this story came from its collaborating source, Judge Barnard, who leaked the details to the *Times* and also revealed the full scope of Wood's financial squeeze. Barnard's revenge against Wood for failing to select Hackett went deeper. He assigned Tweed, who had broken off Tammany's deal with Mozart, as receiver in the Marvine case, and specified payment in gold. The entire episode mortified Wood. People had undeniable evidence of his shady behavior; the public knew his private financial dealings; and, worst of all for a proud man, New Yorkers laughed at how easily Hackett had faced him down.[5]

When the legislature met, Barnard's revelation placed Wood in a familiar position, the center of controversy, a lightning rod for both patent hatred and blind admiration. Since the joint caucus met at a time of shifting political alignments, Wood went to Albany for personal log-rolling and sought Seymour's aid, offering to act as his mouthpiece in Congress.[6] Seymour's thoughts were unclear, but his appointment of Nelson Waterbury, Wood's nemesis, as state judge advocate general spoke volumes about Wood's lack of friends in the Regency.

Intense factional infighting and deep divisions over the war marked every step organizing the caucus. A persistent standoff in the assembly for speaker delayed matters for seventy-eight ballots, amid bitter charges of intimidation and vote-buying. On the floor, some legislators came to blows, others packed guns, and the gallery thronged with imported toughs. Finally, Theophilius Callicot, a King's County Peace Democrat, won on the Ninety-second ballot with Republican Unionist aid through means so suspicious that it caused an official inquiry.[7]

When the joint ballot took place, Republican-Unionists ignored their own shoddy behavior in the speakership contest. Instead, they held Wood solely accountable for the delay and blamed him for having imported "ruffians" to foster legislative anarchy. In the end, the state did elect someone from the city, former Governor Edwin Morgan, not Wood. As soon as voting ended, politicians watched his reaction to see if defeat had cooled his fierce will. They saw neither chagrin nor resignation, but grim resolve to have the last laugh as the leading congressional Peace Democrat and to carry them to national victory. There was something else visible: the Regency's "peculiar relish" at Wood's loss cast deep doubt about any future cooperation.[8]

The political and financial tides that had eroded Wood's position quickly ebbed. While Republican-Unionist maneuvering prevented the assembly from censuring Callicot, sufficient evidence surfaced proving him guilty of accepting their bribes in exchange for influencing the votes of several other Peace Democrats on the joint ballot. Callicot's venality siphoned a little sting out of the *Times's* exposé, making Wood somewhat less repellent. Another factor helped Wood. Drake Mills died in February 1863, leaving a sizable estate. With his wife's share, Wood slowly repaired his sagging fortunes and used part of her inheritance for house-hunting in Washington. He was too practical and proud, however, to rely on her alone. Wood convinced the aldermen to rent part of the first floor of his Nassau Street offices at a temporary lease of $8,200 per year. The First District Court took up the remainder for $1,500.[9]

Now that his destiny lay in the House, Wood tailored loyalism to Peace Democrat specifications. He had to sew with care. Enraging the Republicans was unavoidable, but he also risked splitting Peace Democrats. Unlike extremists such as his brother or Ohio Congressman Alexander Long, Wood had rejected the idea that the Confederates had established their independence. The Union could win, Wood believed, but at a cost that left both victors and vanquished demoralized. Trying to strike a balance between Peace Democratic defeatism and Republican intransigence, Wood presumed a conservative, pro-Union majority existed in the Confederacy willing to negotiate on the basis of constitutional concessions the prewar South had sought.[10]

Much of Wood's ideas were not new but borrowed extensively from Clement L. Vallandigham, the leading Peace Democrat and a former Ohio congressman. Despite minimal doctrinal differences, one major flash point existed between them. Wood was angling to supplant Vallandigham. In this silent power struggle,

Wood evidently reasoned he held the advantages because he was on far better personal terms with Lincoln and Vallandigham lacked a national forum in Congress. On that basis, Wood assumed he might persuade the president to arrange a peace conference, and his prewar southernism might convince Confederates to attend. Yet Vallandigham and Wood shared the same difficulty. The public made no discrimination between extreme Peace Democrats, who were ready for peace *without* reunion, and moderate Peace Democrats who favored peace *and* reunion.[11]

Wood wanted to prove to other conservatives that he had exhausted loyalism before adopting a more drastic course. After fruitlessly asking Lincoln for permission to publish their correspondence the previous December, Wood acted alone. Stumping Connecticut with Horatio Seymour during its spring elections, both men focused on the draft as an unconstitutional measure motivated by a failed government. At Stamford, Wood diverged from this standard tactic. For the first time, he directly censured Lincoln's conduct of the war and hinted without being specific that the president had refused a genuine Confederate offer for an armistice and peace. When Republicans demanded details, Wood shot back that "one of the principle officers of the government" prevented him from issuing supporting "facts."[12]

Back in New York, Wood rented Cooper Union for an April rally of trade unions "opposed to the conscript act, opposed to war for the negro," and "in favor of the rights of the poor." Before the meeting, he completed his conversion as a Peace Democrat. At a Mozart General Committee meeting, Wood announced: "There is no such thing as a 'war democrat.' I hold that any man who supports the policy of this administration cannot be a Democrat."[13]

Little doubt existed about Wood's change of heart after the gathering. Once more invoking Locofocoism, he said that the administration's growing centralization and partisan economic legislation destroyed workers' rights. War Democrats cooperated with Republicans in terrible design. "The only difference will be one set of men to steal instead of the other." Then he shifted emphasis. Peace Democrats, he pointed out, had an untried program to restore the nation and its traditional values. The times demanded bold action in this "evil hour for this country, and for human progress, and for the cause of human liberty throughout the world." If, however, the South did not budge, what should the Union do? Wood's solution was that the president should submit the issue of continuing the war to a plebiscite. The vote "should be final, then and forever. That is my peace programme. I am willing to go with the people."[14]

Beyond expected Peace Democratic accolades for Wood's rather impractical solution, a harsh outcry erupted among fellow Democrats. Upstate, the Regency hustled Seymour away, nervous that their joint campaigning might damage the governor. Tammany hooted at Wood's "latest evolution on the political trapeze" as an individual act. Marble, writing for the swallow-tails, railed that Wood acted "without regard to the welfare of the party at large." Republicans were no less hostile, insisting that Wood had condemned himself as a traitor. Outside the state, the volume of criticism was just as loud. The Mozart regiment repudiated Wood, and when he took a trip to Washington looking for housing, a group of lounging soldiers used "opprobrious language" as he passed.[15]

Denunciations and insults did not cower Wood as new developments seemed favorable to Peace Democrats. His brother started publishing the *New York Daily News* again, and it explained and justified Wood's ideas. Conservative War Democrats, including Tilden and Barlow, using constitutional and legal arguments through their Society for the Diffusion of Political Knowledge, were too unemotional for the masses, but joined Peace men in rejecting the draft and emancipation. Union defeatism was rampant following the Union's inability to capture Vicksburg and the wrenching defeat at Chancellorsville. Towering above everything else, General Ambrose E. Burnside's arrest of Vallandigham in Ohio for traitorous remarks imperiled all Democrats. Wood grasped the significance of these developments. He set a June 3, 1863, "Mass State Convention for Peace and Re-Union" in New York City to mobilize public support.[16]

The meeting exceeded Wood's fondest hopes. Supporting letters poured in from Peace Democrats in other states. Even better, the crowd was so immense that men jostled each other in the main room at Cooper Union to such an extent that organizers set up five stands outside. Nor did Wood disappoint listeners. As he saw it, fighting must cease immediately because under the Constitution only Congress had the right to declare war. Lincoln, acting illegally from the start, had compounded his felony through "damnable crimes against the liberty of the citizen, the rights of property and even the form of government." Wood cited the Vallandigham incident as an example of how unauthorized power had become "monstrous in theory and execrable in practice." Moreover, Lincoln's extralegal actions created a public debt "which must bear down labor, destroy capital, and finally cause national bankruptcy and dishonor." Popular support for the war had subsided, and "force, by a draft, cannot supply indispensable" levies. Even "the over-ruling power of God is against us. We cannot succeed in what we have undertaken." Each day the war went on placed "an additional barrier between us and re-union, and drives another nail in the coffin of the Republic." The only sensible policy was for "calm, prudent and thoughtful men" to join the Peace Democrats in saving what was left of the Republic.[17]

Wood's incisiveness and vigor generated all that he wished. Many Peace Democrats projected him as Vallandigham's replacement, and a steering committee, which Wood headed, scheduled a follow-up meeting the following June just in time for his momentum to peak at the national convention docketed for July 1864.[18] Wood, however, probably had no inkling that these humid days of June and July 1863 marked the first step in the Peace Democrats' decline and the turning point in his struggle with Tammany.

As it turned out, Wood had only convinced the convinced. In fact, the meeting proved a catharsis for Tammany and the Regency. Haunted by ambiguity over their relationship to the rebellion since its outset, War Democrats through the state committee used Wood to settle the issue. They chose military victory as the means to achieve reunion and peace. Other warhawks flew high. "Wood's peace," the *New York Leader* wrote, "means disunion and that only." Ohio Congressman Samuel S. Cox gruffly told Marble not to confuse public anger over Vallandigham's arrest with support for his "peace notions." Another congressman informed Barlow that people scoffed at Wood's quixotic crusade. Lincoln interpreted the meeting as one of eccentrics, plainly draft-dodgers and people the Woods manipulated "as so much capital" to "demand a piece of Tammany Hall." Other Republicans used the phrase "Fernando's farce" as their kindest slur. The *Richmond Examiner* settled the case. Placing no confidence in the Peace Democrats' "best efforts," it announced that the war could only end through the Confederacy's "Peace party, which we call the Army of Northern Virginia."[19]

Wood's ultimate hope to control the Democracy rested on the party's hostility toward conscription. This, too, proved a costly miscalculation. Throughout June and July, the *Daily News* unleashed a torrent of racial and class invectives against the draft, especially the section which allowed wealthier men to escape by paying a $300 commutation fee, a price far beyond ordinary laborers. Stanton, Ben Wood predicted, could only enforce it at bayonet point.[20]

The *Daily News*'s editorials were a self-fulfilling prophesy among the targets of its columns: the city's poor, workers and immigrants alike, demoralized by runaway inflation, distorted racial fears, and a seemingly endless war. On July 13, the first conscript was called. That night, the city exploded with the most vicious riot in its history, one which was foreseeable to perhaps everyone but the Woods and Seymour, who had ignored Mayor Opdyke's pleas for militia protection. Over three days, mobs raged through the city in a bloody orgy of arson, pillage, murder, and racism. By the time fury slacked and the police restored order, helped by the arrival of troops fresh from Gettysburg, partisan finger-pointing began.

Republicans had a handy rogue's gallery. They listed Seymour who underestimated the danger, the Irish for rioting, and the Woods as instigators. War Democrats pleaded innocent. They complained about Stanton's arbitrary centralism, were highly solicitous of the Irish, and absolved Seymour. An icy silence, however, covered their attitude toward the Woods and Peace Democrats. Forced to fend for themselves, the best they mustered was Ben Wood's promise, passed to Stanton through an intermediary, of "no political opposition" when the draft resumed in August.[21]

The riot's insurrectionary timing, coming within days of brilliant Union victories at Vicksburg and Gettysburg, left Fernando Wood's credibility and ambitions tattered. Most New Yorkers, including extremists within the Peace Democracy, took for granted that he had created the riotous environment, just as in the earlier police uprising.[22]

Even the most third-hand rumors seemed valid. Republican David Dudley Field, a leader of the New York Bar, wrote Stanton, "A gentleman visiting my wife and sister now with us rode down in the [street] cars behind Marshall *Isaiah Rynders* and heard him say distinctly to another person that Fernando Wood knew all about the riots before hand." George Wilkes, the editor of *Wilkes' Spirit of the Times,* Wood's former colleague from their days as Locofocos, now on a tortured trek from urban artisanism to right-wing Republicanism, summarized these beliefs in a scorching indictment. The riot, he wrote, was part of a deliberate Confederate diversion fomented by the sinister Fernando Wood and his "cohorts and henchmen," who let "loose the fiends of massacre and rapine on our City."[23]

Wood's immigrant constituency cracked under this intense pressure. Many Irish Catholics and Germans, along with large numbers of middle-class workers, still resented the war's racial, political, and economic consequences. But to silence critics, and out of their own instinct for survival, they rejected Wood and what appeared as his insurrectionary demagoguery, destroying a major part of his power base. Making this defection more painful to Wood, most of these disillusioned groups joined his hated enemies in the McKeon Democracy. By contrast, Tammany gained immeasurable prestige. John Dix, now a major general of volunteers, who was in the city on a fact-finding tour for Stanton, noted: "Tammany Hall, representing more than half the democracy, will stand by the government."[24]

If Wood felt any of this vilification, he did not show it for the next eleven months. In the middle of congressional debate on another subject, however, he mentioned that he was elsewhere when it began. Warming to the subject, he put the onus on Republicans, and flayed conscription as unjust because its class bias penalized poor Democrats. As for the rioters, Radical Republicans misled them as a pretext to declare martial law.[25] Wood's self-justification was insufficient, no matter when he explained. While he was still an unquestioned national force and Mozart remained in operation for another five years, the riot marked the turning point in his local political career. He would never again mount a serious challenge to Tammany Hall.

In the fall, the peculiar nature of city politics prevented Tammany from exploiting Wood's weakness. The reason lay in the sudden surge for the McKeonites, which forced Mozart and Tammany into an uneasy alliance. Purdy and Tweed did not contest Mozart's seating at the state convention, and

Tammany supported placing Wood on the platform committee. Locally, Mozart and Tammany split the ticket, and they prepared a joint fall effort unrelated to national issues.[26]

Few previous campaigns ever began under more inauspicious conditions for Wood and Tammany. In September, Lincoln published their earlier correspondence to a generally skeptical public because the source of Wood's ostensible peace proposal remained obscure. Another incident a month later hurt Wood just as much. Somebody in the post office stole a letter written to him, purportedly by Gazaway Lamar, a Northerner living in Charleston, indicating that both were deeply involved in illegal cotton speculations and bribery of Union officials. With Barnard's disclosure fresh in mind, many New Yorkers snickered at Wood's defense that the letter was a hoax, especially when the *Richmond Examiner* came to his defense. As a consequence, voters punished Mozart, Tammany, and the Regency with impartial disdain. In November elections, conservative Republicans made strong statewide gains. A month later, the McKeonites exploited the aroused anti-Wood mood to elect C. Godfrey Gunther as mayor.[27]

Despite these setbacks, Wood left for Washington in a buoyant mood. As he stopped briefly for a speech at Bergen, New Jersey, his few words indicated where he stood and where he would go: "War is disunion and disintegration," waged under a "centralized despotism" to advance "the fortunes of the most desperate knaves that ever cursed a country," whether Republicans or War Democrats. "It is the duty of the people now to refuse to give another man or another dollar for the purpose of carrying on the war."[28]

Alice Wood also craved life in Washington. Planning to conquer society, she fashioned their new home on H Street, between Thirteenth and Fourteenth, in the grand manner. She even aped her husband's brazenness in courting Mrs. Lincoln, and sought her aid to have the Marine Band play at their first formal reception. Although Stanton prevented that, the Woods did attract over five hundred persons from all levels of government and the diplomatic corps because of his political reputation and her membership in the exclusive New York City aristocracy. Newspapers quickly made Alice Wood a favored hostess. The *Washington Evening Star*'s chatty society writer, after observing the "excellent music" and "magnificent supper" at one gala, hailed the party as "undoubtedly one of the most brilliant events of a brilliant season." Alice enjoyed herself immensely at a cycle of these dinners, theater parties, and balls, creating a sensation with her regal carriage, good breeding, and display of wealth. After a reception at the White House, an ingenuous young visitor from upstate New York wrote home that Mrs. Wood "was one of the attractions of the evening. She wore forty thousand dollars worth of diamonds." Wood encouraged her, and they made a handsome couple. Conscious of his own appearance, he now sported a fashionable military mustache, dyed his greying hair black, and dressed in the latest styles.[29]

Wood valued these diversions for their political effect. Witty, charming, urbane, and dignified in appearance, he cultivated the image of a person who enjoyed the pleasures of the table and the rewards of the good life, hardly the vulgar, treacherous New York politico in hot pursuit of graft and patronage that the press so unflatteringly portrayed. His persona set, Wood renewed old friendships, made new ones, and soothed festering partisan enmities.

During the week before the Thirty-eighth Congress convened on December 7, 1863, Wood signalled that he was not just another congressman of little import. With typical affrontery, he bustled into the White House and lectured Lincoln about appointing a presidential commission, including himself, to show Confederates hard evidence of Union willingness to negotiate. On a related matter, he urged the president to grant amnesty to certain Democratic dissenters, notably Vallandigham, then languishing in Canada after his conviction and banishment. Wood was ready to double-cross both men. Exuding his most persuasive manner, Wood planted the idea in Lincoln's mind that he favored his reelection. As part of his scheme, Wood suggested that Vallandigham's determination to impose a Peace Democratic candidate and platform on the convention would force the party into running two men, guaranteeing the president's victory.[30]

Lincoln evidently saw through Wood's transparent scheme with ease. Dismissing both ideas, he understood that Wood wanted to bring Vallandigham home so his penchant for overstatements would further alienate the public and allow Wood to take his spot. Using such reasoning, Lincoln strung Wood along. The president flattered Wood's ego, but exploited his rivalry with Vallandigham to increase further Democratic disarray.[31]

Few congressmen had any illusion's about Wood's intentions after the session's first days. Defying the obligatory party caucus, he backed Austin A. King of Missouri, a Peace Democrat, instead of War Democrat Samuel Cox, for Speaker. Then, Wood lunged on a collision course with every prowar group. Taking off on Lincoln's special message calling on the public to give "thanks to God for recent victories," Wood said that "a general magnanimity" to the "insurgents" was a more proper religious sentiment. To follow that thought, he introduced a resolution empowering the president to name three peace commissioners so "that this bloody, destructive, and inhumane war shall cease, and the Union be restored on equity, fraternity, and equality under the Constitution." Angry voices rumbled on the floor, but a parliamentary ruling stilled discussion, and the resolution was tabled, 98 to 59.[32] The vote indicated two key points. Peace Democrats did not command the votes to implement their agenda, and Wood was ready to challenge top-ranking House Democrats with longer service.

During the first session, Wood indeed became a major congressional force even if he was a minority member of a minority party, sterile in shaping legislation. His importance lay in the multiple functions of a classic opposition leader. He drove wedges among Republicans, blunted their measures, employed parliamentary footwork to stall passage of hostile measures, sought special committees to investigate purported corrupt administration spending practices, used oratorical skills to hone Peace Democratic appeals, and set party positions to attract voters. In the process, Wood played a significant role in the House's daily operations and as a partisan advocate helped manage the Democracy.

Wood also capitalized on Vallandigham's absence to capture his place as the North's leading Peace Democrat. Utilizing the style he had developed in city politics, Wood simplified his ideas with untiring repetition in terms of nationalistic Peace Democrats versus naive War Democrats and disunionist Republicans. He indeed caught public attention, and his calendar filled with speaking dates.

Wood was more than an obstructionist. In advocating his own proposals and attacking those Republicans submitted, he formed a blueprint to make a negotiated peace possible. Then, too, he designed his speeches as a campaign platform for whomever the party nominated as president, both for restoring the Union and the Democratic party once the war ended.[33]

Wood never wavered from these techniques and goals throughout the first session. Early on, he established his reputation when the House began debate on a bill which tormented Peace Democrats beyond all others, amending and extending conscription. Wood spearheaded Peace Democratic efforts. He harassed Republicans with every delaying tool available to prevent debate, and he loaded the bill with amendments they could not accept. He even showed a streak of ironic humor in one of them, the granting of conscientious objector status to men who opposed the war "until an effort has been made and failed to end it by negotiations."[34]

While the bill's passage was never in doubt, Wood still delivered a systematic denunciation of its provisions by combining Locofocoism with Peace Democratic ideas. He termed bounties as "bribery" to the poor, commutation as brazen class discrimination, and the entire draft an unconstitutional extension of federal power. The public was tired of "this bloody crusade against our own countrymen." Questioning the blind reflex that "any man who speaks of peace is called a traitor or an unconditional submissionist," he emphasized, "I am for restoring the Union" around the doctrine of states' rights. Failure to act was "anti-Christian, utterly anti-humane, and antagonistic to all principles of a republican government."[35]

Republican economic legislation also engrossed Wood for a different but related reason. Believing that Republicans had exploited the war to revive old

Whig programs, he issued a clarion call to rally Democrats around traditional principles. As a latter-day Jacksonian fiscal conservative, Wood demanded a gold and silver standard, the contraction rather than expansion of greenbacks, repeal of the National Bank Act, and tariff reductions. He did support normal government expenditures in terms of spending in general. But, unlike War Democrats, he resisted military appropriations, except to raise the monthly pay of white troops.[36]

In similar ways, Wood linked Peace Democratic objections to a bill that increased internal revenue rates. He agreed disarmingly with Republicans that the government was "embarrassed" and needed "income without borrowing," but countered that such pernicious attacks on private enterprise breached both the Constitution and capitalism. The larger issue was why the government requested more money. The pattern was plain. Issuance of paper money fostered inflation, accelerated the cost of living, drove "specie out of circulation," and discouraged investors from buying bonds because they lacked faith in the government's fiscal wisdom. If Republicans insisted on higher taxes, they must spread the burden in a "just, fair and equitable" manner. As an example of Republican class prejudice, he noted the bill exempted custom-tailored clothing but heavily taxed ready-made clothing, "worn almost exclusively by the poor class."[37] The solution was just as plain, ending the war and returning conservative Democrats to power.

Few items raised Wood's ire more than Radical Republican bills confiscating private Confederate property. Lincoln and his party, Wood pointed out, disagreed on the legal status of Southern states, that is if they were "within or without the Union," and whether the Constitution applied to them. If Lincoln was correct that the Union was indissoluble, then confiscation was clearly illegal. On the other hand, the Radicals, who claimed Confederates were no longer in the Union, tacitly accepted their independence, raising the question of whether the United States had "a right to confiscate the property of a foreign nation."[38] Imponderables so complex had a practical solution through peace negotiations.

Confiscation had a logical extension, the divisive issue of ending slavery and its relationship to defining the status of freed blacks. Wood's position was predetermined. Based on racism, constitutional conservatism, and his belief that freeing slaves foiled compromise, he fought against any alteration of the prewar South's social order. As a result, Wood did not accept the legitimacy of the July 1862 Confiscation Act, which freed all slaves of masters in Confederate service, the Emancipation Proclamation, and vehemently opposed anything that might create black equality.[39]

Wood saw Republican greed behind both confiscation and emancipation. In discussing a bill involving black homesteading on confiscated estates, he remarked that the "direst curse and misfortune" that befell slaves was being "made a football for the ambition of white men to the destruction of their moral and physical well-being." The Sea Island experiment proved the point. "Freemen have been worked as slaves never were for the benefit of Northern speculators and philanthropists." When Republicans freed slaves and handed away illegally seized white Southern property, they assumed "that the Union is forever gone." Nothing was further from the truth, he felt. Peace and reunion could still save the United States and its traditional institutions.[40]

Contemporary observers seized on Wood's rhetoric as the rankest sort of disloyalty and treated Peace Democrats as if they were all the same. This misunderstanding, or maybe political ploy, exploded on April 8 when Republican congressmen, led by Speaker Schuyler Colfax, tried to expel Alexander Long after he made a speech urging Confederate independence. Ill and listless when Long spoke, Wood listened as Republicans pounded away, and he made a short reply the next day. Long, he noted, dealt with "two unfortunate and dreadful results," the extermination of the Southern people or recognition of Confederate independence. Facing those choices, Long chose recognition, and Wood announced, "You may include me in it because I fully concur in that sentiment." As cries of "Agree! Agree!" rang out on the floor, Ohioan Robert C. Schenck accommodated Wood. He seized on Wood's statement to question his patriotism and right to sit in Congress, citing the free-city speech, the sale of arms to Georgia, and the draft riot to document Wood's collaboration with Confederates.[41]

When Wood gained the floor for a more formal speech on April 11, he defended Long but reserved a full reply to Schenck. Long, he countered, had a First Amendment right to express an "honest avowal of opinion," consistent with "humane and Christian" beliefs. At least Long was more candid than prominent Republicans who covered up their wreckage of the "Constitution and the Union." As for himself, Wood partially answered Schenck, emphasizing that he had opposed secession, dissolution, and recognition. Reunion was still possible if people stopped to consider what moderate Peace Democrats said rather than listening to the distortions of Republican and War Democratic propagandists. What was on trial in the House was not Long but the ability of American conservatism to bring "back the Southern states into a condition of fraternity and brotherhood with the North."[42]

Three days later, Speaker Colfax breached normal House procedures. Leaving the rostrum, Colfax engaged Wood in a heated verbal exchange, and scolded him for behaving less as a gentleman than a "gladiator." The House finally voted to censure Long, but the debate tarred Wood and the entire Peace Democratic movement.[43] At that point, he needed another issue to make peace and reunion acceptable. Wood found it on May 3 over the Radical sponsored Wade-Davis bill for reconstructing the South.

Wood adopted his usual conciliatory tone toward the Confederacy and asserted that reconstructing those states as Congress wished along territorial lines was "utterly repugnant to republicanism." Put simply, Congress could not "disfranchise any State" on "any pretext whatever." Each one was still a distinct political community, with an undiminished state constitution and government "deriving authority from the people." In that sense, Congress could only restore the South to its original prewar status. Holding out his familiar Peace Democratic olive branch to each side, Wood implied that peace and reunion to Confederates meant preserving slavery for Confederates, and restoring, not reconstructing, the South to the United States.[44]

Wood then turned to Schenck and Colfax, and transformed their assaults into an apologia of conscience and duty. Throughout his mayoralty, he stressed, the state legislature and judiciary had trespassed on home rule. Schenck misinterpreted his free-city speech because he "did not recommend the withdrawal of the city from the Federal government." His differences were with the state of New York over the misuse of power, which still existed. Local citizens had sold goods to Georgia; the mayor could not regulate free enterprise. The draft riot's causes "can be placed at the door of the Administration or its agents." Such Republicans, he charged, wanted to coerce citizens into obeying an unconstitutional law, and Federal troops, "secretly prompted by radical Republican politicians," fired into innocent people "without discrimination or hesitation."[45]

As for his loyalty, Wood pointed out that he had backed the Union in 1861 and raised a regiment "out of my purse" for "preserving the integrity of the Union." But the war had turned out differently than he expected. Lincoln, Radicals, and War Democrats had voided his loyalism by converting the conflict into a struggle "utterly destructive and ruinous" to vast "numbers of people both North and South." Reading his own version of recent history and employing a Marx-like analysis, Wood maintained that the rebellion's origins lay in the "firebrand theory" of an "irrepressible conflict between 'free labor' and 'capital labor,'" which had "alienated State from State." The war, then, was a Republican pretext for the "unconditional surrender" of one economic system to an alien form. Emancipation was integral to their plot. Running short of time, he ended that all wars were savage, but "the most horrible have been those of a social and religious character."[46]

By the time Congress ended in July, Peace Democrats remained a distinct minority, unable to make any appreciable advances toward negotiations. But evidently Wood was not dismayed. As a legislator and partisan advocate before the bar of Northern public opinion, he had articulated a brand of conservatism which reinforced Democratic principles, prejudices, and programs. He began and ended as a Peace Democrat, embracing issues that confirmed his status as a guardian of the Constitution and a national party leader.

An analysis of Wood's voting pattern confirmed his consistency, even though he missed a number of roll calls due to illness as well as numerous outside speaking engagements. In ninety-one roll calls clearly connected to Republican programs—revenue measures, fiscal issues, tariff increases, confiscation, conscription, public lands, and military funding—he voted with them only 12.1 percent. On twenty-four roll calls affecting blacks, he was easily among the most reactionary Democrats. He cast votes against the proposed Thirteenth Amendment; providing freedmen with homesteads; allowing prisoner exchanges based on equal racial terms; giving the same pay, equipment, and bounties for white and black troops; allowing enlistment of Southern blacks; and even the authorization of Montana as a territory as long as it allowed black suffrage. By contrast, his approval rate ran 95 percent on twenty-two clear Peace Democratic issues—limiting the draft until Lincoln offered an armistice, naming peace commissioners, opposing expelling Long, criticizing the administration for suspending unfriendly newspapers including the *New York World*, limiting executive powers, and rejecting resolutions that the Union had a moral duty to crush the rebellion, plus another putting the House on record in favor of an earnest and successful prosecution of the war. His solitary deviation involved an almost obligatory resolution, which passed 168 to 1, to thank soldiers for their patriotism. When it came to twelve postwar questions involving reconstructing or restoring the Confederacy, Wood was even more perfect, voting 100 percent in favor of restoration under state control.[47]

Wood returned to New York City in early June for the second phase of his "Peace and Reunion" movement. The rally was far less exciting than the previous year, and he surveyed the political landscape for the next two months with a mixture of exhilaration and foreboding.

The Democratic party was still split, but signs indicated the emergence of a broad trend toward peace and reunion. Although Wood still considered Vallandigham a rival, he had returned to Ohio in July, boldly speaking against the war, and the administration left him alone. War weariness had crept over the combatants, making compromise feasible. Already, two sincere but unauthorized Northern peace emissaries had spoken to Jefferson Davis in Richmond, and Greeley had met with purported Confederate agents at Niagara Falls. Just as encouraging, a severe internal Republican squabble erupted when Radicals issued the Wade-Davis Manifesto which attacked Lincoln for pocket-vetoing their bill, forcing the conclusion that only a miracle could save his reelection. No less a partisan than Weed conceded Democratic victory. "The people are wild for Peace," he wrote Seward. There is not "the slightest hope of success."[48]

Locally, party leaders had apparently responded to changing times in a way that fit Wood's plans for converting the party into a Peace Democratic vehicle. In order to maximize party unity, national chairman August Belmont had rescheduled the convention from July 4 to August 29. "The postponement will be productive of good," Wood initially concluded to a colleague. "Our ultra Peace men are now determined that none but a true man shall be nominated. I now feel much encouraged." Samuel Cox foresaw a different set of circumstances. Unremitting military failures, he wrote McClellan, would give *"the Peace men"* the ability either to control the convention or divide it. Even so, Cox believed that in the end the party would unify around a War Democrat if they made some honorable concessions in the platform in "taking all the steps known to civilization, for the attainment of Peace & *Union*."[49]

While some Peace Democrats presumed that these developments had put them in a commanding position, Wood thought otherwise. Realizing that Belmont had changed the dates to buy time for McClellan, not to appease Peace Democrats, Wood now acted. Although McClellan was the front-runner, boomed by Marble and Barlow and funded by swallow-tails' wealth, Wood put Barlow on notice that the general could not win unless he severed his links to the Regency and the War Democrats. "I am *uncommitted*—my friends are uncommitted," Wood wrote. Professing an inclination toward McClellan, he warned Barlow that "I want success—but with a man who will close the war without more fighting—and without disunion." Other Peace Democrats were more blunt, believing it "a palpable inconsistency in supporting a person identified with the war."[50]

The extent to which Wood could influence any nomination, however, was debatable. When the state convention had met in February, Tammany refused to bargain with Peace Democrats and withdrew. Mozart and the McKeonites shared city delegates, but the Regency did not endorse peace and reunion. Instead, Richmond controlled the delegation through the unit rule, barred Wood as a delegate, and labored to nominate McClellan. Another setback struck Wood during midsummer. Mozart shattered into squabbling factions when he was in Washington, and many of his old supporters fused with his bitter McKeonite foes.[51]

Under the circumstances, Wood was willing to accept a partial compromise. Sometime in August he went to see Lincoln and was amazingly frank. Starting with his familiar denunciation of War Democrats as "bastards and imposters," Wood made a stark admission that Peace Democrats "don't expect to elect our candidate for president this fall: the people of the North are not yet ready for peace." Yet, he revealed a larger purpose, restoring the Confederacy and the Democracy under Peace Democratic auspices. When the war ended, "the Democratic party will be the party which will act and assimilate with the dominant party in the South, and so we shall again have our rightful ascendancy." As a result, Wood preferred nominating an unequivocal Peace Democrat, but that was not imperative. What was imperative was to commit the party to peace and

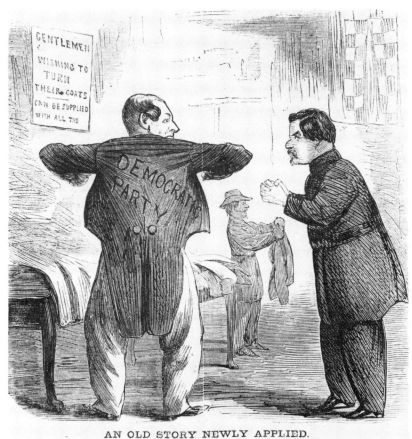

AN OLD STORY NEWLY APPLIED.

FERNANDO WOOD. "Say PEACE! or, by Thunder, I'll split it up the middle!"

Political cartoon depicting Fernando Wood and General George B. McClellan from *Harper's Weekly* 8 (9 July 1864): 448.

reunion.[52] To those ends, he wanted to remove Vallandigham as his rival at the convention, and tried to bait the president into rearresting him. When Lincoln offered no commitment, Wood made another of his patented turnabouts. He pooled forces with Vallandigham, if for no other reason than he was a delegate.

In mid-August, Wood laid out a whistle-stop itinerary to create a Peace Democratic groundswell leading to their possible triumph at the Chicago convention. Departing the city on August 15, he rallied supporters in Albany, took his bandwagon along rocky Republican terrain in central New York to Syracuse, and joined Vallandigham at Dayton for the joint homestretch on to Illinois, stopping at various towns en route. Each time the train halted, Wood directed a message to the heartland of Peace Democratic territory. The eastern Democracy, he said, was unanimously antiwar and determined to achieve immediate peace. "God help the tyrant when the people are arraying against him." Public response was encouraging. When he arrived in Chicago, Wood was confident that even if he could not stop McClellan he could build a case to incorporate peace and reunion in the platform.[53]

The task was difficult. Every report indicated that the general had a firm majority, just short of the magic two-thirds, and his supporters were so sure of victory that they were offering bets with no takers. Still, Wood tried to derail McClellan. His choice fell on the Hamletlike Seymour, who was smitten by the presidential virus, but wavered about opposing the general. Seymour's temperament hardly improved when he heard that Wood purportedly said, "I don't care five cents for Seymour; he is only a convenient tool just now." Before the convention opened, Seymour bowed out and left McClellan's nomination assured. "Wood is most bitter and determined," a friend hurriedly wrote Lincoln, "and declares that his faction will not submit to McClellan on a war platform." At that point, the swallow-tails grew overconfident. To forge the party unity Cox thought probable, they decided to allow the convention to adopt a peace plank, provided it did not compromise the Union.[54]

Such patchwork harmony proved a major blunder. Delegates did select McClellan, but balanced the ticket with Vallandigham's alter ego, George H. Pendleton. The real miscalculation happened on the platform. Vallandigham wrote the second plank, which condemned the war as a costly failure and put the party on record in favor of peace and reunion.[55]

McClellan was cornered and turned to Barlow and other swallow-tails for advice about wording his letter of acceptance. After pondering two preliminary drafts, he finally published a third which enraged Peace Democrats. Since the second plank was mute about resuming the war if compromise failed, McClellan wrote that negotiations could only begin when "our adversaries are ready for peace, upon the basis of Union." Thus, "the Union is the one condition of peace—we ask no more."[56]

Before McClellan's letter appeared, Wood grumbled about his nomination, but supposed he would accept the platform as written. While he awaited the general's reaction, Wood began campaigning. To a rather sparse gathering at Mozart, he admitted that he would have preferred someone else, but pledged support because the second plank vindicated his commitments. On those grounds, "It must be assumed, therefore, that opposition to the war is the national platform of the Democratic party."[57]

But the publication of McClellan's letter struck Wood like a thunderbolt. In reversing the second plank's priorities, by placing reunion before peace, the general had totally undercut him. Ben Wood could not contain his anger. Apparently speaking for his brother, he scourged McClellan as a renegade no Peace Democrat could back, and organized a conference to discuss options. With Fernando Wood strangely absent, Ben Wood and the McKeonites continued their barrage, but failed to formulate any plan beyond announcing they would not support the ticket.[58]

Meantime, Lincoln's miracle happened. Dramatic Union victories at Mobile and Atlanta ended Northern defeatism, ensured that voters would rally behind him as the symbol of national unity, and made a cruel mockery of Peace Democratic cries that the war was a costly failure. The *New York Herald* underscored how badly these factors destroyed the Peace Democrats. It lambasted Fernando and Ben Wood as manifest "dis-unionists," and asserted no one doubted that a mutual understanding existed between the Woods, Vallandigham, and the "rebels." In comparison, Tammany "stands for the Union [and] for the war."[59]

As these cross-currents washed through the electorate, Barlow, who was now McClellan's official campaign manager, informed the general that Ben Wood's "opposition helps, rather than hurts us" because it absolved the ticket from any stigma of disloyalty. Barlow also theorized that Peace Democrats would eventually support McClellan out of normal party allegiance. He was correct. After the fiasco of 1860, the majority of Peace Democrats, both in New York and across the North, except the die-hard Ben Wood and McKeonites, came to the conclusion that they must give the "ticket a cordial support."[60]

The same dictates worked on the shaken Fernando Wood. In a tortuous public slap at his brother, he found a plausible way to support McClellan. At a party rally on Fourteenth Street, Wood observed that the general's letter and the second plank might appear inconsistent and contrary to Peace Democratic views, Yet, the general had rebuffed the extreme Republican position of completely crushing the rebellion and creating a social revolution in the defeated Confederacy. After "examining the letter with care," Wood chose to interpret it as a "resolute determination to adhere to the Union, and a declaration that the Union could only be restored by that exercise of the same spirit which created that which he specified as that of conciliation and compromise." In less foggy words, it did not matter which came first, reunion or peace. When McClellan became president, Peace Democratic ideas would still work. He will, Wood predicted, "be our agent and the creature of our voice." Hence, Wood announced, he would "sustain the nomination" as a loyal Democrat, "so long as he had a voice to speak or a vote to give."[61]

As with so many other instances in his career, Wood brimmed with duplicity. He did not want McClellan to win. The general was beholden to the War

Democrats; his victory would give them the advantage in restoration; and there was a plain distinction between peace and reunion. Although the evidence is murky, Wood apparently sabotaged his own party by secret cooperation with Lincoln.[62]

As if not enough trouble hounded him, Wood lost his touch at the state convention. Six different sets of city delegations sought undivided admittance. Barlow ordered Richmond that only prowar Tammany was "fairly & squarely entitled to represent the party." Richmond bridled at this directive and instinctively sought a compromise. Tammany refused to temporize and won exclusive entry. For Wood, the moment was particularly poignant. Slowly walking down the aisle, shorn of a role in state politics for the first time in over a decade, a serenade of "groans and hisses" ushered him out of the building.[63]

Even deeper gloom surrounded Wood's reelection. He could not unite Mozart, and an expedient bargain with the hated McKeonites aborted. His cup of bitterness filled with one more round. Again a casualty of reapportionment, his new Ninth District included wards represented by incumbent Anson Herrick, his long-time nemesis. When Herrick refused to withdraw, they divided a sure Democratic majority. The elated Republicans, scenting victory, selected a Radical, William Darling. Forced to fight for political survival, Wood concentrated on his own struggle. Nothing helped. His fortunes plummeted so low, the *Herald* caustically observed, that "Fernando Wood is the nominee of Fernando Wood. Fernando Wood is patrolling the district, making speeches for Fernando Wood."[64]

Wood's magic ended on election day. Darling won, 38.9 percent to his 31.7 percent and Herrick's 29.4 percent. The *Leader* was jubilant. Wood's defeat, as both a man and as a symbol, meant that Tammany had finally destroyed Mozart after years of internecine warfare, guaranteed its sovereignty over the party, and crowned Peace Democrats with "odium." Just as important, the Hall helped carry the city for McClellan, and controlled the municipal and county governments in every department except the mayoralty.[65]

Outside New York City, state and national Democratic losses piled up with disheartening regularity. While Democrats were competitive in most elections and McClellan ran better than anyone thought, Republicans regained control of the statehouse, added to their control of Congress, and reelected Lincoln. In their postmortems, Democrats blamed their defeats on misplaced patriotism and frauds, especially Stanton's manipulation of the soldiers' vote and his assigning General Benjamin F. Butler to guard city polls. All were off the mark. With the Union winning and the end of the rebellion drawing near, Lincoln and his party were unbeatable. Peace and reunion remained both an untried option and an unrealistic dream.[66]

Wood found little comfort in this brutal axiom. Peace Democrats were simply on the wrong side of the issues and faced Northern contempt. As a lame duck congressman, Wood could only seek vindication by forces outside his immediate control. At the end of 1864, what shape these forces would take was opaque at best.

TEN

Political Exile

POLITICALLY isolated and suffering from an undisclosed illness, Wood might well have retired from politics to become a full-time real estate magnate. "Fernando is a played-out politician," the *New York Herald* prompted, and "we advise him to die gracefully." Wood, however, had no consciousness of guilt or error. He still believed that he could salvage his position by using the principles, hard work, and even deceit that had gotten him up the political ladder. The tasks were easier said than accomplished. By the time the Thirty-eighth Congress gathered for its second session on December 8, 1864, the prospect of a total Union victory had destroyed the Peace Democrats.[1]

Still, Wood pushed ahead. The previous November, he had responded to rumors that Lincoln and Davis were planning a peace conference by asking the president to select one person "from my wing of the Democratic party." Wood's purpose was to allow at least moderate Peace Democrats some dignity by proving that peace and reunion retained some validity. Gone was Lincoln's need to disrupt the Democracy by encouraging Wood, and he did not bother to answer. With that avenue blocked, Wood sought another means of personal absolution by reviving the politics of loyalty. On January 31, 1865, he introduced a resolution that the president was correct to employ every legal and constitutional means to maintain the Republic. Moreover, Lincoln must not "proffer or accept negotiations" that would recognize "by the remotest implication the existence of any other Federal or Confederate Government within the territory of the United States." Although the House approved it against extremist Peace Democratic opposition, Wood gained no plaudits from either his party or the public. In February, Wood tried again. He made a stunning reversal and voted with prowar groups, 108 to 30, to prevent die-hard Peace Democrats from tabling a resolution congratulating Lincoln for opening peace negotiations leading to "the restoration of the Union" at the Hampton Roads conference.[2]

Wood took one further step. In a perfect reflection of expediency, he told a *New York Tribune* reporter, "It is folly to persist in the application of impractical doctrines instead of accepting those which inevitable fate has forced upon us." His dramatic flip-flop came too late. The Union was winning Republican terms; he remained a political untouchable; and even his brother blasted him for accepting "armed coercion." Under those conditions, Wood again changed direction and reasoned that he must reestablish his credentials as a traditional Democrat.[3]

Debate over adopting the Thirteenth Amendment was one such opportunity. Until January 1865, Democrats had managed to stall it, but then their blocking techniques failed. Lincoln endorsed the amendment's passage; Radicals pushed for a quick vote; and Secretary of State Seward unleashed a powerful lobby among indecisive and rudderless New York Democrats.[4]

William N. Biblo, Seward's chief operative in New York, was optimistic that he could influence some indecisive party leaders, but confessed that he could "not do anything with Fernando Wood nor do I much regret it." To Wood, the amendment was indeed a way for him to reestablish himself among his colleagues. Congress, he said, lacked the power to abolish a state institution. The amendment was "unwise" and "impolitic" because the end of slavery would hinder peaceful reunion and create unremitting white guerrilla warfare. He rested his case on what would happen to individual blacks if slavery were abolished. Adopting the most virulent form of race-baiting, Wood snapped: "The Almighty has fixed the distinction of the races; the Almighty has made the black man inferior, and, sir, by no legislation, by no partisan success, by no military power, can you wipe out this distinction." Wood swayed few minds. The House passed the amendment 119 to 56.[5]

While Wood's words seemed a stale rehashing of the past, he really addressed the future. Conscious that as a practical matter the legal status of blacks needed redefining, he knew that white supremacists in both parties rejected any logical extensions of freedom leading to racial equality. By opposing the Thirteenth Amendment and the Freedmen's Bureau, Wood anticipated the Democracy's coming commitment to political racism. From all indications, it was a tactic with vast emotional potential, one which could crack Republicans, garner a substantial amount of white support for Democrats, and form the basis for reviving the Southern Democracy. Wood's position also fit the party's static view of the Constitution. Marble, in an editorial that Wood should have relished, tied these ideas into a statement of Democratic purpose. The Democracy had never consented to making "the black race as a co-equal of the white race."[6]

Wood followed another traditional Democratic line by advocating a conciliatory peace settlement without vengeance. While Republicans haggled over a reconstruction policy geared to Lincoln's soft approach versus the Radicals' punitive aims, Democrats favored the simple restoration of the prewar South. Wood agreed with his party, and voted on seven roll calls against authorizing either Congress or the president to implement and prescribe reconstruction policies. In that vein, Wood repeated his earlier stand. He maintained that the Southern states had never left the Union, thus their local institutions were "operative" and beyond federal jurisdiction.[7]

As part of his tactics, Wood played Republicans against each other. As moderate Congressman Henry L. Dawes of Massachusetts confided to his wife, "We killed the [revised Wade-Davis Bill] dead—and Fernando Wood killed me dead by complimenting me." While Wood shored up the Democracy's position in Congress, other Democrats upheld his idea of federal noninterference in postwar Southern developments. Speaking for them, state committeeman Joseph Warren, editor of the *Buffalo Daily Courier,* wrote: "Reconstruction is synonymous with radicalism—restoration with conservatism."[8]

At the time, Wood sought other traditional Democratic issues with mass party appeal to blot out his wartime conduct. Fiscal and monetary questions had such potential. Looking to the future, he predicted that forthcoming partisan battles would revolve around conservative economic concerns. As the session approached its last days, he advocated free-market programs regulated by individual initiative around the laws of supply and demand. Although he acknowledged that Democrats did not yet have the votes to convince Republicans "that our present financial system is ruinous," Wood warned Congress that Democrats intended to appeal to an "outside tribunal," voters who better understood "the homely precepts of common sense" than the "fine-spun theories of dreamers, speculators, and peculators."[9]

No matter how Wood shifted, he was an exile within his own party. As a matter of necessity, War Democrats strove for party unity, but feared Peace Democrats had discredited the entire organization. "I don't think we can be too severe on these Peace rascals," Warren cautioned Marble. "They must be driven out of the party at all hazards." Tammany shared Warren's opinion. "Upon the Union men will depend the reorganization of the Democratic party, and to these men will the reins of power be again committed." Wood fully understood. Finding himself in a position far different from anything he had known before, he decided to take a year-long trip to Europe, Italy, and the Holy Land in the hope that time would heal memories.[10]

Whether for politics or pleasure, Wood planned ahead. Since November, he had laid out a tour and sought letters of introduction, particularly from Seward, to gain some sort of semiofficial status. Alice Wood had other interests. Educated at a Paris convent, she looked forward to renewing old friendships and finding a proper school for her young children. After a festive private dinner at the Astor House, the Woods embarked on April 1, 1865.[11]

The Woods had barely begun their journey when news of Lincoln's assassination reached them in London. Sympathy for the martyred president ran high. Harsh cries for vengeance were hurled toward anyone who had contributed, even indirectly, to the circumstances surrounding his death. Wood was counted as one of those because of his Southern sympathies. One evening when the Woods went to supper, a disturbance that broke out among Americans in the room forced them to retire.[12]

From London, the Woods went to Paris and Berlin, but the spirit had gone out of their jaunt. With Andrew Johnson now president, Wood grew increasingly restless. A major political reorganization was under way, and he longed to get involved. Alice Wood must have found his preoccupation annoying. By July, they decided to cut the trip short, ostensibly because she wanted to dispose of a pending case concerning her father's estate and his efforts to foreclose the Stephen Douglas property. They returned the first week of September.[13]

In the interim, a partisan earthquake had shaken both parties. Democrats assumed that President Johnson, who was a prewar Democrat turned Unionist, would return quickly to his real partisan identity. By the time Wood came home, some semblance of order had been restored. Guided by swallow-tails working with Montgomery Blair, the president's chief adviser, the New York Democracy adopted pro-Johnson resolutions at their fall convention in 1865, supported his policy of presidential restoration, and reverted to being apologists for the white South. Only Tammany's refusal to recognize swallow-tails as equals and the continued shunning of Peace Democrats hindered full party unity. Where Johnson stood, however, was not clear. Seward and Weed Republicans, convinced that he shared their desire to establish a conservative Southern Republican movement, adopted a platform closely resembling that of the Democrats.[14]

Wood was equally intent on establishing good relations with Johnson to end his exile. But mere desire was not enough because Peace Democrats were still pariahs. After the assassination, mobs attacked the *New York Daily News*, forcing Ben Wood to relinquish temporarily his editorial control. Documents in captured Confederate archives were even more devastating. They implicated Ben Wood in a plot to disrupt the 1864 election. All these factors convinced party leaders that the Woods were still troublemakers.[15]

Fernando Wood had other ideas, and began a comeback with rumors about a "new ring" he was purportedly forming with Tammany and Weed. At first glance, a deal seemed plausible. Tweed resented swallow-tails' pretensions; Wood needed Tammany's approval to run for mayor in December; and Weed sought conservative Democratic aid to isolate Radicals. Richmond quashed any deal, rudely telling Tammanyites "he would be damn'd of they should dare nominate any peace men." In the end, it became apparent that Wood had circulated these speculations as a trial balloon. When that failed, he published a note that

Mozarters would rely "on their own strength and the rectitude of their own principles."[16]

Despite this statement, Wood was maneuvering to reach an understanding with Tweed along the lines of their wartime agreements. Times had changed. In the November 1865 elections, Mozart substantially endorsed Tammany's entire slate without reciprocity. Ben Wood's race for the state senate proved Mozart's only sign of life. His victory, however, was a "personal triumph," a debt of gratitude the laboring poor and ethnic groups paid for his paper's support of issues important to them, instead of a sign of general exculpation.[17]

Democrats fared poorly statewide as voters handed conservative Republicans astounding majorities. Publicly, swallow-tails still backed Johnson because they had no other option, while they railed in private that he promised so much but delivered so little. Tammany was just as bitter for other reasons. Scorning swallow-tails as political dilettantes, the Hall was intent on showing its power of self-renewal by winning the December mayoralty. Wood welcomed these developments. With Tammany and the swallow-tails competing, he reasoned that Tweed needed some type of reconciliation with Peace Democrats. To that end, he authorized his attorney, George Shea, to explore Tammany's willingness to unite the city Democracy in a common ticket which he would head.[18]

The Hall derided any negotiations. Tweed was aware that Wood dealt from weakness and that swallow-tails hated him. The upshot was that Tweed exploited those feelings to exact pledges of money and influence from them for the man he had already chosen, Recorder John T. Hoffman, the chief officer of the city's criminal court, a popular figure in his own right. Although nominated by Mozart, Wood had no hope of winning without Tammany, and declined with the excuse that New Yorkers were ungrateful "toward him for all the sacrifices he had made for them." Instead, Wood bought time to keep Mozart alive by insisting on John A. Hecker, a wealthy reformer who was paradoxically a Radical Republican.[19]

"Our pending Municipal election," the discerning *Herald* astutely remarked, "is the funniest on record" because "parties, politicians, rings and cliques" are "inexplicably mixed up." Tammany, McKeonites, conservative Republicans, and Mozart played trade-and-barter politics with each other in an expedient battle for raw political power. Yet Fernando Wood was the only issue. Outside of Hecker, the others ran against him, making partisanship even more indistinct.[20]

Hoffman barely won, but Wood was the real loser. Hoffman had tremendous ability, Tammany's blanket support, unquestioned personal integrity up to this point, and immense political skills. These attributes taken together blocked Wood's future mayoral aspirations. Then, too, Hecker's low vote, only 12.2 percent, indicated that Mozart shared Wood's ostracism. Marble was accurate when he observed it was "a shadow of a name."[21]

By the end of 1865, any claims Wood made as a party leader were ludicrous. New Yorkers had again repudiated him, and it seemed his era had passed. For the moment, he acted that way and plunged back into real estate speculations. In a burst of frenzied activity that started shortly before the municipal election and lasted fourteen months, Wood purchased additional property near Wood-lawn, with his wife often listed as a co-purchaser. They encumbered $73,086 in new mortgages, most disposed of in two to eight years. Wood also sold $63,180 in lots, apartments, and homes, generally on the West Side and adjacent to Broadway. Meanwhile, he exploited the growing value of his Nassau Street office building. In December 1865 the Common Council formed a new lease for ten years at an annual fee of $18,000.[22]

Immediately, critics castigated the contract as a swindle, and based their accusations on the suspicious circumstances surrounding how aldermen and lame duck Mayor Gunther had approved the transaction. According to them, Wood bribed aldermen $21,000, and they buried the lease in an omnibus bill for municipal improvements along Ann Street, contiguous to city hall, where the influential *Herald* was located. Gunther signed the bill, supposedly unaware of the contract. When newspapers brought the situation to his attention, Gunther expressed chagrin over the trickery, but explained that any delay would hinder Ann Street's much needed widening and repaving, thus possibly angering Bennett.[23]

Wood maintained the lease was reasonable since good office space was at a premium near city hall. He added in even more self-righteous terms that he was the one being swindled because the rent was too low considering the property was now worth $200,000. There matters rested. Corporation Attorney Richard O'Gorman, Wood's political enemy, refused to use his assigned office on the first floor, claiming it dirty and inadequate, but other city officials used theirs. Wood also found new tenants. A savings bank took the second floor, and sev-eral commercial concerns rented rooms in the basement and third floor. Yet the lease remained a festering problem, soon to develop into another one of the recurrent scandals that scarred Wood's reputation.[24]

It was Johnson, that stubborn, blunt man in the White House, who inadver-tently loosened the chains binding Wood. When the Thirty-ninth congress con-vened in December 1865, a furious battle polarized the nation over the control, meaning, and nature of restoration as opposed to reconstruction. By the sum-mer of 1866, a group of Johnson Democrats and Weed conservative Republi-cans organized a National Union party movement, with his tacit approval, as a vehicle for sustaining presidential policies, and set an August 14 convention date in Philadelphia.

Wood eyed this movement as a golden chance to reclaim his political impor-tance. Grasping Samuel Barlow's admission that Johnson needed all the help he could get, Wood wrote the president: "Myself and friends are desirous of upholding your administration." To make his case stronger, Wood became a delegate and warned Johnson that "you can rely on no support" from either the Regency or the swallow-tails because neither represented "the rank and file." Blair, busy laying the groundwork for the National Unionists, apparently was ready to welcome Wood. Blair told Tilden that right-thinking Americans must "sustain the President's policy leaving the question of names and party organisation to the people." The pro-Johnson *Herald* was even more helpful. "There are no more copperheads and no war men any more," it claimed. "Consequently at the next election new issues will be developed, and a new party must be formed to meet these issues."[25]

Two contrary forces, however, limited the surging National Unionists. Many Democrats steeped in traditional partisanship worried that it might swallow the Democracy; conservative Republicans feared any Peace Democratic involvement would strengthen the Radical charge that the entire movement was one of Northern traitors and ex-Confederates. National chairman Belmont solved one problem by treating the movement as a temporary Democratic expedient. The old Peace Democrats were more troublesome. Tammanyites, the Regency, swallow-tails, and conservative Republicans made it clear that it was "impertinent and indecent" for "such men [as] Fernando Wood" to "present themselves as delegates." Wood did not back down. He told Johnson, "Myself and others have been elected by the *people* [as] delegates to this convention & we do not intend to be excluded."[26]

As the time for the convention neared, the volume of criticism against Wood and others of his ilk made its organizers uneasy. They felt the issues involved in admitting the old Peace Democrats distracted attention from the main priority, backing the president, and validated Radical charges that Johnson's "minions" were "all sliced from the same Copperhead carcass." The situation was so threatening that Barlow complained to Blair that if men such as Wood had any role, "the usefulness of the Convention will in a great degree be destroyed."[27]

Wood accepted the inevitable with "grace." He wrote a widely reprinted letter to Senator James R. Doolittle, a Johnson stalwart and one of the movement's chief sponsors, withdrawing voluntarily, and he took the high ground that he did not wish to disrupt the meeting's "most salutary character." Blaming Radicals for deliberately misrepresenting him to harm National Unionism's "high patriotic object," Wood made no apologies. "I have nothing to regret nor take back as to my course during the war." Neither did he "admit the right of any one to raise that question in the convention."[28]

All the same, Wood partially achieved his objectives. It was no surprise that Greeley berated his move as a "transparent hypocrisy." What counted was that the *Buffalo Daily Courier* lauded Wood's "personal sacrifice for the good of the country," and Marble praised his "judicious" sense.[29] Yet when everything was written, Wood stayed a prisoner of the Civil War. But he had an advantage that no one, including himself, understood. The National Unionists, in treating him as a political outcast, unintentionally revived his career.

In the weeks that followed, the movement did not survive its hybrid character. Weed Republicans were particularly outraged when Tammany manipulated National Unionism to secure Hoffman's gubernatorial nomination. Under intense Radical pressure, they gradually left in disgust, turning the fall contest into a furious outburst of customary partisanship. When National Unionism dissolved, Tammany needed other allies to elect Hoffman. Wood was willing—for a price. He had something valuable the Hall needed, the reawakened support of the city's Irish community.

The situation had its roots during the Civil War when an Irish-American paramilitary group, the Fenian Brotherhood, working with groups in Ireland, had organized in New York City. Devoted to liberating their homeland from British control, they split into moderate and activist factions over a planned raid to capture Canada as ransom for freedom. Over a period of months, activists stockpiled ammunitions and arms. On February 7, 1866, the police, acting on tips from informers, seized their cache and jailed a few Fenian spokesmen.[30]

The arrests drew the two wings together for a protest meeting in Cooper Union five days later. Wood sought and received permission to speak. In this tense atmosphere, he extolled Fenian goals and scorned the British as "religious bigots" who were "bent on the extermination or the conversion of the Irish people." When someone in the crowd shouted "what shall we do?" Wood fired back, "Fight!" You "dare not retreat," he said. Fight "for your homes and your firesides; for your altars and your God; for your kindred and native soil!"[31]

Tammanyites were far less aggressive, and, to the Fenians, far more disappointing. They counselled restraint about violating neutrality laws, and suggested the Irish work through Johnson and Seward for "what is right and best." The Fenians felt betrayed. In contrast to Wood's forthright support, Tammany's sympathy seemed contrived. The Fenians soon had another grievance. In March, the Metropolitans arrested two of their commanders for misusing funds. Although the *New York Leader* paid proper obeisance to Irish independence, it scoffed at their gullibility and mocked Fenian leaders "for deceiving their generous and confiding countrymen."[32]

The situation took a new turn on June 1. More than one thousand Fenians invaded Canada, and were crushed. Johnson acted vigorously, much to their dismay. He issued a cease and desist order with Seward's approval, had fleeing offenders arrested, and sent a military force along the border to prevent further incursions. Most Democrats were no less cool. Forced by their need to defend Johnson, party newspapers almost universally echoed Marble's harsh judgment that the invasion was a "desperate and brainless venture." Conservative Republicans, out of the same impulse, upbraided the Fenians as "cut throats, robbers and murderers." Only the *Daily News* held out a helping hand. "Impelled by the noblest motive—love of country," Fenians had "invaded the territory of their enemy."[33]

As far as the Irish were concerned, everyone connected to the National Union party—Johnson, Seward, Tammanyites, swallow-tails, the Regency, conservative Republicans—exhibited the worst sort of "nativism and know-nothingism." The *New York Irish-American,* totally "sick of the whole tribe of politicians" who spent endless days squabbling over meaningless "public plunder," called on readers henceforth to take up only "honest men, and leave the old hacks to gorge on what they have already acquired." One man escaped Irish contempt, Fernando Wood. To them, his exclusion from the National Union convention was a badge of honor because he lacked any connection to Johnson.[34]

The specter of losing the Irish vote forced Democratic National Unionists to reassess their initial response. They now urged the president to placate Fenians by at least returning their weapons and dropping federal indictments. Johnson did offer some face-saving moves, but the implacable Irish were not swayed. Relations worsened when Tammany did not endorse Charles G. Halpine, a popular Irish newspaperman, for city register, a position worth more than $40,000 from fees collected.[35]

Tammany now realized that time had run out. Of all the men available in the Democracy, only Fernando Wood had the clout to bring the Irish back into the fold, no matter his war record. His days of his exile neared an end, then, but his aid came high. He wanted Tammany's endorsement for the Ninth Congressional District. The Hall kept its end of the bargain. It discouraged Anson Herrick from running and strung along others until too late. When the charade ended, Wood was the sole Democratic nominee. Opposing him was incumbent Republican William Darling.[36]

The district perfectly reflected Wood's normal class, ethnic, and religious base. Consisting of the Twelfth, Nineteenth, and Twenty-second wards, it was a Democratic stronghold. McClellan had carried it for president with 62.2 percent; Hoffman for mayor by 63.2 percent. The area, largely Roman Catholic, contained 20,561 legal voters. The Irish were the largest block at 22.1 percent, closely followed by 21.4 percent Germans. Naturalized citizens made up 54.2 percent, and a large group of potential future voters rested in the district's 20,133 aliens. Blacks formed 1.6 percent. The Ninth was home to a few of the nation's major sugar refiners, and also contained 244 factories, mostly small-scale. Total capitalization of these ventures was $3,670,180. They produced $10,969,065 worth of goods, and employed 6,479 men and 1,489 women. As the Ninth District grew and expanded, its characteristics did not basically change. In the future, Wood held it "in sort of a political mortgage" as a safe district for the remainder of his career.[37]

Wood honored his arrangement, and campaigned arduously for Hoffman. Instructing voters "to avoid anything that might lead to a division of the conservative party at the ensuring election," he urged Mozart, the Germans, and above all, the Irish, to marshal into "one grand and invincible front to the enemy." As for issues, Wood mentioned presidential restoration and congressional fiscal restraint in passing, but fired political racism into a blaze. White labor, he said, strained and sweated earning equality, but Radicals promised "lazy," unfit blacks immediate suffrage, high pay, and "social superiority."[38]

Republicans ran Wood against himself. After reviewing his war record, they contemptuously dismissed him as "a rebel sympathizer and disunionist." Greeley, showing his own brand of intolerance, showered the Fenians with disdain, and wondered why "Copperheads are giving themselves such needless trouble about the Irish vote." In the Ninth District, "the Darling Boys in Blue" wrapped themselves in the American flag and shouted, "we vote as we fought."[39]

By November, National Unionism proved a fiasco. Across the North, voters rejected Johnson's policies and anyone connected to them. Republicans won 42 out of 53 Senate seats, and had an impregnable 143 to 49 majority in the House. Locally, Tammany had little to crow about. It carried the city for Hoffman by more than 50,000, but he ran poorly upstate and could not unseat incumbent Governor Reuben E. Fenton. Republicans retained the legislature, and Halpine gained the coveted register's slot. None of these seemed to bother Wood. He won with 54.2 percent of the total votes cast.[40]

Wood had few moments to savor victory. During the last days of the Thirty-ninth Congress, conservative Republicans compromised with Radicals. By March 3, 1867, they had adopted a package of Reconstruction bills over Johnson's futile vetoes. Since they could not cram their entire program into this session, Republicans scheduled the new Fortieth Congress virtually as the old one ended.

From the outset, Wood had detested congressional Reconstruction as an attack on states' rights and initially assured the president that the "friends of Constitutional liberty" backed him. In return, he and other local Democrats expected Johnson's Custom House patronage. Collector Henry Smythe, however, dispensed spoils more for the sake of business efficiency than politics and disenchanted every hungry Democrat. The Democracy's letdown over spoils was symptomatic of a deeper malaise. For the present, the party encouraged Johnson's defiance of Congress because it did not have any other course. But with the collapse of the National Union movement fresh in mind, Democrats realized increasingly that their identification with Johnson was a distinct liability.[41]

Before Wood left for Washington, his lease with the city flared into tumultu-ous combat which incorporated legal and political chicanery. Nothing had hap-pened until October 1866 when O'Gorman convinced Comptroller Matthew Brennan not to pay Wood any rental fees. Wood filed for a writ of mandamus before his ally, Supreme Court Judge William Leonard, demanding his money. O'Gorman, whose term was expiring, interceded before his replacement, Richard B. Connolly, a former Mozarter and Wood's friend, took office. He hired an attorney, Isaiah A. Williams, and convinced Christopher Pullman, a recently defeated councilman, to file an injunction that alleged the lease was invalid because Wood had obtained it through fraud. O'Gorman then waived a trial, per-suaded that no jury would convict Wood, and submitted the matter to a different Supreme Court judge, George Barnard. Barnard, still on the outs with Wood, was eager to rule against him. He not only found a witness, a so-called Mr. X who was willing to testify that Wood had indeed bribed the aldermen, but substantially ver-ified Mr. X's allegations in a private conversation with Williams.[42]

On February 28, 1867, Judge Leonard ruled in Wood's favor. Basing his deci-sion strictly on the case's merits, he found that the city's use of the building had implied acceptance of the total lease. O'Gorman and Pullman had anticipated the outcome since Leonard was Wood's man, but they felt Barnard's dislike of Wood, coupled with Mr. X, would break the lease and prove Wood's guilt. They underestimated him. Sometime in April, Wood approached Barnard, and they reached an understanding that Wood would support his candidacy for a higher judicial office.[43]

In May, Barnard denied the injunction and issued a peremptory mandamus for Brennan to pay Wood. To appease the public, Barnard granted "that the price was too high and the lease too long." Yet he suppressed any hint of bribery by denying Pullman a chance to present Mr. X's evidence on the grounds that Pullman was no longer a party in the case "because he ceased to be a public officer." O'Gorman and Williams did not let the matter die. They turned to a third Supreme Court judge, Joseph Sutherland, for a stay of Barnard's order, and filed another case on the bribery charge. It went on the next term's Supreme court docket.[44]

At this juncture, everyone connected to these complicated proceedings was soiled. O'Gorman, Williams, Pullman, and Brennan were motivated more by hatred of Wood than an outraged sense of ethics. Judges Leonard and Barnard, along with Connolly, were tainted by friendship of alliances of convenience with Wood. Foremost among these miscreants, as far as his foes and thoughtful citi-zens were concerned, was Fernando Wood. Perhaps without calibrating the lease's sensitive political impact, Wood did not understand how even uncorro-borated testimony made it appear that he had raided the city treasury in "a sharp, and probably a corrupt, bargain," reminiscent of his earlier sordid pursuits of wealth.[45]

Undaunted, Wood went to Washington. Absorbed with proving that his exile was over, he concentrated on reestablishing his credentials as a party leader and prepared to carry on an energetic campaign against Republicans. Little came easily. The first session of the Fortieth Congress met in three brief bursts during March, July, and less than a month between November and December. Republicans carried on where they left off, fine-tuning Reconstruction and assuring the supremacy of the legislative branch. Outnumbered by three to one, Democrats were powerless. The result left Wood in a familiar position, an obstructionist fighting a losing cause.

As Republicans fleshed out the next stage of Reconstruction, Wood voted 100 percent on twenty-one roll calls against them. He opposed the Supplemental Reconstruction Bill, efforts to impeach Johnson, resolutions of thanks to Generals Philip H. Sheridan and Daniel Sickles for their supervision of the Southern states, federal aid for Southern black education, bounty equalization for all former soldiers, including blacks, granting arms to the Republican Tennessee militia, and confiscation of prewar Southern railroads.[46]

In the interim, other New Yorkers, spurred by Marble and Warren, were shocked into a realization that Democratic intransigence might trigger more drastic measures. Reconsidering their position, they counseled white Southerners to accommodate themselves to congressional Reconstruction as the price for rejoining the Union and reestablishing home rule. As for blacks, they expected whites to control them by habit and circumstance. Many former Peace Democrats were unwilling to go that far. They urged whites to stand fast, preferring indefinite Reconstruction rather than surrendering their principles and racism. These differences graphically proved once more that the Democracy was torn by war memories and conflicting advice, and divided over future action.[47]

Wood agreed unexpectedly with the accommodationists. Speaking on March 7, 1867, against Radical Republican James M. Ashley's premature impeachment resolution, Wood made it clear that in defending Johnson he no longer considered the president a Democrat. The agitation over removing him was counterproductive, Wood deduced, because it prevented all Americans from using the time they needed "to look after their individual interests and pursuits." He pleaded with the "House to give the country rest," and asked for a shift in congressional action toward "the real wants of this country," the development of "our mineral, our agricultural, our manufacturing resources." For similar reasons, Wood did not defend Collector Smythe when Republicans formed a special committee to investigate alleged Custom House frauds. Smythe, Wood said, was the president's responsibility; Democrats would defend neither. Wood made the point stronger over the Supplemental Reconstruction Bill. He accepted Reconstruction rather than restoration as a fixed fact, and implored Republicans to settle the issue once and forever. Democrats "want these States back into the Union, even under the conditions which Congress is disposed to impose upon them. Let them know the worst, so that at no distant day we may have the Southern States represented in the Congress of the United States."[48]

None of these sentiments meant that Wood had deserted the white South. During the July session, he was unyielding about Republican efforts to reopen the volatile issue of Confederate treatment of war prisoners, opposed a new investigation of Lincoln's assassination, and rejected a special $1-million appropriation for the Freedmen's Bureau to aid destitute Southern blacks. In each instance, Wood exploited racism and class differences to revive the Democracy's old axis among Northern white workers and the white South. The debate dealing with the relief bill was a case in point. He maintained that whites labored under the same disabilities as blacks. Even admitting that many Southern blacks were impoverished, the solution lay in recreating prewar Northern capital investment patterns, not the Freedmen's Bureau's misplaced charity.[49]

Reconstruction and racism aside, it was essential to Wood's image that the party perceive him as a traditional Democrat. With that in mind, he used Locofocoism to support a bill for government workers mandating an eight-hour day. Nor did he forget the Irish. He authored a resolution praising the Fenians and extending the House's "sympathy to the people of Ireland in their pending struggle for constitutional liberty." Republicans scoffed that the Fenians were doubly unfortunate, pursued by British troops on one side of the Atlantic and Wood, the "model demagogue," on the other. Wood was not dissuaded. After the March break, he traveled to Europe to see one of his sons in a Switzerland school, and stopped in Ireland as sort of a one-man congressional fact-finding committee. Returning home as a self-styled expert, he reported to Congress that the Fenians were indeed patriots, comparable to the Founding Fathers. Any criticism of Fenians was pro-British, promonarchical, and un-American.[50]

The summer of 1867 was a transitional period for Wood and all Democrats. Accommodation collapsed; white Southerners boycotted state elections with Johnson's encouragement; and Southern Republicans and blacks dominated the new reconstructed state governments. New York Democrats did not blame the white South. Rather, they shifted rapidly toward the right, and adopted outright political racism. To symbolize their commitment, the party raised harsh racial objections against Greeley's attempt in July at the state constitutional convention to end the $250 property qualification for black male voters.[51]

Democrats had other grievances on their docket. Beginning in 1865, state Republicans had taken on a new function once the Thirteenth Amendment outmoded their basic organizational glue, the containment of slavery. Under Governor Fenton, they had formed wide-ranging, centralized legislative reforms aimed generally toward New York City. These included a new metropolitan health board, a revised temperance law, the formation of a professional fire department, and a special board to audit city expenditures. Central to each law were state commissions based on the 1857 police model, not home rule. In many ways, these reforms were remarkably progressive in improving the quality of city life. Even so, their politicized nature destroyed whatever value they accomplished because Fenton stacked the commissions with partisan appointees.[52]

Wood emerged as the embattled prophet redeemed in this collision of politics and reform. When he first spoke out as mayor against state centralism twelve years earlier, many New Yorkers dismissed his complaints as those of a would-be dictator. Now, his strictures seemed those of a prescient municipal statesman, especially among Democrats who valued local autonomy, whether it applied to the white South or New York City. The *Herald*, after an analysis of local politics, weighed his rebounding popularity, a popularity so strong that he seemed the Democracy's logical next mayor. Voters agitated by temperance, repelled by centralism, and attracted by political racism, were eager to enlist "beneath the standard of the man who has always stood as their friend and has been recognized as their champion." This "magnificent rascal" was already testing political opinion, it noted, largely by reviving the coalition of Irish and German voters that had first elected him.[53]

A seemingly minor incident in late August proved the paper correct. In order to rid the city of "the nuisance and injury occasioned by slaughter-houses" located near population centers, the new board of health issued regulations for their relocation above Forty-second Street. Wood led the protests. "On the invitation of German butchers and drovers," he defended labor's "trade rights," castigated the board's entire philosophy in slighting home rule, and shrewdly tied German dislike of temperance to the entire question of state control. "I am more and more surprised," he said, "that a people so courageous and respected, so sensitive of their rights, as the citizens of New-York, and so zealous of their power should bow in tame submission to this tyranny of Albany, done by commissions." With "vehement applause" ringing in his ears, no doubt existed that he was in the race for mayor.[54]

As Wood anticipated, Democrats stitched their fall campaign standards with political racism and antitemperance. Tammany refused, however, to give Wood any credit for imminent victories. It dominated the state convention and insulted Wood by convincing delegates to give Mozart only honorary seats. Back in the city, Wood appealed directly to the electorate. Voters, he forecast, "will forgive anything in a public officer, except cowardice." Despite Mozart's poor performance since the draft riot, Wood began preparations for a formal convention. When it met, he used his own brand of gall to instruct delegates to name only men of "character and ability," especially for the court. "Judges were often called upon to decide on political questions, and he was sorry to say a majority of them decided according to their political bias." Yet, Wood still harbored hope that

Tammany would endorse his nomination. For November races, Mozart embraced Tammany's choices, including Albert Cardozo for the Supreme Court, and only made three substitutions, all Irish. At the same time, Wood continued wooing Germans. After Mozart's meeting, he invited the delegates to retire to another "room to hear the music of the champagne corks...prepared for you."[55]

New Yorkers clearly understood that Wood's mobilization of Mozart was secondary to his mayoral campaign. While lecturing Democrats in November "to put bad men out of office and put good men in," most of them realized that he had himself in mind. To make the meaning even more obvious, Wood told a Mozart rally that his main aim was to "be foremost in the work of reconstructing New York" and to redeem it "from the Black Republican discipline."[56]

During the fall, a vicious current of political racism swept the North. In New York, it combined with antitemperance to give Republicans their worst dunking since 1856. The same story held true in the city, with one manifest difference. Tammany won hands down, but Mozart, still a one-man outfit, did not elect a single man.[57]

Wood did not ponder Mozart's sorry showing because in his own mind he had two other key assets: the magic of his name and the willingness to spend freely from his deep pockets. Bursting with confidence, he accepted Mozart's unanimous nomination for his climactic bid for mayor. The three-man field was set when Tammany renominated Hoffman and Republicans selected Darling.[58]

At first, Wood structured his campaign along the lines of political racism, antitemperance, and home rule. Since both Hoffman and Darling opposed black rights and prohibition, however, Wood had to refashion his candidacy around what was left and ran strictly as the paragon of home rule. As for his opponents, Wood dismissed Darling as a waste of time and foolishly considered Hoffman less formidable than he appeared. According to Wood's reasoning, Hoffman was a Tammanyite, and he baited him with the same fervor he used to organize Mozart Hall ten years before.

Politically and psychologically, Wood identified Hoffman as the incarnation of an organization "conceived in fraud and brought forth in corruption." Using charges that his opponents had ironically first raised against him, Wood said that under Hoffman municipal taxes had increased and city services had declined. Even worse according to Wood, Hoffman had connived with corruptionists as a respectable front, a man who saved nickels and dimes but allowed associates to steal millions. By contrast, Wood asserted that "even my enemies cannot but own that I always respected the dignity and character of the office, and left the ermine unsullied." Once safely elected, he swore to restore "the right of self-government" to the people by eliminating the commission system and appointing only honest men to office. Wood put his money on the line to further counterpoint his integrity with Hoffman's "false pretensions." He pledged to reduce expenditures by "20% in each year of my term, provided the necessary power be given to me," and guaranteed a forfeiture of $2 million of his own real estate if he failed.[59]

Oratory was satisfying, but a win involved building coalitions. Wood courted the swallow-tails in the hope that their aversion to Tammany included Hoffman. "Without asking the support of your paper, I have a right to ask that there shall be no assaults," Wood wrote Marble. To "mechanics, laborers and the poor man," Wood reminded them that as their champion "I am the only man living who has been reelected" as mayor in the past twenty-five years. He ended on a theme of much to come. "I am closing my public career. I am yet to erect the monument to which my children may point with pride. This will be the reformation of existing abuses in this City."[60]

Tammany built a different monument for Wood, one constructed of every notorious episode in his past, as distinct from Hoffman, a man "without a blemish in private life, as he is without stain or reproach in his long and trying official career." Marble joined the cry, much to Wood's dismay. Hoffman's reelection, the *New York World* wrote, was vital to protect home rule. Hoffman was just as forceful as Marble on his own behalf. Mouthing words once Wood's, Hoffman explained away his spending record by pointing out that under the charter he had no responsibility for the city's fiscal policies. As for Wood's real estate holdings, Hoffman wondered how any honest public servant could have amassed such a fortune. In Wood, Hoffman concluded, voters saw someone with a public record "without virtue" who deserved a political death "without repentance."[61]

When the campaign deteriorated into name-calling, Wood unexpectedly lost his ethnic constituency. Part of the reason lay in heavy-handed Republican chicanery. They paid lip-service to Darling, knowing he had no chance to win, and secretly sought Wood's election, the *Leader* explained, "to throw a disorganizing element into the next State and national" contests. While Tammany's accusation might have been considered as so much electoral pap, it did not stretch credulity given Greeley's editorials. He wrote that while "Hoffman may be relied upon as the tool of the Ring," Wood "may enact the role again of a first-class Reform Mayor."[62]

This quasi-endorsement was a kiss of death for Wood among the Irish, who never forgot Greeley's nativism. More than that, many of them still feared the lingering memories of the draft riot and were content to see Wood stay in Congress as their stalwart. Then, too, Fenianism was sharp-edged since not all the Irish agreed with its tactics. The *Irish-American*, then, told voters to exercise their franchise strictly according to "individual preferences." Wood lost the German vote in a somewhat similar fashion. Tammany encouraged the mistaken notion that Hoffman was of German descent and kept his Dutch origins quiet. These efforts paid off. The German Democratic Union General Committee, a lobby within the Democracy, endorsed Hoffman.[63]

And, yet, Wood's candidacy was doomed from the start. He ran against a popular incumbent who had done nothing wrong. In fact, Hoffman was Wood's carbon copy without his flawed history on issues that stirred the passions of New York Democrats. Making matters worse, Mozart could not match Tammany's ability to marshal voters, nor its frenetic naturalization mills. As the crowning irony, Tweed's Tammany Hall was just nearing maturity as a machine, aping techniques that Wood had outlined.

Nothing that Wood said or did, then, made any difference. He went down to a humbling defeat. Hoffman carried every ward on the way to a 40,069 majority over Wood, a landslide 60.3 percent of the total. Wood's old coalition now belonged to Hoffman, particularly in East Side wards. Wood gained only 22.8 percent and 21.5 percent respectively in the Irish Fourth and Sixth wards. Within the four German wards, Wood averaged just 17.4 percent. All told, Wood managed only 21.9 percent of the total. Mozart was just as ineffective, winning one of twenty-six offices. Summarizing these results, the exultant *Leader* wrote: "The people are now applauding the exit of Wood, and as a sequel it is announced that he has indefinitely postponed the erection of his monument. Exit Wood!"[64]

Like the proverbial cat, Wood had more than one political life. As Marble grudgingly admitted, he was "a man of great talent and still greater energy."[65] The mortifying mayoral race, however, ended that phase of his career, the attempt to master New York City, and ushered in another. It was hard to imagine local politics without him, but Wood hereafter termed himself strictly a national politician and played no part in future local politics. Rather, he consciously used his considerable abilities to become a truly influential congressman with real national stature.

His departure from the eye of city political storms left many people confused, and they always expected his reincarnation. Indirect evidence suggests that he never considered that option because he and Tammany struck a lasting accommodation. While no records exist of what occurred between them, Wood seemed to accept Tweed's will, and Tammany in return faithfully supported him for Congress for as long as he lived.

On August 3, 1868, Wood signalled the end of one era and the beginning of a second when he officially resigned from Mozart Hall. In an emotional letter to General Committee Chairman William P. Lee, he wrote, "I have for some time contemplated this withdrawal, feeling that personal as well as public considerations render it necessary." By his taking this course, he cautioned, "do not misunderstand me. I do not withdraw from the support of the Democratic party and its candidates." Nonetheless, "I have done with agitation and local contest. My battle against the ruling organization [Tammany] has been fought out to its finality. These are times when we want unity and concert of action."[66] At last, the one-man ruler no longer wanted to be the Democratic party; he was now of the Democratic party.

ELEVEN

The Politics of Frustration

Congressional Democrats, aglow with spectacular wins in the 1867 elections, chafed impatiently awaiting the next presidential election, confident that political racism had ignited a political revolution. What made the situation more intolerable was their inability to thwart Republicans from putting the finishing touches on Reconstruction.[1]

Wood was just as frustrated, and his patience finally snapped. On January 15, 1868, during debate over increasing discretionary powers of the "army of occupation," he lashed out that it was "a bill without a name, a child without a name and probably without a father, a monstrosity, a measure the most infamous of the many infamous acts of this infamous Congress." Before he finished, Speaker Colfax ruled him out of order for violating procedures under the Sixty-second Rule in expressing contempt for the House. Taking the cue, Republicans John A. Bingham of Ohio and Henry Dawes urged Wood's censure unless he apologized. "Mr. Speaker," Wood answered, "I have no explanation to make." Immediately, Republicans moved the censure by a strict party vote, 114 to 39.[2]

Far from harming Wood, the reprimand became a badge of honor among Democrats, a mark of stature as a Democratic congressman of the first rank. Despite the criticism heaped upon him, his outburst was a symptom of how little actual power the party had in Congress. Even the normally hostile *New York World*, while it admitted Wood's language was impolitic, praised his sentiments as true and just.[3]

All the same, Wood lusted for revenge and found a scapegoat in General Oliver O. Howard, head of the Freedmen's Bureau. White Southerners and Northern Democrats despised the bureau as a symbol of federal interference in state sovereignty leading toward black equality. Their fury peaked when Congress expanded the bureau's mandate and empowered it to run military tribunals until states were reconstructed. In March, Wood led party efforts to destroy not only the bureau, but Howard as well.

As Congress began considering a new bill extending the bureau's life, Wood attacked the agency on principles, racism, and class. He flatly denied that the agency was constitutional under the general welfare clause and termed it a costly and unwise social failure that Republicans used to place their "own emissaries and agents in political positions." Overall, it injured freedmen because "it encouraged idleness by affording pecuniary support without labor." Congress had continually supported Southern blacks but ignored the plight of "white workingmen of the North." The reason lay with Howard, according to Wood. Giving credence to rumors that Howard favored "racial amalgamation" and pocketed bureau monies in a secret account, Wood questioned how he had suddenly become "a man of large wealth."[4]

Again the House erupted into disorder. Democrats milled around trying to shake Wood's hand, but Radical Thomas D. Eliot, who had chaired the original committee creating the bureau, gained the floor, crying that Wood had shamed himself by "a slander born of private ill-will and personal unkindness." Where is your proof, Eliot demanded, that Howard favored miscegenation? When Wood lamely replied that he had none at present, the House erupted into raucous laughter. Eliot was not finished mortifying Wood. Howard, he said, had "lost an arm in the service of his country," but "his heart is right." Looking squarely at Wood, Eliot sneered "there are some who have both arms whose hearts are not right." Now Wood became angry. "If the general will give me a committee of investigation," he shot back, "I will prove the charges." The bill's passage settled little; Wood could not let the question die. To all his scores against the bureau, he added another, a personal vendetta against Howard.[5]

Much of Wood's snappish mood reflected how the Republican majority trapped Democrats into defending the unpopular Johnson and prevented them from moving on to more positive issues. The Republican attempt to impeach him illustrated the dilemma. Wood did vote a straight party line on sixteen motions against impeachment, but defended the office, not the man. As Wood saw the situation, the main evil in Johnson's trial and possible removal lay in harming the economy. "The people, taught by the example of Congress, will learn to disrespect and disregard the authority of official power, so necessary for the protection of life, liberty and property."[6]

Wood's connection of impeachment to economic developments was calculated. With Reconstruction basically over, he thought that it was time to move on to issues more germane to the future which could regenerate the Democracy as the nation's majority party. During the discussions over the Freedmen's Bureau, he mentioned in an offhand moment, "I learnt my politics a quarter of a century ago, in the Congress of the United States." Because of that, "I [cannot] unlearn the convictions of my youthful manhood." Transposed into the late 1860s, his was the distinctive creed of a modernized Locofoco, he said. Then he gave the

House his version of how the Constitution set his ideologic roots and molded his understanding of current events. Ours is a government of delegated powers, he explained. That principle "controlled my conduct as a member of Congress" and should have guided the nation during the past nine years. Republicans, however, exploited the war and its consequences to expand federal power in ways the Founding Fathers never intended. Now, in a time of peace, the "decentralization of official rule is indispensable to the preservation of popular rights." In particular, Congress must restore the organic law in regard to the operation of the economy. Quite simply, he said, "Government should not intrude its authority over the contest of private or State corporations."[7]

In combining traditional Democratic principles with a defense of individual initiative through the free enterprise system, Wood chartered his future course around the principles of his Locofoco apprenticeship in political economy: ending excessive taxes; cutting the scope of government; opening free trade; restricting the tariff to revenue purposes; restoring a hard-money currency; withdrawing irredeemable greenback paper currency from circulation; and paying the national debt in gold. As a prototype Bourbon Democrat, Wood became the spokesman for conservative businessmen in his party, and he sought to redefine the Democracy along those lines to erase both his Peace Democratic stigma and vault into congressional prominence.

At heart, Wood was a deflationist and a fiscal conservative, a classic nineteenth-century liberal in the sense that he attempted to prevent any government programs which interfered with the marketplace and any laws which artificially hindered its natural operations. Wood further believed that updating the old polarization between Whigs and Democrats over economic issues would realign the two-party system along the lines of partisan politics that had existed in the 1830s. He ended his own frustration, then, by shifting almost exclusively toward economic questions. In the process, Wood dealt with a significant range of issues which became major public concerns once Reconstruction ran its course, and, after 1873, critical to a depressed national economy.

At first, few Democrats quibbled with Wood's cost-cutting efforts. Working within a broad party consensus, he sought to reduce the military's size, sell unneeded ironclads, decrease or even eliminate the practice of awarding land grants to railroads, and strike some equity in the tariff schedule by exempting domestic manufacturers from Internal Revenue levies which often made imported goods less costly.[8]

Such agreement vanished over the money question and the national debt. To the consternation of most deflationary eastern Democrats, many midwesterners, generally former Peace Democrats led by George Pendleton, were inflationists and formed the Ohio Plan, which proposed that the part of the public debt held by national banks, the principal of Civil War 5-20 bonds, be paid in greenbacks, not gold. The funds the government saved in using paper money and inflating the currency would then form a sinking fund, convertible to greenbacks, to pay the remainder. The Treasury Department worked in a contrary direction. In 1866, Republicans authorized Secretary Hugh McCulloch to convert short term notes into the 5-20s, payable in hard money, and contract greenbacks, thus simultaneously increasing the amount of bonds and reducing inflationary money.

Wood, fearful of splitting the Democracy, asked each party not to politicize "our public credit and currency," making them "questions to be thrust into the popular arena of party determination." His plea went unheeded. The situation was far different from the clear Democratic-Whig alignment of the 1830s. Now, the Democracy was fragmented along sectional and regional lines, the hard-money East versus the soft-money West and South. Those lines foreshadowed divisions lasting for the next decade. Wood was central to the problem because he was a deflationist. "Unlike the stimulant which an irredeemable paper currency affords," he said, specie is of "substantial and positive benefit." Redeeming the national debt in gold, however, was an orthodox Republican tenet. The result often found Wood in the uncomfortable position of supporting Republicans.[9]

Wood's problem came into focus over three monetary bills during the second session of the Fortieth Congress. He voted against the party's midwestern inflationist bloc and with Republicans to reject the use of greenbacks for indebtedness not specified in gold; the gradual withdrawal of interest-bearing bonds in favor of greenbacks; and greenback expansion for the purchase and cancellation of gold interest-bearing bonds. More convinced than ever that inflation harmed economic growth, Wood had begun to hammer out a comprehensive program that forged his new identity. During the next decade, all the lessons he had absorbed about finance, from personal experience and from practical municipal management, were to make him one of the few financial experts in Congress and a key player as Democrats tried resolving their economic ambiguities.[10]

Another important event in Wood's life was taking place back in New York over the resolved status of his lease. With the case before the court, he shuttled between Washington and the city during the spring and summer of 1868, largely at Shea's insistence that his daily presence was necessary for both political and legal reasons.

Both sides had previously presented their briefs to Judge Albert Cardozo. Richard O'Gorman and Isaiah Williams, acting in the "interest of the city," sought to hold Wood criminally accountable for bribery. Shea maintained that the lease was valid and the city was in arrears $27,000 in unpaid rent. Before hearing testimony, Judge Cardozo, who largely owed his position to Wood, ruled the plaintiffs must have ample evidence to prove bribery since they were dealing "with a person's reputation." The plaintiffs, realizing that Cardozo did not have clean hands, used Williams's feigned illness as an excuse to seek a continuance, hoping for a different judge the following term. Cardozo refused, and ruled that the bribery issue was moot because the city had not presented proof, only hearsay. Thus, Wood's judgment for back rent was the only issue. At that point, someone reached O'Gorman and evidently warned him that his political future was in jeopardy if he continued to make things miserable for Wood and Cardozo. O'Gorman then dismissed Williams, took charge of the case, and gave it away. Using a line of prosecution that he knew was without merit, he contended that Wood defrauded the city in rerenting the unused space to gain a double income. The sole question revolved around whether the city used some of its rental space, not all, and if O'Gorman had voluntarily not occupied it. On that, there was no question. Shea presented supporting witnesses who substantiated the fact.[11]

On August 2, Cardozo decided in Wood's favor. Mayor Gunther and the Common Council had accepted "the premises for the term and at the rent mentioned." Even if O'Gorman chose not to use them, the city was liable for the fee set, the full $180,000, and Wood was within his legal rights to rent the offices to others. Cardozo, however, stopped short of giving Wood everything he sought. To appease the public, he ordered the city to pay him the $27,000, but not the interest and court costs Wood wanted.[12]

When the case was over, the *New York Times* spoke for many enraged New Yorkers when it editorialized that the episode was "certainly one of the most flagrant and shameless breaches of trust, on the part of all the officials concerned, that we have ever seen." Yet the paper, for all its moral indignation, was perplexed. The public and other newspapers, it confessed, had scarcely thought the matter "worthy of a passing comment." Yet the paper's judgment was a commentary not only on Wood, but the entire era. True, his basic character flaw, his egotistical ethical myopia, was there for all to see. But in a larger sense, he mirrored the Gilded Age's ethical failures. Wood's real defect was not so much his imperfections, but his inability to rise above what was becoming a national commonplace.[13]

During the summer of 1868, the political pendulum swung against the Democracy. Republicans neutralized political racism by nominating Ulysses S. Grant on a platform which shunned black suffrage and emphasized national reconciliation. Democrats wounded themselves. They selected the chronically hesitant Horatio Seymour on a platform that promised to roll back Reconstruction. Just as damaging, they adopted the Ohio Plan and widened the party's regional economic divisions.[14]

Privately unhappy with both Seymour and the platform, Wood dutifully campaigned in Connecticut and Pennsylvania, appeared but did not speak at rallies in New York City, holidayed at Saratoga, and secured Tammany's renomination by acclamation. This election was dull and predetermined in sharp contrast to past ones. Republicans had selected a token candidate, Francis A. Thomas, and a few insurgent Democrats ran John Savage, Wood's old adversary from the General Committee wars of the 1850s.[15]

Tweed's stakes were much higher. Hoffman was again striving for governor, and the Hall touched off a massive naturalization spree on his behalf. With the connivance of Judges Cardozo, George Barnard, and John H. McCunn, Tammany reputedly registered sixty thousand new voters during October alone. Scandalized Republicans were shocked, but could not halt the process.[16]

When the returns were in, Grant won, but Seymour somewhat salvaged Democratic pride by garnering a respectable total. Locally, Hoffman eked out a narrow victory. In contrast, Wood cruised to an easy triumph, 57.6 percent to Thomas's 35.7 percent, and Savage's 6.7 percent. The elections changed little in congressional dynamics. Northern Republicans, along with their counterparts from the reconstructed states, still controlled the House, 170 to 73, guaranteeing continued Democratic frustration.[17]

When Wood had returned to Congress five years earlier, he and his wife made a determined, if premature, bid to crack Washington society. His seat now safe, they renewed their quest. On December 13, 1868, the Woods bought a spacious mansion, located on the corner of I and Fifteenth Streets for $40,000 in cash. The elongated lot ran 139 feet by 28 feet and included two outbuildings, one a stable large enough to house living quarters for a coachman and four carriages. The main building was three-floored; two parlors on the first, bedrooms on the second, and a ballroom on top. Nearby lived a galaxy of prominent politicos, men with whom Wood formed warm personal, nonpartisan friendships: James G. Blaine, the future Speaker; Senator William A. Buckingham of Connecticut; Maryland Representative Thomas Swan; Hamilton Fish, soon to be secretary of state; and Caleb Cushing.[18]

The Woods immediately turned their home into a social center for "notables of all parties and for those distinguished in various walks of life." At a typical grand reception, a reporter noted, "everything that taste and wealth could procure was lavishly used for the pleasure of the guests and the entertainment could not fail to be exceptionally brilliant." Alice Wood, cascaded with her trademark diamonds, "agreeably" greeted guests, sometimes accompanied by one of her stepdaughters, while her husband, "who reminds one of Henry Clay in courtly bearing and genial grace of manner," made sure everyone enjoyed his "fine" hospitality. Fernando Wood also gave intimate dinners for close friends; Alice Wood held Wednesday card receptions; and they opened their house to New Year's callers.[19]

Entertainment on such a scale was costly. In 1874, the *Times* estimated that congressmen who owned homes in the District spent "about $18,000 to $25,000 for expenses including receptions."[20] Wood was willing to lay out that and more. His wife, sister, daughters, and mother-in-law seemed to revel in society life; these functions, along with the brilliant guests they attracted, proba-bly satisfied his inner need for respect; above all, they served his political ends.

Wood's overwhelming ambition was to become House Speaker when the Democrats returned to power. The politically independent *New York Daily Graphic* speculated that he did have many qualifications for the post: a distin-guished "presence," an "urbane manner," a persuasive style of presenting ideas, and an "alert mind." Yet, his "misfortune" was that his "colleagues and the coun-try" regarded him as "unsafe" due to his well-documented misdeeds. One major reason, then, lay behind Wood's socializing: establishing warm personal rela-tions with members from both sides of the aisle moderated his image, and his well-publicized "self-possession and Clay-like carriage" conveyed the impres-sion that he was "every inch a [future] Speaker."[21]

Republicans started the third session of the Fortieth Congress on Decem-ber 7, 1868, in fine fettle. To ensure the stability of Congressional Reconstruc-tion, they validated the legitimacy of the Louisiana and Georgia electoral votes and continued to admit Southern Republicans. They also gratuitously insulted President Johnson by tabling his annual address before moving on to crown their efforts in the Fifteenth Amendment. Wood and the Democrats were still locked in futile opposition. They scorned the Louisiana and Georgia votes, opposed seating Southern Republican congressmen, backed the president as a final courtesy, and used a variety of devices against the Fifteenth Amendment.

Republicans then pinpointed Democratic ambiguities. First aiming at finance, they sponsored a resolution linking the Ohio Plan to repudiation of the national debt. Wood and the Democrats tried to stall a roll call through a variety of futile parliamentary tricks. On the final vote, however, Wood supported the resolution, including the stipulation that the government was obligated to pay "the public creditor" the full amount "contracted to pay him."[22]

That done, Republicans formed a special committee, headed by Ohioan William Lawrence, to investigate Tammany's alleged fraudulent naturalizations. The committee's Republican majority quickly revealed its ulterior goal. It expanded the question not only to discredit the Hall, but also to revise the entire naturalization and electoral process as a means of lessening the Democ-racy's voting base in the urban North.

Wood was in a no-win situation. Defending Tammany meant guilt by associ-ation; silence was indistinguishable from condoning its behavior. As his way out, he tried fruitlessly through a tabling resolution to prevent the Judiciary Commit-tee from inquiring as to "what amendments to the Naturalization Laws are needed to give greater security to elections." Although he appeared ready to champion the Hall in voting against authorizing the Lawrence Committee, he did not debate the question, and only spoke about protecting the civil rights of "recusant" witnesses. The committee, aided by John Davenport, a young, zealous Republican investigator, predictably issued a majority report that Tammany had illegally naturalized 63,343 new voters, making Hoffman's election suspect. The Democratic minority put the figure at less than sixteen hundred and suggested that whatever frauds existed were bipartisan. At that point, Wood voted for the minority report, but as "a national politician" said nothing in Tammany's support.[23]

Another issue, redistribution of national banknotes, proved more in line with Wood's long-term interests. Under the terms of the 1863 National Bank Act and its refinement in 1864, member banks could issue paper banknotes based on a complicated formula geared to specific amounts for individual banks proportional to their bond holdings and secured by a reserve in "lawful money." By 1869, a sectional lopsidedness developed that favored eastern banks in New England, New York, and Pennsylvania, which had a majority of national banks and printed the bulk of banknotes. As a corrective, the Senate passed bill S. 440 to withdraw $20 million in circulation from states surpassing their limits and redistributing the banknotes to others below quotas, mainly in the South and Midwest.[24]

On February 17, 1869, when S. 440 reached the House, Wood protected New York interests and solidified his fiscal reputation. The sheer fact that eastern banks dominated the system, he maintained, reflected the point that "trade regulates itself." Any inequality resulted from "superior energy, resources, ability [and] local advantages." A wiser course than artificial redistribution through federal interference rested in reestablishing "the constitutional currency of the country, gold and silver."[25]

Money-short midwestern Democrats and newly admitted Southern Democrats resented Wood's stand, and believed sectional economic chaos would result without redistribution. Hard on the heels of a bitter debate, they passed the Coburn Amendment to S. 440, which created a new formula keyed to real and personal property values, proportional to the number of congressmen.

Wood, showing unsuspected ability to work with eastern and midwestern Republicans, especially James A. Garfield of Ohio, chairman of the Committee on Banking and Currency, sparked efforts against revised S. 440. Wood introduced another amendment to defend easterners which stipulated that redemption could take place only in "the principal moneyed centers of the United States." When that did not pass, he moved to table S. 440, a motion that also failed. In the end, the House approved revised S. 440, with Wood voting nay. The most amazing part of its passage was the havoc it wreaked in the customary patterns that had typified Reconstruction. Democrats split 17 yea to 18 nay; Republicans 89 to 59. Equally shocking, both parties fractured along sectional lines. Just 7 out of 76 easterners backed it; 99 of 107 midwesterners and Southerners supported it.[26]

Revised S. 440 died in conference, but redistribution was hardly dead. As for Wood, the consequence of his parliamentary tactics and firm stance came in strong alliances with conservatives in both parties. Along with forging a firm relationship with hard-money Republicans, he repaired his long-strained relationship with Marble, and cemented ties with deflationists Samuel J. Randall of Pennsylvania and Michael C. Kerr of Indiana, both coming Democratic House power brokers.[27]

During these developments, Wood began to emerge as an important figure in the House in other ways. Speaker Colfax had named him to the Committee on Foreign Affairs during the Fortieth Congress, and Wood became its ranking Democrat through attrition and longevity. Then President Grant selected Hamilton Fish, Wood's longtime friend, as secretary of state. Fish was a godsend from Wood's point of view. With Fish in charge of the State Department, Wood settled down to the comfortable prospect of helping mold diplomatic policies, especially by cozying up to the Irish and expanding overseas trade to stimulate economic growth.[28]

As Wood passed his fifty-seventh birthday that February of 1869, Congress was moving away from its commitment to Reconstruction. Radicalism evaporated with Thaddeus Stevens's death. New conservative Republicans emerged, starting with Blaine's election as Speaker. Southerners, at first generally Republicans, were entering in larger numbers, and fresh Democrats appeared. Many men whose careers had spanned the past two decades were gone for a variety of reasons. The House was full of novices, so leadership rested on seniority and seasoning. Wood had both. With his "tall, commanding figure, and his heavy white moustache, which contrasts strikingly with his dark hair," an observer noted, people regarded him as "one of the most adroit and experienced politicians in the House."[29]

Nonetheless, Wood was uneasy because of the New York Democratic delegation's composition. Prior to 1869, he had only one serious competitor for its control in James Brooks, a popular, somewhat erratic, former newspaper editor. Samuel S. Cox was another story. After losing his Ohio seat in 1864, Cox had moved to New York City, built a base among swallow-tails, courted Tammany, and was elected from the Sixth District in 1868. In Cox, Wood faced a man who matched his financial experience, sought similar committee assignments, had the same speakership ambitions, wooed identical Southern whites, and was the swallow-tails' man in Washington. The net result was that Wood redoubled his resolve to become among the handful of House Democratic leaders able to shape policy and bargain with the White House.

To enhance his stature, Wood decided to go overseas as a one-man foreign affairs committee. He told friends that after seeing his children at school in France, he would stop in Ireland to check conditions, go to London to interview

members of the British government about the stalled *Alabama* claims, and end
in Madrid to assess Spain's intention about freeing Cuba. Family problems, however, delayed Wood. Henry Wood, a deputy income tax collector, faced a possible prison term for alleged defalcations, and internal revenue agents pressed
Ben Wood for $30,000 in back taxes on his lottery "policy shops."[30]

Immersed in private matters, Wood slighted congressional duties. His attendance during the waning days of the third session was sporadic, and he missed
56 percent of the role calls in the first session of the Forty-first Congress. While
present he voted to repeal the Tenure of Office Act, objected to seating additional Southern Republicans, and demanded the return of Southern home rule.
Even so, he missed the vital vote on the deflationary Public Credit Act, which
pledged payment in gold, both principle and interest, on the 5-20s, essentially
putting the government on record favoring the "sacredness" of the public debt
and a specie currency.[31]

The Woods left New York City on March 29, spent the entire summer in
Europe, and returned in mid-October. During Wood's absence, Tweed's efforts
to strengthen Hoffman's coming bid for the presidency had ignited Democratic
problems. In particular, Tweed alienated the swallow-tails by his failed attempt
to purge Belmont and Tilden from their respective chairmanships of the national
and state committees. Even Hoffman ran into trouble. After a promising reformist start, he disillusioned the public by signing several special interest bills at
Tweed's behest. Taking advantage of these miscues, a group of dissident Tammanyites, the "Young Democracy," began to challenge Tweed's control of the
Hall. Fortunately, Republicans unwittingly rescued Tweed. The Black Friday
gold corner speculation scandal, which had implicated Grant, increased Democratic chances to win the fall elections and momentarily ended the feuding.

Back in New York, Wood kept on good terms with each party faction. He cultivated swallow-tails by sharing information with Marble that he had gathered in
Europe. As for Young Democrats, Wood courted them through brother Ben, one
of their chief supporters. At the same time, Wood pleased Tweed by pleading for
party unity. Alluding to his trip overseas, Wood told a party rally that "the Irish
people from whom he had just come, anxiously desired to see the Democracy,
who were their only friends, restored to power in this country." With the Black
Friday fiasco fresh in mind, Wood further stressed that Democrats must emphasize Republican "collusion with the worst of Wall-street brokers" and Grant's personal connection to this "conspiracy."[32] Election results confirmed Wood's care.
Voters gave Democrats control of the legislature, giving Tweed the chance to
pass a new city charter and propelling Hoffman toward the White House.

Wood hurried back to the capital alone. These days were unkind to both
Woods. Alice Wood, fatigued by travel, emotionally distraught by conflicts
between her husband and her mother over Drake Mills's estate, and physically

weakened by four pregnancies in six years, evidently suffered the first of several emotional breakdowns. Fernando Wood's health was hardly better. Periodic bouts of rheumatism and bronchitis debilitated his energy, causing friends to urge a vacation before beginning an arduous second session in December.[33]

Rest for Wood was impossible. Cox was too serious a challenger. Since so much rode on the outcome of this intense, if outwardly friendly, rivalry, Wood made two critical decisions. First, he kept close tabs on constituents, introduced bills and resolutions they sought, and dispatched a variety of publications to local leaders educating them about his role in Congress. He even took care while fawning on Hoffman to hint that Democrats must "use their power with caution" in remedying Republican wrongs. Second, he increased efforts to make himself indispensable on issues important to both him and Cox, finance and the white South, while also working on issues on which Cox had little part, the Freedmen's Bureau and foreign relations. Here, Speaker Blaine's friendship proved invaluable. He kept Wood on Foreign Affairs and, as an added favor, put him on the Select Committee on Reconstruction.[34]

As the majority of the former Confederate states returned to the Union, Wood strove to neutralize the mistrust that many Southern Democrats held against their Northern colleagues for supporting the North during the war. His speeches and dilatory tactics contained the old combination of states' rights principles mixed with racism, positions which had long been basic to his political character. He questioned the credentials of Southern Republicans, battled against enforcing the Fourteenth and Fifteenth amendments, and demanded removing political disabilities imposed upon ex-rebels.[35]

Wood's attitude toward finance was less satisfactory to white Southern Democrats. In February 1870, the Senate passed S. 378, which combined $45-million currency expansion in national banknotes for areas that had less than their share, with another $20 million earmarked for redistribution. Garfield, bottling it in committee until June, sponsored a different bill that doubled the currency to $95 million, but retired temporary 3 percent certificates worth $45.5 million as mediums of exchange, and cut greenbacks by $39.5 million.[36]

Pragmatism and principle guided Wood. He did accept the idea of noninflationary currency expansion in theory, recognizing that certain states were economically stagnant because they lacked banknotes. Yet he dismissed redistribution under any guise and blamed Secretary of the Treasury George S. Boutwell for the sectional imbalance. The financial community so distrusted his "maladministration," Wood charged, "that it reflects upon the solvency and credit of the Government itself." When Garfield's bill reached the floor, Wood remarked that Garfield was only interested in strengthening national banks but said little more. On roll calls, he joined easterners in burdening it with so many amendments that Garfield gave up in disgust.[37]

In June, Garfield revived S. 378, and a variety of friendly amendments made it essentially similar to the original one, except the section retiring greenbacks. Again, Wood joined the familiar sectional coalition of easterners versus Southern and midwestern congressman. Nothing worked. The bill passed 98 to 80, and became law after a conference committee increased banknotes $54 million to appease inflationist greenbackers.

Both sides emerged from this bruising battle convinced the other had lost. Although soft-money men were disappointed that the law gave national banks little flexibility to issue new notes and increase credit, they believed that they had established a precedent for future inflation. Deflationists were equally jubilant. They were convinced they had defended national credit and thwarted the greenbackers' attempt to debase the money system, thus hindering economic growth.

For Wood the partisan, everything about the monetary question was treacherous. It disturbed the healing process between Southern and Northern Democrats, estranged midwestern Democrats, and had few possibilities of becoming a clear partisan issue. For those reasons, he had attempted and failed to make S. 378 a litmus test against the administration. When the smoke cleared, Wood made a practical choice. He opposed each bill, and upheld fiscal conservatism to protect the city's business community. Yet he maintained a semblance of party unity, saying little that might antagonize party inflationists, and eyed other financial issues where Democrats agreed.[38]

Refunding the national debt seemed such an issue. Republicans faced a difficult choice concerning the 5-20 bonds, which paid 6 percent interest and represented about three-quarters of the debt, theoretically payable in 1870 and redeemable by July 1, 1873. House and Senate Republicans agreed to consolidate the 5-20s into lower interest bonds of longer maturity, but disagreed over specifics. Senator John Sherman sponsored S. 380, which authorized the Treasury Department to sell three new classes of tax-exempt bonds in multiples of $50 or more, at various times and rates ranging from ten to forty years depending on the type, and required national banks to convert their older 5-20s into the fresh ones. House Republicans proposed H.R. 2176, a single issue of $1 billion redeemable in thirty years, without forced conversion.

While Republicans lined up in opposing camps, Wood's greatest fear was that Democrats did not appreciate the necessity of even paying the 5-20s. As an orthodox Jacksonian political economist, he scorned the national debt for soaking investment capital and preventing growth. Conservative fiscal practice, in his view, mandated prompt refunding and strict adherence to gold. He accepted the main Republican intent, honoring the debt as a sacred obligation, but opposed each bill because they made no pretense of reaching out to Democrats. What Wood pursued was largely symbolic: a show of Democratic fiscal responsibility to assure financiers that they could trust the party to shape a viable refunding package.

Yet, Wood faced massive intraparty opposition. Many Border State, midwestern, and Southern Democrats, often former Peace Democrats or Confederates, were repudiationists who contended that the bonds were unconstitutional consequences of wartime centralism. Others, generally from the South and Midwest, were also inflationists and argued that since many bondholders made purchases in depreciated greenbacks, the principal and interest must be repaid in paper. From the East, a few party ideologues feared the creation of a new monied aristocracy and maintained that paying in gold rewarded speculators with shameful profits on their original paper investments.[39]

On June 27, 1870, Republicans set a five-minute speech limit on H.R. 2167 over Wood's attempt for a longer period. Despite that, he made the most of his allotment. Speaking rapidly, he criticized the Republicans for patching together so important a bill while giving the House so little time for "full and sober deliberations." Any abnormal disturbance of "bonded indebtedness," the "basis of the capital of the country," would divert critical investment funds into the bond market and "derange" existing "mercantile and banking transactions." Doubting that Americans had disposable money in such huge amounts, he warned with a touch of nativism that Europeans would buy the majority, forcing the United States to send $40 million a year overseas in interest payments, thus bankrolling its main economic competitors. Worse, the long maturity was tantamount to a perpetual debt and unceasing taxation because the interest rate was unrealistic. Why not, as a better solution, "use excess revenue to liquidate to some extent the principal of our debt?"[40]

Republicans immediately attacked his assertion that the interest rate was absurd, and scoffed at his notion that only foreigners would benefit. In reply, Wood cited the fact that American banks currently lent money "at least from six to ten percent per annum." Under those conditions, the bill was actually a "foreign loan." Again returning to the idea of applying the surplus, which he estimated at $10 million, to debt reduction, he said that it was poor fiscal management to prevent the Treasury from redeeming even one dollar until the bonds "shall have run at least thirty years." As the defender of ordinary Americans, he ended, "I desire to prevent this indirect fleecing of the tax-payers of this country."[41]

Wood vainly introduced an amendment in the spirit of Locofocoism to prevent the Treasury from selecting private commission agents to market bonds. Other Democrats made similar ineffective moves. The bill passed, 128 to 43, and moved to the Senate. Conferees agreed on a shaky compromise based on S. 380. It again set up three classes of bonds: $1 billion at 4 percent redeemable after 30 years; $300 million at 4.5 percent, redeemable in 15; and $200 million at 5 percent, redeemable in 10. Each bond sold in denominations of $50 or multiples thereof, and were "redeemable in coin of the present value." The House rejected it with many Republicans shifting sides, 103 to 88, largely because of section 7, which forced new banks, many in the South and Midwest, to purchase the bonds at par in gold. A second conference dropped that provision and refunding passed, 139 to 54, along nearly straight party lines.[42]

The entire episode was another exercise in frustration for Wood. Except for the first conference report, refunding was a clear Republican triumph and placed another obstacle in his attempt to construct a Democratic conservative fiscal consensus. While Democrats did exhibit impressive unity on five key roll calls, totaling 86.4 percent of those present against every aspect of refunding,[43] Wood evidently believed most of them opposed it for the wrong reasons. Only a handful agreed with his general concept of backing refunding as a conservative goal, and they assumed he shared their misgivings.

Nothing was further from the truth. In a party where few matched his fiscal acuity, Wood rejected Republican refunding because he recognized its limitations: it froze the debt for at least a generation at an interest rate that indeed proved too high, and prevented debt reduction through the surplus. There was a third fault which neither Wood nor Republicans anticipated. By specifying "coin," each believed that it meant gold because silver was at a premium with gold in the bullion market. Future events proved that miscalculation a source of immense trouble.[44]

Wood was patient. This time around, the Democracy's financial queasiness had robbed him of a means to advance his insights into managing the debt. The issue was not over. Wood meant to reassert his principles when the first batch of bonds became due in 1880.

Easier items on Wood's docket were measures to eliminate internal revenue, cut spending, and decrease the tariff schedule. Each set off a furious burst of partisanship in the second and third session, much to his delight since he stood in the Democratic top echelon.

The income tax annoyed many Democrats as a relic of federal wartime centralism that hindered peacetime economic growth. Given his way, Wood announced, "the sooner we get rid of this onerous and unjust taxation the better." The system was unconstitutional because it invaded privacy, and unjust because it typified class favoritism by allowing rich people exemptions that were unavailable to the poor. When it became clear Republicans would not accept immediate repeal, Wood labored for what was attainable: reducing rates, adding exemptions, and simplifying tax forms. After a running battle that lasted both sessions, Democrats achieved a partial victory. Congress reduced rates by 3 percent, eliminated special taxes, increased exemptions by $1,000, and extended the tax only to 1871 and 1872.[45]

Wood was far more persuasive about spending cuts. Starting with internal improvements as a Locofoco issue, he insisted that subsidizing railroads was a matter of private, not federal, initiative, regardless of political pressure. Issuing a veiled warning, he said the worst type of profligacy lay with the Union Pacific which embraced "all kinds of schemes for government favors of every kind and character." Wood combed through each bill, searching for unneeded expenditures, and used them as excuses to question Grant's competence, such as the Legislative Appropriation Bill. He noted that the administration was "top-heavy with military officers with high salaries," strange for a president who promised an economical government.[46]

Wood was not totally consistent. Like any congressman, he played pork-barrel politics. Republicans made him squirm uncomfortably, yet he traded votes to get authorization for a new city post office. He was just as free over the government's native American policy. Ever since the 1790s, he argued, the nation had immorally followed a program "tantamount to extermination," and only "fruitful of wrong, oppression, and inhumanity." He felt the government should instead spend money for a fresh course "of pacification, of education, of moral culture."[47]

These efforts were a prelude to Wood's ultimate goal, reducing the tariff. In March 1870, Robert C. Schenck, chairman of Ways and Means, introduced a new protectionist bill, H.R. 1086. Wood clamored for recognition and led off debate. Enunciating the principles and vocabulary of Locofocoism, he castigated protectionism as a glaring illustration of Republican special-interest politicking. Tariffs raised the cost of living for poor consumers, overpriced American goods in foreign trade, and created pockets of stubborn unemployment among urban workers. Too, tariffs disproportionately rewarded one group, manufacturers, while they harmed everyone else in violation of the basic tenets of "republican government." The contention that the tariff protected home industry and raised revenue for paying the national debt was "specious sophistry." Actually, the tariff disrupted free trade, made rapid refunding questionable, and raised the melancholy specter of lower national income.[48]

While many Democrats agreed with Wood over the broad aspects of reduction, they broke over what to shave. To avoid any hint of bias, Wood specifically attacked sugar refiners, although he admitted they were the largest employers in his district. Despite what appeared to be politically suicidal, he objected to refiners' efforts to decrease rates on imported raw articles and raise those on clarified and "finer grades of refined sugar." The reason was simple. Refiners in his district, he said, made an unfair return of 200 percent on their investments importing raw sugar. Louisiana Democratic sugar cane producers disagreed. They wanted clarified sugar protected. Schedules in the iron industry were equally divisive because Randall shielded Pennsylvania interests. Wood tried to soften him by suggesting that rates must discriminate between imported scrap iron and finished pig iron as a means to increase jobs for iron workers and lower prices for other industries. Randall was unimpressed. Along with Republican William D. "Pig Iron" Kelley, he rebuffed any effort which might harm his state.[49]

Wood found more Democratic unanimity on items related to class, specifically the comparative schedules for green and black tea. As a way to win the support of prohibitionists, he termed black tea a substitute for "intoxicating beverages," and introduced a resolution to phase it down. The House agreed, as he put it, "so that the poor man's tea shall not pay as high a duty as that of the rich man."[50]

On March 1, just before the third session ended, Wood scored another breakthrough concerning the tariff. He introduced a successful joint resolution, which stampeded the House, to repeal all laws or parts of laws which levied an import duty on coal and placed it on the free list. The move proved immensely popular, coming at a time when the poor suffered through a harsh winter, and drew special praise from the state legislature.[51]

Wood ended with nothing more as protectionism still rode high. Republicans, backed by Democrats from industrial states, easily defeated another of his resolutions, this one that the tariff, granting "exclusive privileges" to certain classes, should be reduced. Wood was not concerned. Again biding his time, he had uncovered a major antiprotectionist device, shifting the issue from direct reduction to increasing the free list. As a result, he once more staked out a position which enhanced his growing stature.[52]

Oddly, Wood's reaction to other Republican measures purportedly involving Southern voting procedures fit into his overall strategy of being a national politician. On May 31, 1870, Grant signed the First Enforcement Act which set up machinery to administer the Fourteenth and Fifteenth amendments. A little over a month later, another bill became law that revised naturalization. Then, on February 28, 1871, the Second Enforcement Act was enacted. It applied only to cities of more than twenty thousand, detailed various types of electoral frauds, and gave federal marshals such as Davenport supervision of the ballot box.

Republicans, despite their ostensible intent to protect black voting rights, framed the laws largely with Tammany's massive 1868 frauds in view. Taken as a whole, they incorporated the Lawrence report, exempted small cities and rural areas where Republicans were strongest, and designated as federal crimes many of the Hall's traditional tactics that Wood had perfected: false registry, repeated votes, premature naturalization, menaced voters, and stolen ballots.[53]

Wood's silence dumfounded New Yorkers. Here were three political bombs that threatened to explode the fabric of local Democratic politics and he said nothing. He did support various dilatory motions, and voted against all three. Yet his expected eloquence was missing, in marked contrast to his emotional speech the next session defending the Ku Klux Klan from yet another enforcement act.

Wood's actions made sense only within the context of city politics. Determined to divorce himself from localism and willing to let Tweed suffer the consequences of what he had caused, Wood had no intention of calling attention to his own culpability.[54]

To Wood, these bills constituted a minor distraction in his single-minded push to dominate the New York delegation. Once more, General Howard was handy. On March 31, 1870, the House was in the midst of discussing a bill to transfer $600,000 from the Freedmen's Bureau to the Bureau of Education when Wood muttered in a low voice something to the effect that Howard had misused funds to enrich himself. The general should have ignored him; rashly he did not. After reading the comments in a newspaper, he wrote Wood to deny the charges and protested that an examination would prove him innocent. Wood complied. Fed with information from one of Howard's enemies, Wood took the floor, listed a catalogue of the general's alleged transgressions, and demanded a full investigation.[55]

Howard's good name was still synonymous with Reconstruction. Republicans scurried to his defense and impaneled a formal inquiry under a subcommittee from Education and Labor chaired by Samuel M. Arnell of Tennessee. For the next seven weeks, from April to July 1870, Wood, occasionally interrupted by roll calls, sat at the elbow of his attorney, Joseph H. Bradley, the future Supreme Court justice, serving as a co-prosecutor, badgering witnesses, and raising doubts about the propriety of Howard's actions. Edgar Ketcham, Howard's counsel, called rebuttal witnesses, all of whom exonerated the general, who sat through the hearings in silence and in full uniform. On July 13, Arnell issued a majority and minority report, and ordered them printed. Before the term ended in March 1871, the House voted in party blocs, 134 Republicans to 52 Democrats, to adopt the majority report which termed Wood's charges a "groundless" character assassination.[56]

Extensive partisan newspaper coverage indicated Wood's intricate purpose. It did not matter to him if Howard were guilty or innocent, nor that he had forever tarnished the general's reputation. What counted was the partisan reaction that Wood generated. Republicans extolled Howard's pure Christian character as something the "malicious" devil Fernando Wood could never understand. In contrast, the *New York Leader* lauded Wood's "boldness and promptness" in upholding the public interest, and Marble sneered that Howard was a pious fraud, a "Bummer." Whatever either side wrote placed Wood exactly where he wanted, in the center of the political spotlight, by himself. For the trifling price of denigrating Howard, he had moved ahead of Cox.[57]

This episode revived Wood's reputation as a conniver. To repair the damage and become the national politician he wished, Wood turned to the international situation. Although the Constitution limited the Foreign Affairs Committee's role in diplomatic affairs, he used a few disposable powers to influence the State Department. As such, he introduced multiple resolutions and bills to regulate oceanic cable companies, stimulate American commerce with the Far East, and safeguard Fenians in British custody who were American citizens. Moreover, Wood sought to guide Secretary of State Fish's policies by shaping diplomatic appropriation bills.[58]

Far more important, Wood became identified with surging popular interest in the Caribbean as a reflection of his Jacksonian belief in manifest destiny and his commitment to the Young America expansionist movement of the 1850s. In 1868, Cubans had begun a revolution against Spain that evolved into the brutal Ten Years War. Wood sympathized with the rebels. Working closely with Republican committee chairman Nathaniel P. Banks, Wood forged a majority report backing the rebels and, on June 14, 1870, made a powerful speech explaining the committee's motives. Cubans fighting for their freedom were bent on forming a republic against Spanish "barbarism and despotism," he said. In time, Cuba would become "our protectorate, if not eventually incorporated in our system." On that basis, Banks and Wood pressed Grant and Fish to recognize rebel belligerency and give them the right to buy arms in the United States. Wood went further. He urged the administration to bar Spanish ironclads from refitting in American naval yards and condemned Spanish atrocities as beyond the bounds of civilized war.[59]

Secretary Fish, fearful of a possible war with Spain and perhaps moved by racial antagonism against the rebels, prodded Grant to issue a special message resisting Banks and Wood. Banks held firm, and attacked his own administration. Wood was close at hand. He avoided any censure of Fish, praised the "patriotic cause in Cuba," drew a parallel with "our own war of independence," and rebuked Grant for not only trying "to coerce but to threaten and insult Congress." Administration pressure crushed Wood's call for national pride. By a vote of 101 to 77, the House beat back the majority report, Democrats 52 to 1 for, Republicans 25 to 100.[60]

The reversal did not harm Wood. He gained another laurel, this one as a Democratic foreign policy spokesman, in addition to already being known as a key party domestic strategist. By the summer, Democratic leaders treated his Cuban position as official party doctrine.[61]

Wood garnered even more prestige by helping Republican Senator Charles Sumner, chairman of the Committee on Foreign Affairs, block Grant's obsession with annexing Santo Domingo. During initial skirmishes in the first and second sessions, Wood fumed on the sidelines as the battle raged in the Senate. Yet, he tried to make his objections known. On political and racist grounds, Wood led a committee revolt against Banks, who now supported Grant, and introduced a resolution that the House had a right to participate in the negotiations since public money was involved. Although Wood's move failed, he repeated the same line in H.R. 1604 which dealt with consular and diplomatic appropriations. On June 30, the issue seemed moot when the Senate defeated the treaty in a tie vote.[62]

At this juncture, Grant wreaked havoc within his party. He turned annexation into a loyalty test, disgraced Sumner, and wielded federal patronage to secure votes. Repercussions touched New York City. Grant placated Senator Roscoe Conkling, a treaty backer, by demoting Custom House Collector Moses Grinnell, a relatively honest man, in favor of Thomas Murphy. Greeley Republicans shouted disapproval. They detested Conkling as an immoral spoils-monger and considered Murphy his unfit tool. In the long run, the appointment set off a massive feud in New York that culminated in Greeley's Liberal Republican revolt against Conkling's Regular Republicans. Wood was elated. As the main speaker at an aroused Tammany rally, he attempted to convince Liberals to coalesce with the Democracy based on their mutual antipathy toward the administration and all its henchmen. Grant, Wood growled, was "totally devoid of executive capacity, without a single qualification for the discharge of his important duties." Although the nascent Liberal Republicans did not respond immediately, Wood thought it only a matter of time before an alliance took hold.[63]

The stubborn Grant was not finished and pushed for annexation through a joint resolution. Wood threw himself into the controversy with zest. By involving the House, Grant had inadvertently made Wood a legitimate participant in a diplomatic issue not previously his proper business. Wood was the Democracy's point man. Coordinating tactics with Sumner, he placed parliamentary hurdles in the path of discussion, and introduced a resolution asking the president for full particulars about the entire affair, hinting that sordid motives were behind annexation. Within Foreign Relations, Wood led another uprising against Banks by rejecting a compromise he had worked out with Grant authorizing a fresh treaty.[64]

As the House settled into turbulent debate, excitement ran high when Wood made a set speech about the entire matter. Putting Grant on the defensive, he stressed the immorality of the president backing a treaty spawned by unscrupulous land speculators who had bribed a corrupt Dominican dictator to secure his compliance. Such greed was behind a treaty of "doubtful constitutionality," one which would increase the national debt at a time when the "people are overridden and overburdened by taxation, internal and external." Wood brought the address to a boiling climax with rabid racism. The people of Santo Domingo were a "degraded" colored race, mixed with African and Spanish Creole blood, a combination that produced a population "utterly incapable of civilization," let alone becoming Americans. Before Wood finished, protreaty forces spotted the flaws in his argument, his Jacksonian commitment to manifest destiny, and the fact Democrats had first used the joint resolution technicality to secure Texas almost thirty years before. Wood equivocated. Democrats were still adamant about carrying the flag everywhere, but only in "brother republics" composed of emigrants "from our own soil."[65]

Proud of his work, Wood sat down, probably confident that the party backed him. The only remaining question was whether Grant could sway a sufficient number of Republicans. He could not. Any possibility of annexing Santo Domingo ended when Congress failed to pass the joint resolution.

It had taken Wood six years, but by March 1871 he was far removed from the broken Peace Democrat of war's end. Partly by design, partly by political chance, he had reversed his political exile, partially overcame the politics of frustration caused by the Democrats' minority status, and evolved into a congressman of prominence, a person who clearly understood party rituals and exhibited great potential leadership. Colleagues recognized these achievements and often selected him chairman of the House caucus. As the *Leader* put it, "The man who comes out of the Forty-first Congress with the greatest applause is Fernando Wood."[66]

Even more satisfying, his reelection turned into a thunderous clap of approval. Old habits died hard. Early in October, some of his followers had infiltrated the Ninth District's Young Democrats' convention, packed the room, pushed through a "sham" nomination, and closed the polls. Those tactics were unnecessary. On election day, Tammany detonated one thousand "compound bombs" in twenty-five areas of the city to awaken voters "to a sense of their duty as citizens," mainly because the deeply partisan Davenport was the supervisor in charge of administering the Enforcement Act. This effort was equally unneeded. The Hall easily elected all candidates, confirming Tweed as the Democracy's "Boss," a role Wood had sought but never gained. As for Wood, his majority over a weak Republican and an ineffectual Young Democrat was over 6,500 more than both Cox and Brooks combined. In short, Wood's future looked far more promising than the past.[67]

TWELVE

Congressional Leader

Wood began the Forty-second Congress with a signal honor. House Democrats selected him as permanent caucus chairman and titular leader. Since the caucus developed party positions on major issues and set floor strategy, Wood was now a true policymaker, ready to mold the Democratic minority into an effective force. Republican disarray accentuated his opportunity. Grant faced a one-term presidency because Liberals and Regulars were hopelessly fractured over general amnesty, tariff reform, civil service, and a new Southern policy.[1]

Wood itched to demonstrate his leadership capabilities. As he wrote Hoffman, "My own experience in organization has enabled me to give direction and force to our movements." His was not an idle boast. Crafting tactics with his usual care, Wood demanded that Democrats attend every session to form "an unbroken opposition front." The result, he continued to Hoffman, gave Democrats, "a close compact organization which enables us to act efficiently in taking advantage of the mistakes of the enemy."[2]

The consequences of Wood's leadership soon became critical. After Congress had sent the Fifteenth Amendment to the states for ratification in February 1869, Democrats split into three camps. Most pragmatic white Southerners acquiesced as the means to end Reconstruction and believed they would eventually control black voters. Extremists largely from the Border States, led by Senator Francis P. Blair, Jr., of Missouri, fought ratification on virulent racial grounds. Centrists followed the example of the New York Democracy which initially opposed the amendment. In March 1870, when all signs indicated that the amendment had sufficient votes, the Democratic-controlled legislature enacted a symbolic law that ended restrictions on black voters to emphasize that the principle of states' rights prevented any further federal interference with home rule.

Democratic extremists did not accept this reasoning. In 1870 they forced congressional Democrats to issue an annual address laced with generalities about the amendment. In April 1871 extremists prepared another statement, this one bristling with defiance. At that point, Wood made his presence felt. As Blair complained to Alexander Stephens of Georgia, moderates "toned [the pronouncement] down to suit the squeamish stomach's [*sic*] of Wood & others from New York."[3]

On April 21, 1871, the caucus under Wood's direction issued an electrifying public statement. Routinely enough, it began with a ritualistic defense of states' rights followed by a standard attack on the administration. The jolting part, however, was a pledge to support "the rights of any portion of the people secured under the Constitution or any of its amendments." Just as striking, Democrats disclaimed "any sympathy" with those who fomented "disorders and violence" to "deny citizens their personal liberty."[4]

This declaration was essentially a trade-off. In acknowledging the Reconstruction amendments as permanent parts of the Constitution, Democrats followed the centrists' course, bowing to the finality of Reconstruction, the permanence of black suffrage, and promised to protect black rights, provided the federal government guaranteed Southern home rule. This formula, later known as the New Departure, set the key element in the Democratic program for winning the presidency in 1872.

As Blair indicated, Wood's centrist position was vital in shaping this statement. Convinced that the party must consign Civil War and Reconstruction issues to the past, Wood had indicated a means for Democrats to move on to new questions, thus neutralizing Republican charges that the Democracy was still a haven for rebels and traitors. On that basis, Wood presumed that Hoffman was the Democracy's logical standard-bearer. Yet that was only possible, he cautioned Hoffman, "if our friends at Albany will continue to be discrete as to legislation."[5]

Grant's supporters were not asleep. Motivated by the desires to heal their party, prop Southern Republicans, and protect blacks, they attempted to reanimate the spirit of Reconstruction through another enforcement bill aimed at suppressing the Ku Klux Klan and identifying it as an arm of the Democratic party. Democrats denied that the bill was needed. They claimed that the Klan was a figment of Republican imagination, rejected any need to give Grant more discretionary powers, and adopted the common line that Southern whites were justified in defending themselves against unwarranted Republican centralism.[6]

Amid the acrimony, Wood added a fresh wrinkle through the New Departure. He pointed out that the party's new policy statement endorsed full citizenship for the "colored race." The real culprits were Southern Republican agencies such as the Freedmen's Bureau and Union Leagues which misled blacks and marshalled them into "a political engine." Democrats considered blacks "free and independent voters," and encouraged them to seek leaders "of their own class." In fact, Republicans had spawned this "monstrous" bill merely to "resuscitate" their party. Left alone, white and black Southerners were capable of racial harmony.[7]

The administration won. The bill passed 93 to 74 along strict party lines, while Wood, who paired no, painfully fretted at home with recurrent rheumatism. Happily for his peace of mind, the *New York Leader* lauded him for acting in the party's best interests. His "logical speech shows," it wrote, "more than ever, the peculiar force of Mr. Wood as a political reasoner, and may be called one of the strongest, in presentation and manner, made in Congress in many a year." The response among thirty-three Liberals was equally gratifying. They boycotted the House vote, apparently indicating they were ready to cooperate with Democrats.[8]

Yet, Wood was wary. Many Southern Democrats distrusted the New Departure and, remembering slippery prewar pledges, still distrusted Northerners, especially men such as Wood who had reneged on their promises. "If you knew the labor, humiliation & self sacrifice which a few Democrats in Congress are obliged to endure, you would pity us," he lamented to Marble.[9]

When the short session ended on April 20, 1871, Wood took another trip overseas and missed the political firestorm the *New York Times* ignited during the summer against the "Tweed Ring." Names once prominent in party circles—Tweed, Sweeny, Hall, Barnard, Connolly, and Hoffman—tumbled into ashes. From the cinders came their replacements, state chairman Samuel Tilden and "Honest" John Kelly, Tammany's new leader.

Fall elections told a grim story. The Committee of Seventy, a self-generated group of reformers, and Apollo Hall Democrats, the Young Democracy's successors, emerged as the new powers in the labyrinth of city politics. The "Tammany scandals" even blighted Democrats in other states, spoiling their charges of corruption against Grant and withering hopes of winning the White House.[10]

Luck and foresight rescued Wood. He was fortunate that brother Ben was a driving force among Apolloites and was able to fend attempts to link him with Tweed. Then, too, Wood's wisdom in rising above the turmoil of localism after abandoning Mozart placed him above the scandal.[11]

On December 1, prior to returning to Congress, Wood spoke at a meeting of the West Side Association, a lobby of uptown real estate developers, and used the opportunity to explain his position. Tammany's defeat, he argued, sprang from "leading citizens of both parties" and an aroused public "demanding that abuses shall be corrected." Taking grim justification in the situation as an elder municipal statesman, he warned that changing leaders was meaningless unless the legislature corrected "inefficient public officers" through a new charter. "What was wanted," based on "his experience as Mayor," was a consolidated strong government," calibrated to home rule, run by a true "Chief Magistrate."[12]

Back in Washington, Wood found Congress crackling with political intrigue. With a presidential election around the corner, Grant tried to court the Liberal Republicans. He promised what they wanted, support for general amnesty, expansion of the recently enacted Civil Service commission, and tariff cuts through horizontal 10 percent rate reductions.

While Liberals pondered Grant's tenders, Tweed's downfall and Hoffman's connection to him demoralized the Democracy. After holding a series of caucuses, Wood conceded that Democrats were unclear about events and how to influence them. He was even shakier about the plan of Missouri Democrats, the "passive policy," which contended the party wait until the Liberals acted and then coalesce with them if their platform and candidates proved acceptable. The situation was so grave that when national chairman Belmont held a strategy session with Democratic congressmen, they could not decide whether to adopt the passive policy or somehow force the Liberals to endorse a Democrat.[13]

Even before that meeting, Wood was not in the best of spirits when he read new committee assignments. Blaine kept him on Foreign Affairs, but also named Cox, apparently to diminish Wood's stature. But then the Speaker increased Wood's importance, appointing him the senior Democrat on the Select Committee for Reform of Civil Service, despite his vote against establishing the commission the previous term.[14]

Wood still held an advantage over Cox as caucus chairman. Using the position for all it was worth, Wood acted as the connection between the congressional establishment and voters. He continued to advocate conservative fiscal measures, and maintained his personal image as the watchdog of federal spending. Politically, he directed the party against bills Democrats could not support, particularly Sumner's proposed civil rights act, and seized every opportunity to humiliate the president and lure Liberals.[15]

Wood also foiled Cox's attempt to make inroads among his working-class constituents. He could not prevent Cox from introducing a bill, that never left committee, creating an eight-hour day for federal workers, similar to the one Wood had earlier proposed. But he neutralized Cox by pushing for a special committee, under Education and Labor, to investigate "the division of profits between capital and labor." Once more summoning the spirit of Locofocoism, Wood repeated "that they who produce nothing get everything, while those who produce everything get nothing."[16]

That Wood understood the political game and how to play it became clear when the Liberals unequivocally rejected Grant's overtures. Wood analyzed this development as an invitation to capture the Liberals, provided the Democracy could convince them that they shared common goals and supported a common candidate. As such, he pressed two issues each backed, a lower tariff and civil service reform, while seeking an acceptable nominee.

Wood opened his offensive with a barrage against the proposed horizontal 10 percent cut, and told Liberals that expanding the free list was more effective. The measure that emerged pleased no one. Free-trade Democrats and Liberals roared that it was a sham, even if rates were indeed lowered 10 percent for most industries. Republican protectionists and a core of about a dozen Democrats, led by Randall, bellowed against any decreases. Although Grant signed the bill, it fit Wood's political calculations.[17] Tariff reform seemed more than ever a Democratic issue, and Liberal refusal to support the bill seemed a precursor of future cooperation.

Wood's stand on civil service looked equally promising. Liberals should measure Grant's sudden conversion to good government, he scoffed, by the large number of "irresponsible" spoilsmen who dominated the administration. By that test, Wood said Congress and the American people must hold Grant " to the most rigid accountability" for each appointment, beginning with the "outrageous" Collector Murphy. Thus, "good men and reformers, without reference to past political issues, are called upon to arrest the demoralization which is now sapping the very foundation of government."[18]

In the midst of these activities, Wood paid a gesture of respect to the memory of Samuel F. B. Morse which said more about his ambitions than any grief over the inventor's recent death. Giving the House a history lesson over how Morse had received federal aid during the Twenty-seventh Congress for developing the telegraph, Wood noted that he was "to-day the only living member of either House of Congress who voted for it."[19] Left unsaid, but clearly implied, was his seniority—the longest in Congress, a link to the giants of the past, and his special status as "The Father of the House," the springboard for becoming Speaker, whenever Democrats won control.

The ultimate item on Wood's list was finding a presidential candidate the Democracy could impose on Liberals. He had in mind Supreme Court Judge David Davis. To Wood's consternation, Liberals rejected Davis and chose the implausible Horace Greeley, whom Wood had never considered. When news of the Cincinnati nomination reached the House, he joined in the "loud and general guffaw" which "broke out all over the floor."[20]

As Democrats veered from loathing to laughter, reality took hold. For Wood, the metamorphosis was especially excruciating. He abominated Greeley as a protectionist, nativist, and partisan who had dogged his very being since the 1830s. And yet, Greeley was the most "available man," a friend of labor, the supporter of general amnesty and the removal of all troops from the South, and a former Radical whose reputation handed Democrats a reasonable means to bury their Peace Democratic stigma. With Hoffman gone and no substitute at hand, the party really had no choice. Once his grim mood lifted, Wood accepted the inevitable, and watched with detachment as the Democrats endorsed Greeley. It was not until three weeks after their July convention, however, that Wood made his position known. He wrote an open letter from his vacation retreat in Saratoga telling the public "all good men, including [myself], are for Greeley."[21]

Wood hoped to duck any further involvement in the campaign, but his congressional prominence made that impossible. In early August, New Yorkers received a franked letter from Wood that contained one of his speeches attacking Grant folded around a copy of Sumner's address to black voters urging them to vote for Greeley. Political necessity demanded more, yet Wood had limits. Bowing to Kelley's insistence, he did serve as keynote speaker at Tammany's first major presidential rally, but his speech was hardly thrilling. A perceptive reporter caught his "uneasiness" as he "astonished" the crowd "by announcing that he intended to speak to Democrats only." After a long harangue about the party's need to maintain its principles, he endorsed Greeley indirectly by commending the Democracy's self-sacrifice. "Our love of a great cause is made paramount to a dislike of an individual."[22]

Wood was more himself in traditional races. Since money translated into political power, he spent liberally to back Democrats in other states, especially the South and Midwest, and organized speakers' tours for gubernatorial nominee Francis Kernan of Utica. In bankrolling these men, Wood did not make the least effort to disguise his revulsion to Greeley, nor did most Democrats care. All evidence pointed toward a rout, and they concentrated on salvaging what they could from the debris.[23]

Meanwhile, reapportionment again jolted Wood's complacent belief in a perfunctory reelection. The remodeled Ninth District, encompassing the Twelfth and Nineteenth wards, along with Blackwell and Randall islands, was strongly Democratic, but contained a number of Apolloites who opposed anyone linked to "the old Tammany gang." Brother Ben saved the day. He convinced potential challengers that Wood was too "strong and valuable" a congressman to sacrifice. Wood also helped himself by receiving the Liberals' endorsement.[24]

Another complication arose. While Grant Republicans ran the worst possible candidate against him, William Darling, now one of Murphy's henchmen, popular disgust against Tammany was still strong. Although Wood won, his plurality was the lowest in six years, 52.2 percent. Most Democrats fared worse. Locally, they lost the city government, legislature, and statehouse. Nationally, Republicans increased their majority in the House, 203 to 88, and Grant easily won. Wood found only one consolation. Cox, who had been redistricted out of his seat, ran at-large and lost. That left Brooks as Wood's sole competitor as New York's ranking congressional Democrat.[25]

The bruising aftermath of such bitter and widespread defeats left Democrats prostrate and adrift, still a hopeless minority. Bereft of a true national leader, they looked to Congress for a rallying point and gave those few Democrats the task of defining possible winning issues.

Wood relished the opportunity, partly as a release from his wife's decaying emotional state. Alice Wood remained at home, wracked by a difficult pregnancy, upset by her mother's recent death and a will disinheriting her, and torn by the impending move of her youngest daughter to her old school in Paris. At this point, Wood needed the emotional support of Ben Wood, his only real friend. But he was of no help, once more distracted by a federal tax lien concerning lottery profits.[26]

Wood found another release in the still-burgeoning real estate market. In the quarter century since he and Anna Wood had bought their pleasant rural retreat in Bloomingdale, the city's massive commercial and population growth turned the area into an even more lucrative investment. The Common Council further increased its value by authorizing the construction of Riverside Park adjacent to the western edges of his holdings and in laying out a new street on his eastern frontage, the magnificent "Boulevard," which ran northwesterly from his other properties near the southwest corner of Fifty-ninth Street. Part of this four-lane street cut through Woodlawn at Seventy-seventh Street. In 1865, the Common Council awarded him $25,000 for an easement. Over the next thirteen years, city assessors did not raise his taxes as the value of Woodlawn escalated, nor did the street department construct the Boulevard through his estate.[27]

Wood again used this property as seed money to plant a second fortune in the early 1870s. For example in 1872, he and Alice transacted nine separate mortgages amounting to $122,850 for plots along Madison Avenue and in the Twenty-second Ward contiguous to Central Park. Most were liquidated within five years. At this stage of life, however, Wood was less interested in accumulating money as an end in itself and more as an instrument of power. In that light, he offered Blaine a loan when he ran into financial problems in October 1873, "having just now a surplus."[28]

Whatever his family and business affairs cost Wood in time and energy was always secondary to politics. After the Liberal debacle, he searched out new issues to scorch Republicans, chiefly those revolving around the corruption-in-government issue. As he told Marble, the Democracy must prove it was the only party which could "serve & maintain an honest integrity."[29]

Wood had in mind the scandal-ridden Crédit Mobilier of America, a corporate front that leaders of the Union Pacific Railroad formed to loot the company of its federally created assets. According to allegations, Congressman Oakes Ames, a company director, had bribed prominent politicians, mainly Republicans, with shares to prevent a congressional probe. To the surprise of his detractors, who always thought ill of him, Wood was aware of the bribery for at least four years, but had kept clean. The consequences left him properly indignant. Congress should hold a full "investigation with open doors," he announced, to assure "the people of the country" that no cover-up was taking place.[30]

Gleeful Democrats were ready to pounce upon implicated Republicans, many of whom lied about their relationship with Ames, notably Vice-President Colfax and Congressmen Blaine, Dawes, Kelley, and Garfield among others. Suddenly,

THE BIGGEST JOKE OF THE SEASON.

Wood's political ploy in introducing a resolution to impeach Vice-President Schuyler Colfax was parodied in *Harper's Weekly* 17 (17 Mar. 1873): 216.

they drew back because Brooks, another Crédit Mobilier director, shared Ames's guilt.[31]

For political and personal reasons, Wood was unsatisfied that justice was being served but was caught in a bind. He wanted to discredit guilty Republicans, proving his respectability in the process, without creating the impression of treachery toward Brooks. Wood found a way: he introduced a resolution to impeach Colfax. The motion failed, 105 to 100. Yet Wood won where it counted, among the public and within the Democracy. The *New York World* was particularly impressed: "That veteran Democrat, Fernando Wood, may be assured that his prompt and decisive action" deserves "the unstinted approbation of every honest American citizen."[32]

Wood won another way. The House formed a select committee that issued a report recommending the censure of Ames and Brooks, not their expulsion. Wood backed the report because censure was unavoidable given the evidence. Although it was a mild slap compared to expulsion, he had not betrayed Brooks. Either way, Brooks was ruined, since his activities, if not precisely illegal, had betrayed the public trust. Wood was not finished. To prove that Republicans were guilty of neglect by not going after bigger game, he pressed the committee to seek "other gentlemen who may be implicated." Republicans, led by John A. Bingham of Ohio, said the matter was settled, and urged the House to discharge the committee. "I do not understand that that is necessarily the case," Wood shot back. There the issue ended. The House quashed his motion, 114 to 104.[33]

Brooks died shortly after he was censured. His death meant that Wood was now the unquestioned leader of the state's Democratic delegation and heir apparent to Brooks's slot on Ways and Means. Yet, Wood still worried that Brooks's followers might somehow resent him, particularly when Cox announced for Brooks's old seat and implied Wood had not really done enough to protect Brooks.[34]

Wood's gambit took place the next term when he eulogized Brooks as the victim of cynical Republicans. Choosing words that defended Brooks and indirectly answered critics, Wood said that the "prevailing error of public judgment" lay in a "distempered and diseased demand for the destruction of reputation" upon mere "shadow of doubt." Brooks deserved better, Wood ended and, by implication, so did he.[35]

Wood discovered to his sorrow that the corruption-in-government issue cut two ways. Before the third session ended in March 1873, congressmen from both parties increased their salaries from $5,000 to $7,500 per year, raised the mileage allowance, and doubled executive and judicial pay. Ben Butler was even more greedy. He added an amendment that made the raises retroactive for two years. After a conference committee approved the bill, Grant signed it with what many considered unseemly haste.[36]

Wood was only peripherally involved. During most of these developments, his wife was in life-threatening labor, and he missed six out of ten roll calls concerning this by-now notorious "salary grab." When present, he voted to boost executive and judicial salaries but supported merely a $1,000 congressional raise and changed his vote when sentiment in the House favored the higher rate. Before leaving Congress on March 3 to join his wife, he paired no twice: once to order reading the conference report that contained Butler's amendment, and then to accept it.[37]

Resentment swept the country over congressional avarice, and voters placed the men who voted for the salary grab in a quandary. Justification was suicidal; silence was equivalent to approval. As a way out, most congressmen blamed Butler, or shifted the onus to the other party. One man, above all others, Fernando Wood, stood in the center of this vortex.[38]

Why Wood became synonymous with back pay and public theft developed out of an unanticipated depression that rumbled through the nation during the late fall of 1873. Voters, lacking an appreciation of what factors caused this, came to a simple conclusion. Republicans were in power, and somehow they were responsible. Democrats, sensing they were on the cutting edge of a major political breakthrough, quickly capitalized on public anger and blamed Republican economic policies. To gain maximum leverage and avoid distracting side issues, Democrats also made repeal of the salary grab official party policy. Their tactics worked in the off-year elections. An avalanche of protest votes buried Republicans.[39]

The same process was afoot in Washington. Democrats had every reason to anticipate control for the Forty-fourth Congress that was scheduled for election in 1874. While the new Forty-third, which was just organizing in December 1873, was still Republican, the heretofore "complementary" Democratic vote for Speaker became critical. While that person would lose surely, he automatically became the leading contender when the Democracy did regain the House. There was another more immediate prize. Based on House usages, the losing Democrat had the choice of any committee assignment. In December 1873, Fernando Wood and Samuel Cox emerged as the front-runners.[40]

Cox, who was back in Congress after carrying Brooks's old district, apparently held the upper hand. He had won largely because he pledged to repeal back pay, and he made it the centerpiece of his efforts to gain the votes for Speaker. In contrast, Wood's muteness on the issue, coupled to his paired votes, seemed a sign of weakness, or even worse, an admission of complicity. During the rousing caucus, Cox put Wood on the spot by demanding he condemn the salary grab. Wood straddled the issue. Unwilling to alienate anyone, especially Southerners who needed the money, he promised to make his position clear at the appropriate time. Cox was furious. He stomped out of the meeting and vowed a floor fight.[41]

Newspapers jumped into the act. Contending that Wood was unfit for high office, the *Times* maintained that his paired no votes were misleading because he apparently told the Republican with whom he had paired that he did support back pay. Wood published a denial. Citing his wife's illness for missing the roll calls, he wrote "had I been present, I should have voted against [the conference report]." Ambiguity was rife among Democratic journalists. They praised Cox, tried to explain how Wood could be both for and against raises, but accepted the unescapable. As the *World* resentfully observed, Wood's overwhelming claims rested on being "the oldest member in point of service and entry into Congress."[42]

Blaine won, 189 to Wood's 75, the remaining seventeen Democrats split between Cox, Georgia's Stephens, and Pennsylvanian Hiester Clymer. As a matter of course, Wood had already demanded his other prize, Brooks's seat on Ways and Means. Writing to Blaine, Wood asserted that he yielded to no man from "this city" in "point of seniority of service, of practical knowledge of the business of that committee," and influence with "the merchant interest of N. York." Cox was equally insistent, citing his college education and lifelong training. The Speaker was nonplussed. He told Cox, "I do not see without a marked personal indignity to Mr. Wood & to the Democratic Party in the House I could refuse the traditional courtesy to him—and thus violate the usage of three generations." Blaine was as good as his word, dutifully awarding Wood the position. For the moment, he was satisfied. Still caucus chairman and on Ways and Means, Wood was, the *Times* acknowledged, the "Democratic leader of the House."[43]

After reflection, however, the paper indicated that Wood's chances of becoming Speaker were probable at best. It editorialized that perhaps he was guilty of nothing more than dissembling over the salary grab. Yet, his personal and political reputation, involving "fraud, corruption and extravagance," produced a man whose "appearance in the field as an advocate of honesty and virtue will be received everywhere with mingled surprise and amusement."[44]

Leadership carried responsibility for setting party goals, but Wood discovered that the "inflationist" Forty-third Congress met in abnormal times. Two overwhelming issues, repealing the salary grab and combating the spreading depression, had lives of their own.

The death of the salary grab was a foregone conclusion when the House opened on December 4, 1873, with a flood of bills to rescind raises. In this deluge of artificial morality, Wood did not criticize, as others did, the men who had sponsored the projected raises. All the same, his compliance was obligatory. He voted to restore salaries to their former levels, returned his own back pay to the Treasury, and noted that his mileage allowance was among the lowest of any congressman.[45]

Depression politics was more tangled. Congressmen, hardly more sophisticated than their constituents about economic matters, were uncertain about what factors caused the depression and how it might be cured. Republicans formed two divergent economic recovery bills. The Senate sponsored S. 617, the Inflation Bill, which sought to stimulate capital investments and consumer purchases by raising greenback volume to $400 million and redistributing $46 million in national banknotes. Grant eventually vetoed it. H.R. 1592 had similar goals through different means. Known as the Free Banking Bill, it originally proposed to lift restrictions on the formation of new national banks, thus increasing the amount of banknotes in circulation. Over the course of debate, various congressmen added other sections, making it a catch-all for conflicting and overlapping amendments.[46]

Wood held firm to deflationary monetarism. He opposed S. 617, joining the familiar regional and nonpartisan bloc of fifty-two out of fifty-three New Yorkers and New Englanders. As for H.R. 1592 and its various amendments, his position was equally consistent. Fusing with eastern deflationists, he supported cancellation of greenbacks beyond their established limits, liquidation of the national debt as rapidly as possible, and specie resumption. None of his motions were incorporated into the final version. On other roll calls, he rejected free banking as an inflationist ploy, an attempt to inflate and redistribute greenbacks, and the bill itself. Ill for most of May and June when Senate and House conferees laboriously hammered out a compromise, he was absent when H.R. 1592 passed and gained Grant's approval. If present, he probably would have supported merely one of its four major sections, the part that put greenback circulation at $382 million, but would have rejected ending reserve requirements for note circulation, the redistribution of $55 million in national bank currency, and free banking.[47]

As Democratic House leader, Wood had an obligation to develop alternative policies. Again, he was consistent and followed the orthodox Jacksonian tenet that the market's unrestricted natural operations would solve the depression. He surmised that the downturn had a plain source and a simple solution. Too much government, too much administration mishandling of the economy, caused "private destitution and paralysis of trade." The antidote lay in setting free capitalism's spirit by reducing the government's size through spending cuts, stabilizing the money supply with resumption of specie currency, and preparing for refunding through the efficient collection of existing taxes. That done, the government's only legitimate function lay in stimulating foreign trade through a revival of the merchant marine, widened trade to Hawaii, lowered tariff schedules, and increased items on the free list.[48]

From purely an economic position, Wood's solutions were debatable. In a political sense, that did not matter since voters continued to pin the calamity on Republicans. Wood's strategy, then, was to force Republicans to defend their questionable monetary and fiscal policies in order to strengthen the public perception that only a political change could set things right.[49]

With Democrats playing for such high stakes, Wood needed proof that Republicans were indeed incompetent and misused federal money. General Howard and the Freedmen's Bureau once more proved handy. The bureau had essentially ceased operations, except for promoting black education and paying bounties to black veterans. Howard, nominally in charge, was on duty in Arizona and detailed subordinates to disburse and invest the Retained Bounty Fund. By late 1873, a series of probes uncovered irregularities in the account. Wood

A composite photograph of the city's delegation to the Forty-fourth Congress appeared in the *New York Daily Graphic*, April 14, 1875.

moved in for the kill. On December 12, he charged the general with defalcation and urged the Committee on Military Affairs to report a "resolution providing for [a court martial] of any officers of the Army implicated."[50]

By the end of January 1874, the House adopted Wood's recommendation, 174 to 64, but lightened it, changing the specifications to a special court of inquiry conducted by fellow officers whom Grant appointed. Although Wood objected that Republicans had rigged the case, he was inwardly satisfied because they had again tied themselves to the general. The inquiry lasted thirty-seven days. Howard was cooperative, gave testimony, and wrote a friend, "I think my enemies will, sooner or later, blow up themselves." In a limited way, he was correct. The court did absolve him and found no cause for Wood's complaint. Whatever it decided was immaterial to Wood. Speaking to the Boulevard Club on July 4, he cited Howard as proof that while Democrats labored to defend the public interest, the "perfidious federal administration" was guilty of ignoring its duties to protect the American people.[51]

Journalistic assessments of Wood's performance as the House's Democratic leader were inevitable given his reputation and the political hothouse that was Congress. The *Times* reported Democrats "were not very happy" because his old corruptionist aura harmed their image-making as the party of honesty, recovery, and reform. The *World* answered in kind: it said Republicans were bitter because Wood "assails the thing which is to be trodden into the dirt, and he is well employed."[52]

This short exchange spoke volumes about congressional dynamics. In the fall elections of 1874, rising popular discontent did sweep Democrats into positions of strength unparalleled since the 1850s. They gained 93 seats in the coming Forty-fourth Congress (giving them control, 181 to 107), slashed Republican dominance of the Senate, returned several Southern states to white control, and seemed ready to retake the White House. In New York, Tilden won the governorship, promptly stamping him as the likely Democratic presidential nominee.

Wood practically yawned through reelection. As so often in the past, his enemies split. Republicans lacked a candidate until the eleventh hour, and a small group of Apolloites ran "the inevitable" John Hardy, a perennial candidate with ties to Tweed. Wood also helped himself. He cultivated Kelly, who had rebuilt Tammany, and conciliated swallow-tails by supporting Tilden.[53]

Winning easily, Wood immediately set his hopes on the Speakership. Staking a direct claim was premature since the Democratic House would not sit for another year, but he was aware as an experienced politician that the ground needed careful sowing. For that reason, he read with satisfaction a column in the popular *New York Daily Graphic*. Wood's "long service in the party," it stated, "his urbanity of demeanor, his peculiar relations with Southern members as well as with the rank and file of Southern Democrats, will make it impossible to organize an effective opposition to his candidacy and election."[54]

Cartoon lampooning the exaggerated courtesy of Samuel S. Cox and Fernando
Wood, contenders for House Speaker, appeared in *Harper's Weekly* 19 (16 Jan.
1875): 61.

Wood had also learned that overconfidence was the ruination of the
ambitious. With little assured, he kept a wary eye on his chief competitors,
Randall, Cox, and Michael Kerr of Indiana, the favorite of Marble and Tilden.

Believing his wisest policy lay in convincing them that the office must seek the person, Wood disarmingly told a reporter that winning the speakership was "too large a question to base on mere personality; find a man who is equal to the task and put him to it."[55]

Returning Democrats launched the second session of the Forty-third Congress on December 7, 1874, with rounds of luncheons and strategy meetings. Republicans soured the happy mood. To prepare for the 1876 presidential election, Senate Republicans passed John Sherman's omnibus Specie Resumption Act (S. 1044) which settled many of the divisive monetary issues which had plagued them for years.

In the House, Republican tacticians prevented debate on S. 1044 and moved an immediate roll call. Wood thrashed around in agony, unable to speak on a topic that had given him a national reputation. Although recognizing that the measure was purely partisan, he would normally have agreed with three of its key provisions: gradual redemption of new banknotes; reduced greenbacks to $300 million; and above all building the gold reserve through the sale of government bonds to redeem greenbacks in specie when resumption began on or after January 1, 1879. He disagreed with two other provisions: restricting national bank circulation to allow free banking, and the minting of silver coins to retire an equal amount of fractional greenbacks. Yet, he might have accepted them as the price for passing the others. At the moment, politics won. Not a single Democrat supported the bill. It passed 136 to 98, with 23 confirmed Republican deflationists, mainly from New England, the Midwest, and South, lining up behind 75 Democrats.[56]

Wood reasserted his version of Democratic political economics on the tariff. Republicans had revived the issue, arguing that the Treasury needed money quickly to ensure resumption, and moved repeal of the 10 percent horizontal reductions. Resentment touching each word, Wood used a variety of statistics to argue that the bill was unnecessary and actually hid new forms of "oppressive" taxation. Since Republicans were unmoved, he appealed as the protector of American "commercial interests" to New York City's trading groups for help. Writing an open letter to the prestigious chamber of commerce, he pointed out that his long experience in Congress proved that the "rates of duty Congress has imposed needs to be thoroughly revised."[57]

Republicans did pass the bill, but his letter impressed the chamber of commerce. Invited to address its anniversary dinner, he made the most of this chance to show these men of wealth that he was like them, a safe, respectable man of substance, far removed from the political buccaneer of the 1850s. Wood employed his most persuasive oratorical style, and took "the future of our metropolis" as his theme. Reiterating his commitment to entrepreneurial freedom, he emphasized that higher tariffs hindered the natural laws of trade. The way out of the depression depended upon "a healthy relation to the other maritime nations of the world."[58]

Never once in this flurry of speeches did he allude to the Speakership, but it was scarcely far from his or the public's consciousness. Doggedly pursuing his dream, Wood avoided giving his enemies a means to embarrass or weaken him by reviving his chief liability, his wartime record. For that reason, he avoided discussing the Supplemental Civil Rights Act of 1875. Even so, Wood further ingratiated himself among Southern Democrats in defending John Young Brown of Kentucky when Republicans moved his expulsion for making "intemperate remarks" during the course of debate.[59]

To nourish further his credentials, Wood stepped up the pace of party-giving during the session. Over the summer, he became slightly more open about his aim, but still firmly gripped his public image as an urbane "old-school Democrat," with "the grace of a gentleman who has nothing further to ask of the gods or gain from his countrymen."[60]

Behind the scenes, nothing was further from the truth. By November, each contender locked in no-holds-barred wrestling for votes. Wood emphasized the importance of his seniority, the longest in Congress, and counted on trade and barter politics for services rendered to garner full support from Southern Democrats and Northern conservatives. It turned out that he proved weak where he assumed strength. Many Southerners, while admittedly grateful for his racist backing of white redeemers, shied away because they feared any support might antagonize Republicans and compromise home rule. Others resented his refusal to back redistribution or the expansion of needed national banks through free banking, and his insistence on hard money. Still more harbored a rankling belief that he had betrayed them during the war. His standing among businessmen was equally soft. Indiana's Michael Kerr shared his conservatism without his political liabilities and had Tilden's backing. Undecided conservatives and some Southern Democrats favored Randall but worried about his protectionism and ambiguous financial views. Cox thought his strength lay in the South and Midwest. He calculated that the odds against Wood would force him to retire, and believed the others would divide the vote, allowing him to slip over the top.[61]

As the day of reckoning neared, Wood indeed knew that he had lost. Fence-sitting Democrats lauded his talents, "elegant manner fit for a speaker," and devotion to principle during his "thirty-five years of congressional fame." Yet those qualities did not outweigh how his notorious personal and political record weakened Democratic attacks on the growing scandals surrounding Grant and made plausible the Republican tactic of waving the bloody shirt against the Democrats to rekindle wartime memories. After reading these signs, Wood withdrew in inner agony, holding his head high with characteristic "dignity."[62]

THE SPEAKERSHIP MAIN—WHO SHALL BE COCK OF THE WALK?

WHILE WALKER WALKS, AND HENLIKE TALKS
HIS "WALK-TALK-TALK,"—"TIS TRUE
THE OTHER THREE, AS CASE MAY BE,
CROW "COX-KERR-WOOD-'LL DO."

SHARP GAFFS OF STEEL ARE ON EACH HEEL,
NOR SHALL HE BE THE SLAIN,
WHOSE SKILL AND LUCK CAN MATCH HIS PLUCK
AND BEST 'IB IN THE "MAIN."

The power struggle for House Speaker was caricatured as a struggle for "cock of the walk" in the *Daily Graphic*, November 19, 1875.

Wood solved one problem but created another. Years of service and intensive financial study, he believed, had entitled him to chair Ways and Means, the

House's most powerful committee. That in turn meant reaching an arrangement with the presumable winner in the few days before the caucus met. A process of elimination followed. Cox was out of the question because he was a local rival. The overconfident Randall was unreliable since he "refused to make a *single* pledge." Anyway, Kerr seemed to have the best chance, yet Wood hesitated because of his tie to Tilden, a deadly foe since the 1850s. Because they had so much in common, however, Wood prepared to back Kerr and banked on his gratitude to allow him to head Ways and Means.[63]

The room where the caucus met jammed nearly beyond capacity as Wood opened the meeting, "looking and acting a little more dignified than usual." Keeping his emotions in check, he called order. When a hush fell, he spoke in a barely audible voice for about a minute about the gravity of the "choice upon the future of the party and the welfare of the country." He then passed the gavel to the new chairman, Lucius Q. C. Lamar, Mississippi's first Democratic post-Reconstruction congressman. Deliberations lasted over an hour and ran three ballots. Through these, Wood was silent, casting his votes for Kerr, the eventual winner.[64]

That night, Wood held a dinner at his home for thirty prominent congressmen, including Kerr, and presumed that he had earned the right to act as "mentor to his Democratic colleagues." Kerr appreciated Wood's hospitality, not his pretensions. Deeply troubled that both Cox and Wood were angling for the chairmanship, Kerr sought Marble's counsel. Meantime, Wood took direct action. He had friends lobby Marble, and introduced a controversial resolution when Congress began that challenged the seating of Republican Frank Morey from Louisiana's Fifth District. The motion passed, but Kerr was appalled. He granted that Republican rigging of Morey's election was scandalous, but resented that Wood had acted without consulting him. Wood had a reason. He hoped to exert maximum pressure on Kerr by demonstrating his power. Wood's gamble failed. Kerr was simply too angered at his solo act to appoint him. The situation ended when Kerr received indirect word from Tilden that Wood was unacceptable. In a stunning blow, Kerr retained Wood on Ways and Means, but selected William R. Morrison of Illinois as the new chairman.[65]

Now that he had the office, Kerr needed to form a cohesive program to prevent the Democratic majority from fragmenting into feuding factions. It was a demanding task, and he eventually focused on one key issue. Putting a heavy burden on Ways and Means, Kerr charged Morrison with implementing tariff reforms to give the American people a sense "of our general purpose, and put upon the Senate the duty of rejection or concurrence."[66]

Wood had a far less sanguine analysis of what the Democracy could accomplish. He informed Senator Thomas F. Bayard of Delaware, Tilden's chief rival for the nomination, that techniques of minority politicking had sapped

Democratic imagination and forced them to relearn "how to frame and carry constructive legislation."[67] Implicit here was Wood's new tactic of watchful waiting. Furious at Kerr, he reasoned that if Morrison failed, he would discredit the Speaker and through him, Tilden.

Wood astutely clarified the party's problems. As one observer complained, "Is there any subject" that Democratic congressmen "can handle with advantage to the public and credit to their party?" This gripe reflected a disconcerting fact. Initially, Democrats were sure of themselves. They set up a score of committees to investigate the scandals hounding Grant, culminating in the impeachment of his close friend, Secretary of War William W. Belknap. Just as easily, they passed a resolution against Grant's third-term ambition. All the same, Democrats floundered over other items. Trying to pass a new general amnesty bill, they handed Republicans an opening to put them on the defensive for coddling purported war criminals. Wood saved Kerr from another embarrassment. Republicans introduced a resolution to give former Union troops federal job preferment, rather than an equal hiring policy that might involve "soldiers of the late Confederate army." Wood knew that Republicans were again trying to identify the Democracy as the party of traitors and rebels, and moved the question to committee. These results left Kerr confused and bitter. He confessed to Marble that House Democrats were not acting sensibly and were hurting Tilden. A large part of this irascible mood mirrored Kerr's deteriorating health, which often forced him to miss sessions, and allowed either Wood or Cox to serve as Speaker pro tem. "At this rate," the *Times* remarked, "Wood will have an early chance of regaining his lost influence in the House."[68]

Feeling somewhat vindicated, Wood was unsympathetic toward Kerr and hostile to Morrison. Despite the coolness between them, Wood offered Morrison help in shaping the new tariff, but Morrison turned exclusively to David A. Wells, the party's leading antiprotectionist theorist. Between them, Morrison and Wells self-destructed. Instead of a thorough revision, they formulated more of a piecemeal measure. It appeased protectionists in adopting specific duties and reimposed rates on coal and tea, but did not go far enough for reformers in cutting manufactured goods or expanding the free list. The House debated the bill for two days before it vanished. This sequence of events found Wood remorseless. A friend told Marble, Wood was "very savage" about Morrison's "neglect to consult him as to the Tariff which he damns up and down, night & day as a clumsy patchwork [through] which he can drive a coach and four. He damns Kerr & damns Morrison."[69]

It was clear to anyone studying the Washington scene that Wood was engaged in an extraordinary vendetta against the party's congressional establishment. Hardly content with humbling Morrison, Wood blasted Cox's Banking and Currency Committee for dragging its feet over preparing the nation for resumption, and ridiculed Randall's lack of preparation in drafting appropriation bills. More disconcerting, Wood joined Kelly, who had broken with Tilden over internal party affairs, to sign a petition which urged delegates to block the governor's presidential bid.[70]

Observers dismissed Wood's maverick streak as petty revenge and overlooked its deeper sources. The New Departure, coupled to the election of 1874, apparently proved to Wood that the Democracy had finally proved its ability to survive. Yet, an even more imperative task remained. Based on his subsequent behavior, he believed that as the United States rushed headlong and unprepared into an unchartered industrial, urbanized, and commercial society, men such as Kerr and Morrison, and even Republicans, blindly led the nation through makeshift expedients, unable to formulate policies or exert fresh ideas. The time had arrived, he noted, for Congress to reach above "degrading servitude" to party and pass legislation "to lead us onward in the important struggle for national grandeur, power, and wealth."[71]

The real problem bothering Wood was that the Democracy was entering a new stage, justifying its survival and ensuring its return to glory, without any concept of what positive direction to take. The solution, in his mind, rested on forming a new dynamic conservative consensus around national issues integral to an emerging modern American economy: tariff reduction, sound finance, sensible taxes, hard money, free trade, and payment of the national debt. Looking forward, he found his guide in the Jacksonian past. "There is not an 'i' that I have not dotted," he announced, "nor a 't' that I have not crossed, in the Democratic alphabet. I entered this House, 36 years ago, and I never wavered, never hesitated."[72] In seeking to redefine the Democracy's image, Wood became instrumental in forging what became known as Bourbon Democracy.

Wood's self-imposed task during the first session was short-lived and barren. It was painfully obvious that the first months of 1876 found him emotionally and physically debilitated. Alice Wood was one cause. Progressive and unresolved mental stresses etched her life as a political wife and mother. How her degeneration affected Wood's psychological equilibrium was unclear, but his health was precarious. In early March, Washington physicians discovered a low "abscess of the throat" that "pressed upon the windpipe and the blood vessels of [his]neck." Local doctors sent for a New York City surgeon, who recommended an immediate operation, otherwise "the patient could not live 24 hours." The procedure, performed without anesthesia, was successful.[73]

Wood needed time for recuperation, but it was in short supply. He had to prepare for his eldest daughter's marriage and another round of character-damaging litigation. Wood pitched into arranging the nuptials with something resembling his old energy, but the weight of legal problems was almost more than he could bear. His troubles began in February 1876 with the creditors of N. Hill Fowler, who alleged that to secure his endorsement for corporation attorney Fowler had bribed Wood in 1863 with $5,000, plus Fowler's entire first year salary and a split of his remaining salary and fees over the course of his term. His creditors sued to recover the total, which they estimated at slightly over $15,000. Forced to attend superior court on almost a daily basis in the early spring, Wood testified that Fowler had been Mozart's finance chairman and voluntarily contributed only a $1,000 assessment, which Mozart repaid with interest. While the court deliberated, Fowler's creditors sued Wood in a separate case, claiming that Wood ordered him to reimburse a Mozart ward worker out of his own pocket for a fraudulent claim. In November, the courts absolved Wood in each case, awarding him damages for legal costs in one, yet he had forfeited a great deal of stamina and reputation. Worse, the cumulative effect of these myriad vexations created a sorry attendance record, amounting to nearly 65 percent missed roll calls.[74]

As if these were not enough, the depression had plunged real estate values downward. Friends reported that Wood suffered deep reverses nearly bordering on bankruptcy. Before he could put his personal house in order, he faced another dilemma of his own making. In May, he told a reporter from the *Baltimore Gazette* that "candor compels me to admit that the animosities" within New York Democracy would disrupt the party and prevent Democrats from carrying the state. "However strong we may be attached to our leading statesmen," either Bayard or Davis was preferable to Tilden, he said. Wood's efforts flopped. Tilden was less than a dozen votes short on the first ballot, and minor switches provided the necessary two-thirds before the second. After the delegates made the nomination unanimous, Kelly gave a gracious speech promising Tammany's full support.[75]

The first session of the Forty-fourth Congress, then, was a disaster for Wood at precisely the hour he had anticipated establishing his leadership. Even in the few instances when he attempted to marshal the Democracy, his darkest fears materialized about its lack of direction.

Wood's major source of unhappiness lay in the baffling money question. Congressman Richard P. Bland of Missouri, chairman of the Committee on Mines and Mining, led one group of midwestern and Southern Democratic inflationists. These men, who were usually farm debtors, strove to repeal the Specie Resumption Act. Failing that, Bland sought the partial remonetization of silver by forcing the Treasury to honor one of the act's provisions, the issuance of fractional silver coins with a simultaneous withdrawal of a comparable amount of greenbacks. Other farmers, underpaid workers, and some businessmen such as ironmaster Peter Cooper formed a second group of inflationists. They organized the Greenback party in May 1876 and were convinced that an expansion of fiat money would cushion further economic distress. Like Bland, the Greenbackers wanted to repeal the Specie Resumption Act, but favored increasing the supply of paper money.

As the party's leading deflationist, Wood rejected Bland's attempt to stampede the Democracy toward inflation. It was true that Wood had opposed the Specie Resumption Act out of mandatory partisanship. Nevertheless, he privately agreed with its deflationary intent. On January 17, 1876, he partially showed his real colors when inflationists introduced a resolution to repeal resumption. They failed, 158 to 112, in a roll call that once more indicated the party's regionally based monetary tensions. Out of 169 Democrats, 103 mainly from the Midwest, South, and Border states, voted for repeal. Wood, along with 12 of 13 New York Democratic deflationists, joined with 54 other Democrats mainly from New England, the Mid-Atlantic, Midwest, and South, and bolted party lines to support 92 Republicans from the same areas in voting nay.[76]

Inflationists then adopted their secondary tactic. Rumor had it that Secretary of the Treasury Benjamin H. Bristow had a sufficient backlog of silver to issue factional coins yet refused. In March, inflationists pounced on his request for funds to replace frayed paper money, and introduced a variety of bills to implement the exchange.

Fellow Democrats expected Wood, given his commitment to hard money, to support silver. In principle, he was a bimetallist, but only when silver stabilized and would not inflate the currency. Since silver was both volatile and inflationary, Wood stunned the silverites. Initially, he moved to have the bills referred to Ways and Means where he could bottle them, rather than to Cox's sympathetic Banking and Currency Committee. When that miscarried, Wood bluntly castigated silver as a fluctuating medium, one which made speculation inevitable and threatened to start a rash of gold hoarding. Making silverites more uncomfortable, he called their tactics "one of the largest humbugs of the day," a mask for rewarding Western bonanza mining kings. Remonetization would only become "a practical proposition" after "we shall resume upon gold coinage."[77]

Ravages of illness stilled Wood's voice as silverites became bolder. Near the session's end, they advocated the complete restoration of silver dollars at 412.5 grams. With a national election around the corner, the party put the proposal on hold and carried the issue over to the following December when Bland reintroduced it in H.R. 4189.

Bland's bill marked the point of no return between Wood and party inflationists. In a depression era, deflation was out of style, while inflation was the debtors' escape valve. When the House voted on H.R. 4189, it passed by the overwhelming margin of 167 to 53, drawing 120 Democrats from the mid-Atlantic, Southern, midwestern, and Border States, along with 44 Republicans, heavily midwesterners, and three Greenbackers. Wood was among merely 17 opposition Democrats, almost entirely easterners, who aligned with 34 Republicans and two independents also mainly from the East.

The bill died in the Senate, but Bland had built a significant platform to launch new forays. As for Wood, the silver question was wrong in every particular and plunged him into a deep minority within the Democracy. As he visualized the issue, it was a fiscally irresponsible panacea that ruptured Democrats, prevented the reestablishment of the prewar alliance of East, South, and West, and frightened some conservative interests into the Republican party.[78]

Wood pushed the adoption of the Hawaiian Treaty as a far better example of national policy issues for next generation Democrats. In 1875, the Grant administration had hammered out a trade agreement with Hawaii based on commercial reciprocity. Since the treaty needed a congressional enabling act, Ways and Means was responsible for steering its passage in the House.

Disunity marred the committee. With David Wells's shadow in the background, Morrison led the minority. He argued that the treaty harmed Louisiana sugar producers and locked the United States into defending the islands in case of attack. He further assailed reciprocity as a protectionist device that lowered federal revenues and subsidized American sugar importers. Wood backed the treaty, and was the principal draftsman of Ways and Means's favorable majority report. Noting these differences, the *Times* commented that Wood had the stronger case but doubted he could prevail. "Morrison is not able to push any measure, but is only strong in holding back and forcing inaction."[79]

Wood brushed Morrison aside. As an early-day imperialist who believed that American commercial penetration would lead to Hawaii's eventual annexation, he presented the enabling bill on March 2. Never before, Wood described himself, had he spoken "with a more decided and positive conviction of the rectitude and correctness of my position" because the treaty had key advantages for everyone involved. Adoption would galvanize national employment by expanding both agricultural and industrial exports, thus stimulating the merchant marine which had not yet recovered from the war. Reciprocity further reduced the costs of imported raw materials, helping both manufacturers and consumers. Turning to the South, he said that its long-sought quest for a transcontinental railroad was feasible since burgeoning trade demanded construction of additional routes. As for lost taxes, Democratic pledges to implement frugal government meant that the Treasury could forego the minimal funds it collected from Hawaii. Then, too, he assured Louisiana that Hawaii produced only "inferior grades," and was no hindrance to the American sugar-growing region. Lastly, Wood called on national pride, pointing out "some remarkable [British] intrigues" to absorb Hawaii unless the United States acted with dispatch. In short, America's new manifest destiny lay in the Pacific.[80]

Morrison's logrolling, Kerr's illness, and the silver question kept the treaty on the back burner until May 8. Wood was not discouraged. He shepherded the enabling bill through the House, lined up lobbyists, and maneuvered for a final

The Forty-fourth Congress as seen by a cartoonist for the *Daily Graphic*, May 2, 1876.

vote. When it came, Wood was disappointed if he considered the treaty a test of the Democracy's capacity for generating new issues. The treaty did pass, 115 to 101, but 47 Democrats were absent. More seriously, a majority of those present were against him, 78 from the Mid-Atlantic, South, and Midwest regions. Only support from the habitual block of 58 commercial-minded Republicans, usually eastern and midwestern, saved the day.[81] Nonetheless, Wood stood on the cutting edge of three long-term goals. He helped prepare the ground for eventual Hawaiian annexation, ripened some Democrats' thoughts about the future, and honed his arguments about expanding American trade.

During the presidential campaign, state pride forced Wood to play the good soldier. Despite his demonstrable aversion to Tilden, he accepted Kelly's invitation to be the main orator at Tammany's Independence Day celebration. As braves listened intently for signs of disloyalty, Wood said he knew Republican nominee Rutherford B. Hayes from their days in Congress as a "respectable man." Yet, Hayes fell short of presidential stature because he lacked the spine to "cope with the rogues in Washington," and went "along with his party," shutting "his mouth and eyes when he saw stealing going-on." By contrast, Tilden was "a practical reformer" about whose "nerve" and integrity "there can be no doubt."[82]

With his own reelection certain, Wood pleaded that he needed time for convalescence and listlessly awaited the verdict. Final results in the electoral college were inconclusive. Tilden won the popular vote, but Republican returning boards in three "unredeemed " Southern states, Florida, Louisiana, and South Carolina, overturned apparent Tilden majorities in Hayes's favor. For nearly the next five months, the nation fretted in a war of nerves. Congress, which had to decide the legality of the disputed returns since the Constitution lacked guidelines for solving the crisis, dissolved into a political and legalistic quagmire.[83] Though Wood could not divine the future, this situation became the final turning point in his career.

Democrats dealt from weaknesses. Republicans controlled the presidency, Senate, Supreme Court, and military. The party's only hope hinged on the House, but complications arose. Kerr had died in August of tuberculosis, and only Tilden's support of Randall as the new Speaker stifled a new round of disruptive personal rivalry. One question was settled, but another remained. Randall was unsure of how Tilden meant to lead the party during this crisis.[84]

Wood did not await Tilden's instructions. Although he remained cool to Tilden as a person, Wood was determined to prevent Republicans from stealing the election. Taking a position as an uncompromising member of the Democracy's extremist Northern Wing, his immediate strategy was to put Republicans on the defensive by proving that the army, acting on President Grant's orders, had interfered with Southern elections, especially in Florida, Louisiana, and South Carolina. With Hayes's election fraudulent from the start, Wood's ultimate goal, which he kept private for almost the next three weeks, was to have Congress authorize new elections in those three states. While he later admitted that the Constitution lacked provisions for such a law, Wood thought that Congress had a constitutional right to safeguard the country by stretching its powers.[85]

On December 7, Wood set his "ultraist" plan in motion at a party caucus. He proposed that Democrats instruct the Judiciary Committee to investigate military movements in the South during the election and "report whether in this respect, there has been any violation of the law by the President." The next day, Wood carried out his threat, introducing a resolution calling on the president to "transmit to this House" full information about the activities of any "military commander or civil officer, with reference to the service of the Army." Republican John A. Kasson of Iowa destroyed Wood's intent, however, when he added the phrase, "if not incompatible with the public interest." It passed with that change, and a select committee began the investigation. At the same time, the Republican-controlled Senate launched its own inquiry into the disputed returns. Yet, Wood was disappointed because Grant could evade a full disclosure and prevent others from presenting damaging facts. Three days later, Wood probed the willingness of Southern Democrats to fight for Tilden and stand firm until the select committee reported. Wood proposed that the party discredit Grant by beginning impeachment proceedings, and "talked of war as he did in 1861." To Wood's consternation, Southern Democrats wanted no part of him. Benjamin H. Hill, a Georgia congressman and former Confederate general, mockingly said that men such as Wood had encouraged secession and then acquiesced as Democratic troops destroyed the Confederacy. Such Northern Democrats were "invincible in peace and invisible in war." They talked tough, but were not willing to take the consequences.[86]

While Hill later denied the statement, his words did reflect the views of many Southern Democrats. Men such as Wood had indeed taught them lessons: the futility of defying the Constitution; the danger of reviving "all ideas of treason as they did in 1861"; and the folly of backing supposed friends who thwarted badly needed federal subsidization of railroads and redistribution. The upshot was that most Southerners put the burden of challenging Republican frauds squarely on the shoulders of Northern Democrats. Republicans were thrilled, and began, Garfield told Hayes, to lay plans "to make inroads into the Democratic camp."[87]

Wood also found this episode instructive, but was uncertain how to respond. He was incredulous about Southern Democrats, furious that Tilden seemed frozen by indecision, frustrated by Kasson's apparent checkmate, and uncertain if the time was ripe to suggest holding new elections. Other Democrats believed the controversy was now farther than ever from solution. As a holding action, the caucus endorsed another of Wood's resolutions, which the House eventually passed, to give the select committee subpoena power since some Louisiana telegraph officials used the right of privacy as an excuse to withhold certain communications. It was now Wood's turn to buy more time. On December 19, he cited the national emergency to urge the House to shorten its traditional Christmas recess, probably to give the select committee more help if needed. But, far from public view, Wood struggled with himself. Those who had watched him for years waited expectantly for continued slashing of Republicans. They waited in vain. Hinting at an inner reassessment, he introduced a petition on January 3, 1877, from New York City bankers and merchants pleading for "an amicable settlement" of the "present political situation."[88]

By the second week of January, the crisis reached new heights. Electoral returning boards in the three Southern states forwarded conflicting reports; both Democrats and Republicans claimed they were the victims of frauds; the Constitution lacked clear guidelines how to count the disputed electoral votes; and rumors spread that extremist Democrats were arming themselves to inaugurate Tilden. In the midst of these developments, Wood finally announced that he was preparing a bill for new elections, but would wait until the House committee issued its report. Response was not encouraging. Other Democrats believed a more practical scheme was to invalidate both sets of returns. With neither man having a majority in the electoral college, the Democratic House would decide the question. Republicans were equally negative. The *Times* retorted that while "it was quite likely" that Wood's idea would receive "considerable attention in certain Democratic quarters," Republicans thought his suggestion was an admission that Tilden could not win and that Democrats only respected the Constitution when it suited their purposes. In fact, the paper continued, Wood was now "reticent," spoke "very guardedly," and "evidently does not have a very exalted idea of the Southern Democracy." Parallel reevaluations gripped the swallow-tails. Cox moaned "We are fighting gigantic fraud; and there is not certainty of success." Barlow was just as chastened. To Bayard he wrote that "as [much] as I desire Tilden's inauguration, I desire the vindication of the law, and a close adherence to the Constitution, much more."[89]

On January 18, Tilden's advisers accepted the Electoral Commission Bill as his sole chance for victory. Under its terms, Congress began the state count alphabetically in joint session. A commission of fifteen, chosen from the three government branches, decided disputed returns, and its decisions were final unless reversed by both the Senate and House. Surprisingly, Wood backed this procedure, although he did not explain why, later rationalizing that he thought the commission would "judicially and impartially" judge the returns. He most likely realized that the select committee was not uncovering the evidence he sought, that he had little Democratic support, and thus lacked sufficient votes to pass his proposal. Even so, the *Times* lauded his fresh stance. All Americans were relieved, it wrote, since Wood, "the representative of the 'invincible' in the peace party," might "have been the first to repudiate in advance any decision that should fail to elect Tilden."[90]

In return for his reasonableness, Wood felt he deserved selection as a Democratic commissioner. Tildenites, however, wanted a more reliable supporter. They objected to Wood on the purported ground that he was not an attorney and that counting the vote involved technical legal skills. Wood took "his defeat very much to heart," but admitted in a discussion of the bill's jurisdiction that it was so complicated that "lawyers, I suppose, are the only competent authority into construction of an act of Congress."[91] Even so, he still meant to make his presence felt but was unsure of the means.

The count went smoothly until it reached Florida. The Republican majority on the commission, by a vote of 8 to 7, refused to "go behind the returns" and ruled for Hayes. The decision rocked Democrats, but Wood kept the decision in perspective. While he joined the futile House Democratic majority in rejecting it, he urged the party to wait for Louisiana and South Carolina where conditions seemed more favorable. Until then, he said Democrats intended no "factious opposition," and were "ready in good faith to carry out" the commission bill.[92]

The count stalled on Louisiana and commissioners again went 8 to 7 for Hayes. Democrats held another caucus, but nothing was clear. Southern Democrats were torn by adamant filibusters, moderates disenchanted with Tilden, and opportunists ready to strike a bargain with Republicans. Northerners were just as rudderless, adrift between those who wanted to go on fighting and others who resented supposed Southern collaboration with Hayes. At the end, the caucus voted 69 to 40, with over 60 abstentions, to continue the count "without dilatory opposition." Wood was indecisive. He realized in his pragmatic mind that Tilden was now a sure loser, but his partisan heart could not accept such a result. Unable to resolve the dilemma, he tried to postpone the caucus. When that tactic failed, he boycotted its vote.[93]

As the House began debating the Louisiana situation, Wood successfully moved a recess, 140 to 130, still evidently being an obstructionist. A different motive became apparent at another muddled caucus. Cooperating with Randall, he watched silently as the Speaker probed the limits of Democratic resistance. House Democrats, Randall mused, could "in an emergency" amend the Presidential Succession Act of 1792 as to make the secretary of state acting president until new elections. Or, the House could recess "from day to day until the amendment was accepted by the Senate, which he thought might be the case." No consensus developed, and Randall finally pointed out that the lack of agreement meant the party, based on the previous caucus, was committed to continuing the count. On that note, the meeting adjourned with little settled.[94]

Against this background, Wood's speech denouncing the commission gushed, as expected, with measured bitterness. He pointed out that Democrats had agreed to arbitrate, believing the panel would be "disinterested, impartial, judicial and non-partisan." Instead, Republican commissioners had "disregarded the law" by accepting blatantly bogus certificates, hence showing itself "partisan in character and insufficient in judgment." By now frenzied with indignation, he shouted, "Why have they done this? This House demands to know why; the American people demand to know why; and history will ask, with wonder and amazement, why?" Wood's phillipic was good for his soul, but his eloquence did not help. House Democrats rejected the decision, 173 to 99, but the count moved inexorably onward.[95]

For the next three days, Wood and the Democratic majority mired proceedings with time-consuming dilatory motions. During this period, Randall invited Wood and a small group of confidants to a meeting in his home for further talks. Secrecy shrouded what they decided, but the next day Randall totally reversed himself, and ruled against any further delays in accepting the finality of Hayes's election. While a small group of zealous Southerners spoke darkly of betrayal, Randall refused to explain, but he probably had multiple, overlapping reasons. He must have realized that the party was too disorganized to force a new election, and that the caucus committed Democrats, perhaps against his inclinations, to continue the count. Moreover, he wanted to retain the Speakership and needed to prove that he was a moderate. Above those, Republicans may have privately assured him that Hayes favored home rule. For whatever reason, Randall's decision was irrevocable.

Wood's shift on the partisan spectrum from extremism to acquiescence was just as incredible and conjectural. He probably shared Randall's reasoning and sensed additional personal benefits. Such a switch could both bury his Peace Democratic stigma and assuage the business community that felt that prolonging the crisis further disrupted the faltering economy. Too, he was aware that some conservative Southern Democratic friends were already dealing with Republicans. It must have struck him that he might as well submit since he could not halt the bargaining. Such a move would repair his damaged ties to them. Sacrificing Tilden was an added fillip. Yet, in the end, Wood's motivation remained speculative because he, as Randall, gave no reasons.[96] What counted were his actions.

On February 24, Wood made an amazing flip-flop. Working with Randall, he led a coalition of conservative Eastern Democrats and Republicans against a dilatory recess over recording the Oregon vote. As events developed, Wood spearheaded the antifilibusters for the remainder of the count, voting and maneuvering against any more recesses, calling for points of order, and refusing to suspend the rules. By the early morning of March 1, Wood was physically worn but "facile and ready," his face drawn in a slight smile, "conspicuous in any crowd by his erect Clay-like figure," towering "in the lead of the conservative

Democrats." Some bitter Southerners, especially William J. O'Brien of Maryland, could not tolerate his switch, and taunted him as "the high priest of the Republican party." Wood, a reporter wrote, "took it all with great good humor." When O'Brien finished, Wood "extended his hand in mock congratulations." O'Brien shook him off, "whereupon Mr. Wood raised his hands over Mr. O'Brien's head as if in the act of conferring a blessing." Comic relief rippled across the floor. "The scene was so funny that the entire House broke out into loud roars of laughter."[97]

As the curtain descended, Randall and Wood stood in the center of the congressional stage, applause ringing in their ears. The *New York Herald* was ecstatic: "Especial praise is due to Speaker Randall for the decisive political courage with which he has ruled against the filibusters on all points, which were vital, and to Mr. Fernando Wood for the magnificent vigor, tact, and skill with which he has led the Democratic opposition to the infuriate obstructionists." Even the usually hostile Republican *New York Tribune* bestowed an unprecedented accolade: "Fernando Wood has made a new reputation." He was one of the few Democrats who "deserved well of their country, and the country will not forget it."[98] By linking his fortunes with Randall, then, Wood finally turned the corner of his post-secessionist career and was in position to implement the policies he deemed crucial to himself, his party, and his nation.

THIRTEEN

An Uncertain Majority

R ANDALL swung into a vigorous campaign to retain the Speakership shortly after the last barrier fell to Hayes's inauguration. Unlike two years earlier, he did everything possible to undercut Cox and Morrison, his chief rivals. Above all, Randall considered Wood indispensable. To a confidant, Randall wrote that although "Wood & I have never spoken on the subject," they made an implicit swap. For his aid, Randall agreed to name Wood "chairman [of] Ways and Means." At the moment, neither considered the chief liability in the deal—their profound differences over the tariff—and pushed ahead with single-minded dedication.[1]

Wood pulled powerful strings of money, organization, and influence. In New York, he lobbied hesitant financiers and congressmen, assuring them that Randall was safe on key fiscal issues. Within Tammany, he secured Kelly's endorsement by warning that Cox's candidacy was futile. During the summer, Wood spent a working holiday at Sharon Springs, pushing Randall among politicians vacationing from other states.[2]

The missing piece was the party's largest bloc of congressmen, sixty-seven Southern Democrats and their uncertain attitude toward Randall after the disputed election. While Randall called in political debts for past help he had given Southerners, Wood tested his own standing among them. It was firm. To most Southerners, Wood's racism was a vital part of their chief priority, preserving the racial order through home rule. His role in the presidential election was beside the point, then, especially since Hayes's Southern policy seemed to abandon blacks to their control.

Wood listened sympathetically to Southern grumbling about Randall's rulings and his negative attitude about subsidizing the Texas and Pacific Railroad. Wood soothed ruffled feelings through a network of congressional associates, and wrote pro-Randall editorials for the prestigious *Charleston News and Courier,* which Ben Wood partially owned, emphasizing Randall's belief in home rule. To three

visiting Georgia congressmen, Alexander Stephens, Robert Toombs, and Pierce
M. B. Young, all former Confederates, Wood hinted that although Randall was
compassionate, he might punish those tempted to stray by reducing their committee assignments.[3]

Wood stayed in constant communication with Randall over these hectic
months, maintaining a steady flow of advice. In a typical letter he lectured, "You
must now be cautious in your expressions with your friends, & avoid all 'interviews' for the Press. Doubtless an effort will be made to get you to say or do
something which will injure you. You cannot keep too quiet, but you must not
lose a point."[4]

As Congress approached its special October 1877 opening, Wood controlled
the sixteen-member New York Democratic delegation, and Cox's backers lamely
hoped that Randall would "fix a committee to suit him." Morrison, who was
barely on speaking terms with Randall but not with Wood, commanded little
more than Illinois's complementary vote. He withdrew, and complained to
Marble that, "Randall and Wood are now in complete control of the democratic
party interests—so far as these interests are committed to the keeping of Congress." Everything now fit. Wood nominated Randall in the caucus; he easily beat
Virginian John Goode, the symbolic Southern candidate; and Randall's reelection
followed, 149 to 132 over Garfield.[5]

Randall honored the bargain, crowning Wood's decades-long quest for
respectability, naming him chairman of Ways and Means and ex officio leader of
the House, the first New Yorker chosen in forty-two years. As the *New York
Tribune* conceded, he had earned the prize because of his "length of service and
parliamentary skill." Now that he had the office, Wood outlined his first goal, tariff revision. In response, the *New York World* wondered how Democrats could
achieve any unified policy since Wood represented a large group which favored
tariff reform while Randall backed protecting domestic industries.[6]

Randall was aware of the discrepancy. He assured Marble that he and Wood
only differed in emphasis, and contended that Ways and Means "is clearly in
favor of the revision of the Tariff in the interest of revenue." On December 1,
1877, Roger Q. Mills of Texas, acting as Randall's surrogate, sought to instruct
Wood about the will of Congress through such a resolution. While it failed, 76
to 67, the seventy-seven Democrats not voting, largely from the Southern and
Mid-Atlantic states, indicated the party's cavernous sectional cleavages and
unclear aims. Wood's vote was even more significant in terms of his relationship with Randall. He joined twelve Democrats, chiefly from the Mid-Atlantic
and South, and sixty-four Republicans from New England and the Midwest
against Mills.[7]

Wood was equally alert to his policy differences with Randall. Despite his dis-
taste for newspapers, Wood used them as a forum to show his independence. As

journalists crowded around his desk, he said mildly that he did not advocate either a "radical change in favor of free trade or protectionism." Yet Wood did challenge Randall. Since previous tariffs lacked clarity, built as they were on a "rickety structure," Wood indicated that he had "made up his mind that we need a new tariff, and that it is idle to attempt to patch up or amend the old one."[8]

Wood did not mention Locofocoism in this exchange, but it was the foundation of his abiding passion to rebuild the Democracy into a modern, conservative force. At the outset of the Forty-fifth Congress, the tariff was not yet a clear-cut partisan issue because each party contained too many internal divisions for such a confrontation. Wood was determined, however, to identify the Democracy as the party of antiprotectionism for ideological and political reasons. He considered tariffs glaring instruments of special privilege, harmful to equal rights. Moreover, tariffs shackled manufacturers and farmers with a competitive disadvantage in overseas markets, lowered employment, and forced consumers to pay artificially higher prices for both domestic and imported commodities. Thus, they prevented capital accumulation necessary to refund the national debt. Revision, in contrast, was the direct antithesis of those factors, the symbolic and practical means to rekindle traditional party principles, unite the sections, and stimulate free enterprise.

Wood was a political realist. He grasped that every political sign indicated that Democrats were divided between protectionists and dogmatic free traders, that he could not count on Randall, and that he faced an insurmountable barrier in a Republican Senate and president. But Wood did not waver. Whatever the political risks, the potential rewards were simply too great.

Wood set to work in a sophisticated, methodical manner. Showing considerable political savvy, he involved each member of Ways and Means in every step he took, beginning with the creation of subcommittees to investigate the entire schedule, item by item, line by line. He then assessed how much revenue the Treasury needed for expenses from tariff collections, considered possible means of equalizing duties between industry and consumers, and examined methods for expanding foreign trade. To stall inevitable lobbyists, he insisted on secrecy and set mid-February as the tentative date for presenting a finished bill. "Making haste slowly," he promised a thorough product not "based upon any wild or speculative theories," but "a practical and useful measure." Meantime, he carefully cultivated Randall. "When the Bill is reported, I think you will approve it, as I am sure the Committee will be glad to have any suggestions from you."[9]

The subcommittee met daily, took testimony only in writing, and remained noncommittal about findings. Reporters, in the absence of hard news, devoted columns of speculation about the bill's ultimate shape. In the midst of these developments, Democrats pleaded for time and rationalized that fair adjustments of "the burden of our custom duties" needed "careful consideration."[10]

Wood's Ways and Means subcommittee investigators were seen as "gratifying their curiosity" by the *Daily Graphic*, January 22, 1878.

Wood did not have time. A powerful lobby from the Industrial League of Pennsylvania, The American Iron and Steel Association, The National Association of Wool Manufacturers, and The National Wool Growers' Association mounted a skillful petition campaign by playing on workingmen's fears that any reforms would further "paralyze financial and business conditions" in a nation still locked in a depression. Other special-interest groups flooded congressmen with suspiciously similar pro-tariff letters. Still others paid traveling expenses for delegations of ironworkers who streamed into Washington to protest against "any reductions whatever." Secretary of the Treasury John Sherman joined the assault with dire warnings that the government could not forego high tariff revenues because of impending specie resumption and the redemption of refunding bonds.[11]

Under this assault, many reform Democrats questioned Wood's competence. Senator Thomas Bayard told David Wells they did not believe that Wood would "get his bill (in *any* shape) through the House at the present session." Wood answered the lobbyists and naysayers with supreme self-confidence. He informed Joseph S. Moore, a prominent member of the Free Trade League, "Whilst it is important to have the people with you, yet the fact that you have not, is no ground for believing that you are wrong." To Wells, Wood added that Democrats must strive for the possible and not attempt too much "and accomplish nothing."[12]

On March 24, 1878, Ways and Means completed the bill, and authorized Wood to present it as H.R. 4106. Two days later, he offered a resolution to make the bill a special order, with debate opening in a week and continuing until completed. While the House passed it, 137 to 114, Wood was uneasy. Out of 156 Democrats, 121 supported him, 10 voted nay, and 25 were absent. Just as troubling, the opposition was solid in protectionist areas: New England, upstate New York, the Republican Midwest, and among Mid-Atlantic Pennsylvania Randall Democrats. Wood did have some reassuring backing in New York City, the Border States, and the South, along with 16 Republicans and 20 votes from Illinois and Indiana Morrison Democrats. But Wood was still on shaky ground. Continued support among Morrison's people was uncertain because they had not forgiven Wood's treachery over Morrison's tariff two years earlier. Even more problematic, several Republicans and Democrats explained they backed the special order only as a courtesy to Ways and Means.[13]

Wood opened formal debate on April 10 with statistics explaining the bill and its probable effect on the economy. Speaking persuasively, he said that Congress had never formalized an orderly system "to procure revenue and to regulate its commerce with other nations." Over the years, the tariff had evolved into an imperfect monster with schedules subject to pressure groups, containing far too many articles, compound duties, and unclear modes of collection which often cheated the government out of legitimate income and fostered smuggling. Its class bias was equally unjust, penalizing poor consumers by overtaxing them and undertaxing the rich. To disarm critics, he insisted that his measure did not correct "all the abuses of the present tariff," but instead offered new principles based

Wood's competence in revising the tariff was questioned by some, and he was depicted as "up to his eyes" in the project by the *Daily Graphic*, March 20, 1878.

upon "a lopping off of the complications and contradictions now existing in the present laws."[14]

For political effect, Wood was disingenuous. His ideas, based on years of thoughtful study and on concepts borrowed from Wells, were in fact innovative, and did threaten many vested interests. H.R. 4106 contained only a dutiable list, and reduced the number of articles from 1524 to 575 at rates based on a percentage of the product's invoiced value, commonly called *ad valorem* rates. Most raw materials were untaxed. Any article not specified was free. In reducing duties, Wood had to neutralize Secretary Sherman and protectionists, who insisted that the bill created a Treasury shortfall. As a partial answer, Wood offered his own figures to show that Sherman misled Congress. More to the point, Wood wanted to shift attention from the direct revenues the tariff generated, where his numbers were suspect, to larger indirect benefits, where he felt he had a stronger case. Removing the "ambiguities of the present tariff," simplifying collection, and ending smuggling, he reasoned, would spur the volume of exports and actually induce higher national economic growth.[15]

The key to his bill lay in an obsessive commitment to expand American industrial and agricultural trade overseas in order to "develop to its full extent the material resources of the nation." To that end, he wanted the free importation of foreign-built ships and shipbuilding material, plus a 10 percent retaliatory surtax against nations that discriminated against American goods.[16]

Protectionist congressmen gave Wood "undivided attention" when he spoke, then whipsawed the bill. Over the next two months, more than fifty, led by William McKinley, a young Ohioan just emerging as the leading Republican pro-tariff theorist, attacked H.R. 4106 as a radical measure which damaged all citizens and especially the Treasury, which could not function with lowered duties. As for Wood's statistical rationalizations, they were "implausible vagaries," sure to condemn the nation to deficit spending far into the foreseeable future.[17]

Wood was at his desk every day as the bill's floor leader, exuding confidence of a 20 to 25 vote majority. What took place on the floor proved secondary to the backroom pressure of logrolling lobbyists, plus the realization that H.R. 4106 stood little chance of winning approval from either the Senate or Hayes. There, Wood lost. He could not convince Randall to prevent a partial protectionist filibuster, nor a distracting, ill-timed Tildenite move to reopen the disputed election through a special investigative committee chaired by New Yorker Clarkson N. Potter. The caucus was just as befuddled. Protectionists objected that Wood had attempted too much, and free traders protested that he had not gone far enough. The caucus responded to these crosscurrents by refusing to bind Democrats to a party line, and allowing each man to vote "according to the interests of his own section."[18]

The end neared on June 4. In a test vote, 131 to 88, the House limited debate to two hours. Defeat came the next day on a simple motion to eliminate the bill's enacting clause. His face frozen in a half-smile, Wood watched the motion pass by 134 to 120. This time, only 113 Democrats backed him— generally from New York City, the Midwest, South, and Border States—while

19, including every Democrat from Pennsylvania and New Jersey, jumped sides, and 24 did not vote. In contrast, only 7 Republicans from the Midwest, South, and Border States defected.[19]

Tariff revision was dead. Immediately, an outburst of critical editorials from both Democrats and Republicans assailed Wood's performance, agreeing that he had overestimated Democratic support, did little to nurture public opinion, advocated few "fixed and tried principles of political economy," and needlessly disturbed business. Perhaps the harshest assessment came from the free-trade *World*. Wood's fatal error, "as we are sorry to be obliged to believe," was that his bill was "neither prepared in time nor pressed with skill and energy."[20] These views oversimplified Wood's failure. No Democrat could as yet manage the party of tomorrow. Intersectional and intrasectional party economic differences, not principles, nor poor guidance, explained his loss. Putting the issue into perspective, the large number of Democrats who had supported Wood indicated that the Democracy was becoming the party of lower tariffs. In the misery of those June days, Wood's efforts were not in vain.

Given his daily duties as Democratic floor leader and the enormous psychic energy he poured into the tariff, Wood's packed schedule left little room to shape other policies. The vacuum gave a group of Midwestern Democratic inflationists an opportunity to introduce a series of monetary and financial measures which he found personally and politically repugnant.[21]

When Hayes had called the Forty-fifth Congress into special session the previous October, silverites were more determined than ever to establish bimetallism by remonetizing "the historic silver dollar of our fathers." Wood was not pleased and had not budged from his position that free and unlimited coinage of silver would destroy the nation's economic vitality.[22]

On November 5, 1877, Bland bypassed Wood and the Ways and Means Committee through a suspension of the rules and introduced a free coinage bill, H.R. 1093. It quickly succeeded, 163 to 34. This massive majority cut across party lines, drawing 90.7 percent of the Democrats and 73.6 percent of the Republicans, from the Midwest, Border States, South, and Far West. Wood bogged down in a deep minority, just one of 10 Democrats and 24 Republicans, concentrated in New York and New England, with a sprinkling from the mid-Atlantic states. H.R. 1093 ran into trouble in the Senate. Republican William B. Allison of Iowa added an amendment so that instead of complete remonetization the Treasury was required to buy not less than $2 million nor more than $4 million a month and coin that into silver dollars at the old rate of 16 to 1.[23]

By February 1878, the focus of conflict shifted back to the House. Wood still opposed Bland-Allison (even though he knew it was a compromise) and various efforts to broaden its scope. In the process, he supported a tabling move, voted against final passage, and backed Hayes's unsuccessful veto. Wood's isolation became clearer on the eight roll calls involving bimetallism. He was merely one of two Democrats and two Republicans who voted against each issue.[24]

Wood's hard-money principles had a happier ending on another monetary issue. On October 31, 1877, Democratic inflationists, this time led by Ohioan Thomas Ewing of the Banking and Currency Committee, introduced a bill to repeal section 3 of the Specie Resumption Act which set the date for resumption on or before January 1, 1879. Wood backed resumption as the best means to guarantee confidence in the money supply, and supported Secretary of the Treasury John Sherman's prudent marketing of bonds to build the necessary reserve.[25]

Wood cast his vote without addressing the House on this issue. In the next session, however, he did explain his attitude about fiat currency. Paper money was acceptable, he said, only if "controvertible into the universally recognized standard of value throughout the civilized world." Warning that any delay in resumption would penalize productive growth, he cautioned that it was unwise "to support a dual money-creating authority, especially when it may frequently happen that values may be unsettled in the differences which may possibly occur."[26]

It came as little surprise, then, when Wood voted on five roll calls against his party on issues connected to resumption. He headed a small Democratic minority against repeal, never larger than 21 percent of the total party vote, which knitted with a bloc of New York, New England, and Midwest Republicans. Although the bill passed, the Senate blocked any further action. When Congress adjourned on June 20, resumption was secure.[27]

Looking backward at an essentially runaway session, Wood had no apology to make. If the true test of his ability as chairman of Ways and Means lay in his ability to legislate, he was ineffectual. Other yardsticks existed. Bearing the brunt of running the House on a day-to-day basis and considering his reputation as a political trickster, he had dramatized his stature as a principled politician on the tariff and finance. Furthermore, while it was true that the party was antiprotectionist and inflationist largely as a result of the depression, the Democracy was not the same organization that it had been ten years before and even less so than it had been in 1877. Despite his apparent faltering, Wood had set tariff and monetary policies in motion that became the touchstones of faith for Democratic conservatives over the course of the next three decades.

However, "ludicrous" was the adjective many people used to describe Wood heading Ways and Means, presuming to guide the nation's financial destiny, while his personal finances seemed so woeful. Men such as Wood, the *New York Daily Graphic* explained, had trouble paying their bills. Lingering bad times made "real estate a drag on the market," and discouraged buyers and creditors, who found themselves in "possession of property which is now considered so undesirable." This description seemed apt. Early in 1878, financial columns of New York City newspapers began to list Wood's disposal of nineteen large parcels, including his original Bloomingdale holdings, which he sold to his eldest son, Joseph L. R. Wood, for the nominal consideration of one dollar. Surely, the public concluded these "deeds of conveyance" indicated that his wealth had deteriorated.[28]

The intensely private Wood said nothing, allowing the public and even his close friends to believe what they wished. He had a personal reason for being tight-lipped. Sometime in 1877, Alice Wood suffered another emotional breakdown and spent the rest of her life institutionalized. Characteristically, Wood never showed any outward strain, nor his own emotional distress, but his wife's condition was potentially hazardous for property they jointly owned. For that reason, he essentially transferred the holdings to his son in order to keep them out of her guardianship and avoid probate.[29]

All the same, Wood's speculative thirst was unquenched. As sole purchaser, he steadily bought parcels along Madison Avenue and on East Fifty-ninth Street. Nor did his interest in uptown development wane. He was still compulsive about developing rapid transit lines in upper Manhattan, the *New York Times* remarked, either to enhance his present property, or "to make it hot for somebody, or some corporation" if he chose to sell in the near future.[30]

Even his Washington social life betrayed little change. He continued to entertain on an extensive scale, aided by a younger sister, his children, and several daughters-in-law, hardly different from "the generous hospitality for which the host has long been noted." There was only one difference. While his presence remained a familiar one in society, propriety silenced questions about his wife.[31]

Over the recess, Wood revived the tariff controversy but in a far more partisan manner. President Hayes, who was pledged to civil service reform, and Senator Roscoe Conkling, the party's premier spoils-monger, were at loggerheads over Conkling's blatant manipulation of patronage in the New York Custom House. While previous investigations had substantiated Wood's contention that corruption and inefficiency marred collections, he conducted his own probe through a Ways and Means subcommittee.[32] What he had in mind was to further widen the Republican breech prior to the fall elections and refurbish his credentials as a party leader.

Republicans either boycotted the inquiry, or, like Garfield, made a token appearance. Wood went it alone, drawing the *Times*'s scoffing comment that no previous inquest had ever been "so harmonious" because he "agrees with himself." While there was little tangible result, beyond proving the common knowledge that Custom House officials were indeed corrupt, Wood's show of integrity came at a time when he and Tammany needed public approval. It was a small but crucial victory. Over the past two years, the tenuous truce between Kelly and the Tildenites had disintegrated. By the fall of 1878, swallow-tails had formed a new organization, the Irving Hall Democracy, to challenge Tammany. These unstable conditions turned the November election into anyone's race just at a time when Republicans appeared vulnerable.[33]

Unlike a few veteran congressmen who took their districts for granted, Wood had kept close tabs on his constituents and expected an easy reelection. After securing Tammany's renomination, he unwisely ignored his challengers, Irving's John Hardy and Republican Wilson Berryman. Wood concentrated instead on helping Kelly. He financed Tammany and spoke with customary vigor at more rallies than at any time since Mozart's demise. Everywhere Wood's message was the same. Tammany "was permanent, like the Democratic party of the country." Irving was a threat to the party's congressional hegemony and compromised the Democracy's chance of success in the 1880 presidential election.[34]

Election returns tumbled Wood into despair. Irving Hall handed Kelly his first major drubbing since taking Tweed's place, and in the Ninth District Wood's blithe assumption of "an automatic re-election" verged on disaster. He did retain his seat, but won by barely 3 percent over Hardy. Other Democrats were equally stunned. In an off-year election, when they assumed that they would pick up congressional seats, they lost six, and the election of twelve Greenbackers promised new troubles for fiscal conservatives. While Democrats still controlled the House, these results broke Wood's habitual stoicism. At a grim postelection Tammany rally, he told Kelly that he intended to put "a black mark upon" everyone who had opposed them.[35]

Wood was now on a collision course with John Davenport, the city's chief supervisor of the Federal Elections Law, whose authority made him the superior of local inspectors. Democrats hated but could not halt his zealotry against fraudulent voting. That fall, Davenport surpassed himself. In the first week of November alone, he or his assistants arrested 530 men for fictitious naturalization papers and "charged them as felons."[36]

Wood was secretly elated at Davenport's interference with home rule, and used him to ambush the president. Once safely in office, Hayes had formed a Southern policy to conciliate whites, largely based on withdrawing remaining Union troops. Although he promised to protect black rights, Hayes's ultimate aim was to build a permanent Southern Republican party geared to attracting white voters. In the 1878 elections, however, Southern whites wielded a combination of physical violence and economic pressure to intimidate black voters. The apprehensive Hayes, with his policy clearly failing, pledged in his annual December message that both the executive and judicial departments would enforce existing elections laws and bring perpetrators to justice.[37]

As part of his normal function as Ways and Means chairman, Wood's duties included the issuance of a proforma resolution to refer the president's message to the Committee of the Whole on the State of the Union. Departing from this routine, Wood shocked Republicans by defending the South on states' rights grounds, and blamed Hayes for waiving the "bloody shirt" in deference to his party's "worst element." If the president really wished to prevent voting fraud he should have censured Davenport's interference with "legally registered" New York citizens, some four thousand of whom he locked in "an iron cage" as "common criminals," rather than diverting attention to "a few unimportant [Southern] disturbances and irregularities."[38]

As Wood surmised, Republicans erupted in partisan fury. Their anger peaked a week later when he introduced a privileged motion authorizing the Judiciary Committee to investigate Davenport. Few mistook Wood's purpose. Wood "blackened" him as a ploy to repeal all the enforcement laws. Senate Republicans, goaded into countermoves, secured approval for a separate panel to deal with Southern outrages and yet another to examine voting procedures in several Northern cities besides New York.[39]

While these committees bogged down taking testimony that in some cases lasted for over a year and accomplished nothing, the real point was that Wood had partially defined Democratic strategy for the 1880 presidential election. In tying Davenport to white Southern home rule, Wood had seized the one issue that tended to unite Democrats, the traditional Northern defense of the white South. Central to his notion, House Democrats attached riders, which basically nullified the elections laws, on two appropriation bills, one for the army, the other for executive, judicial, and legislative expenditures, as a means of forcing Hayes to accept repeal. He did not budge. A deadlock developed, and the president called the new Forty-sixth Congress into special session in mid-March 1879.[40]

Wood probably enjoyed the difficult spot in which he had placed Republicans. Taking the high ground as a prim constitutionalist, he justified the Democracy's actions on the grounds that Congress had final oversight over how "appropriated money" under "existing laws shall be expended by the Government."[41] Thus, the party principle of local sovereignty, whether applied to New York or the white South, became in Wood's mind a fit means to guarantee a united Democracy.

Meantime, Wood continued to mold the party's fiscal conservatism. At the end of February 1879, he mused aloud in the hearing of a *New York Herald* reporter that while he was uncommitted toward any presidential candidate, the country "demanded sound Democratic statesmanship at the head of our national affairs." Since Wood had become identified with a specific program for economic development, it was unclear how he would accomplish his task given the Democratic minefield on finance and the tariff. He tried. Showing moderation now that resumption was secure, Wood sponsored a successful bill to make greenbacks receivable for imports, based on their equality with coins, which meant gold and the limited amount of silver under Bland-Allison. As for the tariff, he let a new bill float without his aid. When it predictably failed, he explained to Wells that nothing more could be accomplished because of the "wild theories" held by "leading members" of Ways and Means. Free traders were furious at his apparent betrayal and did not understand that he had made a pragmatic shift. Having achieved one goal, tying the Democracy to tariff reform, and realizing that it was futile to continue under present conditions, he poised on the threshold of another critical conservative aim, refunding the national debt.[42]

Sherman's 1870 Funding Act neared its first test of confidence in 1879 when the Treasury marketed the last of the 4 percent, thirty-year bonds. Sales soared, largely because he had stockpiled gold to secure resumption, but his task was incomplete. The "new fives" under the Funding Act matured in 1881. These were $469,651,050, along with two other 6 percent "loans" of $145,786,500 and $57,787,750 each.[43]

Since Republicans had crafted this program, financiers lauded their fiscal sagacity and debt-reduction programs. Wood, however, wanted Democrats, through Ways and Means, to counter this impression by proving that they were better than Republicans at negotiating fresh bonds at lower rates, saving the Treasury millions in interest. Wood had another target. Rapid refunding also solved the core internal problem ailing Democrats, stimulating the sluggish economy by manipulating the money supply. In line with his deflationist commitments, he forecast that steady debt reduction freed capital for investments, lowered interest rates, raised wages, and spurred output with proportionate benefits for consumers, farmers, and the unemployed. His goal, then, was similar to inflationists, the expansion of currency, but through conservative means.

On January 15, 1879, Wood introduced H.R. 5477 as an indication of how conservative Democrats meant to facilitate refunding the 4 percent bonds. It commissioned $40 million in $10 certificates, rather than the $50 ones the Republicans had authorized in the original refunding plan, drawing 3 percent interest, payable in lawful money, convertible at any time, with interest accrued. On first glance, his bill made sense. It did not alter refunding, but democratized bond sales by attracting small investors, many of whom Republicans had ignored.

In order to defuse the old internal Democratic opposition to the entire concept of refunding, Wood delivered a long, well-researched speech on the party's need for new fiscal responsibility. Under existing conditions, he said, most refunding bonds sold in European markets, thus creating extensive overseas debts and giving foreigners too much influence over national credit. Letting this situation fester meant that the United States would eventually lose its sovereignty. Congress must reduce dependence on European sales by tapping "the poorer classes," who were eager to find a "secure depository for their surplus earnings." American workers, now national creditors, would then help spur steady economic growth because they "would feel the necessity of protecting" their interests.[44]

Fernando Wood's goal in refunding the national debt was to use conservative measures to expand the currency. His House Resolution was parodied in this cartoon appearing in *Harper's Weekly* 23 (8 Mar. 1879): 5.

In a one-day debate, Democratic antirefunders, along with a few midwestern Republicans, grilled Wood unmercifully about his motives and tried killing the bill with a variety of unfriendly amendments. It passed, however, in its original shape due to Sherman's apparent advice to conservative Republicans that backing Wood would hasten refunding.[45]

The debate and roll calls indicated that Wood was clearly ahead of his party about the relationship he saw between refunding and party revitalization. In his judgment, Democrats had no choice. With the 1870 bonds nearing maturity, maintenance of national credit required full and quick payment. Sound politics dictated that Democrats must contest Republicans on the field of high finance to prove that they were capable of protecting the economy. Locofocoism also came into play in dictating a policy of widening investments for all Americans, not a privileged few. Wood's difficulty, however, was that few Democratic colleagues matched his awareness of financial complexities, nor his candor in facing political reality.

The Forty-fifth Congress ended with little accomplished. Meeting a week later, the new Congress settled housekeeping matters before deciding on an agenda. The caucus selected Randall (with Wood's "active" aid) for Speaker by eighteen votes over Kentucky inflationist Joseph C. S. Blackburn, but the close contest revealed the party's latent animosities. After confirmation by House Democrats, Randall reappointed Wood, making him, the unapproving *Times* wrote, the only chairman who represented the North's "great commercial, financial and political interests." Yet Randall limited Wood's options, "dishonoring the party," one critic growled, by loading Ways and Means with protectionists and a Republican minority under Garfield which supported Sherman's refunding policies. That done, Democrats settled into a familiar routine of bickering. At a round of House caucuses, which Wood often chaired, and joint meetings with Senate Democrats, they fenced over economic issues, ultimately agreeing to confine themselves to continuing the attack on the elections law.[46]

For the next three months, the public watched with growing impatience as Congress passed five appropriations bills followed by Hayes's steadfast vetoes. As overrides failed, Democrats realized they had overplayed their hands and gradually reduced succeeding bills to the point where Hayes got the money he wanted and retained the enforcement laws. Strangely, Wood was barely visible, except for one brief speech where he opposed federal regulation of suffrage rights because "we believe this is a Government of opinion and of law, not of force or of violence."[47]

Wood's lack of participation was due to sickness. He had been unwell since his operation in 1876 and did not improve. Absent most of the session due to repeated attacks of "inflammatory rheumatism," he missed nearly 61 percent of the roll calls. In June, Wood left for European medical treatment while Congress was still in session. Watching him board the ship, a *Times* reporter noted, "His eyes seem hollow and sunken, and his countenance is ghastly."[48]

Wood did not return until November 6, 1879. During his absence, the vendetta between Tammany and Irving had disrupted the entire Democracy. Also, the Potter inquiry had discredited Tilden by implicating him in vote-buying during the disputed election of 1876. The result left New York, the linchpin of the entire Democracy, with no presidential contender and on the verge of becoming a Republican state in 1880.[49]

Wood, true to his word, only wanted the most available man, but was unsure of that man's identity. He did send out a halfhearted feeler to Horatio Seymour, now in comfortable retirement, to become a compromise candidate "to save the party."[50] When Seymour predictably refused, Wood shunned further involvement and allowed events to take their natural course.

While Wood was indifferent to presidential politicking, he was determined to stamp his fiscal ideas on the party's platform. On December 3, he invited the *Herald*'s Washington reporter into "his comfortable residence" and guided the interview toward "the financial situation." Since the depression was lifting, Wood admitted that the public wanted "as little financial legislation as possible." Yet, Democrats must buck up their courage and educate voters about the need for refunding, despite the realization that the issue "never created [political] excitement" because it was a multifaceted question with little grandstand value.[51]

Here, Wood was straightforward. Refunding was not an intramural Democratic fracas, but a typical partisan fight, one that the party must win before Sherman's policies spiraled out of control. Reaching his key point, Wood emphasized that Congress could not dodge the redemption of bonds maturing in 1881. The critical point revolved around his differences with Sherman on the interest rate and years of maturity. Wood said that he favored new 3.5 percent bonds, redeemable after twenty years, to lessen the burden on taxpayers and avoid a perpetual debt. In contrast, Sherman sought 4 percent bonds redeemable after thirty years to reward the already rich and saddle the American people with that perpetual debt. Refunding, therefore, turned on how much money the Treasury required, the amount the nation saved in interest, and which party would be the political and economic beneficiary of those issues.[52]

Sherman recognized Wood's intent and put the burden of proof on him. Trading blows through the press, he doubted that Wood's bonds could be sold at par in the real financial world. But he was "by no means obstinate" and would accept the lower rate "whenever Mr. Wood produces responsible bankers" willing to float them. Not willing to back down, Wood retorted that "it only requires the experiment of putting the bonds on the market" to prove him correct.[53]

Before proceeding, Wood had to handle the thorny tariff. Free-trade Democrats, now led by Cox, hoped "to keep up a lively interest in [it], till there be a better Congress." With little prospect of passage and unwilling to hinder refunding, Wood told Cox his efforts were impolitic. As his way out, Wood urged Ways and Means to discuss the issue, specifically by increasing the free list, but did not prevent pro-tariff members from loading the bill with even more "articles so as to kill it in committee." [54]

That settled, Wood made refunding the key priority of Ways and Means. Since policy-making hinged upon coordinating general fiscal knowledge, special perception of the bond market, and the management of his committee into an effective political coalition, he enlisted the aid of friendly bankers, gave each member a chance to air views, and sought a broad spectrum of support. The process took from December to February, but his effort bore fruit. Outside of Morrison and Garfield, a bipartisan consensus emerged. On February 18, 1880, Wood introduced H.R. 4592, but procedural delays prevented debate until March 4 when he secured a special order.[55]

The way Wood framed H.R. 4592 indicated whose interests he wanted to advance and protect. At the outset, the bill negated the Republican version of refunding by applying its terms to any bonds bearing more than 4.5 percent interest which "may hereafter become redeemable." It empowered the Treasury to issue fresh $500 million bonds, at 3.5 percent, redeemable after twenty years and payable in forty in lieu of the Funding Act's bonds and its additions now coming due, including his $10 certificates. He also proposed an additional $200 million in notes of 3.5 percent redeemable after two years and payable in ten. The Treasury, using these bonds and notes, would exchange them for older bonds at higher interest than 4.5 percent, but of longer maturity, par for par, based upon previous rates of interest and dates of maturity, to speed refunding and save money. Since the bill wiped out his $10 certificates, Wood protected small investors with an option of conversion. He further required that only these 3.5 percent refunding bonds were "receivable as security for national-bank circulation." Finally, he accepted the deflationist intent of the 1870 Refunding Act, implicitly stating that the new bonds were subject to its provisions.[56]

As the bill's sponsor, Wood asked, "Has not the time arrived when the United States can say to the lenders of money how much interest it will pay, instead of saying as heretofore, What rate of interest will you accept?" Answering himself, Wood maintained his lone purpose was to "liquidate the existing public debt," which absorbed one-third of government income, in the quickest way, at the lowest cost, and with least damage to public credit. Cutting the interest rate, he calculated, saved the United States $14 million a year, thereby shrinking taxation and preventing monopolistic bank "syndicates" from growing richer at public expense. The new bonds were feasible after a careful examination and were a safe depository for private American investors because federal credit was at a high watermark due to resumption and government surpluses. As for future refunding, Wood estimated that the market could handle 3 percent bonds. "This generation," he concluded, could not "liquidate" the total public debt, but its obligation lay in "reducing the burden to the lowest possible weight" for future generations.[57]

Wood's demand for rapid refunding, however desirable or even unavoidable, was not enough. While he spoke, a large number of congressmen milled around the floor, either not listening or talking among themselves. While observers admitted that speeches and debates had "very little to do nowadays with the fate of a bill," they nevertheless recommended that Congress "not abandon the subject, which is too important to be neglected." Such words were unheard. After a desultory debate on March 20, the House referred H.R. 4592 back to Ways and Means.[58]

Congress had indeed dodged a major question. Outside of Wood, the forces of inertia were too strong. Most Republicans and other Democrats did not wish to introduce the issue with a presidential election coming. Inflationists refused to accept it unless Wood specified paper or silver. Democratic ideologues feared refunding further consolidated federal power. Current bondholders worried that Wood's scheme jeopardized their payments. Some few free trade Democrats punished Wood for dragging his feet over the tariff. To complete the circle, few voters could fathom refunding and their leaders would not act until public opinion hardened.

The still-haggard Wood was phlegmatic, and confessed "to having been in doubt about the possibility of carrying his plan successfully through [the present] Congress." This episode, then, marked the opening skirmish in a fight he hoped to win in the third session. Yet something was wrong. Deep in his soul, he had to admit that time was running out.[59]

On the surface, Wood was still the confident congressional impresario, sure that he could master any man or issue. Since December, he had plunged into his customary frenetic behavior. While shaping refunding, he introduced twelve bills and fifty-nine petitions from constituents, and he was constantly on his feet moving parliamentary motions. His spirit was willing, but not his body. Now in constant pain, he received three leaves of absences for evening sessions. By June, he crumbled. "Hon. Fernando Wood is confined to his house in New York City," because of "overwork," the *Washington Evening Star* announced, "but hopes to be out in a few days."[60]

During his convalescence, Wood watched with detachment as the party washed the bloody shirt by nominating General Winfield Scott Hancock for president. Several planks, however, did reflect Wood's influence: attacks on the enforcement laws and government centralism; home rule for the South; and an

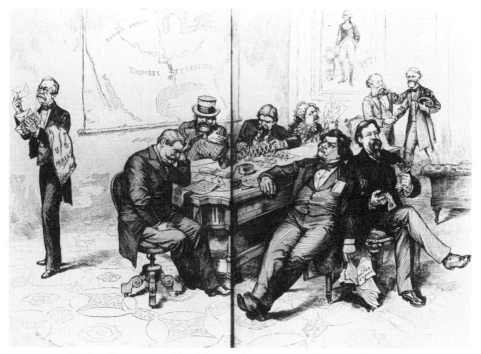

During the 1880 presidential campaign, a cartoon depicting "possible" changes in the cabinet included Wood as postmaster general (left). *Harper's Weekly* 24 (30 Oct. 1880): 696–97.

explanation that the Democracy sacrificed Tilden to prevent a recurrence of "the horrors of a civil war." More to the point, the third plank incorporated key parts of Wood's fiscal program: an indirect acceptance of refunding through a phrase pledging "the strict maintenance of the public faith," and another calling for "honest money," defined in deflationist terms, "gold and silver, and paper convertible to coin."[61]

Wood remained an outsider that fall. His solitary contribution to the presidential campaign came in a public letter urging "the necessity of a change of rulers." As for his reelection, Wood depended upon his "personal popularity" and Kelly's support in beating Irving Hall's Hardy and Republican John L. N. Hunt.[62]

It was not a good year for Democrats. Tammany and Irving fused on the presidential ticket but substantially disagreed on local races. Combined they carried the city for Hancock, but Tammany again lost ground to Irving.

Garfield gained the presidency, and his party recovered the House by thirty-two seats. Wood barely withstood the avalanche. He won by only 1,529 out of 28,552 votes cast, gaining 37.9 percent to Hardy's 32.6 percent and Hunt's 28.9 percent.[63]

December found Wood back in Washington in a fatalistic mood. Journalists, who now made a habit of turning to him for bits of information, covered up the fact that he appeared "infirm" and "ancient," the old bounce gone from his step, and simply reported he was still "handsome" and full of purpose. Such was the image he tried projecting before Republicans returned to power, telling colleagues of ambitious goals to cut federal spending, widen the free list, and, beyond all else, pass refunding. Behind that public mask, Wood knew his time was short. Chafing with frustration over delays in reaching refunding, he fell into an embarrassing shouting match with Maine's Thomas B. Reed over what Wood termed Republican "obstructionism" involving the electoral count. Randall proved a friend. Fearing another ineffectual session, he instructed Democrats that they must gain credit for disposing of refunding "in a business-like manner." Equally vital, he "commended" Wood and emphasized "that no bill before Congress was more important."[64]

On December 14, 1880, Wood reintroduced H.R. 4592 and pressed for prompt passage. Over the course of the next week, opponents raised procedural barriers and introduced a number of distracting revenue bills, while others were absent, preventing even a quorum. Growing desperate, Wood appealed directly to Sherman. "I hope you will indicate to your friends the importance of speedy action on the subject." When Sherman offered nothing, Wood's composure snapped. One day before the two-week Christmas break, he threatened a motion limiting all general debate on the bill to one day, unless the House immediately went into the Committee of the Whole on refunding. At that point, James B. Weaver of Iowa, the recent Greenback candidate for president, muddled the entire question. He launched a bitter personal attack against Wood and Randall for trying to stampede deliberations, and ended with a general denunciation of all deflationists. As cries of "shame" filled the air, the sergeant-at-arms restored order, and congressmen bogged down over whether to censure or expel Weaver. Amid the confusion, the House shelved refunding until after the break.[65]

The joyous Christmas season and New Year festivities, long a time of happiness for the Wood household, passed in quiet. Writhing in physical and emotional pain, Wood was bedridden when Congress reopened on January 5, 1881, and he designated Virginian John Tucker, a colleague on Ways and Means, as his replacement. When Wood could return was problematic, and observers doubted the bill could pass without him. Even Wood was uncertain, and confided to Randall that he was "quite a cripple." Three days later, his face "showing the traces of his recent illness," Wood took his seat, "at great personal risk," somehow finding willpower in his obsession to make refunding the capstone of his career.[66]

During his absence, several congressmen had formulated amendments, some friendly, some not, and they tried reading his face for clues about which ones he would accept. The first amendment reduced bonds by $100 million, increased notes $100 million, and slashed interest to 3 percent. Wood accepted all three. Their advantages, he reasoned, lay in reducing interest payments and hence avoiding any chance of a permanent debt. Republicans disagreed. They believed the volume of bonds was too low and that the interest rate was unrealistic in terms of the market. The amendment passed, 149 to 104, along strict party lines: 94.8 percent Democrats in favor, 87.8 percent Republicans opposed.[67]

Wood did not approve the second amendment coming from Bland. As a means of reviving the inflation question, Bland specified that before the government issued new bonds or notes, the Treasury must redeem older ones coming due in silver dollars of 412.5 grams "and all the gold over and above $50,000,000, now held in the Treasury for redemption purposes." In a brief but sharp attack, Wood defended fiscal conservatism, suggested that inflation was unnecessary due to rebounding prosperity, and joined the familiar bloc of deflationary Democrats and Republicans in defeating Bland, 140 to 111.[68]

Section 5 contained the most critical amendment. It forced national banks to purchase and deposit only the 3 percent bonds as security for banknote circulation. In addition, the amendment repealed section 4 of the Free Banking Act of 1874 which allowed national banks to increase capital and circulation according to need. As objecting Republicans pointed out, section 5 limited banknote circulation, threatened the stability of the entire National Bank system, and raised the specter of cash shortages in the money market.

Wood said little. Many Democrats, who were hostile toward central banking on principle, privately told him they would begin a filibuster if he disapproved, delaying refunding until the next session. Ordinarily, such a threat would have aroused his ire. Now, Wood was cowed. He grew progressively weaker each passing day. One sympathetic reporter noticed, "He required assistance to get up the stairs and it was with difficulty that he could walk from the door to his seat, or sit in it or rise from it during the debate." Wood voted for the revision, then, although his motives were unclear. He may have rationalized that Democrats would not support refunding without it; or, perhaps, he was merely being consistent in light of his long record against the National Bank Act. Whatever his reasons, the roll call indicated that his hands were tied. Strict partisanship prevailed. Section 5 passed, 137 to 119. Democrats voted 96.1 percent in favor, only 1 Republican approved, and Greenbackers, who wanted to limit the National Bank System in any possible way, gave it 10 out of 11 votes.[69]

The climactic vote came on the morning of January 19. The House, by a vote of 135 to 125, handed Wood his ultimate victory. An impressive Democratic majority of 92.5 percent finally put the party on record in favor of a major conservative goal. The result, observers agreed, was a tribute to both Wood's fiscal sagacity and Randall's arm-twisting. The opposition was equally firm. Republicans cast a negative vote of 91.7 percent along with 10 Democratic inflationists led by Bland. Greenbackers, by 91.2 percent, joined them because the final version contained few tangible assurances of inflationary currency.[70]

Shortly afterwards, Wood left Washington for the last time. "By advice of friends & physicians I shall leave here for the Hot Springs of Arkansas," he informed Randall. But duty bulked large on his mind. "If I do not return in time for any conference there may be on the Funding Bill," he ended, "I hope you will appoint members who will never yield the rate of interest [of] 3%." Two weeks later, time finally ran out. On his sixty-ninth birthday, February 14, 1881, Wood died.[71]

Wood did not live to see his victory turn to ashes. On March 3, after Senate modification and passage, Hayes vetoed the measure. Although he disagreed with the 3 percent interest rate, Hayes was willing to allow the market to settle the question. Even so, he pilloried the bill as a "radical change in the banking law" and based his veto on section 5. In Hayes's judgment, it was not an "essential part of a refunding measure" and "imperiled the national banking system." One last time, it seemed as if Wood's congressional career had ended in frustration.[72]

FOURTEEN

The Man and His Career

THE train carrying Fernando Wood's remains moved from Hot Springs to Washington, accompanied by several of his children and delegations from the board of aldermen and Congress. After a brief memorial service in Washington, the cortege moved to New York City where he was buried in Trinity Cemetery in a family plot next to Anna D. Wood.

Even in death, Wood remained a focus of controversy. Conflicting assessments involved not only his personal character and career, but more particularly his accomplishments.

Not surprisingly, the rules of the congressional club made Wood a paragon. Foes were silent as fellow Democrats lauded his rise from humble beginnings, his principles, and his multiple services to city, state, and nation. Others hailed his "warm, courteous and hospitable nature," and praised his strong commitment to "the best interests of the financial management of the country." Perhaps the most surprising and gracious eulogy came from Elbridge G. Lapham, an upstate New York Republican, soon to replace Roscoe Conkling in the Senate. "Years had tempered the ardor of [Wood's] zeal as a politician, and ripened his judgement for the discharge of the more dignified duties of a statesman," Lapham said. "We shall miss his manly presence among us; and it may be many years before, in these respects, we shall look upon his like again."[1]

Outside of Congress, the words were more biting. *The Nation* and its editor, the cultivated and moralistic Edwin L. Godkin who let little escape his notice, wrote a brief obituary whose theme was that Wood was only distinguished because "he was the first municipal 'Boss.'" *New York Daily Graphic* agreed: Wood "was a very remarkable man," it said, but he had few durable principles, and even those he sacrificed to tactical maneuvers. The *New York Times* issued the harshest evaluation: Wood had "ceased some time since to be a conspicuous figure in American life, and his disappearance from the scenes of active life will not cause a commotion so wide-spread as it would have twenty years ago."[2]

The truth lay between these extremes. Much of Wood's life was admirable. He was indeed a self-made man, and his political career was a testament to durable Democratic principles rooted in Locofocoism. During the height of his municipal career in the 1850s, Wood was the dominant figure in New York City, its first true professional politician, a man who constructed a firm political coalition among the city's underclass of workers and immigrants through personal magnetism, gritty determination, and a Jacksonian commitment to be a tribune of the people. These qualities became particularly apparent when he organized Mozart Hall or campaigned with the innovative skill to refine old political rules, invent new ones, and to win by them.

Wood became mayor in 1855 at a time when New York City's rapid growth overwhelmed the municipal government and its traditional leaders, and cast doubt on the ability of New Yorkers to govern themselves. He confronted these multiple crises with far more energy, self-confidence, and imagination than any of his predecessors, leaving a legacy that anticipated several of the varied and often contradictory strands that composed the later Progressive Movement.

Wood foreshadowed one aspect of progressivism, urban liberalism, by sponsoring an extensive social-welfare program through the regulatory role of government. Sincerely troubled by the deteriorating quality of urban life and endemic class tensions, his solutions rested on decisive executive leadership, working up from ordinary voters to a vigorous and aggressive mayor, who headed an effective bureaucracy accountable to him. Integral to this process, Wood championed the working class, particularly by involving it in the distribution and use of political power.

Yet Wood, like some later Progressives, blended liberal reforms with conservatism. He had no quarrel with the acquisitive spirit of his age, and feared the consequences of too centralized a government. Having earned a fortune through his own efforts, he made a concerted effort to become a businessmen's mayor and served their needs by stressing efficiency in government and attacking the growing corruption among aldermen. While he shared the business community's desire for lower taxes, however, he realized the city needed more funds to underwrite expanded city services and merely recommended more effective modes of collection. At the same time, Wood's Locofoco commitment to equal opportunity tugged him in a contrary direction. Even as he accepted growing inequalities as inevitable consequences of the free-market system, he warned businessmen that they risked unremitting class warfare unless they duplicated his social conscience and placed human rights over property rights.

Wood's crusade against Tammany Hall paralleled a similar strain of progressivism aimed at structural changes in urban politics. His actions contradicted the old adage that municipal politics revolved around a struggle between bosses and reformers. To the contrary, Wood was both a prototype machine boss and a reformer. In those roles, Wood used the municipal government's constitutional and institutional diffusions of power to consolidate decision-making in himself. Reflecting Locofocoism, however, he formed Mozart Hall to return authority to ordinary voters that corrupt vested interests in Tammany Hall had stolen from them. Yet, Wood was typically inconsistent. While many of his goals were idealistic, they also had a practical side. Purifying politics through Mozart Hall had as much to do with increasing his power as it had with attacking Tammanyites.

He presaged another Progressive characteristic, an antidemocratic bias. Although he never went as far as some elitist Progressives who distrusted the urban masses, Wood's personality, egotistical obsession with strong executive leadership, and policies served a similar end. Even though he favored more public involvement in decision-making, he clearly set its bounds.

In the largest sense, then, Wood was a unique mayor, a city builder who was involved in every facet of the city's life. By focusing authority in himself, the person best able to guarantee the city's civic betterment, Wood sought to conserve individual private rights, expand the scope of social services, foster investments in human capital, devise sound municipal taxation and spending procedures, safeguard public order, defend consumers, protect working-class interests, and ensure steady economic growth through a new version of municipal mercantilism that guarded the city's vital trade links with the Southern states.

In terms of immediate improvements in the quality of urban life, Wood admittedly fell short of his goals. His shabby flaws, his willingness to pander to the worst of human instincts, his ego, ethical lapses, inconsistencies, racism, and tactical trickery made far more enemies than friends and clouded his overall accomplishments. As a result, his opponents in the Common Council enacted few of his ideas and stalled others. Beyond even those, Wood was never a boss in the ultimate sense because he could not centralize power by totally controlling Tammany and the city and state governments.

Taken in context, Wood's true achievements should not be measured in specific gains and losses within the years that he served as mayor. A more valid test lay in the long-term significance of his programs on subsequent mayors who adopted and refined what he had begun. In that sense, he did improve the quality of urban life by serving as a model for future city builders and urban progressives. Even more, his consistent defense of the working class, as in his relief programs, proved that one man's demagogue was another's champion of the people. In short, Wood was a mayor of true historical significance.

The way Wood achieved prominence after his mayoralty also set him apart from the majority of fellow mayors during the nineteenth century. Of the approximately 450 men elected as mayors of the fifteen largest American cities between 1808 and 1900, Wood numbered among a tiny band who used the position to climb into higher office. Voters selected eight as governors, legislatures named two for the United States Senate, and one became president, Grover Cleveland of Buffalo. While Wood's public service was limited to the House of Representatives along with thirteen others, he was nevertheless distinctive. None matched his eight postmayoral terms, nor did any duplicate his distinctive role as a key party strategist and congressional leader.[3]

Despite his failures, Wood was a major, if underappreciated, force within the national Democratic party. His long political career, spanning nearly fifty years, was in many ways a microcosm of its operations during his lifetime, with all its principles, programs, hopes, and shortcomings.

Wood learned his political craft through the schools of Jacksonianism and the radical politics of the Locofocos. Through such education, he absorbed a lifelong definition of equality which shaped his consciousness, the idea that ordinary people ought to have equal political, social, and economic rights regardless of ethnicity or class. In the prewar period, Wood was an apologist for the white South and slavery, but he did represent and reflect the views of a large number of Democratic voters. During the Civil War, Wood, like Lincoln, believed in a permanent Federal Union. Yet, the perplexing problem of how to remain a loyal American and a loyal Democrat limited Wood's vision and contributed to the party's divisions and defeats. His difficulty was that while he sought an undivided Union, he pictured it in antebellum terms as a white man's republic, functioning under constitutional restraints, grounded upon static socioeconomic and racial institutions. Once the realities of war undermined his commitments, Wood lacked the ability to adjust. By 1863, he was a national spokesman for an America that no longer existed. During the early stages of congressional Reconstruction he remained a reactionary striving for the values of the past.

Wood finally made his peace in 1871 with this transformed nation when he became instrumental in orchestrating the party's adoption of the New Departure. In his mind, Democrats had survived the war and its consequences, but faced the larger challenge of justifying that survival and facing the future. To those ends, he urged the Democracy to reconstitute itself as a potent force in modern American life by dropping racial issues for economic ones. His ideas drew inspiration from Locofocoism and its stress on equal opportunity for the many, not the few. Becoming an articulate advocate for a revived version of Jacksonian political economy in a new era of industrial and business growth, he redirected the party back to its traditional free-market policies: hard money, deflation, tariff reduction, decentralized banking, reduced government, and strict payment of the national debt.

True, Wood's congressional achievements were unimpressive. Few major bills bore his name. That situation was expected because he was a member of a hopeless minority for five out of eight postwar terms. During this unproductive period, his sole option was that of a congressional gadfly, pestering Republicans with dead-end obstructionism. These years, however, were not wasted and were instead marked by productivity along other lines: the advocacy of deflationary fiscal issues, hard work on foreign relations, detailed labor on esoteric but demanding budgetary and taxation items, a sincere desire to soften class conflict, a passionate commitment to pay the national debt, and a determined drive to spur the economy by lowering the tariff and opening foreign markets. Reconciling his years of preparation for leadership with his limited accomplishments as chairman of Ways and Means was more difficult. In that position, he suffered more failures than victories. Even his final vindication, Chester A. Arthur's administration's enactment of refunding based on his ideas, came too late.

Ultimately, Wood must be judged within the framework of what was possible. After the Democracy regained the House in 1875, conflicting regional needs, mainly economic, buffeted congressional leaders and the programs they sought. As the *Times* aptly remarked in 1878, minority Democrats had been united in a "compact body" around the easy task of negativism. Once in power, the party's centrifugal forces made it "an uncertain majority," unable "to hold its members together long enough to carry any partisan measure."[4] The result did not excuse Wood's failures so much as explain them. Given existing conditions, no one could keep the Democracy's competing factions together long enough to pass a consistent program.

Wood's failures, then, were less his than his party's. Like any politician, he should be evaluated on how well he saw the purpose of politics and its relationship to government, the ability of society to function effectively without destroying its fabric and to allocate a fair share of power to its component parts. Here lay Wood's importance. Although he was a Democratic conservative, Wood was not a tool of special interests or a standpatter. Nor was he a politician who concentrated on insignificant spoils and mean-spirited partisanship that supposedly typified what Mark Twain called the Gilded Age. Rather, he sought forward-looking means to stimulate economic growth and free the spirit of American enterprise. Even if his ideas were not immediately successful, he did reshape the party leading toward the triumph of the Bourbon Democrats under Grover Cleveland. When the Democracy moved into the 1880s and beyond, it was the party that Wood did so much to mold as the one of sound money, home rule, deflation, and antiprotectionism.

ABBREVIATIONS USED IN NOTES

AHR	*American Historical Review*
CU	Columbia University, New York, N.Y.
CWH	*Civil War History*
HSP	Historical Society of Pennsylvania, Philadelphia
JAH	*Journal of American History*
JSH	*Journal of Southern History*
LC	Library of Congress, Washington, D.C.
MHS	Massachusetts Historical Society, Boston
MVHR	*Mississippi Valley Historical Review*
NA	National Archives, Washington, D.C.
NYH	New York History
NYHS	New-York Historical Society, New York, N.Y.
NYHSQ	*New-York Historical Society Quarterly*
NYPL	New York Public Library, New York, N.Y.
NYSL	New York State Library, Albany
OAHQ	*Ohio Archeological and Historical Quarterly*
OHS	Ohio Historical Society, Columbus, Ohio
PSQ	*Political Science Quarterly*
UR	University of Rochester, Rochester, N.Y.
UV	University of Virginia, Charlottesville

NOTES

1. THE BEGINNING

1. Donald MacLeod, *Biography of Honorable Fernando Wood, Mayor of New York City* (New York: O. F. Parsons, 1856), hereafter cited as *Wood*; Edward K. Spann, *The New Metropolis: New York City, 1840–1857* (New York: Columbia Univ. Press, 1981), 502.

2. See, for example, *New York Daily Graphic*, May 1, 1874; *New York Times*, Feb. 15, 1881; *New York Herald*, Feb. 15, 1881.

3. MacLeod, *Wood*, 17–29; George R. Prowell, *The History of Camden County, New Jersey* (Philadelphia: L. J. Richards and Co., 1886), 741; John S. Wood, *An Index of Wood Families in America* (Baltimore: Garrett & Massie, 1966), 2; William H. McMahon, *South Jersey Towns: History and Legends* (New Brunswick: Rutgers Univ. Press, 1973), 146–47, 277.

4. MacLeod, *Wood*, 29–31; Wood, *Index of Wood Families*, 206. For further information on Wood's family background, see: A. Van Doren Honeyman, ed., *Documents Relating to the Colonial History of New Jersey, First Series, Calendar of New Jersey Wills, Administration, Etc.* (Somerville: The Unionist-Gazette Association, 1918), 1–11, and Frank H. Stewart, *Notes on Old Gloucester County, New Jersey* (Baltimore: Genealogical Publications Company, 1977), 1–4.

5. MacLeod, *Wood*, 33–35; *Times*, Nov. 18, 1860, Oct. 4, 1862.

6. *Congressional Globe*, 27th Cong., 1st sess., 1841, 10: "App," 290–91, hereafter *Cong. Globe*; MacLeod, *Wood*, 35–39; Wood, *Index of Wood Families*, 23.

7. MacLeod, *Wood*, 39; *Times*, Oct. 31, 1860; *New York Sun*, Oct. 18, 1861; David A. Long, "The New York Daily News, 1855–1906: Spokesman for the Underprivileged," Ph.D. diss., Columbia University, 1950; Robert C. Toll, *Blacking Up: The Minstrel Show in Nineteenth-Century America* (New York: Oxford Univ. Press, 1974), 32, 56, 198. For Benjamin Wood's residencies, see: James Robinson, *The Philadephia Directory* (Philadelphia: W. Woodhouse, 1807–11, 1816, 1817); John A. Paxton, *The Philadelphia Directory and Register* (Philadelphia: B. & T. Kite, 1813, 1818, 1819); *Kite's Philadelphia Directory for 1814* (Philadelphia: B. & T. Kite, 1814); and Edward Dawes, *The Philadelphia Directory for 1817* (Philadelphia, 1817).

8. MacLeod, *Wood*, 36.

9. Ibid.

10. Ibid., 37–39, 42.

11. Fernando Wood to Samuel J. Randall, July 20, 1877, Samuel J. Randall Papers, Van Pelt Library, University of Pennsylvania, Philadelphia.

12. *Sun*, Dec. 2, 1857; *Times*, Mar. 31, 1860, Sept. 4, 1864; *Daily Graphic*, Oct. 29, 1877; *Herald*, Feb. 15, 1881; *New York Herald Tribune*, Sept. 18, 1927; *New York Evening Post*, July 27, 1901; Charles S. Haswell, *Reminiscences of an Octogenarian of the City of New York (1816–1860)* (New York: Harper & Brothers, 1897), 509–10; John Foord, *The Life and Public Service of Andrew Haskell Green* (Garden City: Doubleday, Page & Company, 1913), 47–49; William J. Rorabaugh, "Rising Spirits: Immigrants, Temperance, and Tammany Hall," *CWH* 22 (June 1976): 139–57.

13. MacLeod, *Wood*, 41–42; [E. A. Hutchinson], *A MODEL MAYOR: Early Life, Congressional Career, & Triumphant Municipal Administration of Hon. Fernando Wood, Mayor of New York City* (New York: American Family Publishers, 1855), 10.

14. *Fernando Wood v. Anna W. Wood*, New York County Court of Chancery, June 14, 1839, Index no. BM-W2127, New York City Hall of Records; MacLeod, *Wood*, 42–45; *Sun*, Jan. 8, 1861.

15. Thomas Longworth, *Longworth's American Almanac, New-York Register, and City Directory for 1832* (New York: Thomas Longworth, 1832), 725; *Times*, Oct. 31, Nov. 18, 1860; *Sun*, Oct. 18, 1861; *New York World*, Feb. 2, 1880; MacLeod, *Wood*, 45.

16. *World*, Feb. 15, 1881; [Anson Herrick], *A Condensed Biography of Fernando Wood* (New York, 1866), 3–4.

17. Fernando Wood to William J. Crum, Dec. 26, 1839, Fernando Wood Papers, NYPL; [Joseph A. Scoville], *The Old Merchants of New York City. By Walter Barrett, Clerk. First Series* (New York: Carleton, Publisher, 1863), 10, 149–54; Herrick, *Wood*, 2–4.

18. Edward Pessen, "The Egalitarian Myth and American Social Reality: Wealth, Mobility, and Equality in the 'Era of the Common Man,'" *AHR* 76 (Oct. 1971): 989–1034; Edward Pessen, "Who Governed the Nation's Cities in the 'Era of the Common Man'?" *PSQ* 87 (Dec. 1972): 591–614; Amy B. Bridges, *A City in the Republic: Antebellum New York and the Origins of Machine Politics* (New York: Cambridge Univ. Press, 1984), 125–40.

19. "Tammany Society Membership List," Edwin Kilroe Collection, Columbia University; Jerome Mushkat, *Tammany: The Evolution of a Political Machine, 1789–1865* (Syracuse: Syracuse Univ. Press, 1971), 1–3.

20. *Working Man's Advocate*, Jan. 3, Apr. 11, 1835; *The Man*, Feb. 9, 19, 21, Mar. 19, 25, Apr. 3, 1835; *Evening Post*, Nov. 7, 21, 1835, May 20, 1836; Fitzwilliam Byrdsall, *The History of the Loco-Foco, or Equal Rights Party* (New York: Clement and Packard, 1842); Leo Hershkowitz, "The Loco Foco Party of New York: Its Origins and Career, 1835–1837," *NYHSQ* 46 (July 1962): 305–29; Edward Pessen, "Who Has Power in the Democratic Capitalistic Community? Reflections on Antebellum New York City," *NYH* 58 (Apr. 1977): 138; Sean Wilentz, *Chants Democratic: New York City and the Rise of the American Working Class, 1788–1850* (New York: Oxford Univ. Press, 1984), 219–325.

21. Byrdsall, *Loco-Foco Party*, 15–17; "Radicalism," *The United States Magazine and Democratic Review* 3 (Oct. 1839): 99–111; William Trimble, "The Social Philosophy of the Loco-Foco Democracy," *American Journal of Sociology* 26 (May 1921): 705–21; Carl Degler, "The Locofocos: Urban 'Agrarians,'" *Journal of Economic History* 16 (Sept. 1956): 322–33; Edward Pessen, *Most Uncommon Jacksonians* (Albany: State Univ. of New York Press, 1961); John B. Jentz, "The Anti-slavery Constituency in Jacksonian New York City," *CWH* 27 (June 1981): 101–22.

22. *Evening Post*, Nov. 3, 4, 1837; Herrick, *Wood*, 5.

23. *New York Plaindealer*, June 13, 1837; *Evening Post*, June 15, 1837; William L. Marcy to Prosper M. Wetmore, June 16, 1837, William L. Marcy Papers, LC.

24. *New-York Times*, Apr. 15, Sept. 8, 11, 1837; Jesse Hoyt to Martin Van Buren, Apr. 30, 1837, Marcy to Van Buren, May 25, 1837, Silas Wright to Van Buren, June 4, 1837, Martin Van Buren Papers, LC; *Evening Post*, Aug. 21, 25, 31, Sept. 5, 8, 1837; Silas Wright to Azariah C. Flagg, Sept. 5, 1837, Azariah C. Flagg Papers, NYPL; Donald C. Cole, *Martin Van Buren and the American Political System* (Princeton: Princeton Univ. Press, 1984), 285–316.

25. *Evening Post,* Aug. 2, Sept. 7, 8, 1837; *Herald,* Sept. 5, 9, 1837; *New York American,* Sept. 7, 1837; *New-York Times,* Sept. 11, 1837; William K. Paulding to Van Buren, Sept. 10, 1837, Van Buren Papers.

26. *Evening Post,* Sept. 12, 16, 20, 1837; *Herald,* Sept. 14, 16, 21, 1837; Enos P. Throop to Van Buren, Sept. 16, 1837, Marcy to Van Buren, Sept. 18, 1837, Van Buren Papers; Byrdsall, *Loco-Foco Party,* 162.

27. *Evening Post,* Sept. 22, 1837; *Herald,* Sept. 22, 1837.

28. *Evening Post,* Oct. 11, 27, 1837.

29. *Herald,* Oct. 31, Nov. 3, 1837; *Evening Post,* Oct. 31, 1837; Churchill C. Cambreleng to Van Buren, Nov. 15, 1837, Van Buren Papers; Preston King to Flagg, Nov. 21, 1837, Flagg Papers; *New Era,* Nov. 29, 1837; William Trimble, "Diverging Tendencies in the New York Democracy in the Period of the Locofocos," *AHR* 24 (Apr. 1919): 396–421; Judah B. Ginsburg, "Barnburners, Free Soilers and the New York Republican Party," *NYH* 57 (Oct. 1975): 475–500.

30. *Evening Post,* Dec. 20, 27, 1837, Jan. 4, Nov. 30, Dec. 18, 1838, Dec. 24, 1839.

31. *Albany Argus,* Jan. 4, Oct. 2, 1840; *Evening Post,* Jan. 5, 7, 21, Mar. 25, Apr. 3, 7, 17, May 2, 8, Sept. 5, 14, 19, Oct. 2, 7, 1840; *Herald,* Sept. 9, Oct. 12, 1840.

32. William F. Havemeyer to Van Buren, Oct. 12, 1840, Van Buren Papers; Howard Furer, *William Frederick Havemeyer: A Political Biography* (New York: American Press, 1965).

33. *Fernando Wood v. Anna W. Wood;* Herrick, *Wood,* 5; *New York World,* Feb. 15, 1881.

2. FOUNDATIONS

1. Horace Greeley to William H. Seward, Sept. 30, 1840, William H. Seward Papers, Department of Rare Books and Special Collections, Rush Rhees Library, UR; *Albany Argus,* Oct. 7, 1840; *New York Herald,* Oct. 12, 1840; James M. Edwards to Flagg, Oct. 18, 1840, Flagg Papers; *New York Evening Post,* Oct. 23, 24, 1840; James Glentworth, *A Statement of the Frauds on the Election Franchise in the City of New York* (New York, 1840).

2. *New York American,* Sept. 6, 7, 10, 1840; *Evening Post,* Sept. 7, 9, 10, 1840; *Morning Courier and New York Enquirer,* Oct. 31, 1840.

3. *New York American,* Oct. 31, 1840.

4. *Herald,* Nov. 2, 3, 1840; *Evening Post,* Nov. 2, 3, 7, 1840; *Albany Argus,* Nov. 14, 1840; *Refutation of the Whig Slander Against Mr. Fernando Wood* (New York, 1840).

5. *Evening Post,* Nov. 2, 3, 1840; *Morning Courier and New York Enquirer,* Nov. 2, 1854; Abijah Ingraham, *A Biography of Fernando Wood. A History of the Forgeries, Perjuries, and Other Crimes of Our "Model Mayor"* (New York, 1856).

6. *Evening Post,* Nov. 2, 3, 7, 1840; *Herald,* Nov. 7, 1840; Stanley B. Parson, William W. Beach, and Dan Hermann, *United States Congressional Districts 1788–1841* (Westport, Conn.: Greenwood Press, 1978), 336.

7. See, for example, Herrick, *Wood,* 4; Marian H. Adams to Robert W. Hooper, Dec. 20, 1877, Adams Family Papers, MHS.

8. *Cong. Globe.,* 27th Cong., 1st sess., 1841, 10:37; Samuel A. Pleasants, *Fernando Wood of New York* (New York: Columbia Univ. Press, 1948), 18–19; *Daily Graphic,* May 1, 1874; *Herald,* Feb. 15, 1881.

9. Wood voted against the following: various procedural motions eliminating the Gag Rule; introducing petitions abolishing slavery and the internal slave trade in the District of Columbia; freeing slave sailors beyond state limits; opposing censure of John Quincy Adams for presenting a petition from forty-six persons from Haverhill, Massachusetts, praying for peaceful dissolution of the Union; denying imprisonment for black sailors in Southern ports; opening diplomatic relations

with Haiti; allowing free blacks and mulattoes to settle in the Florida Territory; preventing an attempt to censure Joshua Giddings; and granting blacks full citizenship under naturalization laws. Wood's votes can be found in the Inter-University Consortium for Political and Social Research, 27th Congress, University of Michigan. See also Joel H. Silbey, *The Shrine of Party: Congressional Voting Patterns, 1841–1852* (Pittsburgh: Univ. of Pittsburgh Press, 1967), 161, and Thomas B. Alexander, *Sectional Stress and Party Strength: A Study of Roll Call Voting Patterns in the United States House of Representatives, 1836–1860* (Nashville: Vanderbilt Univ. Press, 1967), 45–46.

10. Fitzwilliam Byrdsall to John C. Calhoun, Nov. 6, 1842, Feb. 22, 1847, John C. Calhoun Papers, Clemson University Library, Clemson, S.C.; *Herald*, Aug. 16, 22, 1843; Arthur M. Schlesinger, Jr., *The Age of Jackson* (Boston: Little, Brown and Company, 1950), 406–9; Matthew A. Fitzsimons, "Calhoun's Bid for the Presidency, 1841–1844," *MVHR* 28 (June 1951): 39–60. See also Charles H. Ambler, "Correspondence of Robert M. T. Hunter," *American Historical Association, Annual Report for the Year 1916* (Washington: GPO, 1918), 2:39–66, hereafter cited as Hunter corresp., *AHA*.

11. Wood to Van Buren, Jan. 29, Feb. 20, 1843, Van Buren Papers.

12. Thomas A. Carr to Martin Van Buren, May 15, Sept. 15, 1843, Van Buren Papers; John Van Buren to Marcy, Mar. 8, 1854, Marcy Papers.

13. Robert J. Rayback, *Millard Fillmore: Biography of a President* (Buffalo: Henry Stewart, 1959), 118–23.

14. *Herald*, July 12, 1841; *Evening Post*, July 12, 1841; *Cong. Globe*, 27th Cong., 1st sess., 1841, 10:175–76.

15. *Cong. Globe*, 27th Cong., 1st sess., 1841, 10:278–81; John Quincy Adams, *Memoirs of John Quincy Adams, Comprising Portions of his Diary from 1795 to 1848*, ed. Charles F. Adams (Philadelphia: J. B. Lippincott, 1877), 10:541.

16. *Cong. Globe*, 27th Cong., 1st sess., 1841, 10: App., 279–80; Wood's votes included opposition to the repeal of the Independent Treasury; forming a new national bank; passing the $12 million loan; rechartering banks in the District of Columbia; incorporating subscribers to a fiscal bank of the United States; increasing federal appropriations; expanding the issuance of Treasury notes; approving the Uniform Bankruptcy Act; reimbursing Cherokee claimants; reducing the price of public land; subsidizing steamboats on the Great Lakes; improving internal waterways; and extending the National Road. See also Silbey, *The Shrine of Party*, 49–66, 239–44; Alexander, *Sectional Stress and Party Strength*, 38–50, 155–76; and Edward K. Spann, "Gotham in Congress: New York's Representatives and the National Government, 1840–1854," *NYH* 57 (July 1986): 305–28.

17. *Cong. Globe*, 27th Cong., 3d sess., 1843, 12:146, 231; *Cong. Globe*, 42d Cong., 2d sess., 1872, pt. 3:2168; Emily E. Briggs, *The Olivia Letters* (New York: Neal Publishing, 1906), 303.

18. *Evening Post*, Sept. 10, 1841, May 13, 14, 23, 1842; *Herald*, Sept. 7, 1842; *Cong. Globe*, 27th Cong., 1st sess., 1841, 10:37, 228.

19. *Evening Post*, Feb. 10, 1842; *Cong. Globe*, 27th Cong., 2d sess., 1842, 11:210, App. 131–33.

20. *Evening Post*, Feb. 10, 11, 1842; *Herald*, Feb. 11, 1842.

21. *Times*, Dec. 10, 1859; *Herald*, Dec. 10, 1859; Herrick, *Wood*, 5; Elliott G. Storke, *History of Cayuga County, New York, 1789–1879* (Syracuse: D. Mason & Co., 1879), 219.

22. *Evening Post*, Aug. 31, Sept. 21, 1842; *Herald*, Sept. 20, 21, 22, 1842; *Morning Courier and New York Enquirer*, Sept. 22, 1842; Joseph A. Scoville to Robert M. T. Hunter, Sept. 11, 1842, Emanuel B. Hart to Hunter, Oct. 5, 1842, Hunter corresp., *AHA* 2:44, 50; Robert B. Rhett to John C. Calhoun, Oct. 3, 1842, in *The Papers of John C. Calhoun, 1841–1843*, ed. Clyde N. Wilson (Columbia: Univ. of South Carolina Press, 1984), 10:485–86; Walter B. Hugins, "Ely Moore: The Case History of a Jacksonian Labor Leader," *PSQ* 65 (Mar. 1950): 105–25. Following

the Sixth census, the Twenty-seventh Congress passed a new reapportionment bill on June 25, 1842, to base districts on a fixed ratio of one representative for every 70,680 persons, and specified each district must be contiguous. This act forced states to create specific congressional districts. Wood opposed the bill and voted on eighteen roll calls against its provisions, preferring a ration of 50,179. See *Congressional Quarterly's Guide to the Congress of the United States: Origins, History and Procedures* (Washington, D.C.: Congressional Quarterly Service, 1973), 502.

23. *Herald,* Oct. 18, 19, 22, 24, 26, Nov. 10, 1842; *Evening Post,* Oct. 22, 29, 1842; *Morning Courier and New York Enquirer,* Oct. 29, 1842; Henry Tunney to Wood, Jan. 29, 1843, Wood Papers, NYHS; Thomas Whelan to Hamilton Fish, Oct. 19, 1850, Hamilton Fish Papers, LC; Herrick, *Wood,* 5-6.

24. Wood to Calhoun, July 17, 1846, Calhoun Papers; Calhoun to James R. Brady, May 7, 1844, Miscellaneous Papers, Virginia Historical Society, Richmond.

25. Wood to Henry A. Wise, Feb. 9, 1844, Letters of Application and Recommendation during the Administrations of John Tyler, James K. Polk, Zachary Taylor, and Millard Fillmore, NA.

26. James F. Randolph to Abel Upshur, Feb. 13, 1844, Elisha Whittling to Upshur, Feb. 23, 1844, NA; Wood to Calhoun, Apr. 28, 1844, Calhoun Papers.

27. Calhoun to Wood, May 8, 1844, Calhoun Papers.

28. Wood to Calhoun, Mar. 19, Sept. 18, Dec. 26, 1845, Nov. 12, 1846, July 23, 1847, Calhoun Papers.

29. *Population Schedules of the Seventh Census of the United States, 1850* (Washington, D. C.: National Archives and Records Service, 1959), microfilm, M 422, reel 559; Thomas Moorehead, *Mercantile Register for 1848-9* (New York: John P. Prall, 1848). Wood was unlisted in William A. Darling, *List of Persons, Co-partnerships & Corporations, who were Taxed on Seventeen Thousand Five Hundred Dollars, and Upwards in the City of New York in the Year 1850* (New York: John F. Whitney, 1851).

30. Wood to James K. Polk, June 1, July 11, 19, Aug. 26, Sept. 20, Oct. 16, Nov. 4, 8, 1844, James K. Polk Papers, LC.

31. Wood to Robert M. T. Hunter, Nov. 20, 1844, Miscellaneous Letters, Manuscript Div., Alderman Library, UV; Wood to Polk, Dec. 23, 1844, Jan. 11, May 29, July 27, Sept. 13, Oct. 11, 15, 1845, Polk Papers; Norman A. Graebner, "James K. Polk: A Study in Federal Patronage," *MVHR* 38 (Mar. 1952): 613-32; John Niven, *Martin Van Buren: The Romantic Age of American Politics* (New York: Oxford Univ. Press, 1983), 570-79.

32. James Brady to James Buchanan, Dec. 10, 1844, William B. Taylor to George Platt, Mar. 24, 31, Apr. 2, 1845, Wood to Buchanan, Mar. 15, 1845, Ely Moore to Buchanan, July 29, 1845, Andrew H. Mickle to Buchanan, July 29, 1846, Wood File, NA.

33: Elijah Purdy to Buchanan, Jan. 20, 1848, William Straham to Buchanan, Jan. 22, 1848, William C. Bouck to Buchanan, Jan. 27, 1848, Straham to George Sanders, Jan. 27, 1848, Wood to [?], Feb. 23, 1848, Wood File, NA; Wood to Polk, Feb. 24, 1848, Polk Papers.

34. Wood to Polk, Sept. 29, 1848, Polk Papers; Wood to Fish, Feb. 27, 1849, Fish Papers.

35. *New York Times,* July 22, 1854; Edward D. Durand, *The Finances of New York City* (New York: Macmillan, 1898), 373; Robert Ernst, *Immigrant Life in New York City 1825-1863* (New York: Columbia Univ. Press, 1949); Edward Pessen, *Riches, Class, and Power Before the Civil War* (Lexington: D. C. Heath, 1973); Spann, *The New Metropolis,* 94-241; Bridges, *City in the Republic,* 3-60.

36. Wood's home ward was an example of uneven land usages and residential patterns. See Assessors' Property Evaluation, 22d Ward, 1860, New York City Municipal Archives.

37. *Daily Graphic,* May 1, 1874; *Times,* Oct. 31, 1878.

38. *Times,* Sept. 14, 1877; Final Judicial Settlement of the Account of the Executors of the Will of Fernando Wood, Feb. 8, 1884, New York Surrogate's Court, Hall of Records, New York City Archives and Record Center.

39. Wood's real estate transactions are found in the Municipal Real Estate Libers, from 1848 to 1881, located in the New York City Archives and Record Center. These multiple volumes contain full details about his purchases, mortgages, sales, and deeds.

40. Memorandum of Agreement, Mar. 20, 1852, Thomas O. Larkin Papers, Bancroft Library, University of California, Berkeley; *New York Sun*, Nov. 29, 1856; Albert Ramsey to Buchanan, Oct. 25, 1858, James Buchanan Papers, HSP; *New York Daily News*, Sept. 12, 1859; Wood to Stephen A. Douglas, Oct. 3, 1859, in *The Letters of Stephen A. Douglas*, ed. Robert W. Johannsen (Urbana: Univ. of Illinois Press, 1961), 477 (hereafter cited as *Douglas Letters*); *New York World*, Feb. 15, 1868; *Times*, Sept. 14, 1877. See also Volume of Deeds, old ser., vol. 2, book 483, May 28, 1851, 483–86, San Francisco Hall of Records, for the Wood-Larkin exchange. For more information on Wood and Larkin, see George P. Hammond, *The Larkin Papers. Personal, Business, and Official Correspondence of Thomas Oliver Larkin, Merchant and United States Consul in California* (Berkeley: Univ. of California Press, 1964), 9:87, 93, 149, 173, 190–91, 223, 241, 248.

41. Moses V. Beach, *The Wealthy Citizens of New York*, 13th ed. (New York, 1855); William H. Boyd, *Boyd's New York City Tax-Book, Being a List of Persons, Corporations & Co-Partnerships, Resident and Non-Resident, Who were Taxed According to the Assessors' Book, 1856 and 1857* (New York: William H. Boyd, Publisher, 1857); Reuben Vose, *The Rich Men of New York*, 2d ser. (New York, 1861); Durand, *Finances of New York City*, 372–73. See also Edward Pessen, "The Wealthiest New Yorkers of the Jacksonian Era," *NYHSQ* 54 (Apr. 1970): 145–72.

42. *Population Schedules of the Eighth Census of the United States, 1860* (Washington, D.C.: National Archives and Records Service, 1959), microfilm reel 820, p. 24.

43. *Herald*, Nov. 15, Dec. 6, 1851; Herrick, *Wood*, 6–7.

44. *New York Commercial Advertiser*, Oct. 18, 1848; *Herald*, Oct. 18, 20, 1848, Aug. 13, Sept. 14, Oct. 10, Nov. 2, 1849; *San Francisco Alta California*, Mar. 15, 22, May 24, July 19, Aug. 9, Dec. 1, 1849; Roger W. Lotchin, *San Francisco, 1846–1856: From Hamlet to City* (New York: Oxford Univ. Press, 1974). In 1849, various New York City newspapers published reports listing amounts of specie received from California by individuals. This practice generally ended by 1850 when merchants such as Wood shipped their specie through banks. Thus, his earnings after 1849 are impossible to find.

45. Ingraham, *Wood*, 7–14; Herrick, *Wood*, 6–7.

46. *Herald*, Nov. 14, 15, Dec. 6, 8, 20, 22, 1851; *Times*, Dec. 15, 23, 1851; Samuel Owen, *The New-York Legal Observer* (New York: Samuel Owen, Publisher, 1852), 61–63.

47. *Times*, Mar. 3, 1856; *New York Tribune*, Mar. 3, 1856.

48. *Evening Post*, Nov. 3, 1854; *Times*, Nov. 4, 1854, Sept. 7, 1862; *Tribune*, Nov. 6, 9, 1854.

49. *Herald*, Sept. 28, 1856; *Morning Courier and New York Enquirer*, cited by *Daily News*, Sept. 12, 1859.

50. *Sun*, July 28, 1855, Sept. 12, 1859; *Daily News*, Jan. 16, Feb. 17, Oct. 15, 1860; *Daily Graphic*, May 1, 1874; *Times*, Sept. 14, 1877, Oct. 31, 1878.

51. *Herald*, Sept. 13, 23, Oct. 30, Nov. 1, 5, 7, 1849; *New York Sunday Times and Noah's Weekly Messenger*, Nov. 4, 1849; Marcy to Prosper Wetmore, Nov. 13, 1849, Daniel S. Dickinson to Marcy, Jan. 29, 1850, Marcy Papers; *The Softs, the True Democracy of the State of New York* (New York, 1856); Roy F. Nichols, *The Democratic Machine, 1850–1854* (New York: Columbia Univ. Press, 1923), 19–22.

52. *Herald*, Jan. 14, 26, Feb. 12, 16, 17, 19, 1850; *Commercial Advertiser*, Feb. 13, 18, 1850; Lorenzo Shepard to Marcy, Feb. 20, 1850, Marcy Papers; *Noah's Weekly Messenger*, Feb. 24, 1850.

53. *Herald*, Feb. 20, 22, 1850; *Evening Post*, Feb. 20, 1850.

54. *Herald*, Mar. 1, 3, 11, Apr. 5, 1850; *Commercial Advertiser*, Mar. 4, 1850.

55. *Herald*, Apr. 14, 16, 29, May 1, 6, 7, 1850.

56. *Herald*, May 10, 13, 20, 23, June 21, Sept. 10, 1850; Marcy to Horatio Seymour, July 28, 1850, Horatio Seymour Papers, NYSL; Holman Hamilton, *Prologue to Conflict: The Crisis and Compromise of 1850* (New York: W. W. Norton & Company, 1966).

57. *Herald*, July 18, 22, 26, 31, Aug. 1, 7, 15, 24, Sept. 10, 11, 14, 27, 29, 1850; Marcy to Wetmore, Sept. 9, 1850, Marcy Papers; *Albany Argus*, Sept. 16, 1850; Edwin Croswell to Seymour, Oct. 8, 1850, Seymour Papers.

58. *Herald*, Oct. 8, 10, 12, 1850; *Evening Post*, Oct. 12, 1850; *New York Atlas*, Oct. 13, 20, 1850. At this point, Anson Herrick, owner and editor of the *New York Atlas*, supported Wood.

59. *Tribune*, Oct. 12, 16, 26, 1850; *Herald*, Oct. 13, 14, 16, 18, 1850; *Morning Courier and New York Enquirer*, Oct. 26, 1850.

60. *Commercial Advertiser*, Oct. 12, 17, 1850; *Herald*, Oct. 13, 14, 16, 1850; *Evening Post*, Oct. 16, 1850; *Tribune*, Oct. 16, 29, 1850.

61. *Herald*, Oct. 26, 1850; *Evening Post*, Oct. 31, 1850; *Noah's Weekly Messenger*, Nov. 3, 1850; Philip Foner, *Business and Slavery: The New York Merchants and the Irrepressible Conflict* (Chapel Hill: Univ. of North Carolina Press, 1941), 34–54.

62. *New York Atlas*, Nov. 3, 10, 1850; *Commercial Advertiser*, Nov. 4, 1850; *Tribune*, Nov. 2, 5, 1850.

63. *Herald*, Nov. 4, 1850; *Evening Post*, Nov. 4, 1850.

64. *Herald*, Nov. 6, 7, 1850; *Noah's Weekly Messenger*, Nov. 10, 1850; *New York Atlas*, Nov. 10, 1850; Jabez Hammond to Seymour, Nov. 10, 1850, Seymour Papers; Marcy to Buchanan, Nov. 10, 1850, Buchanan Papers; *Buffalo Daily Courier*, Nov. 25, 1850.

65. *Evening Post*, Nov. 7, 1850.

3. FIRST VICTORY

1. *Populations Schedules of the Eighth Census*, reel 820, p. 74.

2. *San Francisco Alta California*, May 22, 1852; Louis Rasmussen, *San Francisco Ship Passenger Lists* (Colma, Calif.: San Francisco Historical Record & Geneological Bulletin, 1965), 1:74; Pleasants, *Wood*, 26; Lotchin, *San Francisco*, 174–177.

3. *Herald*, Mar. 30, Apr. 19, June 3, Sept. 8, 9, 10, 22, 27, Oct. 7, 9, 12, 16, 17, 22, Nov. 1, 3, 5, 8, 12, 19, 1853; Isaac Fowler to Franklin Pierce, Aug. 15, 1853, Samuel J. Tilden Papers, NYPL; Seymour to Marcy, Nov. 5, 13, 1853, Herman Redfield to Marcy, Dec. 10, 14, 1853, Marcy Papers; Edward West to Stephen A. Douglas, Nov. 15, 1853, Stephen A. Douglas Papers, Regenstein Library, University of Chicago; Roy F. Nichols, *Franklin Pierce: Young Hickory of the Granite Hills* (Philadelphia: Univ. of Pennsylvania Press, 1931), 232–38; Mark L. Berger, *The Revolution in the New York Party System, 1840–1860* (Port Washington: Kennikat Press, 1973), 1–16.

4. Wood to Marcy, Nov. 24, Dec. 1, 1853, Marcy Papers.

5. *Evening Post*, Jan. 3, 19, 1854; *Herald*, Jan. 6, 10, 1854.

6. *Herald*, Jan. 7, 30, Feb. 1, Mar. 10, May 14, 24, 1854; *Evening Post*, Jan 25, Feb. 4, 1854; John Van Buren to Marcy, Mar. 8, 1854, Marcy Papers; *New York Times*, May 25, 1854.

7. Shepard to Marcy, Jan. 18, 28, Feb. 7, Mar. 4, 6, 1854, Cochrane to Marcy, Jan. 18, 28, Feb. 7, Mar. 4, 6, 1854, Marcy Papers; *Evening Post*, Mar. 15, 16, 1854; *Herald*, Mar. 16, 17, 18, 1854.

8. Shepard to Marcy, Jan. 18, 1854, Marcy Papers; *Herald*, Jan. 30, Feb. 4, 8, 13, 14, Mar. 16, 1854.

9. *Herald*, Mar. 26, Aug. 13, Nov. 2, 3, 1854; *New York Tribune*, Apr. 2, 1854; *Times*, Aug. 26, 1854; *Evening Post*, Oct. 4, Nov. 3, 1854.

10. *Herald*, Mar. 25, 26, Apr. 10, July 25, 1854; Shepard to Marcy, July 6, 9, 10, Wood to Marcy, July 12, 1854, Marcy Papers; *Evening Post*, July 11, 13, 1854.

11. *Herald*, Mar. 25, Apr. 13, July 1, 5, 31, Aug. 1, Sept. 8, Nov. 2, 3, 1854; *Tribune*, Apr. 2, 1854; *Times*, Oct. 10, 1854.

12. *Herald*, July 1, 5, 14, 16, 1854; *New York Times*, Aug. 26, 1854; *New York Irish-American*, Oct. 28, 1854; *Evening Post*, Oct. 28, 1854; *Tribune*, Oct. 23, 1854; Louis D. Scisco, *Political Nativism in New York State* (New York: Columbia Univ. Press, 1901), 62–107; Thomas J. Curran, "Seward and the Know-Nothings," *NYHSQ* 41 (Apr. 1967): 141–59.

13. *Evening Post*, June 5, 1854; Wood to Marcy, July 12, 1854; *Times*, Sept. 21, 23, 1854; *Journal of Commerce*, Sept. 29, 1854.

14. *Evening Post*, Oct. 6, 10, 1854; *Herald*, Oct. 10, 1854; *Times*, Oct. 10, 13, 23, 1854; *Tribune*, Oct. 10, 21, 1854.

15. *Times*, Oct. 13, 28, 1854; *Herald*, Oct. 10, 21, 1854; *Evening Post*, Oct. 12, 27, 1854; *Tribune*, Oct. 12, 21, 27, 1854.

16. *Times*, Oct 20, 26, 1854; *Herald*, Nov. 3, 1854.

17. *Morning Courier and New York Enquirer*, Oct. 11, 1854; James L. Crouthamel, *James Watson Webb: A Biography* (Middletown: Wesleyan Univ. Press, 1969).

18. *Morning Courier and New York Enquirer*, Oct. 31, Nov. 1, 2, 3, 4, 1854.

19. *Evening Post*, Oct. 31, 1854.

20. *Evening Post*, Nov. 1, 3, 4, 9, 1854; *Morning Courier and New York Enquirer*, Nov. 4, 6, 1854; *Tribune*, Nov. 1, 3, 4, 6, 8, 9, 1854; *Times*, Nov. 1, 2, 3, 4, 7, 8, 1854.

21. *Herald*, Nov. 2, 3, 1854; *Times*, Nov. 2, 4, 7, 1854; *Irish-American*, Nov. 4, 1854; *Morning Courier and New York Enquirer*, Nov. 4, 1854; *Evening Post*, Nov. 5, 1854; *Tribune*, Nov. 6, 1854.

22. *Herald*, Nov. 8, 1854; *Morning Courier and New York Enquirer*, Nov. 9, 1854.

23. The key to Wood's victory lay in a coalition based on the relationship of his percentage of the vote to the percentage of immigrants and low per capita wealth in each ward. The resultant multiple coefficient of correlation was 0.649. Since naturalized voters formed 48 percent of the electorate, his high positive coefficient of correlation, 0.762, proved vital. By contrast, his high negative correlation among the native-born was -0.774. Statistical material derived from: *Hunt's Magazine and Commercial Review* 31 (1854): 489; John Hardy, *The Manual of the Corporation of the City of New York for 1870* (New York: New York Printing Company, 1870), 733; Ernst, *Immigrant Life*, 192–93, 223; Bridges, *A City in the Republic*, 43, 67, 84, 115.

24. *Times*, Nov. 8, 11, 1854; *Morning Courier and New York Enquirer*, Nov. 11, 1854.

25. *Tribune*, Nov. 11, 1854; Alexander, *Political History of New York*, 2:200–204; Hendrik Booraem V, *The Formation of the Republican Party in New York: Politics and Conscience in the Antebellum North* (New York: New York Univ. Press, 1983), 13–64.

26. *Tribune*, Nov. 15, 1854.

27. *Evening Post*, Nov. 11, 1854. For a different interpretation of Wood's motivation see Spann, *The New Metropolis*, 358–66.

28. *Daily News*, Nov. 29, 1859.

29. Information for this section is derived from: "The Great Want of New-York City," *New-York Quarterly* 3 (Apr. 1854): 80–101; *Tribune*, Nov. 13, 1854; *Times*, Dec. 11, 1854; "New-York Government," *New-York Quarterly* 4 (Apr./July 1855): 1–20; James R. Bayley, *A Brief Account of the Catholic Church on the Island of New York* (New York: E. Dunigan & Brothers, 1853); David T. Valentine, *The Manual of the Corporation of the City of New York for 1854* (New York, 1854); Isaac C. Kendall, *The Growth of New York* (New York, 1865); Friedrich Knapp, *Immigration and the Commissioners of Emigration of the State of New York* (New York, 1870); Stephen Byrne, *Irish Immigration to the United States* (New York: Catholic Publication Society, 1873); Margaret Myers, *The New York Money Market: Origins and Development* (New York: Columbia Univ. Press, 1931); Ernst,

Immigrant Life, 25–184; Bayrd Still, *Mirror for Gotham: New York as Seen by Contemporaries from Dutch Days to the Present* (New York: New York Univ. Press, 1956); Allan R. Pred, *The Spatial Dynamics of U.S. Urban-Industrial Life* (Cambridge: MIT Press, 1966); John R. Duffy, *A History of Public Health in New York City, 1625–1886* (New York: Russell Sage Foundation, 1968); Ira Rosenwaike, *Population History of New York* (Syracuse: Syracuse Univ. Press, 1972); Diana Ravitch, *The Great School Wars: New York City 1805–1973* (New York: Basic Books, 1974); Spann, *The New Metropolis*, 1–340; Hendrik Hartog, *Public Property and Private Power: The Corporation of the City of New York in American Law, 1730–1870* (Chapel Hill: Univ. of North Carolina Press, 1983), 179–236; Wilentz, *Chants Democratic*, 296–389; Cristine Stansell, *City of Women: Sex and Class in New York 1789–1860* (New York: Alfred A. Knopf, 1986).

4. THE MODEL MAYOR

1. *New York Times*, Jan. 3, 1855; Hutchinson, *MODEL MAYOR*, 17–22.

2. *Times*, Jan. 3, 1855.

3. Ibid.

4. *Times*, Jan. 10, 25, Feb. 1, 1855; *Daily News*, Jan. 4, Aug. 23, Oct. 9, 1860; *Herald*, Mar. 9, 1874; Hutchinson, *MODEL MAYOR*, x–xi.

5. *Times*, Jan. 18, Feb. 4, 9, 23, 1855.

6. *Sun*, July 28, Aug. 14, 1855; *Times*, Aug. 3, 1855.

7. *Daily News*, Jan. 6, 1855; Wood to Marcy, Mar. 20, 1855, Marcy Papers; *Times*, May 28, 29, June 13, July 10, 18, Aug. 29, 1855; Wood to Erastus Corning, June 28, 1855, Simon Gratz Collection, HSP; James F. Richardson, *The New York Police: Colonial Times to 1901* (New York: Oxford Univ. Press, 1970), 90.

8. *Times*, Jan. 6, 10, 24, Feb. 1, 8, 12, Aug. 10, 1855; Wood to Alfred B. Parker, Feb. 9, 1855, Miscellaneous Papers, Houghton Library, Harvard University; *Evening Post*, Feb. 24, 1855.

9. *Times*, Jan. 9, 15, 25, 30, Feb. 9, 21, May 21, 1855; *Herald*, Mar. 31, 1855; *Sun*, Aug. 28, Oct. 19, 1855; Stansell, *City of Women*, 162–91; Timothy Gilfoyle, Jr., "Strumpets and Misogynists: 'Brothel Riots' and the Transformation of Prostitution in Antebellum New York City," *NYH* 58 (Jan. 1987): 46–67.

10. *Tribune*, Jan. 15, 29, 31, Feb. 1, Apr. 3, 21, Aug. 22, 1855; *Daily News*, Apr. 30, 1855; *Times*, Apr. 7, 17, 19, 28, May 3, 5, 20, 22, June 20, 26, July 7, 1855; John A. Krout, "The Maine Law in New York Politics," *NYH* 17 (July 1936): 260–71; David Ellis, "'Upstate Hicks' Versus 'City Slickers,'" *NYHSQ* 43 (Apr. 1959): 202–19.

11. *Tribune*, Sept. 4, 1855; *Times*, Sept. 4, 22, 1855; MacLeod, *Wood*, 257–70; Spann, *New Metropolis*, 374.

12. *Times*, Jan. 1, 2, 3, 11, 1855; *Tribune*, Jan. 12, 1855; *Herald*, Jan. 2, 1855; MacLeod, *Wood*, 157–62. See also Joel T. Headley, *The Great Riots of New York, 1712–1873* (New York: E. B. Treat, 1873); Paul A. Gilje, *The Road to Mobocracy: Popular Disorder in New York City, 1763–1834* (Chapel Hill: Univ. of North Carolina Press, 1987).

13. *Times*, Apr. 7, May 31, June 2, 4, 6, Sept. 18, 1855; *Sun*, July 23, 1855.

14. *Times*, Mar. 6, 1855; Richardson, *New York Police*, 85–87. The *Times* published Wood's letter to Raymond on Mar. 6, 1855.

15. *Times*, Feb. 16, Mar. 12, Apr. 9, June 4, 1855.

16. *Times* Apr. 6, May 5, 28, 1855; *Herald*, Apr. 24, 1855; Spann, *New Metropolis*, 368–72.

17. *Times*, Mar. 22, 1855; Richardson, *New York Police*, 85.

18. *Times*, Feb. 6, May 23, July 11, Aug. 2, Sept. 24, 1855; *Herald*, July 3, 19, Aug. 2, 9, Oct. 10, 1856; *Sun*, July 19, 1855; *Tribune*, Nov. 13, 14, 1855; Spann, *New Metropolis*, 379.

19. *Times*, May 29, June 8, Oct. 16, 1855; *Herald* May 29, 30, 1855.

20. *Times*, Oct. 11, 1854, May 9, June 27, Sept. 3, 7, Oct. 8, 16, 1855; *Sun*, July 23, Sept. 21, 1855; *Herald*, July 24, 1855.

21. *Times*, July 19, Oct. 8, 1855; *Sun*, July 24, Sept. 25, 29, 1855; *Herald*, Sept. 25, 1855.

22. *Tribune*, Jan. 6, 17, Feb. 8, 1855; *Times*, Feb. 20, May 9, 21, 1855.

23. *Evening Post*, Mar. 22, 23, 1855, Aug. 22, 1873; *Times*, Mar. 24, 1855, Sept. 13, 1867; *Daily News*, July 10, 1856; *New York World*, Aug. 21, 1873; Wood to Tilden, May 22, 1876, Tilden Papers; *Herald*, May 7, 1875; Laura Wood Roper, *FLO: A Biography of Frederick Law Olmstead* (Baltimore: Johns Hopkins Press, 1973), 119, 126–31; Ian R. Stewart, "Politics and the Park: The Fight for Central Park," *NYHSQ* 61 (July/Oct. 1977): 152–53.

24. *Times*, Feb. 18, 27, 28, Mar. 8, May 14, 1855.

25. *Times*, Jan. 20, May 3, June 11, July 24, 1856; *Tribune*, Mar. 23, 1855; Hutchinson, *MODEL MAYOR*, 13–14, 51–62.

26. *Times*, Mar. 13, 20, 30, Apr. 2, 9, June 4, July 17, Sept. 11, 13, Oct. 1, 1855.

27. *Times*, Apr. 5, 7, May 31, June 2, 5, 6, 1855; James F. Richardson, "Mayor Fernando Wood and the New York Police Force, 1855–1857," *NYHSQ* 50 (Jan. 1966): 12.

28. *Times*, July 6, Aug. 11, Sept. 18, 1855.

29. *Times*, Sept. 26, Nov. 15, 24, Dec. 12, 28, 1855; Richardson, *New York Police*, 88–89.

30. Shepard to Marcy, May 12, 29, Sept. 8, 1855, Marcy Papers; *Times*, Oct. 17, 18, 22, 23, 29, Nov. 1, 2, 1855; *Evening Post*, Nov. 2, 1855; *Herald*, Nov. 2, 1855.

31. *Times*, Nov. 10, 1855, Jan. 8, 1856; *Daily News*, Dec. 7, 1855.

32. *Times*, Jan. 8, 9, Feb. 5, 9, 12, 13, 22, Mar. 5, 12, Apr. 8, 1856; *Sun*, Jan. 8, 9, 1856.

33. *Times*, Feb. 3, 4, 1856; *Sun*, Feb. 4, 5, 6, 7, 1856; *Herald*, Feb. 19, 1856; Spann, *New Metropolis*, 375–77.

34. *Daily News*, July 8, 11, 1856; Spann, *New Metropolis*, 377.

35. *Times*, Sept. 4, 1855; *Herald*, Jan. 2, 1856; Durand, *Finances of New York City*, 372–74.

36. *Times*, Feb. 5, 1856.

37. *Herald*, Feb. 5, 1856.

38. *Times*, Jan. 2, 8, 1856; *Tribune*, Jan. 8, 1856; *Herald*, Jan. 8, Feb. 5, 1856; *Sun*, Feb. 7, 20, Mar. 14, 1856.

39. *Times*, Jan. 8, Feb. 5, 1856; Spann, *New Metropolis*, 377–78.

40. *Sun*, Jan. 21, Feb. 5, 7, 20, Mar. 14, Apr. 16, 1857; *Times*, Feb. 5, 1856; Wood to William H. Clark, Mar. 31, 1856, Wood Papers, NYPL.

41. *Morning Courier and New York Enquirer*, Jan. 8, 1856; *Times*, Jan. 21, Feb. 6, 9, 12, 13, 23, Mar. 13, Apr. 8, 1856.

42. *Sun*, Mar. 4, 22, 24, 1856; *Times*, Mar. 13, Apr. 8, 1856; Richardson, "Mayor Wood and New York Police," 12–15.

43. *Herald*, Apr. 30, 1856; *Times*, May 19, 20, July 17, 1856; *Sun*, May 20, 1856.

44. *Times*, Jan. 9, 1856; *Sun*, Feb. 1, 1856.

45. Wood to Wise, Oct. 29, 1855, Ben Perley Poore Papers, Haverhill Public Library, Haverhill, Mass.; Marcy to Buchanan, Sept. 2, 1855, Sickles to Buchanan, Nov. 25, 1855, Jan. 3, Feb. 3, 19, 1856, Anson Herrick to Buchanan, Feb. 13, 1856, George Sanders to Buchanan, Mar. 25, 1856, James W. Webb to Buchanan, Apr. 27, 1856, Moses Beach to Buchanan, Apr. 28, 1856, Buchanan Papers.

46. Sickles to Buchanan, Jan. 3, 1856, Wood to Buchanan, Apr. 23, May 26, 1856, John Dix to Buchanan, Apr. 25, 1856, Buchanan Papers; David Disney to Douglas, Feb. 26, 28, 1856, Douglas Papers; *Times*, Apr. 24, 25, 1856; *Sun*, May 24, 1856.

47. *Daily News*, May 25, 1856; Wood to Buchanan, June 2, 6, 1856, Buchanan Papers.

48. Seymour to Buchanan, June 6, 1856, Sickles to Buchanan, July 1856, Buchanan Papers; Wood to Seymour, July 26, 1856, Seymour Papers, NYHS; *Sun*, Aug. 1, 1856; DeAlva S. Alexander, *A Political History of New York* (New York: Henry Holt & Company, 1924), 2:232–33.

49. Herrick to Buchanan, June 8, 1856, John Van Buren to Buchanan, June 10, 1856, Buchanan Papers; *Daily News*, June 17, 1856.

50. Sanders to Buchanan, June 27, 1856, Sickles to Buchanan, July 26, 1856, Buchanan Papers; *Albany Argus*, June 27, 1856.

51. Wood to Buchanan, June 6, 28, July 13, 1856, Buchanan Papers; Wood to Seymour, July 26, 1856, Fairchild Family Papers, NYHS.

52. *Herald*, July 31, Aug. 1, 1856; *Daily News*, July 31, Aug. 6, 1856; *Times*, Aug. 6, 1856.

53. Wood to Buchanan, Aug. 2, 17, 1856, Buchanan Papers.

54. *Times*, Aug. 8, 1856; Cochrane to Buchanan, Aug. 19, 1856, Sickles to Buchanan, Aug. 28, 1856, Buchanan Papers.

55. *Herald*, Sept. 3, 1856; *Times*, Sept. 3, 4, 1856; *Evening Post*, Sept. 3, 4, 1856; *Tribune*, Sept. 3, 1856.

56. *Times*, Sept. 9, 12, 16, 27, 1856; *Tribune*, Sept. 16, 20, Oct. 8, 1856; Wood to Buchanan, Sept. 17, 1856, Buchanan Papers; *Herald*, Sept. 20, 1856; *Sun*, Oct. 4, 8, 1856.

57. *Herald*, Sept. 6, 9, 12, 16, 17, Oct. 14, 1856; *Sun*, Oct. 20, 1856; *Times*, Oct. 23, 28, 1856; *Tribune*, Nov. 5, 1856.

58. *Herald*, Oct. 4, 8, 9, 24, 1856; *Times*, Oct. 8, 9, 13, 23, 28, 1856; *New York Irish-American*, Oct. 25, 1856; *Tribune*, Oct. 8, 9, 10, 14, 21, 22, 28, 1856; "Abijah Ingraham," *A Biography of Fernando Wood. A History of the Forgeries, Perjuries and Other Crimes of Our "Model Mayor"* (New York, 1856).

59. *Sun*, Oct. 4, 17, 18, 1856; *Times*, Oct. 28, 1856.

60. *Herald*, Sept. 28, 29, 1856; *Tribune*, Sept. 29, 1856.

61. *Herald*, Sept. 23, 1856; *Times*, Oct. 4, Dec. 20, 1856, Feb. 5, Apr. 18, 1857, Nov. 26, 1859; Spann, *New Metropolis*, 380–82.

62. *Daily News*, Aug 21, 1856; *Tribune*, Oct. 8, 20, 1856; *Times*, Oct. 8, Nov. 24, 1856; *Herald*, Oct. 8, 31, Nov. 5, 7, 1856; *Evening Post*, Oct. 31, Nov. 4, 1856; Richardson, *New York Police*, 94–95; Leonard Chalmers, "Fernando Wood and Tammany Hall: The First Phase," *NYHSQ* 52 (Oct. 1968): 386–400.

63. Wood to Buchanan, Oct. 9, 22, 1856, Rynders to Buchanan, Oct. 27, 1856, Patrick Lynch to Buchanan, Nov. 11, 1856, Buchanan Papers; *Irish-American*, Oct. 25, Nov. 15, 1856; *Tribune*, Oct. 30, Nov. 1, 1856; *Herald*, Oct. 31, Nov. 2, 1856; *Times*, Nov. 3, 1856; Wood to Joseph S. Moore, May 3, 1878, Wood Papers, NYPL.

64. *Tribune*, Nov. 3, 5, 24, Dec. 10, 1856; *Evening Post*, Nov. 3, 4, Dec. 10, 1856; *Times*, Nov. 3, 4, 5, 6, 24, 1856; *Herald*, Nov. 5, 1856; *Sun*, Nov. 5, 1856.

65. *Times*, Nov. 5, 6, 7, 1856; *Evening Post*, Nov. 5, 1856; *Tribune*, Nov. 6, 7, 1856. Wood's 1854 coalition was still firm. His multiple coefficient of correlation increased to 0.778, as did his coefficient of correlation 0.831, among immigrants. Another pattern persisted. His negative correlation among the native-born rose to -0.779. The statistic material derived from: Hardy, *Manual of the Corporation of the City of New York for 1870* (New York: New York Printing Company, 1870), 734; Ernst, *Immigrant Life in New York City*, 192–93, 223.

66. *Sun*, Nov. 14, 25, 27, Dec. 16, 18, 19, 20, 27, 30, 1856.

67. Wood to Buchanan, Nov. 8, 28, 1856, Buchanan to Wood, Dec. 1, 1856, Buchanan Papers.

68. Buchanan to James Gordon Bennett, Dec. 29, 1856, Henry Wikoff to Buchanan, Dec. 30, 31, 1856, Buchanan Papers.

69. *Herald*, Dec. 3, 1856, Feb. 6, 22, 1857; *Sun*, Jan. 3, 1856; *Times*, Jan. 3, 8, Feb. 6, 1857; *Evening Post*, Jan. 8, 1857.

70. *Sun*, Dec. 22, 1856, Jan. 7, 20, 1857; *Times*, Jan. 7, 24, 27, 1857.
71. Wood to Corning, Nov. 30, 1856, Gratz Collection.
72. *Times*, Jan. 2, 6, 1857; *Sun*, Jan 5, 6, 1857; *Herald*, Jan. 6, 1857.
73. *Times*, Jan. 6, 1857.

5. THE POLITICAL MAYOR

1. William B. Maclay to Edmund Burke, Dec. 16, 1857, Edmund Burke Papers, LC; Wood to Buchanan, Jan. 8, 1857, Buchanan Papers.
2. *Sun*, Jan. 13, Feb. 6, 9, 24, Mar. 4, 12, 19, 23, 30, 1857.
3. Mushkat, *Tammany*, 1–3.
4. *Times*, Jan. 3, 8, 9, Feb. 6, 14, 15, 23, Mar. 3, 1857.
5. *Herald*, Feb. 6, 14, 15, 21, 23; *Statement of the Majority of the Grand Council of the Tammany Society, or Columbian Order, in Reply to a Protest of the Minority; Also the Addresses and Resolutions of the Grand Council Adopted February 14, 1857, Relative to the Political Use of Tammany Hall* (New York, 1857). The seven sachems were Isaac Fowler, Elijah Purdy, Thomas Dunlap, James Conner, André Froment, Joseph Marsh, and William Kennedy.
6. *Sun*, Apr. 20, 21, 1857; *Times*, Apr. 22, 1857; Wikoff to Buchanan, Apr. 22, 1857, Buchanan Papers.
7. *Times*, Apr. 14, 18, 19, 20, 22, May 5, 12, June 10, 13, 19, July 24, Aug. 28, 1857; *Sun*, May 5, June 1, 4, 6, 10, 26, 30, Aug. 18, 29, Sept. 1, 4, 8, 10, 1857; *Herald*, July 25, 27, 1857; *Irish-American*, Aug. 8, 1857.
8. Roy F. Nichols, *The Disruption of American Democracy* (New York: Macmillan, 1948), 93–98.
9. Redfield to Erastus Corning, Jan. 9, 1857, Erastus Corning Papers, Albany Institute of Art and History, Albany, N.Y.; Redfield to Buchanan, Jan. 29, 1857, Seymour to Buchanan, Jan. 29, 1857, Sickles to Buchanan, Feb. 23, 1857, Dickinson to Buchanan, Feb. 23, 26, 1857, Buchanan Papers; *Times*, Mar. 16, 19, 1857; *Herald*, Mar. 16, 19, 1857.
10. *Times*, Mar. 23, 1857.
11. *Sun*, Mar 14, 1857; *Times*, Mar. 14, 23, 1857.
12. *Times*, Mar. 17, 23, 1857; *Herald*, Mar. 23, 1857.
13. Wikoff to Buchanan, Jan. 9, 13, 1857, Buchanan Papers; *Times*, Mar. 20, 25, 26, 1857; *Herald*, Mar. 26, 1857; Nichols, *Disruption of American Democracy*, 85.
14. *Times*, Mar. 26, 1857.
15. Gideon Tucker to Burke, Mar. 16, 1857, Burke Papers; Samuel L. M. Barlow to Buchanan, July 18, 1857, Buchanan Papers; *Times*, Apr. 18, 1857; Philip S. Klein, *President James Buchanan* (University Park: Pennsylvania State Univ. Press, 1962), 280. Buchanan also appointed three of Wood's most implacable enemies: Isaiah Rynders (marshal), George Sanders (naval agent), and Emanuel Hart (surveyor of the port).
16. Wikoff to Buchanan, Mar. 27, 1857, Buchanan Papers.
17. *Times*, Jan. 28, Feb. 12, Mar. 3, 13, 27, 1857; *Herald*, Mar. 24, 27, 1857; *Sun*, Apr. 3, 11, 1857.
18. *Times*, Jan. 1, 9, 25, 28, Feb. 9, 24, 25, Mar. 31, Apr. 1, 2, 6, 7, 10, 1857; *Herald*, Jan. 25, Feb. 19, 1857; *Sun*, Feb. 19, 1857.
19. *Times*, Jan. 15, 28, 30, Feb. 19, Mar. 3, 1857; *Sun*, Feb. 19, Mar. 4, 1857.
20. *Times*, Feb. 26, Mar. 13, 18, 24, 27, 1857; *Sun*, Apr. 3, 11, 12, 1857; Dean Richmond to Tilden, Apr. 2, 1857, Tilden Papers.

21. *Times*, Apr. 13, 14, 15, 1857; *Herald*, Apr. 28, 1857; Valentine, *Manual. . .for 1857*, 68–84; James Bryce, *The American Commonwealth* (New York: Macmillan, 1888), 2:335–36; Spann, *New Metropolis*, 385–86; Hartog, *Public Property and Private Power*, 236–39.

22. *Times*, Mar. 24, Apr. 14, 15, 16, 1857; *Morning Courier and New York Enquirer*, Apr. 17, 1857; *Sun*, Apr. 20, 1857; Richardson, "Wood and the New York Police," 26–33; Richardson, *New York Police*, 96–103.

23. *Herald*, Apr. 13, 16, 17, 1857; *Times*, Apr. 13, May 7, 1857; *New York Evening Post*, May 21, 1857; *Sun*, June 2, 1857; Spann, *New Metropolis*, 387–88.

24. *Times*, Apr. 18, 1857; Valentine, *Manual. . .for 1857*, 85-88; Alexander B. Callow, Jr., *The Tweed Ring* (New York: Oxford Univ. Press, 1965), 21, 78–79; John M. Allswang, *Bosses, Machines, and Urban Voters: An American Symbiosis* (Port Washington: Kennikat Press, 1977), 41–59. Figures for patronage derived from "Schedule of Officials, Whose Salaries are Paid from City and County Treasury," in Valentine, *Manual. . .for 1861* (1861), 252–84. Ira M. Leonard, "The Politics of Charter Revision in New York City, 1845–1847," *NYHSQ* 62 (Jan. 1978): 51, sets the number of patronage jobs during the 1840s at approximately two thousand. See also Bridges, *City in the Republic*, 132–33, 191.

25. *Herald*, Apr. 17, 24, 1857; Joseph T. Miller to Wood, July 18, 1857, Joseph T. Miller Papers, Rush Rhees Library, UR; Paul O. Weinbaum, "Temperance, Politics, and the New York City Riots of 1857," *NYHSQ* 59 (July 1975): 246–70; William J. Rorabaugh, "Rising Spirits: Immigrants, Temperance, and Tammany Hall," *CWH* 22 (June 1976): 139–57. In the Senate, an alliance of Know-Nothings and Republicans overpowered the Democrats by nearly 7 to 1. In the Assembly, the ratio was less, about 3 to 1, but Democrats were still impotent. See *Journal of the Senate of New York at their Eightieth Session* (Albany: Charles Van Benthuysen, 1857), 504, 784, 831, 944–46, 957, 983; *Journal of the Assembly of the State of New York at their Eightieth Session, 1857* (Albany: Charles Van Benthuysen, 1857), 1245, 1255, 1288, 1298–1300, 1301, 1390, 1393–94, 1473. For another view, see L. Ray Gunn, *The Decline of Authority: Public Economic Policy and Political Development in New York State, 1800–1860* (Ithaca, N.Y.: Cornell Univ. Press, 1988).

26. *Sun*, May 4, 15, 1857; *Times*, May 13, 16, June 5, 1857.

27. Wood to Sedgwick, Apr. 21, 1857, Miscellaneous Papers, Houghton Library; *Sun*, May 5, 1857; *Times*, May 5, 6, 23, July 5, 7, 14, 1857.

28. *Sun*, Apr. 18, 23, 24, 25, 28, May 15, 26, 1857; *Herald*, Apr. 18, 21, May 14, 15, 1857; *Times*, May 1, 2, 12, 13, 16, June 3, 4, 1857; Richardson, *New York Police*, 103-4.

29. *Times*, May 19, 22, 1857; *Tribune*, May 20, 1857; *Sun*, May 20, 1857; *Journal of Commerce*, May 23, 1857.

30. *Times*, Apr. 19, 23, 24, 28, May 5, 6, 7, 8, 19, 26, 27, 28, 1857; *Sun*, Apr. 24, 26, 28, 29, 30, May 4, 12, 16, 21, 27, June 12, 1857; Wood to Augustus Schell, June 1, 1857, Augustus Schell Papers, NYHS; Rynders to Buchanan, June 19, 1857, Buchanan Papers; *Herald*, July 10, 1857.

31. *Times*, Apr. 18, 20, 22, May 7, 8, 12, June 23, 1857.

32. *Times*, May 29, 1857.

33. *Sun*, June 11, 12, 15, 1857; *Herald*, June 16, 17, 18, 19, 24, 25, 26, 1857.

34. *Times*, June 10, 11, 19, 1857; Gustavus Myers, *The History of Tammany Hall* (New York: Boni & Liveright, 1917), 182; Denis T. Lynch, *"Boss" Tweed: The Story of a Grim Generation* (New York: Boni & Liveright, 1927), 187.

35. *Tribune*, June 15, 16, 17, 1857; *Times*, June 16, 17, 1857; Spann, *New Metropolis*, 392–93.

36. *Times*, June 18, 19, 24, 26, July 11, 31, 1857, Apr. 13, 16, 17, 18, 19, 20, 21, 1858.

37. *Sun*, June 15, 17, 19, 1857; *Times*, June 17, 19, 20, 1857.

38. *Times*, June 29, July 1, 3, 4, 8, 1857; DeAlva S. Alexander, *A Political History of the State of New York* (New York: Henry Holt & Company, 1906–1924), 2:184; Richardson, *New York Police*, 107-8.

39. *Herald*, June 29, July 1, 3, 5, 1857; *Times*, July 3, 4, 6, 7, 8, 13, 14, 1857; Headley, *The Great Riots*, 129–34; Spann, *New Metropolis*, 393–94.

40. *Times*, July 6, 7, Aug. 7, 1857; *Tribune*, July 6, 9, 1857.

41. *Herald*, July 21, Aug. 4, 1857; *Times*, July 21, 22, Aug. 5, 6, 7, 14, Sept. 1, 1857.

42. Wikoff to Buchanan, July 22, Aug. 6, 30, 1857, Sanders to Buchanan, July 26, 1857, Sickles to Buchanan, Sept. 8, 1857, Buchanan Papers; *Times*, Aug. 14, 28, 31, Sept. 2, 1857; *Sun*, Aug. 28, Sept 3, 1857.

43. *Sun*, July 20, Aug. 23, Sept. 8, 1857; *Times*, July 20, Aug. 1, Sept. 8, 1857; Sickles to Buchanan, Sept. 8, 29, 1857, Buchanan Papers; Wood to Daniel Dickinson, Sept. 14, 1857, Wood Papers, NYHS.

44. Parker to Buchanan, Sept. 4, 1857, Buchanan Papers; *Herald*, Sept. 12, 13, 14, 18, 1857.

45. *Sun*, Sept. 11, 12, 15, 1857; *Times*, Sept. 12, 14, 16, 1857.

46. *Sun*, Sept. 28, 30, Oct. 2, 9, 10, 15, 16, 17, 30, 1857; *Daily News*, Oct. 13, 1857; *Herald*, Oct. 15, 16, 1857.

47. *Sun*, Oct. 16, 1857; *Times*, Oct. 22, 1857.

48. *Sun*, Sept. 17, Oct. 7, 14, 15, 22, 1857; *Times*, Oct. 8, 9, 14, 15, 16, 1857; *Hunt's Merchant's Magazine and Commercial Review* 37 (1857): 582; Samuel Rezneck, "The Influence of Depression Upon American Opinion, 1857–1859," *Journal of Economic History* 2 (May 1942): 1–23.

49. *Sun*, Oct. 23, 1857.

50. *Times*, Oct. 23, 27, Nov. 5, 6, 9, 10, 1857; *Evening Post*, Oct. 23, 27, Nov. 4, 10, 1857; *Herald*, Nov. 6, 8, 10, 11, 12, 13, 18, 1857; George T. Strong, *The Diary of George Templeton Strong*, ed. Allan Nevins and Milton H. Thomas (New York: Macmillan, 1952), 1:369–70.

51. *Sun*, Nov. 3, 6, 7, 10, 11, 12, 19, 20, 21, 1857; John Dix to Buchanan, Nov. 10, 1857, Buchanan Papers; Leah Feder, *Unemployment Relief in Periods of Depression: A Study of Measures Adopted in Certain American Cities, 1857 through 1922* (New York: Russell Sage Foundation, 1936), 32–35.

52. *Herald*, Nov. 6, 8, 10, 11, 12, 13, 18, 25, 1857; *Sun*, Nov. 10, 1857.

53. *Irish-American*, Nov. 14, 1857; *Times*, Nov. 14, 1857; Sickles to Buchanan, Nov. 20, 1857, Buchanan Papers.

54. *Herald*, Nov. 16, 18, 21, 1857; *Tribune*, Nov. 18, 21, 1857.

55. *Evening Post*, Nov. 9, 1857; *Sun*, Nov. 10, 12, 16, 19, 1857; *Times*, Nov. 21, 1857; Sickles to Buchanan, Nov. 28, 1857, Daniel F. Tiemann to Buchanan, Dec. 8, 1857, Buchanan Papers.

56. *Sun*, Nov. 21, 25, 26, 1857; *Herald*, Nov. 25, 1857; *Tribune*, Nov. 25, 1857.

57. *Times*, Nov. 24, 1857.

58. *Evening Post*, Nov. 24, 1857; *Times*, Nov. 24, 1857.

59. *Herald*, Nov. 23, 24, 1857; *Times*, Nov. 28, 29, 1857; *Sun*, Nov. 28, 30, Dec. 1, 1857; *Tribune*, Nov. 28, 29, Dec. 1, 1857.

60. *Sun*, Nov. 28, 1857.

61. *Times*, Nov. 28, Dec. 3, 1857; *Sun*, Dec. 1, 4, 1857; Spann, *New Metropolis*, 395–96; Leonard Chalmers, "Tammany Hall, Fernando Wood, and the Struggle to Control New York City, 1857–1860," *NYHSQ* 53 (Jan. 1969): 16–18.

62. *Times*, Dec. 2, 1857; *Herald*, Dec. 2, 3, 1857.

63. Wood's normal coalition had begun to slip. His multiple coefficient of correlation dropped to 0.687. He partially decreased his negative coefficient of correlation among the native-born to -0.724, but his marginal decrease among immigrants, 0.776, proved the key to Tiemann's victory. Statistical material derived from: *Hunt's Merchant's Magazine and Commercial Review* 37 (July–Dec. 1857): 342; Hardy, *Manual...for 1870*, 734; Ernst, *Immigrant Life*, 192–93, 223.

64. *Sun*, Dec. 3, 1857; Belmont to John Slidell, Dec. 8, 1857, Buchanan Papers.

6. THE SOUTHERN CANDIDATE

1. *Sun,* Dec. 4, 5, 1857, Apr. 5, 1858; *Times,* Dec. 4, 1857; *Irish-American,* Dec. 19, 1857.

2. *Sun,* Dec. 9, 1857; *Herald,* Dec. 9, 25, 1857, Jan. 2, 7, 8, 11, 12, 1858; *Times,* Jan. 7, 1858; *Daily News,* Jan. 8, 1857.

3. *Times,* Dec. 17, 24, 1857; *Sun,* Dec. 17, 18, 24, 1857; Sickles to Buchanan, Dec. 21, 1857, Dickinson to Buchanan, Dec. 26, 1857, Buchanan Papers; *Tribune,* Dec. 24, 1857.

4. Sickles to Buchanan, Dec. 21, 1857, John Dix to Buchanan, Mar. 5, 1858, Buchanan Papers; *Daily News,* Jan. 9, 1858; *Times,* Jan. 18, Mar. 5, 1858; Wood to Wise, Jan. 23, 1858, Poore Papers; *Sun,* Feb. 10, May 18, 1858; *Irish-American,* Apr. 3, 1858; Wood to Wise, June 18, 1858, Wood Papers, NYHS.

5. *Daily News,* Jan. 8, Feb. 9, Apr. 2, Aug. 30, 1858, Jan. 31, 1859, Apr. 15, 1861; William Cassidy to Tilden, Jan. 14, 1858, Tilden Papers; *Sun,* Feb. 10, Mar. 27, 1858, Feb. 12, 1859.

6. *Sun,* Mar. 27, 1858; *Daily News,* Apr. 2, 19, 1858; *Times,* Apr. 8, 18, 1858.

7. Cochrane to Buchanan, Dec. 31, 1857, Buchanan Papers; *Times,* Mar. 12, Apr. 5, 14, 19, May 25, 1858; *Herald,* Apr. 2, 18, 1858; *Evening Post,* Apr. 10, 1858.

8. *Sun,* Mar. 25, Apr. 7, 14, 19, 20, 1858; *Times,* Apr. 8, 10, 14, 19, 20, May 25, June 8, 1858; *Herald,* Apr. 20, 1858; Dix to Buchanan, Apr. 20, 1858, Buchanan Papers; *Daily News,* Apr. 24, 1858.

9. *Sun,* May 18, 1858; *Times,* June 11, 19, Aug. 5, 1858; Sickles to Buchanan, Aug. 5, 1858, Howell Cobb to Buchanan, Aug. 6, 1858, Buchanan Papers.

10. *Times,* May 10, Sept. 13, 1858; *Sun,* May 27, June 4, 1858; *Daily News,* Sept. 14, 1858.

11. *Daily News,* Jan. 8, 9, 19, Aug. 30, Oct. 4, 27, Dec. 6, 20, 1858, Jan. 7, 22, 1859; *Herald,* Mar. 4, 1859.

12. *Times,* Sept. 2, 7, 8, 16, 1858.

13. Wood to Buchanan, Sept. 8, 10, 27, 29, 1858, Buchanan to Wood, Sept. 9, 1858, Buchanan Papers.

14. Sickles to Buchanan, Aug. 5, Sept. 8, Oct. 18, 1858, Nathaniel Fowler to Buchanan, Sept. 8, 1858, John Cochrane to Buchanan, Sept. 13, 1858, Buchanan Papers.

15. Sickles to Buchanan, Aug. 5, 1858, Buchanan Papers; *Daily News,* Aug. 9, 28, 30, Sept. 5, 9, 13, 16, 17, 18, 1858; *Herald,* Sept. 3, 4, 5, 16, 17, 1858; *Times,* Aug. 26, Sept. 4, 5, 1858; *Irish-American,* Oct. 30, 1858.

16. Wood to Buchanan, Oct. 1, 6, 8, 15, 1858, Kelly to Buchanan, Oct. 12, 1858, Buchanan to Wood, Oct. 18, 1858, Albert Ramsey to Buchanan, Oct. 25, 1858, Sickles to Buchanan, Oct. 31, 1858, Buchanan Papers; *Daily News,* Oct. 13, 15, 28, Nov. 2, 1858; *Times,* Nov. 1, 1858.

17. *Daily News,* Nov. 3, 7, 8, 16, 25, Dec. 2, 4, 1858; *New York Leader,* Nov. 20, 27, Dec. 11, 1858.

18. Albert Ramsey to Fowler, Nov. 6, 8, 1858, Albert Ramsey Papers, NYHS; Nichols, *Disruption of American Democracy,* 213.

19. Ramsey to Buchanan, Oct. 25, Nov. 27, 1858, Purdy to Buchanan, Dec. 17, 1858, "Paper signed by John Kelly, John Cochrane, Isaac V. Fowler, Augustus Schell, William D. Kennedy, Richard B. Connolly, etc.," Dec. 17, 1858, Buchanan Papers; *Herald,* Dec. 18, 19, 20, 21, 1858; *Leader,* Dec. 25, 1858; Wood to Anna Ella Carroll, May 9, 1860, Anna Ella Carroll Papers, Maryland Historical Society, Baltimore.

20. *Daily News,* Dec. 16, 20, 21, 31, 1858; *Herald,* Dec. 31, 1858; *Leader,* Jan. 8, 29, 1859.

21. *Herald,* Jan. 1, 14, 25, 28, 29, 1859; *Leader,* Jan. 1, 29, 1859; *Sun,* Jan. 20, 1859.

22. *Times,* Jan. 28, 29, 31, Feb. 28, 1859; *Leader,* Feb. 5, 1859; *Sun,* Feb. 5, 1859; *Daily News,* Feb. 10, Mar. 22, June 4, 1859; *Herald,* Feb. 28, Mar. 15, May 5, 1859; Gideon Tucker to Burke, Mar. 16, 1859, Burke Papers; William A. Swanburg, *Sickles The Incredible* (New York: Charles Scribner's Sons, 1956), 36–37.

23. *Sun*, Oct. 16, 1857, Mar. 1, 1860; *Herald*, Dec. 10, 1859; Benjamin Wood to George H. Paul, June 14, 1861, George H. Paul to Pamela Paul, June 29, Aug. 18, 1861, George H. Paul Papers, Wisconsin Historical Society, Madison; *Population Schedules of the Eighth Census*, reel 820, p. 74.

24. *Daily News*, Jan. 19, Mar. 2, 7, 8, Apr. 2, 1859; L. B. Spinola to Wood, Mar. 8, 1859, Wood Papers, NYPL; *Sun*, Mar. 13, Apr. 7, 25, 1859; *Herald*, Apr. 14, 20, 1859; Mark W. Summers, "'A Band of Brigands': Albany Lawmakers and Republican National Politics, 1860," *CWH* 30 (June 1984): 101–19.

25. *Sun*, Feb. 2, Apr. 11, 15, May 6, 1859; *Daily News*, Mar. 21, Apr. 2, 5, 8, 9, 10, 21, 23, May 26, 1859.

26. *Herald*, May 12, 15, June 4, 16, 1859; *Sun*, June 1, 2, 1859; *Evening Post*, June 1, 1859; *Daily News*, June 18, July 4, 1859.

27. Wood to Wise, Mar. 13, 1859, Henry A. Wise Papers, Alderman Library, University of Virginia; Wood to Wise, Apr. 5, 11, 1859, Wood Papers, NYHS; Thomas Dyer to Douglas, June 5, 1859, Douglas Papers; *Daily News*, June 25, July 13, 20, 1859; *Sun*, June 25, 30, July 20, 1859; *Herald*, June 30, July 9, Sept. 2, 1859; Wood to Wise, July 6, 1859, Brock Collection, Huntington Library.

28. Wood to Wise, Jan. 5, 1857, Jan. 23, 1858, Poore Papers; *Herald*, Aug. 4, 5, 9, 1859; *Sun*, Aug. 4, 13, 1859; *Daily News*, Aug. 8, 1859; Wood to Douglas, Sept. 30, 1859, Douglas Papers; Craig M. Simpson, *A Good Southerner: A Life of Henry A. Wise of Virginia* (Chapel Hill: Univ. of North Carolina Press, 1985), 188–89.

29. *Daily News*, Aug. 4, 5, 10, 15, 16, 20, 1859; Dyer to Douglas, Aug. 6, 1859, Connolly to Douglas, Aug. 19, 1859, Douglas Papers; *Herald*, Aug. 7, 11, 1859; *Sun*, Aug. 11, 18, 1859; Wise to Wood, Sept. 10, 1858, Henry A. Wise Papers, Virginia State Library, Richmond.

30. *Daily News*, Aug. 9, 11, 13, 22, Sept. 1, 2, 9, 1859; *Herald*, Aug. 22, 30, Sept. 2, 1859; *New York Weekly Tribune*, Aug. 13, 20, 1859; *Times*, Sept. 2, 1859.

31. *Herald*, Sept. 6, 7, 15, 16, 1859; *Sun*, Sept. 9, 10, 14, 16, 17, 1859; *Times*, Sept. 15, 16, 17, 1859; *Daily News*, Sept. 16, 17, 1859; *New York Weekly Tribune*, Sept. 17, 1859; Alexander, *Political History* 2:257–58.

32. *Herald*, Sept. 16, 28, Oct. 4, 1859; *Sun*, Sept 17, 20, 23, 28, Oct. 17, 1859; *Times*, Sept. 17, 19, 1859; *Weekly New York Tribune*, Sept. 24, 1859; *Irish-American*, Sept. 24, 1859; *Evening Post*, Oct. 17, 1859.

33. *Herald*, Jan. 31, 1859; *Daily News*, May 7, 1859; *Times*, Sept. 3, 1859; Nichols, *Disruption of American Democracy*, 260; John E. Simpson, *Howell Cobb: The Politics of Ambition* (Chicago: Adams Press, 1973), 129–30.

34. *Sun*, Sept. 3, Oct. 6, 7, 1859; *Herald*, Oct. 1, 13, 14, 28, Nov. 4, 1859; *Times*, Oct. 8, 13, 1859; *Daily News*, Oct. 14, 1859; Peter Cagger to Corning, Nov. 1, 1859, Corning Papers.

35. *Times*, Oct. 4, 5, 31, Nov. 10, 19, 11, 23, 25, 1859; *Irish-American*, Nov. 5, 26, 1859; *Tribune*, Nov. 11, 21, 1859; *Sun*, Nov. 11, 14, 18, 1859; Barlow to James T. Brady, Nov. 15, 1859, Samuel L. M. Barlow Papers, Huntington Library, San Marino, Calif.; Havemeyer to Tilden, Nov. 20, 1859, Tilden Papers.

36. *Sun*, Nov. 19, 21, 23, 24, Dec. 1, 2, 1859; *Times*, Nov. 22, 24, 26, Dec. 2, 1859; *Daily News*, Nov. 22, 23, 1859; *Tribune*, Nov. 22, Dec. 2, 1859; *Herald*, Nov. 22, 26, 28, 1859; *Irish-American*, Nov. 26, 1859; William C. Bryant to John Bigelow, Dec. 14, 1859, in *The Letters of William Cullen Bryant*, ed. William C. Bryant II and Thomas G. Viss (New York: Fordham Univ. Press, 1984), 4:129–130.

37. *Daily News*, Oct. 6, 14, Nov. 21, 23, 24, 1859; *Herald*, Oct. 19, 1859.

38. John A. McMaster to Douglas, Oct. 30, A. D. Banks to Douglas, Oct. 30, 1859, Douglas Papers; *New York Evening Post*, Nov. 21, 1859; Joseph Peabody to Barlow, Nov. 30, 1859, Barlow Papers.

39. John W. Botts to Carroll, Nov. 12, 1859, Carroll Papers.

40. *Times*, Oct. 4, 5, 22, Nov. 7, 10, 11, 18, 25, 26, 29, 1859; *Evening Post*, Oct. 17, Nov. 17, 1859; *Herald*, Nov. 19, 26, 1859; *Weekly New York Tribune*, Nov. 25, Dec. 19, 1859; *Sun*, Nov. 26, 29, Dec. 1, 3, 1859.

41. Charles Daly to Wood, Oct. 3, 1859, Lyman Tremaine to Wood, Oct. 11, 1859, Oswald Ottendorfer to Wood, Nov. 7, 1859, Richard Busteed to Wood, Nov. 14, 1859, Wood Papers, NYPL; *Daily News*, Oct. 10, 27, Nov. 3, 9, 15, 17, 1859; Wood to [?], Dec. 1, 1859, Miscellaneous Papers, John Hay Library, Brown University, Providence, R.I.; Chalmers, "Struggle to Control New York City," 24–32. Copies of Wood's lithographed letter can be found in a number of archives.

42. *Daily News*, Oct. 19, 20, Nov. 25, 1859; *Sun*, Oct. 19, 20, 1859; *Times*, Oct. 21, 29, 1859; *Weekly New York Tribune*, Nov. 5, 1859; *Herald*, Nov. 7, 14, 1859.

43. Wise to Wood, Oct. 2, 1859, Wise Papers, Virginia Historical Society, Richmond; Wood to Wise, Nov. 2, 1859, Frederick J. Dreer Collection (John Brown Papers), HSP; *Weekly Tribune*, Nov. 5, 12, 25, Dec. 3, 1859; *Herald*, Nov. 14, Dec. 6, 1859.

44. Wise to Wood, Nov. 4, 1859, Dreer Collection; *Daily News*, Dec. 5, 1859; Simpson, *Good Southerner*, 203–18.

45. *Daily News*, Nov. 29, 1859; Spann, *New Metropolis*, 365.

46. *Sun*, Nov. 24, Dec. 7, 1859; *Daily News*, Nov. 25, Dec. 17, 1859; *Herald*, Dec. 4, 7, 1859; *Evening Post*, Dec. 7, 8, 1859; *Times*, Dec. 7, 17, 1859.

47. *Herald*, Dec. 8, 1859. Wood's normal coalition continued to erode. His multiple coefficient of correlation dropped to 0.488. At the same time, his standing among immigrants was down to 0.198. He partially made up for that loss by a slight increase among native-born voters, -0.589. Statistical material derived from: *Times*, Sept. 9, 1859; David Valentine, *Manual of the Corporation of the City of New York for 1860* (New York, 1860), 230; *Herald*, Mar. 13, 1861; Hardy, *The Manual . . . for 1870*, 735; *Reports of the Industrial Commission on Immigration, including Testimony, with Review and Digest and Special Reports and on Education, including Testimony, with Review and Digest* (Washington, D.C.: GPO, 1901), 15:455, 486.

48. *Daily News*, Dec. 7, 8, 1859, Jan. 16, 1860; *Herald*, Dec. 8, 1859; *Times*, Jan. 21, 1860.

49. *Daily News*, Dec. 7, 8, 15, 1859, Jan. 4, 1860; *Sun*, Dec. 7, 8, 1859; *Times*, Dec. 7, 17, 1859; *Evening Post*, Dec. 7, 8, 1859; John Dix to Buchanan, Dec. 7, 1858, Buchanan Papers; *Richmond Examiner*, Dec. 9, 1859, cited by *Daily News*, Dec. 11, 1859; *Times*, Dec. 15, 24, 31, 1859; *Irish-American*, Dec. 17, 1859; *London Times*, Dec. 20, 1859, cited by *Daily News*, Jan. 11, 1860; Sanders to Douglas, Dec. 28, 1859, Douglas Papers.

50. *Daily News*, Dec. 7, 1859.

51. *Times*, Dec. 10, 13, 1859; *Herald*, Dec. 10, 1859; *Daily News*, Dec. 10, 1859; *Sun*, Dec. 13, 17, 1859.

52. *Times*, Dec. 13, 20, 1859; James Beekman to Wood, Dec. 14, 1859, Bishop John Hughes to Wood, Dec. 16, 1859, Stout to Wood, Dec. 29, 1859, Tucker to Wood, Dec. 29, 1859, Barr to Wood, Dec. 30, 1859, Wood Papers, NYPL; *Daily News*, Dec. 17, 20, 21, 1859.

7. THE SOUTHERN MAYOR

1. *Daily News*, Jan. 3, 4, 1860; *Herald*, Jan. 4, 1860.

2. *Times*, Jan. 4, 6, 1860; *Daily News*, Feb. 11, 1860.

3. *Herald*, Jan. 2, 21, 1860; *Daily News*, Jan. 2, 12, 1860; *Times*, Feb. 29, Mar. 21, 1860.

4. *Daily News*, Jan. 6, 11, 1860; *Times*, Jan. 6, 27, Mar. 7, 13, 1860; *Herald*, Jan. 16, 1860.

5. *Times*, Jan. 17, 25, Feb. 6, 28, Mar. 2, 1860; Richardson, *New York Police*, 116–17.

6. *Daily News*, Jan. 20, Feb. 18, Mar. 17, 1860.

7. *Times*, Jan. 9, 14, 23, Feb. 3, 14, 20, 1860; *Daily News*, Jan. 23, 30, Feb. 27, Mar. 8, Apr. 9, 1860, Jan. 1, 1861; *Herald*, Feb. 19, Mar. 4, 1860; David Valentine to Wood, Apr. 10, 1860, Wood Papers, NYPL.

8. *Times*, Feb. 3, 6, 28, Mar. 2, 5, 8, 9, 21, Apr. 12, 19, 25, 26, 1860; *Daily News*, Mar. 6, 1860; *Herald*, Apr. 11, 19, 1860; Richardson, *New York Police*, 118–22.

9. Wood to Anna Ella Carroll, Jan. 30, Feb. 10, 1860, Carroll Papers; *Times*, Jan. 2, Feb. 1, 1860; *Journal of Commerce*, Jan. 5, 1860; Samuel P. Powell to Wood, Jan. 30, 1860, Wood Papers, NYPL; *Herald*, Feb. 1, 24, Apr. 14, 1860; *Daily News*, Feb. 6, 10, 11, 17, 18, 1860; Wood to Robert Tyler, Mar. 8, 1860, Wood Papers, NYHS.

10. Connolly to Douglas, Jan. 19, 1860, Wood to Douglas, Jan. 21, 1860, Sanders to Douglas, Feb. 5, 1860, Cagger to Douglas, Feb. 14, 1860, Douglas Papers; Dickinson to Burke, Jan. 26, 1860, Burke Papers; Butterworth to Barlow, Feb. 14, 1860, Seymour to Barlow, May 15, 1860, Barlow Papers; Douglas to Wood, Feb. 16, 1860, Brock Collection, Huntington Library, San Marino, Calif.; *Daily News*, Feb. 18, 1860; *Herald*, Apr. 23, May 1, June 19, 1860; Ramsey to Buchanan, Apr. 26, 1860, Rynders to Buchanan, May 11, 1860, Buchanan Papers.

11. *Daily News*, Jan. 26, Feb. 3, 6, 7, 8, 9, 1860; Fernando Wood, *Speech of Fernando Wood delivered Before the Meeting of the National Democratic Delegation to the Charleston Convention, at Syracuse, February 7, 1860* (New York, 1860).

12. *Times*, Feb. 9, Mar. 2, 10, 22, 26, 1860; *Daily News*, Feb. 10, 17, 23, 1860; Judah Benjamin to Barlow, Apr. 15, 1860, Barlow Papers; *Herald*, Apr. 18, 1860; *Tribune*, Apr. 28, 1860.

13. Wood to Carroll, Jan. 30, Feb. 10, Mar. 7, 20, 1860, Carroll Papers; *Daily News*, Mar. 5, 8, 12, 20, 21, 22, 23, 24, 25, 28, 30, Apr. 2, 3, 4, 5, 11, 1860; *Herald*, Apr. 4, 1860.

14. *Daily News*, Feb. 28, Apr. 13, 18, 25, 26, 28, 30, 1860; *Times*, Apr. 16, 19, 23, 27, 1860; William B. Hesseltine, ed., *Three Against Lincoln: Murat Halstead Reports the Caucuses of 1860* (Baton Rouge: Louisiana State Univ. Press, 1960), 5–6, 8, 16.

15. *Herald*, Apr. 23, 24, 27, May 1, 1860; *Times*, Apr. 23, 24, 25, 26, 27, 1860; *Tribune*, Apr. 26, 1860.

16. *Herald*, Apr. 24, 25, 28, 1860; *Times*, Apr. 25, 26, 28, May 2, 1860; *Tribune*, Apr. 28, 1860; Hesseltine, *Three Against Lincoln*, 21, 31, 32, 34, 43. Wood received full votes from Alabama, Georgia, Mississippi, and Texas. Arkansas gave him 3 of 7.5; Missouri, 1 of 9; North Carolina, 5 out of 10; Tennessee, 9 of 12; Virginia, 3.5 of 15; and the pro-Buchanan Californians, 3.5 of 4. He received none from Florida, Kentucky, Louisiana, or South Carolina.

17. *Times*, Apr. 29, May 1, 2, 3, 4, 1860; *Daily News*, Apr. 30, May 1, 4, 1860; *Herald*, May 1, 11, 1860; *Journal of Commerce*, May 10, 1860.

18. *Daily News*, Apr. 30, May 1, 1860.

19. Nichols, *Disruption of American Democracy*, 288–304; Joseph J. Hemmer, Jr., "The Democratic National Conventions of 1860: Discourse of Disruption in Rhetorical-Historical Perspective," Ph.D. diss., University of Wisconsin, 1969.

20. *Times*, May 1, 3, 4, 1860; *Daily News*, May 7, 1860.

21. *Herald*, Apr. 29, June 13, 17, 20, 21, 29, Dec. 7, 1860; Dix to Buchanan, May 9, 1860, Buchanan to Mrs. James J. Roosevelt, Feb. 14, 1863, Buchanan Papers; Barlow to Corning, May 19, 1860, Corning Papers; Philip G. Auchampaugh, "The Buchanan-Douglas Feud," *Journal of the Illinois Historical Society* 24 (Apr.–July 1932): 44.

22. *Times*, Apr. 13, May 7, 8, 15, 16, 17, 18, 29, 30, 31, June 1, 2, 15, 1860; *Daily News*, May 17, June 15, 16, 1860.

23. *Times*, June 13, July 16, Nov. 28, 1860.

24. *Daily News*, July 16, 17, Aug. 8, 1860; *Times*, Sept. 11, 12, 18, 26, Oct. 2, 1860.

25. *Daily News,* May 16, July 11, Aug. 25, Oct. 10, 11, 12, 1860. The Prince of Wales, the future King Edward VII, traveled under the name of Lord Renfrew.

26. Sanders to Douglas, Feb. 5, 1860, Douglas Papers; Dix to Buchanan, May 14, June 4, 1860, Buchanan Papers; *Times,* May 15, 1860; *Herald,* May 16, 19, 1860; Croswell to Corning, May 19, 1860, Corning Papers; *Tribune,* May 26, 1860; Fowler to Barlow, June 21, 1860, Barlow Papers; Montgomery Blair to Abraham Lincoln, Jan. 16, 1863, Robert Todd Lincoln Papers, LC.

27. *Daily News,* June 20, 21, 1860.

28. *Herald,* June 22, 23, 27, 1860; Douglas to Richmond, June 23, 1860, *Douglas Letters,* 493; *Daily News,* June 2, 26, 27, 1860; Hesseltine, *Three Against Lincoln,* 185–278; Nichols, *Disruption of American Democracy,* 312–20; Damon Wells, *Stephen Douglas: The Last Years, 1857–1861* (Austin: Univ. of Texas Press, 1971), 232–40.

29. *Daily News,* June 29, 1860.

30. *Herald,* June 28, 1860; *Daily News,* July 7, 1860; Reinhard H. Luthin, *The First Lincoln Campaign* (Cambridge: Harvard Univ. Press, 1944), 212–13.

31. *Times,* June 27, July 3, 17, Aug. 17, 1860; Schell to Corning, June 28, 1860, Corning Papers; Tucker to Buchanan, June 29, 1860, Dickinson to Buchanan, June 30, 1860, Wikoff to Buchanan, July 12, 1860, Buchanan Papers; *Herald,* July 2, 3, 4, 13, 19, 29, Aug. 10, 1860; *Daily News,* July 7, 13, 19, 23, 25, 1860; Milledge L. Bonham, Jr., "New York and the Election of 1860," *NYH* 15 (Apr. 1934): 124–43.

32. *Herald,* June 27, 28, July 3, 19, 1860; *Daily News,* July 6, 1860; *Times,* July 7, 13, 1860; Wells, *Douglas,* 244–46.

33. *Irish-American,* June 30, 1860; André Froment to Barlow, July 7, 1860, Seymour to Barlow, July 26, 1860, Barlow Papers; *Herald,* July 13, 14, 1860; Rynders to Buchanan, Aug. 13, 1860, Buchanan Papers.

34. *Herald,* July 15, 1860; *Daily News,* July 16, 1860; Sherman to Corning, July 17, 1860, Belmont to Corning, Aug. 1, 1860, Corning Papers; Dix to Buchanan, July 17, 1860, Gouveneur Kemble to Buchanan, July 25, 1860, Buchanan Papers; *Journal of Commerce,* July 19, 26, 1860; Belmont to Douglas, July 28, 1860, Douglas Papers; Foner, *Business and Slavery,* 169–270.

35. Washington Hunt to John Bell, Aug. 19, 1860, in Louis Sears, "New York and the Fusion Movement of 1860," *Journal of the Illinois State Historical Society* 16 (Apr.–July 1923): 60–61; Dix to Buchanan, July 17, 1860, Buchanan Papers; Sidney D. Brummer, *Political History of New York State During the Period of the Civil War* (New York: Columbia Univ. Press, 1911), 79–80.

36. *Times,* July 12, 1860; *Daily News,* Aug. 1, 1860; *Herald,* Aug. 1, 1860.

37. *Herald,* Aug. 4, 13, 15, 17, 21, 31, 1860; *Daily News,* Aug. 6, 9, 13, 15, 1860; *Journal of Commerce,* Aug. 9, 23, 1860; *Times,* Aug. 9, 17, 1860.

38. Belmont to Douglas, July 28, 1860, Douglas Papers; Calvert Comstock to Barlow, Aug. 9, 22, 1860, Barlow Papers; *Journal of Commerce,* Sept. 13, 1860; Belmont to Tilden n.d. [1860?], Tilden Papers; *Daily News,* Aug. 16, 17, 31, Sept. 1, 10, 1860; *Herald,* Sept. 2, 7, 8, 11, 16, 24, 1860.

39. *Times,* Sept. 2, 11, 17, 21, 22, 25, Oct. 1, 2, 3, 16, 1860; *Herald,* Oct. 1, 2, 3, 16, 21, 24, 30, 1860; James J. Roosevelt to Buchanan, Sept. 30, 1860, Buchanan Papers; Cagger to Tilden, Oct. 24, 1860, Tilden Papers.

40. *Times,* Aug. 14, 15, 30, Oct. 11, 1860; *Daily News,* Sept. 3, 8, 13, 14, 21, 24, 25, 26, Oct. 1, 3, 9, 15, 19, 1860.

41. *Daily News,* Jan. 5, 16, 1861; *New York Leader,* Feb. 21, 1863; Cornelia Roosevelt to Buchanan, Apr. 10, 1863, Buchanan Papers; [Joseph A. Scoville], *The Old Merchants of New York City. By Walter Barrett, Clerk. Second Series* (New York: Carleton, Publisher, 1864), 1:192–93; Abby B. Mills, "Last Will and Testament," Oct. 25, 1872, liber 189, pp. 406, 424, Surrogate's Court, New York County, Hall of Records.

42. Barlow to Cagger, Sept. 5, 1860, Cagger to Barlow, Sept. 6, 18, 20, 1860, Oct. 8, 1860, John Stryker to Barlow, Sept. 10, 1860, James T. Brady to Barlow, Sept. 20, 24, 1860, Barlow Papers; *Herald*, Sept. 18, 1860; *Daily News*, Sept. 18, 1860; Nathan Paine to Buchanan, Sept. 27, 1860, Buchanan Papers; Robert W. Johannsen, *Stephen Douglas* (New York: Oxford Univ. Press, 1973), 792–94.

43. *Times*, Sept. 17, 18, 25, 27, Oct. 6, 7, 9, 1860; *Herald*, Oct. 3, 4, 9, 14, 16, 19, 25, 31, 1860; Sherman to Corning, Oct. 27, 1860, Corning Papers.

44. *Times*, Oct. 3, 23, 26, 29, 31, Nov. 3, 6, 1860; *Irish-American*, Oct. 6, 1860; *Daily News*, Oct. 21, 23, 29, Nov. 3, 1860; Wood to Barlow, Oct. 23, 1860, Barlow Papers.

45. *Times*, Nov. 7, 8, 9, 1860; *Daily News*, Nov. 7, 9, 13, 1860; *Herald*, Nov. 7, 8, 1860; *Leader*, Nov. 10, 1860; Dale Baum and Dale T. Knobel, "Anatomy of a Realignment: New York Presidential Politics, 1848–1860," *NYH* 65 (Jan. 1984): 61–81.

46. *Times*, Nov. 15, 16, 23, 30, Dec. 5, 6, 1860; *Herald*, Nov. 16, 30, Dec. 5, 6, 1860; *Daily News*, Nov. 21, Dec. 3, 28, 1860; Valentine, *Manual. . .for 1861*, 99.

47. *Times*, Nov. 13, 20, 21, 22, 28, Dec. 4, 1860, Jan. 1, 2, 1861.

48. *Times*, Dec. 28, 29, 31, 1860, Jan. 1, 2, 5, 12, 14, Mar. 9, 1861; *Daily News*, Dec. 28, Jan. 1, 9, 10, 17, Mar. 2, 1861.

49. *Times*, Jan. 8, 10, 11, 12, 14, 16, 17, 19, 23, 25, Feb. 4, 6, 11, 13, Mar. 2, 15, 16, Apr. 12, 13, 1861; *Daily News*, Jan. 9, 10, 11, 17, 29, Mar. 2, Apr. 13, 1861; *Herald*, Mar. 16, Apr. 14, 1861.

50. *Daily News*, Nov. 15, 17, 24, 27, Dec. 3, 25, 1860; *Tribune*, Nov. 25, 1860.

51. *Daily News*, Mar. 1, Dec. 8, 15, 22, 1860; Dix to Horatio King, Nov. 25, Dec. 14, 1860, Horatio King Papers, LC; Wood to Fish, Dec. 11, 1860, Fish Papers; Wood to Tilden, Dec. 12, 1860, Cochrane to Tilden, Dec. 20, 1860, Tilden Papers; *Herald*, Dec. 21, 1860.

52. Cochrane to Barlow, Dec. 5, 12, 19, 1860, Barlow to Cochrane, Dec. 8, 1860, Judah Benjamin to Barlow, Dec. 9, 1860, Barlow Papers; *Times*, Dec. 13, 1860; Buchanan to Bennett, Dec. 20, 1860, Buchanan Papers; *Daily News*, Dec. 20, 1860; Kemble to Corning, Dec. 29, 1860, Corning Papers; Tyler G. Anbinder, "Fernando Wood and New York City's Secession from the Union: A Political Reappraisal," *NYH* 68 (Jan. 1987): 67–92.

53. *Times*, Jan. 8, 1861.

54. Ibid.

55. Ibid.

56. *Sun*, Jan. 8, 1861; *Daily News*, Jan. 8, 9, 1861; *Herald*, Jan. 8, Apr. 12, 1861; *Times*, Jan. 8, 9, 11, 26, 1861; *Tribune*, Jan. 8, 1861; *Richmond Examiner*, Jan. 10, 1861; *Leader*, Jan. 12, 1861; Foner, *Business and Slavery*, 288–96; James Heslin, "'Peaceful Compromise' in New York City, 1860–1861," *NYHSQ* 44 (Oct. 1960): 349–62.

57. *Irish-American*, Jan. 19, 26, 1861; *Sun*, Jan. 19, Feb. 2, 1861; *Journal of Commerce*, Jan. 30, Mar. 7, 1861; *Times*, Feb. 1, 1861; *Leader*, Feb. 2, 9, 1861; *Daily News*, Feb. 2, 22, Mar. 24, 1861; John Cisco to Dix, Feb. 2, Buchanan to Dix, Mar. 18, 1861, John A. Dix Papers, Butler Library, Columbia University, New York.

58. *Daily News*, Jan. 11, 12, 15, 17, 21, 24, Feb. 1, 9, Mar. 1, 5, 15, Apr. 1, 13, 15, 1861; *Richmond Examiner*, Mar. 1, 1861.

59. *Daily News*, Jan. 16, 25, 26, Feb. 9, 13, 1861; *Sun*, Jan. 23, 1861; John Kennedy to Thurlow Weed, Jan. 24, 1861, Thurlow Weed Papers, UR; *Herald*, Jan. 25, 1861; *Times*, Jan. 26, 1861; *Irish-American*, Feb. 23, 1861.

60. *Daily News*, Feb. 20, 21, 1861; *Sun*, Feb. 20, 21, 1861; John Adams Dix, *Memoirs of John Adams Dix*, ed. Morgan Dix (New York: Harper & Brothers, 1883), 1:386–87; Andrew A. Freeman, *Abraham Lincoln Goes to New York* (New York: Coward-McCann, 1960), 109–12.

61. *Times*, Feb. 21, 1861.

62. *Leader,* Apr. 20, 1861.

63. *Leader,* Mar. 23, 1861; *Daily News,* Apr. 6, 1861.

8. THE POLITICS OF LOYALTY

1. *Journal of Commerce,* Apr. 15, 1861; *Sun,* Apr. 16, 17, 21, 1861; Buchanan to Dix, Apr. 19, 1861; *Herald,* Apr. 21, 1861.

2. *Daily News,* Apr. 16, 19, 23, June 11, 1861; *Times,* Apr. 17, June 20, 1861; *Irish-American,* Apr. 20, 1861; *Sun,* Apr. 23, May 3, 1861; *Leader,* May 4, 11, 18, 1861; *Times,* June 5, 1861; Wood to Haws, June 19, 1861, Wood to Bronson, Jan. 13, 1864, Historical Documents Collection, Queens College, Flushing, N.Y.; Wood to Joseph Mansfield, July 2, 1861, Wood Papers, NYHS.

3. Bennett to Wood, Apr. 19, 1861, Wood Papers, NYPL; *Sun,* Apr. 14, 1861; *Daily News,* Apr. 14, 1861; Wood to Haws, Apr. 29, 1861, Historical Documents Collection; *Times,* July 6, 1861; Wood to Robert Anderson, July 22, 1861, Robert Anderson Papers, LC; Wood to Lincoln, Apr. 29, 1861, Lincoln Papers; John A. Stevens, *The Union Defense Committee of the City of New York* (New York: Published by the Committee, 1885).

4. *Sun,* Apr. 16, 1861.

5. *Daily News,* Apr. 22, May 1, June 21, July 22, Aug. 1, 1861; Dickinson to John C. Spencer, May 7, 1861, in Daniel S. Dickinson, *The Speeches, Correspondence, Etc. of the Late Daniel S. Dickinson,* ed. John Dickinson (New York: G. P. Putnam & Sons, 1867), 550–51; *Leader,* May 16, 1861; *Times,* May 23, June 28, 1861; *Sun,* Aug. 7, 1861; William Hartman, "Custom House Patronage Under Lincoln," *NYHSQ* 41 (Oct. 1957): 440–57; William G. Carleton, "Civil War Dissidence in the North: The Perspective of a Century," *South Atlantic Quarterly* 55 (Summer 1966): 390–402; Richard O. Curry, "'The Union As It Was': A Critique of Recent Interpretations of the Copperheads," *CWH* 13 (Mar. 1967): 23–39; Robert Azbug, "The Copperheads: Historical Approaches to Civil War Dissent," *Indiana Magazine of History* 66 (Mar. 1970): 40–55; John T. Hubbell, "The Northern Democrats and Party Survival, 1860–1861," *Illinois Quarterly* 36 (Sept. 1973): 22–33; Joel H. Silbey, *A Respectable Minority: The Democratic Party in the Civil War Era, 1860–1868* (New York: W. W. Norton & Company, 1977), 3–61.

6. *Daily News,* July 23, 1861; *Sun,* July 24, 1861; *Times,* July 24, Aug. 13, 1861; *Leader,* July 27, 1861; *Journal of Commerce,* Aug. 1, 1861; *Tribune,* Oct. 12, 1861.

7. *Daily News,* May 24, July 25, Aug. 10, 1861; *Times,* July 9, 11, 12, Oct. 1, 1861.

8. *Daily News,* May 2, 4, 9, 15, 17, 31, June 3, 1861; *Times,* May 17, June 3, July 29, Aug. 20, 1861.

9. *Times,* June 28, Aug. 20, 23, 27, 28, Sept. 2, 1861; *Daily News,* June 28, Aug. 23, 24, 27, 28, Sept. 14, 1861; *Sun,* Aug. 6, 7, 16, 27, 1861; *Tribune,* Aug. 17, 1861.

10. *Leader,* June 15, 1861; *Daily News,* Aug. 6, 9, 10, 1861; *Herald,* Aug. 7, 9, 12, 1861; *Times,* Aug. 7, 10, 12, 16, 1861; *New York Evening Post,* Aug. 7, 1861; Weed to Lincoln, Aug. 18, 1861, Lincoln Papers; Isaac Sherman to Weed, Sept. 8, 1861, Weed Papers.

11. *Times,* Sept. 1, 6, 1861; *Daily News,* Sept. 3, 4, 7, 10, 1861; *Journal of Commerce,* Sept. 4, 1861; *Sun,* Sept. 4, 5, 6, 9, 1861; *Herald,* Sept. 6, 9, 1861; *Leader,* Sept. 7, 1861; Brummer, *Political History,* 158–64.

12. *Daily News,* Sept. 10, 1861.

13. *Daily News,* Sept. 11, 1861.

14. *Richmond Examiner,* Sept. 10, 11, 1861.

15. *Leader,* Sept. 14, 21, 28, Oct. 12, 26, Nov. 2, 1861; *Times,* Sept. 19, Oct. 4, 9, 20, 23, 28, 1861; *Sun,* Oct. 8, 9, 10, 25, 28, Nov. 2, 1861; Richard O'Gorman to Wood, Oct. 16, 1861, Weed to Wood, Oct. 29, 1861, Wood Papers, NYPL.

16. *Times*, Nov. 2, 1861; Edward James to Wood, Nov. [?], 1861, Wood Papers, NYPL.

17. *Times*, Nov. 4, 5, 11, 1861; *Sun*, Nov. 6, 1861; *Herald*, Nov. 6, 8, 1861; Hall to Wood, Dec. 23, 1861, Wood Papers, NYPL; Hall to Weed, Dec. 31, 1862, Weed Papers.

18. *Times*, Feb. 15, Mar. 5, 12, 14, 19, Apr. 19, 22, 27, July 25, 1861; *Daily News*, Mar. 6, 22, 1861; *Evening Post*, Mar. 21, 1861.

19. *Daily News*, Apr. 4, 12, 1861; *Tribune*, Apr. 10, 11, 12, 1861; *Sun*, Apr. 19, 1861; *Times*, June 23, 28, Sept. 7, 1861.

20. *Times*, June 21, 28, July 6, Sept. 24, Oct, 22, 1861; *Sun*, Oct. 22, 1861.

21. *Times*, July 25, Sept. 10, 1861, Jan. 7, 22, 30, Mar. 29, Apr. 23, 24, 25, 29, May 10, 19, June 23, 1863, Sept. 9, 1865.

22. *Sun*, Sept. 21, Nov. 16, 1861; *Times*, Sept 21, 1861; *Leader*, Sept. 21, 28, Oct. 12, 1861; Mar. 1, June 21, 1862; *Tribune*, Oct. 11, 1861; *Herald*, Oct. 17, Nov. 4, 1861; Havemeyer to Dix, Nov. 8, 1861, Dix Papers.

23. *Times*, Nov. 15, 20, 25, 27, Dec. 2, 3, 1861; *Sun*, Nov. 15, 19, 20, 26, 27, 1861; *Leader*, Nov. 16, 23, 1861; *Herald*, Nov. 17, 26, 1861. Havemeyer to Dix, Nov. 23, 1861, Dix Papers; Develin to Weed, Dec. 3, 1861, Weed Papers.

24. *Sun*, Nov. 22, 29, 30, 1861; *Tribune*, Nov. 27, 29, 30, Dec. 1, 1861; *Times*, Dec. 1, 1861.

25. *Sun*, Nov. 22, 23, 25, 1861; *Times*, Nov. 25, 28, 1861.

26. *Herald*, Nov. 28, 1861.

27. Ibid.

28. Ibid.

29. *Sun*, Nov. 30, 1861.

30. Barlow to Henry Bacon, Nov. 18, 1861, Belmont to Barlow, Dec. 10, 1861, Barlow Papers; *Sun*, Nov. 22, Dec. 6, 1861; Wood to Seward, Nov. 27, 1861, William H. Seward Papers, UR; Frederick W. Seward to Wood, Nov. 29, 1861, Wood Papers, NYPL; Wood to Caleb Cushing, Nov. 29, 1861, Cushing to Wood, Dec. 6, 1861, Sidney Webster to Wood, Dec. 15, 1861, Caleb Cushing Papers, LC; *Leader*, Nov. 30, 1861; *Times*, Dec. 1, 1861; *Richmond Examiner*, Dec. 2, 1861; Claude M. Fuess, *The Life and Times of Caleb Cushing* (New York: Harcourt, Brace and Company, 1923), 2:284 (hereafter *Caleb Cushing*); Pleasants, *Wood*, 129–30.

31. *Times*, Dec. 4, 1861; *Herald*, Dec. 8, 1861; *Richmond Examiner*, Dec. 11, 1861. Wood's decline was most apparent in how badly his original coalition had changed since 1854. His multiple coefficient of correlation plummeted to 0.283, his coefficient of correlation among immigrants now stood at 0.237, and he improved among native-born voters to -0.315. Statistical material derived from: *Herald*, Mar. 13, 1861; Valentine, *Manual. . .for 1862* (New York, 1862), 162; *Reports of Industrial Commission* 15:455,486; Hardy, *Manual. . .for 1870*, 735.

32. *Times*, Jan. 3, 1860; *Sun*, Dec. 6, 1861, Jan 7, 1862; Opdyke to Wood, Dec. 13, 1861, Wood Papers, NYPL.

33. *Times*, Dec. 4, 1861; *Leader*, Dec. 7, 14, 28, 1861; *Sun*, Jan. 8, 1862.

34. Wood to Hiram Barney, Sept. 19, 1861, Miscellaneous Papers, Huntington Library; *Richmond Examiner*, June 11, 1863.

35. Wood to Lincoln, Jan. 12, 1862, Lincoln Papers; Fletcher Pratt, *Stanton: Lincoln's Secretary of War* (New York: W. W. Norton & Company, 1953), 127–35.

36. *Times*, Nov. 18, 1860, Jan. 25, 1862; Mills to Wood, Sept. 28, 1861, James Lawson to Wood, Oct. 28, 1861, Wood Papers, NYPL; *Sun*, Oct. 18, 1861; *Leader*, Feb. 1, 1862; *Population Schedules of the Ninth Census of the United States*, 1870, Washington, D.C.; National Archives and Record Service, 1959, microfilm, reel 1915, p. 592.

37. Manton Marble to Martin B. Anderson, Apr. 9, June 11, 1861, Mar. 6, May 12, Oct. 19, 1862, Martin B. Anderson Papers, Department of Rare Books and Special Collections, Rush Rhees Library, UR; Wood to Barlow, Aug. 29, Dec. 10, 1862, Aug. 29, 1863, Barlow to Marble,

June 15, 1863, June 13, 1868, Barlow Papers; Wood to Marble, Sept. 4, 1863, Manton Marble Papers, LC; George T. McJimsey, *Genteel Partisan: Manton Marble, 1834–1917* (Ames: Iowa State Univ. Press, 1971), 39–42. Wood's real estate transactions are recorded in the various New York City Liber volumes.

38. *Times*, Jan. 17, May 19, 1862; *Leader*, Jan. 18, Feb. 15, 22, Mar. 1, 1862.

39. *Times*, Jan. 21, Mar. 3, Apr. 18, 22, 1862; *Leader*, Mar. 1, 22, 29, Apr. 12, 19, June 14, 21, 28, 1862.

40. Belmont to Barlow, Feb. 10, Apr. 22, 1862, Ward to Barlow, Mar. 16, 18, 22, Apr. 27, May 3, June 27, 1862, Barlow to Frank Blair, Apr. 24, 1862, Barlow to Ward, Apr. 29, 1862, Barlow to Belmont, Aug. [n.d.], 1862, Barlow Papers; Webster to Cushing, Apr. 12, 1862, Cushing Papers; Belmont to Weed, July 20, 26, 1862, Seward Papers; Lincoln to Belmont, July 31, 1862, Lincoln Papers; Irving Katz, *August Belmont: A Political Biography* (New York: Columbia Univ. Press, 1968), 108–12.

41. *Herald*, Jan. 19, 1862; *Times*, Feb. 28, 1862; William C. Prime to George B. McClellan, Sept. 6, 1862, George B. McClellan Papers, LC; William R. Thayer, *The Life and Letters of John Hay* (Boston: Houghton-Mifflin Company, 1908), 1:130–31; William S. Myers, *General George Brinton McClellan: A Study in Personality* (New York: D. Appleton-Century Company, 1934), 310–11. For a different view, see Stephen W. Sears, *George B. McClellan: The Young Napoleon* (New York: Ticknor & Fields, 1988), 354–55, 448.

42. *Times*, Apr. 19, May 21, 1862; Wood to Barlow, May 9, 1862, Barlow to Prime, June 23, 1862, Barlow to Henry Wadsworth, June 26, 1862, Barlow Papers; *Leader*, May 10, 24, 31, June 14, 28, 1862; Barney to Lincoln, May 16, 1862, Lincoln Papers; *Irish-American*, May 24, 1862; *Journal of Commerce*, June 26, 1862.

43. *Times*, July 2, 1862.

44. Ibid.

45. *Herald*, July 2, 3, 1863; *Times*, July 3, 1863.

46. *Herald*, July 5, 11, Sept. 5, 1862; *Leader*, July 5, 12, Aug. 9, 30, 1862; *Times*, July 9, 10, Aug. 14, 1862.

47. *Herald*, Sept. 11, 1862; *Times*, Sept. 11, 12, 1862; *Leader*, Sept. 13, 1862.

48. *Times*, Sept. 11, 12, 1862, Jan. 16, 23, 1863; *Leader*, Sept. 13, 1862; *Albany Argus*, Jan. 16, 1863; Brummer, *Political History*, 227–48.

49. Henry Raymond to James Wadsworth, Oct. 4, 1862, Wadsworth Family Papers, Rush Rhees Library, UR; *Herald*, Oct. 9, 31, 1862; *Tribune*, Oct. 15, 30, 1862; *Times*, Oct. 15, 28, 31, 1862.

50. *Leader*, June 14, 1862; *Times*, June 23, July 16, 1862; *Tribune*, Sept. 16, Oct. 30, 1862; Belmont to Barlow, Oct. 2, 12, 1862, Barlow Papers; *Herald*, Oct. 8, 14, 23, 29, 1862; *Journal of Commerce*, Oct. 15, 16, 22, 1862; McClellan to Barlow, Oct. 19, 1862, McClellan Papers; *Evening Post*, Oct. 23, 1862; Washington Hunt to Samuel Ruggles, Oct. 29, 1862, Washington Hunt Papers, NYSL.

51. Wood to Weed, July 26, 1862, Gratz Collection; Wood to Lincoln, Aug. 20, Sept. 12, 1862, Lincoln Papers.

52. *Leader*, Sept. 13, 1862.

53. *Times*, Oct. 4, 1862.

54. *Leader*, Oct. 11, Nov. 1, 1862; *Herald*, Oct. 15, 18, 31, 1862; *Times*, Oct. 15, 18, 23, 28, 31, Nov. 2, 4, 1862; *Documents Relative to the Withdrawal of Nelson J. Waterbury from the Canvass in the Eighth Congressional District* (New York: 1862).

55. *Herald*, Nov. 5, 6, 1862; *Times*, Nov. 5, 1862; *Journal of Commerce*, Nov. 6, 1862; *Leader*, Nov. 8, 1862.

56. *Journal of Commerce*, Sept. 20, Oct. 18, 1862; *Leader*, Oct. 4, 18, 25, Nov. 15, 22, Dec. 6, 1862; *Times*, Oct. 7, 29, Nov. 11, 15, 18, Dec. 1, 2, 3, 1862; *Irish-American*, Nov. 1, 1862; *Herald*, Nov. 18, 20, 21, 23, 30, Dec. 1, 1862.

57. *Times*, Nov. 11, 1862; *Leader*, Dec. 13, 27, 1862; Marble to Anderson, Dec. 18, 1862, Martin Anderson Papers.

58. *Richmond Examiner*, Nov. 6, 10, 1862.

59. Wood to Lincoln, Dec. 8, 17, 1862, Lincoln to Wood, Dec. 12, 1862, Lincoln Papers.

60. *Times*, Aug. 4, Sept. 16, 22, Nov. 8, 1862, Jan. 16, Mar. 26, 28, 1863; *Leader*, Nov. 1, 1862, Feb. 7, 1863; Richard L. Banks to Corning, Jan. 8, 1863, Corning Papers; Henry Wadsworth to Barlow, Feb. 3, 1863, Barlow Papers; Silbey, *Respectable Minority*, 100–109.

9. THE PEACE DEMOCRAT

1. *Times*, Sept. 7, 25, Dec. 16, 1862, Jan. 1, 24, 1863; *Leader*, Jan. 3, 1862; Pleasants, *Wood*, 27. For Wood's real estate transactions, see various municipal liber volumes.

2. *Times*, Jan. 7, 22, 30, Feb. 3, Mar. 30, Apr. 23, 24, 25, 29, 30, 1862.

3. *Times*, Jan. 24, 1863.

4. *Leader*, Jan. 3, 1863.

5. *Times*, Jan. 24, 1863.

6. *Leader*, Jan. 3, 10, 1863; Richard L. Banks to Corning, Jan. 8, 1863, Corning Papers.

7. *Leader*, Jan. 3, 10, 17, 24, 1863; *Albany Argus*, Jan. 16, 24, 1863; *Times*, Jan. 16, 17, 20, 23, 24, 25, 26, 30, 31, Feb. 3, 1863; *Herald*, Jan. 16, 23, 1863; *Evening Post*, Jan. 17, 26, 31, 1863. (Callicot's first name appears variously as Theophilius and Timothy.)

8. *Herald*, Feb. 4, 5, 6, 1863; *Times*, Feb. 4, 5, 1863; *Leader*, Feb. 7, 1863; Brummer, *Political History*, 264–74.

9. *Leader*, Feb. 21, 1863; Cornelia Roosevelt to Buchanan, Feb. 26, Apr. 10, 1863, Buchanan Papers; *Herald*, Apr. 17, 18, 21, 1863; General Expense Vouchers of the City of New York, 1864, Historical Documents Collection.

10. *Leader*, Jan. 31, Feb. 21, Mar. 28, 1863; *Herald*, Feb. 15, 1863; *Times*, Mar. 11, 13, 25, Apr. 3, Sept. 5, 1863; Silbey, *Respectable Minority*, 91, 100.

11. *Proceedings of the Great Peace Conference Held in the City of New York June 3, 1863: Speakers, Addresses, Resolutions & Letters from Leading Men* (New York, 1863); Frank L. Klement, *The Limits of Dissent: Clement L. Vallandigham and the Civil War* (Lexington: Univ. of Kentucky Press, 1970); Silbey, *Respectable Minority*, 89–114. Vallandigham lost his congressional seat in 1862.

12. Belmont to Tilden, Jan. 24, 1863, Tilden to John Taylor, Feb. 26, 1863, Tilden Papers; Wadsworth to Barlow, Feb. 3, 1863, Barlow Papers; Wood to Lincoln, Feb. 6, 1863, Lincoln Papers; *Herald*, Feb. 15, 1863; *Times*, Mar. 11, 12, 13, 22, 26, 28, Apr. 2, 1863.

13. *Herald*, Mar. 25, 1863; *Times*, Mar. 25, Apr. 3, 8, 1863.

14. *Times*, Apr. 8, 1863.

15. *Times*, Apr. 5, 9, 13, 28, May 8, 9, 11, June 8, 1863; *New York World*, Apr. 8, 9, May 8, 1863; *Leader*, Apr. 11, 18, May 9, 1863; *Tribune*, Apr. 11, 1863.

16. *Leader*, Jan. 24, Apr. 11, May 2, 16, 23, 30, 1863; *World*, May 19, 1863; *Times*, May 20, 21, 27, 29, 31, June 1, 2, 1863; Christopher Dell, *Lincoln and the War Democrats: The Erosion of Conservative Tradition* (Rutherford, N.J.: Fairleigh Dickinson Univ. Press, 1975), 195–217.

17. *Times*, June 4, 1863.

18. *Times*, June 5, July 3, 1863; *Leader*, June 6, Aug. 29, 1863; *Herald*, Sept. 12, 1863.

19. *Leader*, May 30, June 6, 1863; *Times*, June 1, 5, 7, 8, 14, 1863; Cox to Marble, June 1, 1863, Marble Papers; Thomas Barnett to Barlow, June 6, 10, 1863, Barlow Papers; *Richmond Examiner*, June 27, 1863.

20. *Daily News*, June 20, 23, July 2, 3, 10, 11, 1863; *Leader*, June 13, July 4, 11, 1863; *Herald*, June 15, 1863; Purdy to Seymour, June 26, 1863, Opdyke to Seymour, June 30, 1863, Seymour Papers; *Times*, July 1, 1863; Basil Leo Lee, *Discontent in New York City, 1861–1865* (Washington, D.C.: Catholic Univ. Press, 1943); Williston Lofton, "Northern Labor and the Negro During the Civil War," *Journal of Negro History* 34 (Oct. 1949); 251–73; Albon P. Man, Jr., "Labor Competition and the New York Draft Riot of 1863," *Journal of Negro History* 36 (Oct. 1951): 375–405; Eugene C. Murdock, "Horatio Seymour and the 1863 Draft," *CWH* 11 (June 1965): 117–41.

21. *Daily News*, July 6, 9, 16, 17, 18, 1863; *Tribune*, July 14, 16, 17, 18, 1863; *Times*, July 14, 18, 25, 1864; *Leader*, July 18, 25, 1863; Dix to Stanton, July 20, 1863, Stanton Papers; John Rathbone to Marble, Aug. 13, 1863, Marble Papers; Adrian Cook, *The Armies of the Streets: The New York City Draft Riots of 1863* (Lexington: Univ. of Kentucky Press, 1974).

22. *Daily News*, July 20, 21, 22, 25, 1863; *Tribune*, July 23, 1863; *Leader*, Aug. 1, 1863; *Times*, Aug. 8, 1863.

23. David D. Field to Stanton, July 23, 1863, Stanton Papers; Alexander Saxton, "George Wilkes: The Transformation of a Radical Ideology," *American Quarterly* 33 (Fall 1981): 437–58.

24. *Irish-American*, July 18, 25, Aug. 23, 1863, Nov. 23, 30, 1867; Dix to Stanton, July 20, 1863, Stanton Papers.

25. *Cong. Globe*, 38th Cong., 1st sess., 1864, pt. 3:2075.

26. *Leader*, Aug. 29, Sept. 5, 12, 19, 26, Oct. 3, 17, 24, Nov. 7, 1863; *Herald*, Sept. 10, 11, 12, Oct. 8, 10, 13, 15, 25, 28, 1863; *Times*, Sept. 10, 11, Oct. 9, 22, 27, Nov. 4, 1863.

27. *Herald*, Sept. 8, Nov. 4, Dec. 2, 1863; *Times*, Sept. 8, 13, Oct. 7, 12, Nov. 11, 28, 29, Dec. 4, 1863; *Leader*, Oct. 10, Nov. 14, 21, 28, Dec. 5, 1863; Charles Halpine to Dix, Nov. 1863, Dix Papers.

28. *Times*, Nov. 25, 1863; Wood to Frank Kilton, Dec. 4, 1863, Eldridge Collection, Huntington Library.

29. Cornelia Roosevelt to Buchanan, Feb. 26, Apr. 10, 1863, Buchanan Papers; Henry Dawes to Electa Dawes, Jan. 28, 1864, Henry Dawes Papers, LC; *Times*, Jan. 28, Feb. 4, 1864; *Washington Evening Star*, Jan. 30, 1864; Mary J. Mason to Mary Nearing, Mar. 25, 1864, Berry Family Papers, Olin Library, Cornell University; Ben: Perley Poore, *Perley's Reminiscences of Sixty Years in the National Metropolis* (Philadelphia: Hubbard Brothers, Publishers, 1884), 2:212–14; Margaret Leech, *Reveille in Washington 1860–1865* (New York: Harper & Brothers, 1941), 280, 309; Justin G. Turner and Linda L. Turner, *Mary Todd Lincoln: Her Life and Letters* (New York: Alfred A. Knopf, 1972), 167–68.

30. John G. Nicolay and John Hay, *Abraham Lincoln: A History* (New York: The Century Co., 1890), 7:394–95.

31. Wood to Lincoln, Apr. 29, 1864, Lincoln Papers; *Times*, July 16, 1864; *Herald*, Sept. 4, 1864.

32. Cox to Marble, Dec. 5, 1863, Marble Papers; *Times*, Dec. 8, 1863; *Leader*, Dec. 19, 1863; *Cong. Globe*, 38th Cong., 1st sess., 1864, pt. 1:21.

33. *Times*, Jan. 11, Mar. 4, June 22, 1864; *Leader*, Jan. 16, 30, 1864; J. B. Vatties to Alexander Long, Feb. 22, 1864, Alexander Long Papers, Cincinnati Historical Society; *Daily News*, Apr. 21, 1864; Wood to D. M. Woolsey, June 15, 1864, Wood Papers, NYHS; Noah Brooks, *Washington, D.C. in Lincoln's Time*, ed. Herbert Mitgang (New York: Collier Books, 1962), 108; Allan G. Bogue, *The Congressman's Civil War* (New York: Cambridge Univ. Press, 1989), 106.

34. *Cong. Globe*, 38th Cong., 1st sess., 1864, pt. 1:94, 398, 600.

35. Ibid., pt. 4:3281, 3282.

36. Ibid., pt. 1:150, 168, 170, 173, 217–18, 270–73, 282, 284, 309, 311, 313, 661, 690–92, 731, 737, 777; ibid., pt. 2:1653, 1658, 1793, 1858–59.

37. Ibid., 1722, 1786, 1787, 1790, 1816, 1835–37, 1848–50, 1939, 1943; ibid., pt. 4:2996, 3019.

38. Ibid., pt. 1:352–54.

39. Ibid., 352.

40. Ibid., pt. 3:2233, 2249, 2251.

41. Ibid., pt. 2:1517.

42. Ibid., 1535, 1556–57.

43. Ibid., 1627; *Daily News*, Apr. 9, 18, 1864; *Times*, Apr. 9, 11, 15, 1864.

44. *Cong. Globe*, 38th Cong., 1st sess., 1864, pt. 3:2074.

45. Ibid., 2075.

46. Ibid., 2075–76.

47. Leonard P. Curry, "Congressional Democrats, 1861–1863," *CWH* 12 (Sept. 1966): 213–29; John L. McCarthy, "Reconstruction Legislation and Voting Alignments in the House of Representatives, 1863–1869," Ph.D. diss., Yale University, 1970, 52; Jean H. Baker, "A Loyal Opposition: Northern Democrats in the Thirty-seventh Congress," *CWH* 25 (June 1979): 139–55; Michael Les Benedict, *A Compromise of Principle: Congressional Republicans and Reconstruction, 1863–1869* (New York: W. W. Norton & Company, 1973), 339–40. For Wood's votes see roll calls from the 38th Cong., 1st sess., 1864, Inter-University Consortium, University of Michigan.

48. Greeley to Edwin D. Morgan, June 10, 1864, Edwin D. Morgan Papers, NYSL; Greeley to Lincoln, July 7, Aug. 8, 9, 1864, Francis Blair to Lincoln, July 21, 1864, Weed to Seward, July 21, 1864, Lincoln Papers; *Daily News*, Aug. 9, 1864; Cox to Marble, Aug. 9, 1864, Marble Papers.

49. Wood to Lincoln, Apr. 29, 1864, Lincoln Papers; Seymour to Francis Kernan, May 21, 1864, Francis Kernan Papers, Olin Library, Cornell University; Vallandigham to Long, June 14, 1864, Long Papers; Cox to McClellan, June 9, Aug. 14, 1864, Barlow to McClellan, June 16, 1864, McClellan Papers; Richmond to Marble, June 16, 1864, Cassidy to Marble, June 25, 1864, Marble Papers; Wood to Burke, June 23, 1864, Burke Papers; Ward to Barlow, July 1864, Barlow Papers; Barlow to Marble, Aug. 24, 1864, Marble Papers.

50. Marble to James Wall, Mar. 30, 1864, Marble Papers; Wall to Long, June 7, 1864, Long Papers; Wood to Barlow, June 15, 1864, Barlow Papers; Raymond to Seward, June 21, 1864, Seward Papers; Russell to Corning, Aug. 15, 1864, Corning Papers; Niven to McClellan, Aug. 17, 1864, McClellan Papers; William F. Zornow, *Lincoln and the Party Divided* (Norman: Univ. of Oklahoma Press, 1954), 109–10.

51. *Leader*, Feb. 20, 27, Mar. 5, 12, 19, 26, Apr. 2, May 14, June 4, July 30, Aug. 4, 1864; *Herald*, Feb. 25, 29, Mar. 23, July 29, Aug. 6, 1864; *Albany Argus*, Feb. 26, 29, 1864; *Tribune*, Mar. 14, 1864; *World*, Mar. 23, 1864; Brummer, *Political History*, 371–74.

52. Brooks, *Washington, D.C. in Lincoln's Time*, 108–9.

53. *Leader*, Aug. 6, 20, 1864; Long to Alexander Boys, Aug. 9, 1864, Boys Family Papers, OHS; George Morgan to McClellan, Aug. 14, 1864, McClellan Papers; *Tribune*, Aug. 19, 21, 28, 29, 1864; *Herald*, Aug. 19, 21, 22, 27, 28, 29, 1864; *Times*, Aug. 21, 27, 28, 31, 1864; *Richmond Examiner*, Aug. 30, Sept. 1, 1864.

54. John V. L. Pruyn, "Diary," Aug. 8, 1864, Albany Institute; Barlow to Marble, Aug. 21, 24, 1864, Marble to Barlow, Aug. 27, 1864, Marble Papers; Belmont to Marble, Aug. 29, 1864, Barlow Papers; Barlow to McClellan, Aug. 29, [September?] 1864, McClellan Papers; Brooks to Lincoln, Aug. 29, 1864, Lincoln Papers; *Herald*, Aug. 31, 1864; William F. Zornow, "McClellan and Seymour in the Chicago Convention," *Journal of the Illinois Historical Society* 43 (Winter 1950): 282–95.

55. *Herald*, Sept. 1, 2, 3, 1864; *Leader*, Sept. 3, 1864; Pendleton to Belmont, Sept. 27, 1864, McClellan Papers; William F. Zornow, "Clement L. Vallandigham and the Democratic Party in 1864," *Historical and Philosophic Society of Ohio* 29 (Jan. 1961): 21–37.

56. Belmont to McClellan, Sept. 3, 1864, Barlow to McClellan, Sept. 3, 1864, Vallandigham to McClellan, Sept. 4, 1864, McClellan Papers; Cassidy to Barlow, Sept. 12, 1864, Barlow Papers;

Charles R. Wilson, "McClellan's Changing Views on the Peace Plank of 1864," *AHR* 38 (Apr. 1933): 498–505.

57. *Times*, Sept. 7, 1864.

58. *Herald*, Sept. 3, 4, 5, 13, 15, 1864; *Evening Post*, Sept. 4, 13, 1864; *Daily News*, Sept. 9, 12, 15, 1864; *Buffalo Daily Courier*, Sept. 12, 13, 17, 1864.

59. *Leader*, Sept. 10, 17, 1864; John A. Trimble to Pendleton, Sept. 10, 1864, John A. Trimble Papers, OHS; *Herald*, Sept. 11, 13, 15, 1864; *Daily News*, Sept. 12, 1864; Marble to McClellan, Sept. 12, 1864, McClellan Papers.

60. Barlow to McClellan, Sept. 14, 1864, Pendleton to Belmont, Sept. 27, 1864, Parker to McClellan, Sept. 30, 1864, Cox to McClellan, Oct. 11, 21, 1864, McClellan Papers.

61. *Times*, Sept. 18, 23, 1864.

62. *Herald*, Sept. 4, 1864; Wood to Lincoln, Sept. 10, 24, Wood to [?], Oct. 6, 1864, Lincoln Papers.

63. Barlow to Richmond, Sept. 13, 1864, Barlow Papers; *Herald*, Sept. 15, 16, 17, 18, 1864; *Leader*, Sept. 17, 24, 1864.

64. *Times*, Oct. 7, 12, 20, 26, Nov. 9, 10, 1864; *Leader*, Oct. 8, 22, 29, Nov. 5, 12, 1864; *Herald*, Oct. 19, 24, Nov. 6, 8, 1864; *Irish-American*, Oct. 23, Nov. 12, 1864.

65. *Leader*, Nov. 5, 12, 1864; *Herald*, Nov. 8, 1864; *World*, Nov. 8, 9, 1864; *Times*, Nov. 9, 10, 1865.

66. Barlow to McClellan, Nov. 9, 1864, Cox to McClellan, Nov. 9, 1864, McClellan Papers; Bayard to Barlow, Nov. 12, 1864, Barlow Papers; Dix to Lincoln, Nov. 12, 1864, Lincoln Papers; *Albany Argus*, Nov. 12, 27, 1864; *Daily News*, Nov. 12, 1864; *Daily Courier*, Nov. 30, 1864; Oscar O. Winther, "The Soldier Vote in the Election of 1864," *NYH* 25 (Oct. 1944): 440–58; Louis T. Merrill, "General Benjamin Franklin Butler in the Presidential Campaign of 1864," *MVHR* 33 (Mar. 1948): 537–70; Silbey, *Respectable Minority*, 136–76.

10. POLITICAL EXILE

1. *Herald*, Jan. 12, 1865; Wood to George Shea, Mar. 2, 1865, Wood Papers, NYPL.

2. Wood to Lincoln, Nov. 18, 1864, Lincoln Papers; *Cong. Globe*, 38th Cong., 2d sess., 1865, pt. 1:572, 617, 619; Brooks, *Washington, D.C. in Lincoln's Time*, 191–92; Ludwell Johnson, "Lincoln's Solution to the Problem of Peace Terms, 1864–1865," *Journal of Southern History* 34 (Nov. 1968): 576–86.

3. *Daily News*, Jan. 10, Feb. 7, 14, 1865; *Tribune*, Feb. 1, 1865; Cox to Marble, Feb. 13, 1865, Marble Papers.

4. *Daily News*, Nov. 18, 1864, Jan. 3, 5, 12, Feb. 10, 1865; Cox to Marble, Dec. 7, 21, 1864, Marble Papers; Blair to Barlow, Jan. 7, 1865, Barlow to Cox, Feb. 9, 1865, Barlow to Belmont, Feb. 14, 1865, Barlow Papers; *Leader*, Jan. 7, 14, 21, Feb. 4, 1865; *Evening Post*, Jan. 10, Feb. 1, 1865; *Herald*, Jan. 23, 1865; *Albany Argus*, Feb. 22, 1865; LaWanda Cox and John H. Cox, *Politics, Principles, and Prejudice 1865–1866* (New York: Antheneum Press, 1969), 1–30.

5. Bilbo to Seward, Jan. 10, 1865, Seward Papers; Wood to Shea, Jan. 15, 1865, Wood Papers, NYPL; *Daily News*, Feb. 2, 1865; *New York World*, Feb. 3, 1865; *Cong. Globe*, 38th Cong., 2d sess., 1865, pt. 1:194, 195, 238; Samuel S. Cox, *Union – Disunion – Reunion: Three Decades of Federal Legislation, 1855 to 1885* (Providence, R.I.: J. A. & R. A. Reid, 1886), 320–29; P. J. Staudenraus, "The Popular Origins of the Thirteenth Amendment," *Mid-America* 50 (Apr. 1968): 108–15.

6. *World*, Mar. 18, 1865; Silbey, *Respectable Minority*, 189–95; Phyllis F. Field, *The Politics of Race in New York: The Struggle for Black Suffrage in the Civil War Era* (Ithaca, N.Y.: Cornell Univ. Press, 1982), 147–86.

7. *Cong. Globe,* 38th Cong., 2d sess., 1865, pt. 2:937–41.

8. Henry Dawes to Electa Dawes, Feb. 22, 1865, Dawes Papers; James Dixon to Horace Greeley, Apr. 14, 1865, Horace Greeley Papers, LC; *Buffalo Daily Courier,* Jan. 30, 1865; Herman Belz, *Emancipation and Equal Rights: Politics and Constitutionalism in the Civil War Era* (New York: W. W. Norton & Company, 1978), 75–108.

9. Vallandigham to Long, June 11, 1865, William Rodgers to Long, Dec. 12, 1865, Long Papers; Long to John A. Trimble, Dec. 7, 1865, John A. Trimble Papers, OHS; *Cong. Globe,* 2d sess., 1865, pt. 2:875–76, 929, 1037, 1163–64, 1168, 1198–99; Silbey, *Respectable Minority,* 190–96.

10. *Leader,* Feb. 18, Mar. 4, 1865; Warren to Marble, Mar. 23, 1865, Marble Papers.

11. Wood to Shea, Mar. 9, 31, 1865, Wood Papers, NYPL.

12. Wood to Shea, Apr. 18, 1865, Wood Papers, NYPL; *World,* Feb. 15, 1881; Pleasants, *Wood,* 165.

13. *Times,* May 4, 1865; *Daily Courier,* May 6, 1865; George Comfort to Andrew Johnson, June 30, 1865, Andrew Johnson Papers, LC; Wood to Shea, July 24, 1865, Wood Papers, NYPL; *World,* Sept. 8, 1865.

14. Montgomery Blair to Samuel Barlow, Apr. 28, June 25, 31, July 24, 1865, Barlow Papers; *Herald,* July 28, 1865; *World,* Sept. 1, 6, 7, 10, 14, 1865; *Times,* Sept. 20, 22, 1865; Weed to Seward, Sept. 23, 30, 1865, Johnson Papers; William R. Brock, *An American Crisis: Congress and Reconstruction, 1865–1867* (New York: Harper & Row, 1963), 1–152.

15. *Daily News,* Apr. 22, 1865; *Times,* June 3, 17, 25, 1865; *Herald,* June 9, 16, 18, 1865; *Leader,* June 10, 1865; Isaac Toucey to Buchanan, Aug. 15, 1865, Buchanan Papers.

16. *Herald,* June 8, 9, Oct. 2, 15, Nov. 3, 1865; Blair to Johnson, June 16, 1865, Johnson Papers; Blair to Barlow, July 21, Sept. 15, 1865, Barlow Papers; *Daily News,* Sept 7, Oct. 17, 19, 1865; *World,* Oct. 19, 27, 1865; *Leader,* Oct. 21, 24, 1865; Wood to Weed, Nov. 5, 1865, Weed Papers, NYPL; Weed to Morgan, Dec. 27, 1865, Morgan Papers; Glyndon G. Van Dusen, *William Henry Seward* (New York: Oxford Univ. Press, 1967), 421–31.

17. *Daily News,* Sept. 14, Dec. 8, 1865; Ben Wood to Thomas Florence, Sept. 27, 1865, Johnson Papers; *Times,* Oct. 3, 6, 16, 19, 21, 29, Nov. 3, 4, 6, 1865; *Leader,* Oct. 28, 1865; *World,* Nov. 7, 8, 1865.

18. *Leader,* May 6, July 18, Nov. 11, 1865; Barlow to Blair, Nov. 8, 13, Dec. 21, 1865, Blair to Barlow, Nov. 12, 18, 1865, Barlow Papers; *Times,* Nov. 16, 17, 19, 21, 1865; Cochrane to Blair, Nov. 19, 1865, Blair Papers.

19. Hoffman to Barlow, Nov. 2, 1865, Barlow Papers; *Leader,* Nov. 11, 18, 25, Dec. 1, 19, 1865; *Times,* Nov. 12, 22, 24, 25, Dec. 1, 2, 4, 1865; Barlow to Tilden, Nov. 15, 1865, Tilden Papers; *Tribune,* Nov. 23, 25, Dec. 4, 1865.

20. *Herald,* Nov. 26, Dec. 3, 5, 1865; *Irish-American,* Nov. 11, 18, 25, Dec. 2, 1865; *Evening Post,* Nov. 22, 1865; *World,* Nov. 22, 23, 1865; *Daily Courier,* Nov. 27, 1865; *Times,* Nov. 30, Dec. 2, 1865.

21. *World,* Nov. 27, Dec. 6, 17, 1865; *Herald,* Dec. 6, 1865; *Times,* Dec. 7, 1865; *Leader,* Dec. 9, 1865.

22. General Expense Vouchers, Dec. 1864, Historical Documents Collection. See various municipal liber volumes for Wood's real estate transactions.

23. *Times,* Dec. 16, 19, 1865, Feb. 23, Mar. 1, 1867; "The Ermine in the Ring: A History of the Wood Lease Case," *Putnam's Magazine Supplement* (Nov. 1868): 1–6.

24. *Times,* May 9, 1867; "Ermine in the Ring," 6–10.

25. Wood to Johnson, Feb. 24, Apr. 5, May 28, 1866, Johnson Papers; Blair to Tilden, Apr. 15, 1866, Tilden Papers; Wood to Franklin Pierce, May 29, 1866, Franklin Pierce Papers, LC; *Evening Post,* May 29, 1866; Barlow to Blair, June 15, 1866; *Herald,* July 9, 1866.

26. Wood to Johnson, May 28, Aug. 1, 1866, Johnson Papers; Belmont to Barlow, June 26, July 17, 1866, Barlow Papers; Wood to Randall, July 7, 1866, Wood Papers, NYPL; *Times*, July 11, 17, 19, 21, 26, 27, 31, 1866; *World*, July 12, 24, 1866; Cox to [?], July 22, 1866, Cox Papers; *Tribune*, July 27, 30, Aug. 1, 1866.

27. Gideon Welles to Burke, Aug. 3, 1866, Burke Papers; *Times*, Aug. 4, 10, 1866; Barlow to Blair, Aug. 9, 1866, Barlow Papers; *Leader*, Aug. 11, 1866.

28. *Washington Evening Star*, Aug. 13, 14, 1866; *Times*, Aug. 14, 15, 1866; Dix to Johnson, Aug. 16, 1866, Johnson Papers; *Daily Courier*, Aug. 17, 1866; *Journal of Commerce*, Aug. 18, 1866; *Irish-American*, Aug.18, 1866; Raymond to Seward, Aug. 19, 1866, Seward Papers.

29. *Tribune*, Aug. 15, 16, 1866; *Daily Courier*, Aug. 14, 15, 1866; *World*, Aug. 14, 15, 1866; Thomas Wagstaff, "The Arm-in-Arms Convention," *CWH* 14 (June 1966): 102–4; Albert Castel, *The Presidency of Andrew Johnson* (Lawrence: Regents Press of Kansas, 1979), 77–98.

30. *Daily News*, Sept. 18, 1865; *Irish-American*, Sept. 22, Oct. 28, 1865; *Evening Post*, Nov. 20, Dec. 9, 1865; *Leader*, Dec. 16, 1865; *World*, Feb. 8, 13, 1866; William G. Hanchett, *IRISH/ Charles G. Halpine in Civil War America* (Syracuse: Syracuse Univ. Press, 1970), 153–54.

31. *Times*, Feb. 13, 1866.

32. *Leader*, Mar. 3, 31, May 12, June 9, 1866; *Evening Post*, Mar. 6, 9, 1866; *World*, Mar. 10, 1866.

33. *Evening Post*, June 1, 4, 13, 1866; *World*, June 2, 8, 1866; *Herald*, June 3, 12, 1866; *Times*, June 6, 1866; *Daily Courier*, June 6, 8, 15, 1866; *Albany Evening Journal*, June 7, 15, 1866; *Daily News*, June 20, 1866; Brian Jenkins, *Fenians and Anglo-American Relations During Reconstruction* (Ithaca, N.Y.: Cornell Univ. Press, 1969), 106–74.

34. *Irish-American*, June 16, 23, 28, Aug. 4, 28, Sept. 1, 22, 1866.

35. Tilden to Johnson, Sept. 20, 1866, Halpine to Johnson, Nov. 15, 1866, Johnson Papers; *Albany Argus*, Sept. 27, 1866; *Daily Courier*, Oct. 16, 1866; Kelley to Tilden, Oct. 22, 1866, Roswell P. Flower to Tilden, Oct. 22, 1866, Tilden Papers; Weed to Seward, Oct. 26, 1866, Seward Papers; *Irish-American*, Oct. 28, 1866. Richmond had died in Tilden's home of a heart attack on Aug. 25, 1866. Tilden then became the new state chairman.

36. *Leader*, Sept. 15, 20, Oct. 20, Nov. 3, 1866; *World*, Oct. 10, 11, 19, 26, 1866; *Times*, Oct. 18, 19, 28, 29, 31, 1866; *Herald*, Oct. 25, 1866.

37. *Herald*, Nov. 7, 1876. The class structure of the Ninth Congressional District, 1865, can be represented as follows: large private business, 1,255 people, 3.9 percent; small private business, 4,099, 12.6; professionals, 855, 2.7; government employees, 907, 2.8; artisans/mechanics, 5,255, 16.6; semi-skilled labor, 8,994, 28.7; unskilled labor, 10,377, 32.7. Sources: Document No. 13, Board of Supervisors, Aug. 15, 1866, Frederick B. Hough, *Statistics of Population of the City and County of New York, as shown by the State Census of 1865, with the Comparative Results of This and Previous Enumerations, and Other Statistics Given by the State and Federal Census, From the Earliest Period* (New York: The New York Printing Company, 1866), 241–80; Franklin B. Hough, *Census of the State of New York for 1865* (Albany: Charles Van Benthuysen & Sons, 1867), xxv, 2, 124–31.

38. *World*, Sept. 7, Oct. 17, 24, 1866; *Times*, Sept. 8, Oct. 17, 24, 1866; *Leader*, Nov. 3, 1866.

39. *Tribune*, Aug. 26, Nov. 1, 1866; *Daily Courier*, Aug. 28, 1866; *Times*, Oct. 4, Nov. 1, 2, 1866; *World*, Nov. 5, 1866.

40. *Times*, Nov. 2, 7, 9, 1866; *Herald*, Nov. 6, 7, 9, 1866; *World*, Nov. 6, 1866; Hoffman to Tilden, Nov. 7, 1866, Sandford E. Church to Tilden, Nov. 10, 1866, Tilden Papers; Eric L. McKitrick, *Andrew Johnson and Reconstruction* (Chicago: Univ. of Chicago Press, 1960), 421–47.

41. *Leader*, Feb. 2, Mar. 16, 1867; Waterbury to Johnson, Feb. 18, 1867, Wood to Johnson, Feb. 21, Apr. 7, May 12, 1867, Halpine to Johnson, Feb. 25, 1867, Johnson Papers; Marble to

Blair, Mar. 11, 1867, Marble Papers; Church to Tilden, Mar. 8, 14, 1867, Tilden to [?], Apr. 19, 1867, Tilden Papers; Barlow to Blair, Mar. 20, 1867, Barlow Papers; Charles O. Lerche, Jr., "Congressional Interpretations of the Guarantee of a Republican Form of Government during Reconstruction," *JSH* 15 (May 1949): 192–211; Benedict, *Compromise of Principle*, 210–22.

42. *Times*, Feb. 23, 1867; *Herald*, Feb. 23, 1867; "Ermine in the Ring," 7–20.

43. *Herald*, Mar. 1, 1867; *Times*, Mar. 1, 1867; "Review of 'The Ermine in the Ring,'" *North American Review* 108 (Jan. 1869): 305–7.

44. *Times*, May 7, 9, 14, 18, 1867; *Herald*, May 7, 9, 18, 1867.

45. *Times*, May 9, 1867.

46. Roll calls derived from Inter-University Consortium, 40th Cong., 1st sess., 1867.

47. Silbey, *Respectable Minority*, 187–202; Edward L. Gambill, *Conservative Ordeal: Northern Democrats and Reconstruction, 1865–1869* (Ames: Iowa State Univ. Press, 1981), 87–104.

48. *Cong. Globe*, 40th Cong. 1st sess., 1867, pt. 1:19, 20, 24, 124, 126, 129–31, 255, 284, 289, 540, 546, 618, 619.

49. Ibid., 83, 86.

50. Ibid., 33, 36, 188, 392, 393, 561; *Times*, Mar. 12, 14, 30, 1867.

51. *World*, May 21, June 21, July 11, 20, Aug. 12, Sept. 2, 1867; William Russ, Jr., "Registration and Disfranchisement under Radical Reconstruction," *MVHR* 21 (Sept. 1934): 163–80; Michael Perman, "The South and Congress's Reconstruction Policy, 1866–67," *Journal of American Studies* 4 (Feb. 1971): 181–200; Michael Les Benedict, "The Rout of Radicalism: Republicans and the Election of 1867," *CWH* 18 (Dec. 1972): 334–44.

52. James C. Mohr, *The Radical Republicans and Reform in New York during Reconstruction* (Ithaca, N.Y.: Cornell Univ. Press, 1973), 1–152.

53. *Herald*, Aug. 14, 1867.

54. *World*, Aug. 30, 1867; *Times*, Sept. 12, 13, 1867; *Tribune*, Sept. 12, 13, 1867.

55. *Times*, Sept. 3, 24, Oct. 4, 6, 9, 10, 15, 16, 18, 19, 1867; *Leader*, Sept. 7, 28, 29, 1867; *World*, Sept. 18, Oct. 19, 24, 28, 1867; *Herald*, Oct. 8, 30, 1867; *Tribune*, Oct. 12, 28, 1867; *Irish-American*, Oct. 26, 1867.

56. *Herald*, Oct. 1, 1867; *Times*, Oct. 12, 14, 27, 30, 1867; *World*, Oct. 15, 1867; Wood to Tilden, Oct. 18, 1867, Tilden Papers.

57. Blair to Barlow, Sept. 9, 16, 1867, Barlow Papers; *World*, Nov. 2, 4, 6, 1867; *Herald*, Nov. 4, 9, 1867; *Times*, Nov. 5, 6, 7, 1867; Hoffman to Johnson, Nov. 5, 1867, Johnson Papers; Warren to Marble, Nov. 9, 1867, Marble Papers; Homer A. Stebbins, *A Political History of the State of New York, 1865–1869* (New York: Columbia Univ. Press, 1913), 159–266.

58. *Times*, Nov. 7, 13, 19, 20, 27, 1867; *Herald*, Nov. 12, 17, 19, 1867; *Tribune*, Nov. 14, 16, 1867; *Evening Post*, Nov. 18, 1867; *World*, Nov. 19, 1867.

59. *Times*, Nov. 14, 17, 30, 1867; *World*, Nov. 14, 1867.

60. Wood to Marble, Nov. 8, 1867, Marble Papers; *Times*, Nov. 30, 1867.

61. *Leader*, Oct. 12, Nov. 9, 30, 1867; *World*, Oct. 15, Nov. 9, 18, 23, 27, 28, Dec. 2, 1867; *Herald*, Nov. 8, 9, 27, 28, 1867; *Daily Courier*, Nov. 11, 1867; *Times*, Nov. 20, 22, 23, Dec. 2, 1867; *Evening Post*, Nov. 22, 30, 1867.

62. *Tribune*, Nov. 17, Dec. 2, 1867; *Leader*, Nov. 16, 23, 1867; *Daily Courier*, Nov. 18, 27, 1867; *Tribune*, Nov. 17, Dec. 2, 1867.

63. *Times*, Sept. 13, Nov. 10, 11, 12, 23, 28, Dec. 3, 1867; *New York Irish-Citizen*, Nov. 23, 1867; *Irish-American*, Nov. 23, 30, 1867; *Herald*, Nov. 30, 1867; Florence E. Gibson, *The Attitudes of the New York Irish toward State and National Affairs, 1848–1892* (New York: Columbia Univ. Press, 1951), 216–18.

64. Wood to [?], Nov. 30, 1867, Wood Papers, NYHS; *Daily Courier*, Dec. 3, 1867; *Times*, Dec. 3, 4, 1867; *Evening Post*, Dec. 4, 1867; *Herald*, Dec. 4, 1867; *Albany Argus*, Dec. 4, 7, 1867.

In essence, Hoffman had captured and reversed Wood's 1854 coalition. The best means to see that development lay in contrasting Wood's multiple coefficient of correlation, 0.035, to Hoffman's 0.518. Statistical material derived from: Hough, *Statistics of Population*, 54, 78, 241–43; Hough, *Census. . .for 1865*, xxv, 124–31, 192–94, 731; Hardy, *Manual. . .for 1870*, 738.

65. *World*, Dec. 4, 1867.

66. *Times*, Aug. 3, 1868.

11. THE POLITICS OF FRUSTRATION

1. Wood voted against the following: establishing equal rights for blacks in the District of Columbia; ratifying the Fourteenth Amendment; selling land in the Sea Islands to freed blacks; continuing the Freedmen's Bureau; admitting Republican representatives from reconstructed Alabama; changing the quorum for the Supreme Court; commending Sheridan and Grant for their conduct; endorsing congressional Reconstruction; excluding unreconstructed states from the electoral college; giving the Reconstruction Committee the power to appoint temporary state officials; calling for speedy reconstruction of Virginia, Mississippi, Texas, and other states; and appointing black diplomatic agents to Liberia and Haiti.

2. *Cong. Globe*, 40th Cong., 2d sess., 1868, pt. 1:543, 546, 551, 661–65.

3. *Times*, Jan. 14, 16, 1868; *Buffalo Daily Courier*, Jan. 17, 1868; *World*, Jan. 16, 1868.

4. *Cong. Globe*, 40th Cong., 2d sess., 1868, pt. 2:1994, 1996.

5. Ibid., 1997; *Times*, Mar. 20, 21, 28, 1868.

6. *Cong. Globe*, 40th Cong., 2d sess., 1868, pt. 2:1393, 1401–2, 1425–26, 1905, 2021; ibid., pt. 3:2072, 2074–75, 2081.

7. Ibid., pt. 2:1993; ibid., 3d sess, 1869, pt. 1:429, 681, 682.

8. Ibid., 2d sess., 1868, pt. 2:1201, 1219–20, 1272, 1278, 1281, 1319, 1421, 1791, 1796; ibid., pt. 3:2102, 2106; ibid., 3d sess., 1869, pt. 1:289–90, 359–61.

9. Ibid., 2d sess., 1868, pt. 3:2817–18; Max L. Shipley, "The Background and Legal Aspects of the Pendleton Plan," *MVHR* 24 (Sept. 1937): 329–40; Walter T. K. Nugent, *The Money Question During Reconstruction* (New York: W. W. Norton & Company, 1967).

10. *Cong. Globe*, 40th Cong., 2d sess., 1868, pt. 1:212–13, 1761, 1902. In setting up these regional codes, New York appears as a separate unit; New England (Connecticut, Maine, Massachusetts, New Hampshire, Rhode Island, and Vermont); mid-Atlantic (New Jersey, Pennsylvania); Southern states (Alabama, Arkansas, Florida, Georgia, Louisana, Mississippi, North Carolina, South Carolina, Tenessee, Texas, Virginia, West Virginia); Midwest (Indiana, Illinois, Iowa, Kansas, Michigan, Minnesota, Nebraska, Ohio, Wisconsin); Border States (Delaware, Kentucky, Maryland, Missouri); Far West (California, Nevada, Oregon, and later Colorado). See also George L. Anderson, "The South and Problems of Post–Civil War Finance," *JSH* 9 (Aug. 1943): 181–95; Stanley Coben, "Northeastern Business and Radical Reconstruction: A Reexamination," *MVHR* 46 (June 1959): 67–90; Glenn M. Linden, "'Radicals' and Economic Policies: The House of Representatives, 1861–1873," *CWH* 13 (Mar. 1967): 51–65.

11. *Times*, Jan. 30, Feb. 26, May 12, June 2, 3, 8, 9, 15, 23, 24, 27, 1868.

12. *Times*, Aug. 2, 1868; "Ermine in the Ring," 21–81.

13. *Times*, June 8, 1868; *Daily Graphic*, Dec. 4, 1875.

14. Vallandigham to Blair, June 13, 1868, Blair Family Papers, LC; *Evening Post*, June 29, July 28, 1868; *Herald*, July 2, 3, 4, 5, 8, Aug. 16, 1868; *New York Commercial Advertiser*, July 13, 1868; *Daily Courier*, July 28, 1868; *World*, Oct. 15, 1868; Edward McPherson, *The Political History of the United States of America during the Period of Reconstruction: April 15, 1865-July 15, 1870* (Washington, D.C.: Philips & Solomons, 1871), 368; Charles Coleman, *The Election of 1868: The*

Democratic Effort to Regain Control (New York: Columbia Univ. Press, 1933); Martin E. Mantell, *Johnson, Grant, and the Politics of Reconstruction* (New York: Columbia Univ. Press, 1973).

15. Wood to Tilden, July 21, 1868, Tilden Papers; *Leader,* Aug. 8, Sept. 5, Oct. 24, 1868; *World,* Aug. 10, Sept. 14, 18, 21, Oct. 6, 20, 22, 27, 31, 1868; *Times,* Sept. 1, Oct. 9, 10, 13, 22, 23, 25, 26, 28, 29, 1868; *Washington Evening Star,* Oct. 1, 9, 30, 1868; *Herald,* Oct. 23, 1868.

16. *Evening Post,* Sept. 24, Oct. 17, 23, 1868; Sweeny to Tilden, Oct. 12, 1868, Tilden Papers; John Davenport, *The Election and Naturalization Frauds in New York City, 1860–1870* (New York: Printed by the author, 1894); Gustavus Myers, *The History of Tammany Hall* (New York: Boni & Liveright, 1917), 217–18; Callow, *The Tweed Ring,* 211–12.

17. *Herald,* Nov. 4, 5, 7, 1868; *Times,* Nov. 5, 1868.

18. Wood to Elihu B. Washburne, [1869], Elihu B. Washburne Papers, LC; *Evening Star,* Jan. 23, 1874, Dec. 8, 1878; General Index Trusts & Leases, Liber D, Number 4, 1868–69, pp. 332–33, Records of Deeds, District of Columbia; David S. Muzzey, *James G. Blaine: A Political Idol of Other Days* (New York: Dodd, Mead & Company, 1934), 64; Fuess, *Caleb Cushing,* 2:376–78.

19. *Evening Star,* Jan. 9, Mar. 1, 1869, Jan. 18, Feb. 25, 1870, Jan. 11, 19, 24, 25, Dec. 30, 1871, Jan. 12, 26, Dec. 31, 1872, Feb. 12, 1874, Feb. 13, 1877, Feb. 9, 1878; *Times,* Jan. 23, 30, 1871; *Herald,* Dec. 7, 1873; Briggs, *Olivia Letters,* 291–92.

20. *Times,* Mar. 28, 1874.

21. *Evening Star,* Feb. 25, 1870, Dec. 5, 11, 1874; *Herald,* Dec. 15, 1875; *Daily Graphic,* Oct. 29, 1877.

22. McPherson, *Political History,* 391–98.

23. Wood cast eight votes against creating the Lawrence Committee and its operations, and in favor of issuing both a majority and minority report. *Cong. Globe,* 40th Cong., 3d sess., 1869, pt. 1:428; ibid., pt. 2:832–34, 878. See also *Leader,* Jan. 16, Feb. 13, 20, 27, Mar. 6, 1869; *Irish-American,* Feb. 20, Mar. 6, 1869; *Evening Post,* Feb. 23, 1869; U.S. Congress, House of Representatives, Select Committee on Alleged New York City Electoral Frauds, *Alleged New York City Electoral Frauds,* 40th Cong., 3d sess., 1869, Report no. 31.

24. Fritz Redlich, *The Molding of American Banking: Men and Ideas* (New York: Hafner Publishing Company, 1951), 2:99–121; Robert P. Sharkey, *Money, Class, and Party: An Economic Study of Civil War and Reconstruction* (Baltimore: Johns Hopkins Press, 1959), 221–37; John A. James, "Financial Underdevelopment in the Post Bellum South," *Journal of Interdisciplinary History* 11 (Winter 1981): 443–54.

25. *Cong. Globe,* 40th Cong., 3d sess., 1869, pt. 2:1321–22.

26. Ibid., 1333.

27. *World,* Nov. 19, Dec. 20, 1868; *Evening Post,* Feb. 8, 1869; Wood to Marble, Feb. 12, Mar. 26, July 26, 1869, Marble Papers; Poore, *Perley's Reminiscences,* 2:212–14.

28. Wood to Fish, Oct. 31, 1870, June 1, 16, 1874, Feb. 4, 1876, Fish Papers; *Cong. Globe,* 40th Cong., 1st sess., 1867, pt. 1:33, 511; ibid., 2d sess., 1868, pt. 1:213, 473; ibid., 3d sess., 1869, pt. 1:9, 26, 75, 456.

29. James D. McCabe, Jr., *Behind the Scenes in Washington* (Philadelphia: National Publishing Company, 1873), 212–13; Margaret S. Thompson, *The "Spider's Web": Congress and Lobbying in the Age of Grant* (Ithaca, N.Y.: Cornell Univ. Press, 1985), 71–115.

30. *Times,* Jan. 7, Feb. 5, Nov. 30, 1869; *Washington Evening Star,* Nov. 30, 1869.

31. *Cong. Globe,* 41st Cong., 1st sess., 1869, pt. 1:10, 36, 40, 60, 79, 125–26, 149, 281–84, 337, 398, 404–5; Irwin Unger, *The Greenback Era: A Social and Political History of American Finance, 1865–1879* (Princeton, N.J.: Princeton Univ. Press, 1964), 43; Sharkey, *Money, Class, and Party,* 124–34. The short session ran from Mar. 4 to Apr. 9, 1869. Wood's last day of attendance was Mar. 29, 1869.

32. *Times*, Oct. 17, 20, 26, 28, 29, 1869; Wood to Marble, Oct. 27, 1869, Marble Papers; *World*, Oct. 28, 31, 1869.

33. *Evening Star*, Jan. 10, 1870; *World*, Feb. 15, 1881; Abby B. Mills, "Last Will and Testament," 406, 424.

34. *Times*, Dec. 22, 1869, Jan. 13, July 5, 1870; Wood to John T. Hoffman, Jan. 14, 1870 (facsimile copy), in Alexander, *Political History of New York*, 3:270, Huntington Library; *World*, Jan. 27, Feb. 15, Apr. 30, Oct 31, 1870; Cox to Marble, Feb. 27, 1870, Marble Papers; Wood to Tilden, Mar. 21, 1870, Tilden Papers; Wood to John Foley, Mar. 21, 1870, Wood Papers, NYPL; Wood to Fish, Oct. 31, 1870, Fish Papers; Wood to Barlow, Dec. 16, 1870, Barlow Papers.

35. *Cong. Globe*, 41st Cong., 2d sess., 1870, pt. 1:9, 10, 14, 244–45, 362, 433–37, 492, 720; ibid., pt. 2:1463, 1707, 1770, 1790; ibid., pt. 3:1946, 1970, 2281, 2291–94; ibid., 3d sess., 1871, pt. 2:1274.

36. McPherson, *Political History*, 587–96; Terry L. Seip, *The South Returns to Congress: Men, Economic Measures, and Intersectional Relationships, 1868–1879* (Baton Rouge: Louisiana State Univ. Press, 1983), 179–82.

37. *Cong. Globe*, 41st Cong., 2d sess., 1869, pt. 1:75, 583; ibid., 1870, pt. 2:1263; ibid., pt. 5:4178, 4244.

38. Ibid., 4434, 4435, 4471, 4477–78, 4484; McPherson, *Political History*, 585.

39. John Sherman, *John Sherman's Recollections of Forty Years in the House, Senate and Cabinet: An Autobiography* (New York: Werner Co., 1895), 1:450–57; David R. Dewey, *Financial History of the United States* (New York: Longmans, Green, 1928), 326–56; Herbert S. Schell, "Hugh McCulloch and the Treasury Department," *MVHR* 17 (Dec. 1930): 404–21.

40. *Cong. Globe*, 41st Cong., 2d sess., 1870, pt. 6:5019, 5020; McPherson, *Political History*, 586–96.

41. *Cong. Globe*, 41st Cong., 2d Sess., 1870, pt. 6:5025.

42. Ibid., 5068; McPherson, *Political History*, 586–87, 597–604.

43. *Herald*, July 6, 1870; *Evening Post*, July 6, Aug. 22, 1870; *Irish-American*, July 16, 1870; *Leader*, Sept. 24, 1870; McPherson, *Political History*, 603–4.

44. Robert T. Patterson, *Federal-Debt Management Policies, 1865–1879* (Durham, N.C.: Duke Univ. Press, 1954), 78–112; Nugent, *Money Question*, 30–31, 83, 85; Seip, *South Returns to Congress*, 153–57.

45. *Cong. Globe*, 41st Cong., 2d sess., 1870, pt. 4:2936–37; ibid., pt. 5:3993, 4029, 4095–96; ibid., pt. 6:5414; ibid., 3d sess., 1871, pt. 3:1851–52, 1928.

46. Ibid., 2d sess., 1870, pt. 1:583–877; ibid., pt. 2:956, 958, 1198, 1235, 1241–42, 1271–72, 1380–82, 1411, 1492, 1801–2; ibid., pt. 4:3267–71; ibid., pt. 6:4850–51, 5425; ibid., 3d sess., 1871, pt. 2:1443, 1525–33, 1648; ibid., pt. 3:1973–75.

47. Ibid., 2d sess., 1870, pt. 1:558; ibid., pt. 2:1640, 1648, 1773–75.

48. Ibid., pt. 3:2100–2103.

49. Ibid., 2433, 2475, 2684, 2797; ibid., pt. 4:2912, 3414. See also James L. Huston, "A Political Response to Industrialism: The Republican Embrace of Protectionist Labor Doctrines," *JAH* 70 (June 1983): 35–57.

50. *Cong. Globe*, 41st Cong., 2d sess., 1870, pt. 3:2357, 2378; ibid., 3d sess., 1871, pt. 3:1762; *Leader*, Mar 4, 1871.

51. *Times*, Mar. 1, 1871; *World*, Mar. 1, 2, 14, 1871; *Cong. Globe*, 42d Cong., 1st sess., 1871, pt. 1:23, 55–56, 81.

52. Ibid., 41st Cong., 2d sess., 1870, pt. 1:99.

53. *World*, May 23, June 22, Aug. 19, 1870; *Leader*, May 28, 1870; *Evening Post*, June 27, 1870; McPherson, *Political History*, 546–57, 616–17; Everette Swinney, "Enforcing the Fifteenth Amendment, 1870–1877," *JSH* 28 (May 1972): 202–18; Harold A. Hyman, *A More Perfect Union:*

The Impact of Civil War and Reconstruction on the Constitution (Boston: Houghton-Mifflin, 1975), 525–28.

54. *Cong. Globe,* 41st Cong., 1st sess., 1869, pt. 1:59; ibid., 2d sess., 1870, pt. 2:1268; ibid., pt. 5:3853–55, 4266–67; ibid., 3d sess., 1871, pt. 2:994–95, 1185, 1285; ibid., pt. 3:1859; ibid., 42nd Cong., 1st sess., 1871, pt. 2: App., 74–78.

55. Ibid., 41st Cong., 2d sess., 1870, pt. 3:2460–63; Oliver O. Howard to Wood, Apr. 1, 1870, Oliver O. Howard Papers, Bowdoin College Library, Brunswick, Maine.

56. *Cong. Globe,* 41st Cong., 3d sess., 1871, pt. 3:1850; *Times,* Apr. 7, 17, 20, 25, May 8, 10, June 14, July 7, 14, 16, 1870; Howard to Samuel M. Arnell, Apr. 19, 1870, Howard to Robert Carson, Apr. 30, 1870, Howard to Edgar Ketchum, June 24, 28, July 19, 28, 1870, Ketchum to Howard, July 9, 1870, Howard to Benjamin F. Butler, Aug. 4, 1870, Arnell to Howard, Mar. 2, 1871, Howard Papers; Oliver O. Howard, *Autobiography of Oliver Otis Howard* (New York: Baker & Taylor Co., 1907), 2:436–44; John A. Carpenter, *Sword and Olive Branch: Oliver Otis Howard* (Pittsburgh: Univ. of Pittsburgh Press, 1964), 202–8.

57. *Leader,* Apr. 9, May 23, 1870; *World,* Apr. 7, 16, 20, 21, 25, 26, May 9, July 7, 12, 13, 14, 1870; *Times,* July 14, 1870; *New York Tribune,* July 14, 1870.

58. *Cong. Globe,* 41st Cong., 2d sess., 1870, pt. 1:22, 64, 99, 102, 615; ibid., pt. 2:1185, 1268, 1400; ibid., pt. 4:3261; ibid., 3d sess., 1870, pt. 1:271.

59. Ibid., 2d sess., 1870, pt. 1:102; ibid., pt. 2:1268; ibid., pt. 5:4442, 4481; *Leader,* Jan. 22, 1870; *Times,* Feb. 15, Mar. 4, 1870; Nathaniel P. Banks to Dix, May 7, 1870, George Cogswell to Banks, July 4, 1870, Nathaniel P. Banks Papers, LC; Philip S. Foner, *A History of Cuba and Its Relations with the United States* (New York: International Publishers, 1963), 2:162–223; William S. McFeely, *Grant: A Biography* (New York: W. W. Norton & Company, 1981), 297–99, 344.

60. *Cong. Globe,* 41st Cong., 2d sess., 1870, pt. 5:4478–80; McPherson, *Political History,* 619–21; Allan Nevins, *Hamilton Fish: The Inner History of the Grant Administration* (New York: Dodd, Mead & Company, 1936), 176–230, 258–78, 318, 371; Fred H. Harrington, *Fighting Politician: Major General N. P. Banks* (Westport, Conn.: Greenwood Press, 1970), 189–92.

61. *Times,* June 17, 1870.

62. *Cong. Globe,* 41st Cong., 2d sess., 1870, pt. 1:615; ibid., pt. 4:3263; David Donald, *Charles Sumner and the Rights of Man* (New York: Alfred A. Knopf, 1970), 443–53; McFeely, *Grant,* 297–98.

63. *Evening Post,* July 1, 2, 9, 12, Aug. 15, 22, Sept. 7, 1870, July 2, 24, Sept. 14, 1870; *Tribune,* July 2, Aug. 27, Sept. 8, Oct. 20, 1870; *World,* Oct. 28, 1870; David M. Jordan, *Roscoe Conkling of New York: Voice in the Senate* (Ithaca, N.Y.: Cornell Univ. Press, 1971), 133–65.

64. *Cong. Globe,* 41st Cong., 3d sess., 1871, pt. 1:309, 381–83; *Times,* Jan. 5, 7, 9, 12, 1871; *Leader,* Jan. 14, 1871; Harrington, *Fighting Politician,* 189–91.

65. *Cong. Globe,* 41st Cong., 3d sess., 1871, pt. 1:385–88.

66. *Leader,* Mar. 4, 1871.

67. *Times,* Aug. 29, Oct. 14, 19, 21, 23, 25, 28, Nov. 4, 5, 8, 9, 1870; *Tribune,* Oct. 7, 1870; *Evening Post,* Oct. 14, 1870; *World,* Oct. 16, Nov. 10, 1870; *Commercial Advertiser,* Oct. 20, 1870; *Leader,* Oct. 22, Nov. 5, 1870; *Irish-American,* Nov. 5, 1870.

12. CONGRESSIONAL LEADER

1. Wood to Barlow, Dec. 6, 1870, Barlow Papers; Horace White to Montgomery Blair, Dec. 10, 1870, Blair Papers; *World,* Feb. 28, Mar. 14, 1871; *Times,* Mar. 5, 1871; *Washington Evening Star,* Mar. 3, 28, 1871.

2. *World,* Feb. 28, 1871; Wood to Hoffman, Mar. 17, 1871, facsimile in Alexander, *Political History,* 3:232, Huntington Library. Wood followed his own advice about attendance, missing only 9 of 86 roll calls.

3. Francis P. Blair, Jr., to Alexander H. Stephens, Mar. 10, May 3, 1871, Alexander H. Stephens Papers, LC; Lawrence Grossman, *The Democratic Party and the Negro: Northern and National Politics, 1868-92* (Urbana: Univ. of Illinois Press, 1976), 1-22.

4. *World,* Apr. 21, 1871; *Herald,* Apr. 22, 1871.

5. Wood to Hoffman, Mar. 17, 1871, facsimile in Alexander, *Political History,* 3:232, Huntington Library; Grossman, *Democratic Party,* 22-25. See also Stephen Hoyes, *The Political Situation Resulting from the Late State Election. (Herald Interview with Peter B. Sweeny)* (New York: The Jackson Association, 1869).

6. *Cong. Globe,* 42d Cong., 1st sess., 1871, pt. 1:245-47, 317-19, 387-88, 508, 520-23, 749, 801; Allen W. Trelease, *White Terror: The Ku Klux Klan Conspiracy and Southern Reconstruction* (New York: Harper & Row, 1971); William Gillette, *Retreat from Reconstruction, 1869-1879* (Baton Rouge: Louisiana State Univ. Press, 1979), 26-52.

7. *Cong. Globe,* 42d Cong, 1st sess., 1871, pt. 2: App., 74-78.

8. *Herald,* Jan. 14, Mar. 8, 9, 24, 25, Apr. 10, 22, May 3, 11, 1871; *Evening Post,* Jan. 23, Mar. 8, 13, 24, Apr. 12, 1871: *World,* Mar. 10, Apr. 8, 1871; *Tribune,* Mar. 16, 1871; *Leader,* Apr. 1, 1871; *Irish-American,* Apr. 22, 1871; Edward McPherson, *Hand-Book of Politics for 1872* (Washington, D.C.: Philips & Solomons, 1872), 85-91.

9. Wood to Marble, Feb. 24, 1871, Marble Papers.

10. Mark D. Hirsch, "More Light on Boss Tweed," *PSQ* 60 (June 1945): 267-78; Seymour J. Mandelbaum, *Boss Tweed's New York* (John Wiley & Sons, 1965), 1-86; Callow, *The Tweed Ring,* 253-78; Leo Hershkowitz, *Tweed's New York: Another Look* (New York: Anchor Press, 1977), 167-275.

11. *Times,* July 5, Sept. 12, Oct. 6, Nov. 2, 3, 1871; *Buffalo Daily Courier,* Sept. 20, 1871; *Herald,* Oct. 2, 1871; *World,* Oct. 7, 30, 1871.

12. *Times,* Dec. 2, 1871.

13. Wood to Marble, Dec. 5, 1871, Marble Papers; *World,* Dec. 7, 1871; *Times,* Jan. 17, 1872; *Herald,* Jan. 11, Mar. 31, 1872; Belmont to Carl Schurz, Apr. 1, 1872, Carl Schurz Papers, LC.

14. *Times,* Dec. 7, 1871; *Cong. Globe,* 42d Cong., 2d sess., 1872, pt.1:31.

15. *World,* Mar. 6, 1873; *Cong. Globe,* 42d Cong., 2d sess., 1872, pt. 1:16, 60, 102-4, 223-24, 229, 322, 439, 540-41, 741-42, 750; ibid., pt. 2:1058-59, 1402-3, 1502, 1609, 1614-19; ibid., pt. 3:2108-11, 2312-16, 2563; ibid., pt. 4:2697-98, 2702, 2885.

16. Ibid., pt. 1:102, 104, 223, 257.

17. *Irish-American,* Apr. 27, 1872; Henry Dawes to Electa Dawes, May 4, 1872, Dawes Papers; *Cong. Globe,* 42d Cong., 2d sess., 1872, pt. 3:2550-55; ibid., pt. 4:2999; Frank W. Taussig, *The Tariff History of the United States* (New York: G. P. Putnam's Sons, 1931), 179-89.

18. *Cong. Globe,* 42d Cong., 2d sess., 1872, pt. 1:31; ibid., pt. 2:1135-37; Ari Hoogenboom, *Outlawing the Spoils: A History of the Civil Service Reform Movement, 1865-1883* (Urbana: Univ. of Illinois Press, 1861), 1-110.

19. *Cong. Globe,* 42d Congress, 2d sess., 1872, pt. 3:2168.

20. John Wentworth to David Davis, Feb. 8, 16, 24, Mar. 17, Apr. 23, 26, 1872, Thomas Ewing to Davis, Feb. 22, 1872, Jeremiah Black to Davis, Feb. 28, 1872, Cox to Davis, Mar. 8, 1872, Wood to Davis, Apr. 21, 25, 1872, David Davis Papers, Illinois State Historical Society; *Daily News,* Feb. 29, 1872; *World,* Apr. 18, 1872; Marble to Chamberlain, May 3, 1872, Marble Papers; *Times,* May 4, 1872; David Montgomery, *Beyond Equality: Labor and the Radical Republicans, 1862-1872* (New York: Alfred A. Knopf, 1967), 387-409.

21. Marble to Schurz, Apr. 23, 1872, Blair to Schurz, May 28, 1872, Schurz Papers; *Daily News*, May 6, June 2, 8, July 1, 1872; Belmont to Samuel Bowles, May 7, 1872, David A. Wells Papers, LC; *Herald*, May 17, 1872; Cox to Weed, May 22, 1872, Weed Papers; *Times*, June 12, July 2, 8, 1872; Belmont to Marble, July 11, 1872, Marble Papers; *Evening Post*, Aug. 3, 1872; Matthew T. Downey, "Horace Greeley and the Politicians: The Liberal Republican Convention in 1872," *JAH* 43 (Mar. 1867): 727-50.

22. *Times*, Aug. 2, 22, Sept. 13, 1872; *World*, Sept. 11, 12, 13, 1872; Earle D. Ross, *The Liberal Republican Movement* (New York: Henry Holt and Company, 1919), 155-56.

23. *Daily News*, Sept. 16, 17, 23, 1872; *Times*, Sept. 17, 25, 28, Oct. 2, 1872; *World*, Sept. 28, Oct. 10, 1872.

24. *Irish-American*, Sept. 21, Nov. 2, 1872; *Evening Post*, Sept. 24, Oct. 10, 28, 1872; *Times*, Oct. 22, 24, 28, Nov. 1, 1872; *World*, Oct. 28, 1872.

25. *Times*, Oct. 20, 25, 30, Nov. 2, 7, 1872, Jan. 1, 1873; *World*, Oct. 21, Nov. 3, 4, 7, 1872; *Herald*, Nov. 6, 7, 8, 1872; Cox to James G. Blaine, Nov. 19, 1872, James G. Blaine Papers, LC; Hoffman to Samuel J. Randall, Dec. 28, 1872, Randall Papers; David Lindsey, *"Sunset" Cox: Irrepressible Democrat* (Detroit: Wayne State Univ. Press, 1959), 136-37 (hereafter *Cox*).

26. *Times*, Dec. 12, 1872; *Evening Star*, Jan. 9, 14, 1873; Wood to Washburne, Apr. 23, Dec. 1873, Washburne Papers; *World*, Dec. 3, 1873; Abby B. Mills, "Last Will and Testament," 406. Abby B. Mills died on Oct. 25, 1872.

27. *World*, Feb. 15, 1868, Jan. 1, 1871, July 30, 1872; *Times*, Feb. 4, 1872, Oct. 31, 1878; Wood to Tilden, May 22, 1876, Tilden Papers; Moses King, *King's Handbook of New York City, 1893* (Boston: Moses King, Publisher, 1893), 193.

28. Wood to Blaine, Oct. 29, 1873, Blaine Papers. Wood's transactions are recorded in multiple municipal libers, New York City Hall of Records.

29. Wood to Marble, Apr. 22, 1873, Marble Papers.

30. *Times*, Dec. 4, 19, 1872; *Herald*, Jan. 6, 9, 21, Feb. 6, 1873; *Daily Courier*, Jan. 6, 10, 25, Feb. 19, 1873; *World*, Feb. 18, 1873; *Cong. Globe*, 42d Cong., 3d sess., 1873, pt. 1:259-60.

31. *World*, Jan. 10, 24, 30, 1873; *Irish-American*, Jan. 25, 1873; Eugene Casserly to Marble, Jan. 29, 1873, Marble Papers; *Daily Courier*, Jan. 31, 1873; *Herald*, Feb. 3, 20, 24, 27, 1873.

32. Wood to Marble, Feb. 19, 1873, Marble Papers; *Times*, Feb. 21, 22, 1873; Wood to Blaine, Mar. 28, 1873, Blaine Papers; *Cong. Globe*, 42d Cong., 3d sess., 1873, pt. 2:1544-45; *World*, Feb. 19, 21, 1873.

33. *World*, Mar. 6, 1873; *Cong. Globe*, 42d Cong., 3d sess., 1873, pt. 2:1842-44.

34. *Irish-American*, May 10, 1873; Cox to Marble, Oct. 13, 1873, Marble Papers; *Tribune*, Oct. 27, 1873; Lindsey, *Cox*, 140-42.

35. *Cong. Record*, 43d Cong., 1st sess., 1874, 2, pt. 1:532.

36. *Herald*, Mar. 2, 3, 1873; *Times*, Mar. 2, 3, 18, 1873; *Sun*, Mar. 15, 1873; *Evening Post*, Mar. 18, Apr. 11, 1873; Hans L. Trefousse, *Ben Butler: The South Called Him BEAST!* (New York: Twayne Publishers, 1957), 225-26.

37. *Times*, Jan. 10, 1874; *Cong. Globe*, 42d Cong., 3d sess., 1873, pt. 3:1977, 2007, 2100, 2105.

38. *Times*, Apr. 4, 1873; *Evening Post*, Apr. 24, 1873; *Irish-American*, May 10, 1873; *World*, Oct. 4, Dec. 3, 1873; Cox to Tilden, Dec. 1, 1873, Tilden Papers.

39. *Times*, May 4, 11, Oct. 8, 1873; *World*, June 27, Oct. 8, Nov. 10, 25, Dec. 2, 3, 1873; *Herald*, Aug. 13, Nov. 6, 10, 1873; *Irish-American*, Oct. 11, 1873; *Daily Courier*, Nov. 26, 1873; John Bigelow to Morgan, Nov. 27, 1873, Morgan Papers.

40. *Times*, Nov. 10, 11, 18, 25, Dec. 1, 2, 1873; *Daily Courier*, Dec. 1, 1873; *World*, Dec. 4, 1873.

41. *Daily Graphic*, Nov. 28, Dec. 1, 3, 1873; *Times*, Nov. 30, Dec. 1, 1873; *Daily Courier*, Dec. 1, 1873; *World*, Dec. 4, 1873.

42. *Times*, Dec. 1, 3, 4, 5, 6, 1873; *Daily Courier*, Dec. 3, 4, 6, 1873; *Sun*, Dec. 5, 1873; *Tribune*, Dec. 5, 1873; *World*, Dec. 3, 6, 1873; McPherson, *Hand-book. . .for 1874* (1874), 38.

43. *Herald*, Nov. 30, Dec. 1, 4, 6, 9, 10, 14, 1873; *Daily Courier*, Dec. 6, 8, 11, 12, 13, 1873; *World*, Dec. 6, 8, 10, 15, 17, 1873; Wood to Blaine, Nov. 10, 1873, Cox to Blaine, Nov. 5, Dec. 2, 1873; Blaine to Cox, [Nov.] 1873, Blaine Papers; *Times*, Dec. 5, 10, 12, 15, 18, 1873.

44. *Times*, Mar. 9, 1874.

45. McPherson, *Hand-Book. . .for 1874*, 20–39.

46. Unger, *Greenback Era*, 213–48.

47. *Cong. Record*, 43d Cong., 1st sess., 1874, 2, pt. 4:3002, 3003, 3007, 3019, 3072, 3073, 3078; *Herald*, Jan. 22, 1874; *Times*, Jan. 27, Mar. 24, 26, Apr. 16, June 21, 1874; *Evening Post*, Mar. 24, 26, 1874; *Daily Courier*, Mar. 27, 1874; *World*, Apr. 8, 1874; Seip, *South Returns to Congress*, 189–200.

48. *Times*, Jan. 8, 13, 17, Feb. 7, 28, Mar. 8, 1874; *Herald*, Jan. 8, 1874; *World*, Jan. 19, Mar. 8, 10, 1874; Wood to Marble, Mar. 4, 1874, Marble Papers; *Cong. Record*, 43d Cong., 1st sess., 1874, 2, pt. 1:91, 92, 106–7, 180–81, 199, 501–4; ibid., pt. 2:1538, 1731, 1958; ibid., pt. 3:2051–57, 2869–70; ibid., pt. 4:3042, 3175, 3377; ibid., pt. 5:4040–43, 4272–75.

49. *Herald*, Mar. 8, 1874; *Times*, Mar. 9, 15, 16, 1874; *Daily Courier*, Mar. 10, 1874; *World*, Mar. 10, 1874.

50. *World*, Oct. 24, 29, Dec. 13, 1873; *Cong. Record*, 43d Cong., 1st sess., 1874, 2, pt. 1:168–69; Carpenter, *Sword and Olive Branch*, 220–29.

51. *Herald*, Dec. 13, 17, 18, 1873, Jan. 21, July 5, 1874; *Evening Star*, Dec. 16, 17, 18, 24, 1873; *Times*, Dec. 19, 1873, Jan. 31, Feb. 14, Mar. 4, 23, Apr. 6, May 1, 1874; Nelson Miles to Howard, Jan. 4, 1874, Howard to Earnest F. Hoffman, Jan. 4, 1874, Howard Papers; *Daily Graphic*, May 12, July 7, 1874; *Cong. Record*, 43d Cong., 1st sess., 1874, 2, pt. 2:1064–70; Howard, *Autobiography*, 2:444–45.

52. *Times*, Mar. 9, May 21, 1874; *World*, Mar. 17, 1874.

53. *Herald*, Nov. 4, 5, 7, 1874; *Albany Argus*, Nov. 4, 6, 1874; *World*, Nov. 4, 10, 1874; Barlow to Tilden, Nov. 14, 1874, Tilden Papers; Schenck to Blaine, Dec. 18, 1874, Blaine Papers; Earle D. Ross, "Samuel Jones Tilden and the Revival of the Democratic Party," *South Atlantic Quarterly* 19 (Jan. 1920): 43–54.

54. *Times*, Oct. 16, 23, 28, Nov. 1, 3, 6, 7, 19, 1874; *Herald*, Nov. 1, 2, 5, 1874; *Daily Graphic*, Nov. 14, 1874.

55. Kerr to Wells, Oct. 5, 1874, Wells Papers; Cox to Thomas F. Bayard, Nov. 13, 1874, Thomas F. Bayard Papers, LC; Wood to Barlow, Nov. 23, 1874, Barlow Papers; *Evening Star*, Nov. 23, 1874; Wood to Douglas Taylor, Dec. 28, 1874, Miscellaneous Papers, Huntington Library.

56. *Cong. Record*, 43d Cong., 2d sess., 1875, 3, pt. 1:172; James G. Bennett, Jr., to Wells, Nov. 17, 1874, Wells Papers; Bayard to Marble, Dec. 2, 1874, Marble Papers; *Times*, Dec. 10, 13, 1874, Jan. 7, 8, 12, 13, 1875; Unger, *Greenback Era*, 249–85; Irwin Unger, "Businessmen and Specie Resumption," *PSQ* 74 (Mar. 1959): 46–70; James K. Kindall, "Economic Factors in Specie Resumption: The United States, 1869–79," *Journal of Political Economy* 69 (Feb. 1961): 30–48; Richard H. Timberlake, Jr., "Ideological Factors in Specie Resumption and Treasury Policy," *Journal of Economic History* 24 (Mar. 1964): 29–52.

57. *Herald*, Feb. 1, 11, 12, 1875; *Cong. Record*, 43d Cong., 2d sess., 1875, 3, pt. 2:1185–88, 1210.

58. *Herald*, Feb. 1, May 7, 1875; *Times*, May 7, 1875.

59. *Cong. Record*, 43d Cong., 2d sess., 1875, 3, pt. 2:990.

60. *Evening Star*, Jan. 12, 25, 29, 30, Feb. 4, 10, Nov. 15, 1875; *Herald*, Feb. 1, 1875; *Daily Graphic*, Feb. 8, 12, Sept. 1, Nov. 13, 1875; *Times*, Sept. 17, Nov. 8, 19, 1875; Wood to Banks, [1875], Miscellaneous Papers, Brown University.

61. Cox to James R. Comly, Mar. 23, 1875, James R. Comly Papers, OHS; Charles A. Dana to Chauncey Black, Mar. 23, Aug. 25, Nov. 15, 1875, Randall to Jeremiah S. Black, Apr. 9, Sept. 2, Nov. 2, 8, 1875, Jeremiah S. Black Papers, LC; *Daily Graphic*, Sept. 29, Nov. 15, 1875; Wells to Marble, Oct. 18, Nov. 30, 1875, William H. Hurlbert to Marble, Nov. 28, 1875, Marble Papers; *Herald*, Nov. 15, 26, 1875; Michael Kerr to Blaine, Nov. 21, 1875, Blaine Papers; Albert V. House, Jr., "Northern Congressional Democrats as Defenders of the South During Reconstruction," *JSH* 6 (Feb. 1940): 51–66; Albert V. House, Jr., "The Speakership Contest of 1875: Democratic Response to Power," *JAH* 42 (Sept. 1965): 252–68.

62. *Times*, Nov. 2, 17, 26, 27, 30, Dec. 1, 2, 1875; *Daily Graphic*, Nov. 13, 15, 29, 30, Dec. 4, 1875; *Herald*, Nov. 27, 29, 30, 1875.

63. Randall to Chauncey Black, Nov. 23, 1875, Apr. 25, 1877, Black Papers; Kerr to Marble, Nov. 21, 28, 1875, Wells to Marble, Nov. 30, 1875, Marble Papers; *Herald*, Dec. 1, 2, 4, 6, 1875; *Cong. Globe*, 42d Cong., 3d sess., 1873, pt. 1:382.

64. *Times*, Dec. 5, 1875; *Herald*, Dec. 5, 1875; House, "Speakership Contest," 256–74; James B. Murphy, *L. Q. C. Lamar, Pragmatic Patriot* (Baton Rouge: Louisiana State Univ. Press, 1983), 123.

65. *Herald*, Dec. 6, 7, 10, 13, 14, 15, 20, 21, 22, 24, 1875; *Times*, Dec. 7, 8, 9, 11, 14, 15, 20, 21, 22, 24, 1875; Kerr to Marble, Dec. 7, 18, 21, 1875, Hiram Calkins to Marble, Dec. 15, 16, 1875, Marble Papers; *Cong. Record*, 44th Cong., 1st sess., 1876, 4, pt. 1:169–71; McJimsey, *Genteel Partisan*, 173–74; Joe G. Taylor, *Louisiana Reconstructed, 1863–1877* (Baton Rouge: Louisiana State Univ. Press, 1974).

66. Kerr to Wells, Dec. 31, 1875, Jan. 12, 1876, Wells Papers.

67. Wood to Bayard, Dec. 10, 1875, Bayard Papers, cited by Lindsey, *Cox*, 151.

68. Robert Minturn to Wells, Feb. 21, 1876, Garfield to Wells, Feb. 24, 1876, Charles Nordhoff to Wells, Mar. 15, 1876, William Robinson to Wells, Mar. 16, 1876, Wells Papers; *Herald*, Jan. 6, 7, 12, 18, Feb. 18, 1876; Cox to Marble, Feb. 9, 28, 1876, Kerr to Marble, Mar. 31, May 3, 1876, Marble Papers; *Times*, Jan. 11, 12, 27, 30, 31, Feb. 10, 16, 18, May 8, 1876; *Cong. Record*, 44th Cong., 1st sess., 1876, 4, pt. 2:269, 382.

69. *Times*, Jan. 19, Feb. 2, 6, Apr. 12, May 13, 30, 1876; *Herald*, Jan. 31, Feb. 1, 2, 8, Mar. 5, May 15, 26, 1876; [?] to Marble, Feb. 3, 1876, Marble Papers; Wells to James Moore, Feb. 4, 1876, Barlow Papers; *Daily Graphic*, Feb. 9, 1876; William R. Morrison to Wells, Feb. 20, 1876, Wells Papers; Tom E. Terrill, "David A. Wells, The Democracy, and Tariff Reduction," *JAH* 46 (Dec. 1969): 540–55.

70. *Herald*, Jan. 6, 7, 10, Apr. 11, 14, 24, May 22, 1876; *Evening Star*, Feb. 16, 1876; *Daily Graphic*, Mar. 1, 1876; *World*, Apr. 10, 27, 28, 1876; Bayard to Wells, May 27, 1876, Bayard Papers.

71. *Herald*, May 15, 1876; *World*, Oct. 17, 1876; *Cong. Record*, 45th Cong., 2d sess., 1878, 7, pt. 3:2402.

72. Ibid., 44th Cong., 1st sess., 1876, 4, pt. 2:302; Albert V. House, Jr., "Republicans and Democrats Search for New Identities, 1870–1890," *Review of Politics* 31 (Oct. 1969): 466–76.

73. *Evening Star*, Jan. 5, 7, 1876; *Daily Graphic*, Jan. 8, 15, 28, Mar. 16, Apr. 3, 1876; *Times*, Mar. 20, 1876.

74. *Evening Star*, Mar. 1, 1876; *Times*, Mar. 5, May 27, July 2, Nov. 11, 23, 28, 1876; *Daily Graphic*, Apr. 5, 19, 22, 1876; *Herald*, May 27, 1876; *World*, Nov. 11, 1876. A slightly different version of Fowler's alleged bribery of Wood appeared in the *Times*, Jan. 24, 1863.

75. *Daily Graphic*, Feb. 22 1876; Church to Kernan, Apr. 3, 1876, Kernan Family Papers; Barlow to Bayard, May 14, 1876, Bayard Papers; *Baltimore Gazette*, May 21, 1876, cited in *Times*, May 22, 1876; Richard Taylor to Barlow, May 24, 1876, Barlow Papers; Robinson to Tilden, May 28, 1876, "Anti-Tilden Circular, June 1876," Tilden Papers; *World*, Feb. 15, 1881; Alexander C.

Flick, *Samuel Jones Tilden: A Study in Political Sagacity* (New York: Dodd, Mead & Company, 1939), 283; Keith I. Polakoff, *The Politics of Inertia: The Election of 1876 and the End of Reconstruction* (Baton Rouge: Louisiana State Univ. Press, 1973), 70–93.

76. *Cong. Record*, 44th Cong., 1st sess., 1876, 4, pt. 2:444; Allen Weinstein, *Prelude to Populism: Origins of the Silver Issue, 1867–1878* (New Haven, Conn.: Yale Univ. Press, 1970), 33–123.

77. *Cong. Record*, 44th Cong., 1st sess., 1876, 4, pt. 2:777; ibid., pt. 4:2048, 2998.

78. Ibid., 2d sess., 1877, 5, pt. 2:172; Weinstein, *Prelude to Populism*, 177–203.

79. *Times*, Feb. 9, 11, 1876; Donald M. Dozer, "Opposition to Hawaiian Reciprocity, 1876–1888," *Pacific Historical Review* 14 (June 1945): 157–83; Tom E. Terrill, *The Tariff, Politics, and American Foreign Policy, 1874–1901* (Westport, Conn.: Greenwood Press, 1973), 17–21.

80. "Notes on Fernando Wood's Speech [1876]," Elisha H. Allen Papers, LC; *Cong. Record*, 44th Cong., 1st sess., 1876, 4, pt. 3:1419–26, 1460, 1461, 1490.

81. Wood to Fish, Feb. 4, Mar. 25, 1876, Fish Papers; Wood to Allen, May 23, 1876, Allen Papers; *Cong. Record*, 44th Cong., 1st sess., 1876, 4, pt. 4:2124–25, 2281; ibid., pt. 5:3031, 3036–37; Merze Tate, *Hawaii: Reciprocity or Annexation* (East Lansing: Michigan State Univ. Press, 1968), 108–30.

82. *Times*, July 5, 1876.

83. *Herald*, Oct. 8, 22, Nov. 3, 9, 1876; *Times*, Oct. 1, 4, 7, 11, 15, 20, 21, 24, 26, Nov. 3, 9, 1876; *World*, Oct. 7, 16, 24, 31, Nov. 6, 8, 1876; Henry Dawes to Electa Dawes, Jan. 11, 1877, Dawes Papers. Wood defeated George W. DeCunha by 6,721 votes cast out of 21,575, or 65.6 percent to 34.4 percent. *Times*, Nov. 9, 1876.

84. *Herald*, Nov. 8, 24, 28, Dec. 3, 1876; *Daily Graphic*, Nov. 27, Dec. 1, 4, 1876; *Evening Star*, Nov. 28, Dec. 3, 1876; *Times*, Nov. 28, 30, Dec. 3, 1876; Samuel Ward to Randall Dec. 3, 8, 1876, Randall Papers; Randall to Tilden, Dec. 3, 1876, Tilden Papers.

85. *Times*, Jan. 7, 1877.

86. *Herald*, Dec. 6, 7, 8, 12, 13, 1876; *World*, Dec. 7, 8, 9, 12, 1876; *Evening Star*, Dec. 7, 8, 1876; *Times*, Dec. 7, 8, 9, 10, 12, 14, 25, 1876; *Daily Graphic*, Dec. 18, 1876; *Cong. Record*, 44th Cong., 2d sess., 1877, 5, pt. 1:68, 71; ibid., "Use of the Army in Certain Southern States," H. Exec. Doc. 30; George C. Rable, "Southern Interests and the Election of 1876: A Reappraisal," *CWH* 26 (Dec. 1980): 353.

87. Garfield to Hayes, Dec. 12, 1876, cited by Margaret Leech and Harry J. Brown, *The Garfield Orbit* (New York: Harper & Row, 1978), 290–93; *Herald*, Dec. 13, 14, 1876; *Daily Graphic*, Dec. 14, 1876, Jan. 10, 1877; William H. Smith to Henry Boynton, Dec. 15, 22, 1876, William Roberts to Smith, Dec. 16, 1876, William H. Smith Papers, OHS; *Times*, Dec. 21, 1876; Michael Les Benedict, "Southern Democrats in the Crisis of 1876–1877: A Reconsideration of *Reunion and Reaction*," *JSH* 46 (Nov. 1980): 489–520.

88. *Evening Star*, Dec. 7, 9, 11, 19, 20, 30, 1876; *Times*, Dec. 8, 1876; *Sun*, Jan. 4, 1877; *Herald*, Jan. 4, 1877; *World*, Jan. 5, 7, 1877; *Cong. Record*, 44th Cong., 2d sess., 1877, 5, pt. 1:241, 244, 245, 296, 406; Mark D. Hirsch, "Samuel J. Tilden: The Story of a Lost Opportunity," *AHR* 56 (July 1951): 788–802.

89. *Times*, Jan. 7, 8, 9, 1877; *Herald*, Jan. 7, 8, 15, 1877; Barlow to Bayard, Jan. 10, 1877, Bayard Papers; Cox to Wells, Jan. 14, 1877, Wells Papers; *Sun*, Jan. 15, 1877.

90. *World*, Jan. 18, 24, 25, 1877; *Daily Graphic*, Jan. 19, 20, 1877; *Sun*, Jan. 19, 1877; *Tribune*, Jan. 26, 1877; *Times*, Jan. 27, Feb. 13, 1877; *Herald*, Jan. 27, 1877; Manton Marble, "A Secret Chapter of the Political History," [1878], Marble Papers; *Cong. Record*, 44th Cong., 2d sess., 1877, pt. 3:1702; Abram S. Hewitt, "Secret History of the Disputed Election, 1876–77," in *Selected Writings of Abram S. Hewitt*, ed. Allan Nevins (New York: Columbia Univ. Press, 1937), 167–71; Polakoff, *Politics of Inertia*, 221–86.

91. *World*, Jan. 17, 18, 19, 23, 25, 26, 27, 28, 29, 30, 1877; *Evening Star*, Jan. 23, 26, 1877; *Times*, Jan. 23, 25, 30, 1877; *Sun*, Jan. 25, 28, 1877; *Cong. Record*, 44th Cong., 2d sess., 1877, 5, pt. 1:633, 814-17; ibid., pt. 2:925-28, 1269.

92. *Sun*, Feb. 1, 10, 12, 1877; *Herald*, Feb. 10, 13, 14, 1877; *Times*, Feb. 11, 12, 1877; *Evening Star*, Feb. 12, 13, 1877; *Tribune*, Feb. 13, 1877; *World*, Feb. 13, 1877; *Cong. Record*, 44th Cong., 2d sess., 1877, 5, pt. 2:1491-92; Jerrell H. Shofner, "Florida Courts and the Disputed Election of 1876," *Florida Historical Quarterly* 48 (July 1969): 24-46.

93. *Evening Star*, Feb. 16, 19, 1877; *World*, Feb. 17, 18, 1877; *Times*, Feb. 17, 18, 1877; Andrew J. Kellar to Smith, Feb. 20, 1877, Smith Papers.

94. *Times*, Feb. 17, 20, 1877; *Tribune*, Feb. 19, 1877; *Evening Star*, Feb. 19, 20, 1877; *Herald*, Feb. 20, 1877; C. Vann Woodward, *Reunion and Reaction: The Compromise of 1877 and the End of Reconstruction* (New York: Doubleday & Company, 1956), 193-94.

95. *Cong. Record*, 44th Cong., 2d sess., 1877, 5, pt. 3:1702-3.

96. *Daily Graphic*, Feb. 22, 1877; *Herald*, Feb. 23, 24, 1877; *Sun*, Feb. 23, 24, Mar. 3, 1877; *Evening Star*, Feb. 23, 24, 26, 1877; *World*, Feb. 25, 1877; Woodward, *Reunion and Reaction*, 201-6; Polakoff, *Politics of Inertia*, 309-13; Allan Peskin, "Was There a Compromise of 1877?" *JAH* 60 (June 1973): 67.

97. *Herald*, Feb. 27, 1877; *Evening Star*, Feb. 28, Mar. 1, 2, 1877; *World*, Mar. 1, 2, 1877; *Daily Graphic*, Mar. 1, 29, 1877; *Tribune*, Mar. 1, 2, 1877; *Times*, Mar. 1, 5, 1877; *Cong. Record*, 44th Cong., 2d sess., 1877, 5, pt. 3:1945, 1990, 2037-67; House, "Northern Congressional Democrats," 67-68.

98. *Herald*, Mar. 2, 1877; *Tribune*, March 3, 1877.

13. AN UNCERTAIN MAJORITY

1. Randall to Chauncey Black, Apr. 11, 22, 25, May 13, Aug. 14, Sept. 11, 1877, Jeremiah S. Black Papers; *Daily Graphic*, Apr. 26, May 29, June 4, 1877; Cox to Wells, May 22, 1877, Wells Papers.

2. Wood to Randall, Apr. 26, 27, 28, May 2, 21, June 1, July 7, Aug. 8, 17, Sept. 14, 20, Oct. 1, 1877, John Cagle to Randall, May 19, 1877, Edward Cooper to Randall, Oct. 4, 1877, Randall Papers.

3. Wood to Randall, Apr. 13, July 8, 9, 11, 16, 28, Aug. 21, 25, 1877, Henry Waterson to Randall, Apr. 19, 1877, E. Key Buchanan to Randall, Sept. 16, 1877, William Holman to Randall, Aug. 14, 1877, Randall Papers; *World*, Oct. 7, 1877.

4. Wood to Randall, Mar. 29, May 8, July 20, 1877, Randall Papers.

5. Morrison to Marble, Apr. 13, Oct. 20, 1877, Marble Papers; William O. Pelton to Randall, May 15, October 10, 1877, Ward Hunt to Randall, Sept. 20, 1877, Edward Cooper to Randall, Oct. 8, 1877, Marble to Randall, Oct. 14, 1877, Randall Papers; Wood to Rutherford B. Hayes, Aug. 27, 1877, Rutherford B. Hayes Papers, Rutherford B. Hayes Presidential Center, Fremont, Ohio; *Daily Graphic*, Sept. 12, Oct. 5, 6, 7, 13, 16, 17, 1877; *Times*, Oct. 5, 8, 9, 11, 12, 14, 15, 16, 1877, Dec. 9, 1879; *World*, Oct. 9, 12, 14, 16, 1877; *Herald*, Oct. 7, 12, 14, 16, 1877; *Tribune*, Oct. 12, 15, 1877; *Evening Post*, Oct. 13, 1877; Seip, *South Returns to Congress*, 283-86.

6. *Evening Post*, Oct. 15, 1877; *Times*, Oct. 15, 22, 29, 30, 31, 1877; *Herald*, Oct. 16, 28, 29, 30, 1877; *Washington Evening Star*, Oct. 17, 18, 1877; Randall to Wells, Oct. 20, 1877, Wells Papers; Randall to Chauncey Black, Nov. 2, 1877, Black Papers; *Tribune*, Oct. 30, 1877; *World*, Oct. 30, 31, 1877.

7. Randall to Marble, Nov. 3, 1877, Marble Papers; McPherson, *Hand-Book. . .for 1878* (1878), 201-2; *Cong. Record*, 45th Cong., 2d sess., 1878, 7, pt. 1:812.

8. *Herald*, Nov. 17, 1877; *Daily Graphic*, Nov. 17, 1877.

9. *Evening Star*, Nov. 10, 1877, Jan. 11, 31, Feb. 1, 5, 19, 1878; *World*, Nov. 22, Dec. 3, 10, 1877, Jan. 6, 9, 12, 18, 20, Mar. 3, 6, 8, 11, 18, 1878; *Times*, Dec. 1, 10, 1877, Jan. 30, 31, Feb. 8, 9, 10, 25, 28, Mar. 1, 1878; Wood to Wells, Dec. 10, 1877, Wells Papers; Wood to Bayard, Feb. 5, 1878, Bayard Papers; Wood to Randall, Feb. 10, 1878, Randall Papers; *Daily Graphic*, Mar. 18, 1878.

10. *World*, Jan. 9, 10, 23, 24, 28, 31, Feb. 1, 25, 26, 27, Mar. 2, 1878; *Herald*, Jan. 14, 25, 1878; *Daily Graphic*, Jan. 15, 21, Feb. 4, 5, 1878; *Evening Post*, Jan. 24, Feb. 2, 1878; *Times*, Jan. 31, Feb. 2, 14, Mar. 4, 16, 22, 1878; *Evening Star*, Feb. 19, Mar. 2, 1878; Cox to Wells, Apr. 2, 1878, Wells Papers; William S. Rosecrans to Wood, Apr. 15, 1878, Wood to Rosecrans, Apr. 26, 1878, William S. Rosecrans Papers, Bancroft Library, University of California, Berkeley, California.

11. *Herald*, Jan. 23, 31, Feb. 6, 8, 10, 12, 15, Mar. 3, 6, 8, 12, 1878; *Tribune*, Jan. 22, 26, 31, Feb. 12, 19, Mar. 26, 1878; *Evening Post*, Jan. 25, 31, Feb. 15, 16, 25, Mar. 10, 1878; *Daily Graphic*, Jan. 31, Feb. 6, 7, 9, 16, 18, Mar. 5, 9, 19, 1878; William Wood and Company to Wood, Feb. 9, 1878, Wood to Randall, May 1, 1878, Randall Papers; *Times*, Feb. 9, 19, Mar. 6, 8, 11, 1878; *World*, Feb. 10, 12, 22, Mar. 26, 1878; E. L. Day to James A. Garfield, Feb. 18, 1878, Joseph Carter to Garfield, Feb. 22, 1878, Martin Townsend to Garfield, Mar. 4, 1878, A. R. Seagrave to Garfield, May 25, 1878, James A. Garfield Papers, LC.

12. Bayard to Wells, May 8, 1878, Seymour to Wells, May 25, 1878, Wells Papers; *World*, Mar. 26, 27, 1878; *Daily Graphic*, Apr. 11, 1878; Arthur Austin to Bayard, Apr. 22, 1878, Bayard Papers; Wood to Moore, May 3, 1878, Wood Papers, NYPL; Wood to Wells, Mar. 21, 1878, Wells Papers.

13. *Evening Star*, Mar. 25, 1878; *Times*, Mar. 26, 27, Apr. 4, 8, 17, 1878; *World*, Mar. 27, 1878; *Evening Post*, Mar. 27, Apr. 3, 1878; *Herald*, Mar. 27, Apr. 3, 1878; *Daily Graphic*, Mar. 25, 27, 1878; Morrison to Wells, Jan. 14, 1882, Wells Papers; *Cong. Record*, 45th Cong., 2d sess., 1878, 7, pt. 3:2036.

14. Ibid., 2393-94, 2401-2.

15. Ibid., 2395.

16. Ibid., 2401.

17. *Herald*, Apr. 10, 1878; *World*, Apr. 10, 20, May 1, 8, 1878; *Tribune*, Apr. 10, 15, May 7, 8, 1878; *Times*, Apr. 10, 24, May 8, 1878; *Evening Post*, Apr. 10, May 8, 1878; *Daily Graphic*, Apr. 18, May 14, 1878; *Cong. Record*, 45th Cong., 2d sess., 1878, pt. 3:2540-57; ibid., pt. 4:3280-93, 3329-47.

18. *Evening Post*, Apr. 13, May 10, 16, 20, 30, 1878; *Times*, Apr. 15, 18, 21, May 8, 9, 15, 1878; *World*, Apr. 18, 27, 30, May 9, 13, 20, 1878; *Evening Star*, Apr. 18, May 3, 9, 15, 21, 29, 1878; *Herald*, Apr. 18, 21, May 8, 9, 14, 15, 17, 19, 24, 29, 30, 31, 1878; *Tribune*, May 10, 29, 1878.

19. *Times*, May 30, June 5, 1878; *World*, June 5, 1878; *Herald*, June 6, 1878; *Cong. Record.*, 45th Cong., 2d sess., 1878, 7, pt. 5:4095-96, 4154-55.

20. *Evening Star*, June 5, 14, 15, 1878; *Evening Post*, June 6, 1878; *Tribune*, June 6, 19, 1878; *Herald*, June 6, 18, 1878; *Times*, June 6, 18, 20, 1878; *World*, June 6, 18, 20, July 3, 1878; Barlow to Marble, June 10, 1878, Barlow Papers.

21. Smith to Hayes, Aug. 2, 1877, Smith Papers; *Tribune*, Oct. 30, 1877; *World*, Nov. 6, 1877; *Daily Graphic*, Mar. 19, 1878; *Herald*, June 17, 1878.

22. *Tribune*, Nov. 6, 7, 1877, Feb. 19, 1878; *World*, Dec. 8, 11, 12, 19, 1877, Feb. 12, 22, Mar. 11, 1878; *Times*, Feb. 9, 1878; *Daily Graphic*, Feb. 16, Mar. 1, 1878; Belmont to Garfield, Mar. 2, 1878, Garfield Papers.

23. *Cong. Record*, 44th Cong., 1st sess., 1876, 4, pt. 4:2048, 2998; ibid., 45th Cong., 2d sess., 1878, 7, pt. 5:4448, 4500; J. Laurence Laughlin, *The History of Bimetallism in the United States* (New York: D. Appleton and Company, 1897), 200-213.

24. *Cong. Record*, 45th Cong., 1st sess., 1877, 6, pt. 2:241; ibid., 2d sess., 1878, 7, pt. 2:1283–84, 1285, 1420, 2014–16; ibid., pt. 3:2712.

25. A. Burton Hepburn, *History of Coinage and Currency in the United States and the Perennial Contest for Sound Money* (New York: Macmillan, 1903), 230–33; Unger, *Greenback Era*, 353–73; Walter T. K. Nugent, *Money and American Society, 1865–1880* (New York: Free Press, 1968), 229–34.

26. *Cong. Record*, 45th Cong., 3d sess., 1879, 8, pt. 1:405.

27. Ibid., 1st sess., 1877, 6, pt. 2:204–5, 213, 632; ibid., 2d sess., 1878, 7, pt. 5:4620, 4834.

28. *Daily Graphic*, Jan. 12, 1877; *Times*, Jan. 28, July 11, Oct. 31, 1878; *World*, Feb. 16, 17, 1881.

29. Fernando Wood, "Last Will and Testament," Feb. 23, 1881, Probate Account of Proceedings, Jan. 4, 1885, Surrogate's Court, New York City Hall of Records.

30. *Times*, July 11, 1878. See various municipal libers, 1877–81, for Wood's real estate transactions.

31. *Daily Graphic*, Oct. 16, 1877, Feb. 12, 1878; Marian H. Adams to Robert W. Hooper, Jan. 13, Feb. 10, 1878, Jan. 27, 1879, Adams Family Papers; *Evening Star*, Dec. 31, 1878, Feb. 8, 1879, Jan. 8, 16, Feb. 13, 1880.

32. W. Hemphill Jones to Garfield, June 17, 1878, Garfield Papers; *World*, Sept. 5, 6, 13, 14, 18, 19, 24, 1878; Hayes to Comly, Oct. 29, 1878, Comly Papers; *Cong. Record*, 45th Cong., 2d sess., 1878, 7, pt. 5:4515–16; William Hartman, "The New York Custom House: Seats of Spoils Politics," *NYH* 34 (Apr. 1953): 149–63; Harry Barnard, *Rutherford B. Hayes and His America* (Indianapolis: Bobbs-Merrill, 1954), 450–56; Ari Hoogenboom, *The Presidency of Rutherford B. Hayes* (Lawrence: Regents Press of Kansas, 1988), 127–51.

33. Barlow to Bayard, July 18, Nov. 18, 1878, Bayard Papers; Wood to Randall, Aug. 10, 22, 1878, Randall Papers; *World*, Aug. 18, Sept. 20, Oct. 19, 1878; Wood to Garfield, Aug. 5, 17, 1878, Garfield Papers; *Times*, Sept. 4, 6, 13, 18, 19, 24, 25, 26, 27, Oct. 1, 1878; Barlow to Marble, Sept. 22, 1878, Marble Papers; Arnold Nye to Kernan, Sept. 22, 1878, William Dorsheimer to Kernan, Oct. 11, 1878, Kernan Papers; *Sugar Frauds: Investigation of the Committee on Ways and Means at New York City Custom House, September 17 and 18, 1878* (Boston: Henry A. Brown, 1878).

34. Wood to Randall, Sept. 20, Oct. 21, 26, 1878, Randall Papers; *Evening Post*, Oct. 15, 1878; *Times*, Oct. 15, 16, 22, 23, 27, 30, 31, Nov. 2, 4, 1878; *Tribune*, Oct. 19, 23, 30, Nov. 4, 1878; *World*, Oct. 22, 23, Nov. 6, 1878; *Herald*, Oct. 29, 30, Nov. 3, 4, 8, 1878.

35. *Tribune*, Nov. 5, 8, 1878; *Times*, Nov. 7, 1878; *Herald*, Nov. 8, 1878; Wood to Randall, Nov. 9, 1878, Randall Papers. Wood won, 37.3 percent, to Hardy's 33.6 and Berryman's 29.1.

36. *Times*, Mar. 22, Nov. 15, 17, 20, 1878; *World*, Mar. 23, Dec. 2, 1878; *Herald*, Nov. 5, 6, 1878; *Evening Post*, Dec. 3, 1878.

37. James D. Richardson, ed., *A Compilation of the Messages and Papers of the Presidents of the United States, 1789–1907* (New York: Bureau of National Literature and Art, 1908), 7:494; Gillette, *Retreat from Reconstruction*, 335–64.

38. *Cong. Record*, 45th Cong., 3d sess., 1879, 8, pt. 1:9–11.

39. Garfield to Hinsdale, Dec. 2, 1878, in *Garfield-Hinsdale Letters: Correspondence Between James Abram Garfield and Burke Aaron Hinsdale*, ed. Mary L. Hinsdale (Ann Arbor: Univ. of Michigan Press, 1949), 12; *Times*, Dec. 3, 4, 14, 18, 19, 21, 1878; *Tribune*, Dec. 3, 4, 14, 1878; *World*, Dec. 3, 5, 19, 1878; *Evening Post*, Dec. 13, 1878; *Herald*, Dec. 13, 14, 18, 1878; *Cong. Record*, 45th Cong., 3d sess., 1879, 8, pt. 1:127, 128, 175.

40. *Herald*, Jan. 17, Feb. 15, Mar. 3, 4, 1878; *Evening Star*, Feb. 18, 21, Mar. 4, 1879; Wood to Bayard, Mar. 3, 18, 1879, Bayard Papers; Bayard to Barlow, Feb. 22, 1878, Barlow Papers; *Times*, Apr. 8, 25, Nov. 26, 1879; House of Representatives, Committee on the Judiciary, "Charges Against John I. Davenport," 45th Cong., 3d sess., H. Rept. 135.

41. *Cong. Record*, 45th Cong., 3d sess., 1879, 8, pt. 2:1063.

42. Garfield to Comly, Dec. 14, 1878, Comly Papers; *Evening Star*, Jan. 7, Feb. 18, 20, 1879; *Times*, Jan. 7, 8, 10, 13, 14, 15, 23, 27, 31, Feb. 4, 7, 11, 22, 27, Mar. 3, 5, 6, 23, 1879; *Herald*, Jan. 8, 11, 14, 15, Feb. 28, Mar. 2, 1879; *World*, Jan. 15, 16, Feb. 11, 27, 1879; Wood to Randall, Jan. 18, 1879, Randall Papers; Wood to Garfield, Feb. 20, 1879, Garfield Papers; Wood to Wells, Mar. 24, 1879, Wells Papers.

43. Sherman, *Recollections*, 2:701–10, 795–96; Henry C. Adams, *Public Debt: An Essay in the Science of Finance* (New York: D. Appleton and Company, 1898), 201–32; Dewey, *Financial History*, 299–358; Nugent, *Money and Society*, 132–39; Patterson, *Federal-Debt Management*, 78–112.

44. *Cong. Record*, 45th Cong., 3d sess., 1879, 8, pt. 1:463–67.

45. Ibid., 474, 476, 477.

46. Hayes to Comly, Jan. 18, 1879, Comly Papers; *Herald*, Mar. 3, 6, 9, 16, Apr. 3, 12, May 3, 13, 14, 1879; *World*, Mar. 7, 12, 17, 18, Apr. 12, May 1, 2, 15, 1879; Barlow to Randall, Mar. 11, 1879, John Coyle to Randall, Mar. 13, 1879, Blaine to Randall, Mar. 31, 1879, Randall Papers; *Evening Star*, Mar. 21, 26, 29, Apr. 17, 1879; *Times*, Mar. 21, 24, 28, Apr. 12, 1879; Bayard to Barlow, Mar. 22, 1879, Barlow Papers; Randall to Wells, Apr. 23, 1879, Wells Papers; Moore to Bayard, May 6, 1879, Bayard Papers.

47. *World*, Apr. 6, May 12, June 26, 1879; *Herald*, Apr. 29, 1879; *Evening Star*, Apr. 28, 29, May 12, June 26, 1879; McPherson, *Hand-Book. . .for 1880* (1880), 100–144; *Cong. Record*, 46th Cong., 1st sess., 1879, 9, pt. 1:123–24; Charles R. Williams, *Diary and Letters of Rutherford B. Hayes* (Columbus: The F. J. Heer Printing Company, 1924), 3:528–64.

48. *Evening Star*, Apr. 21, May 6, 1879; *Tribune*, Apr. 29, 1879; *Times*, May 21, June 19, 1879; *Herald*, June 19, 1879; *Cong. Record*, 46th Cong., 1st sess., 1879, 9, pt. 1:341.

49. Dorsheimer to Bayard, Jan. 31, 1879, Ward to Bayard, June 3, 20, 1879, Belmont to Bayard, Nov. 10, 1879, Barlow to Bayard, Nov. 10, 1879, Bayard Papers; *Evening Star*, Apr. 8, Nov. 6, 1879; Henry McKay to Kernan, Sept. 18, 1879, Waterbury to Kernan, Sept. 18, 1879, Hurlbert to Kernan, Oct. 21, 1879, Kernan Family Papers; Waterbury to Randall, Sept. 23, 1879, Lester Faulkner to Randall, Sept. 26, Oct. 4, Nov. 6, 1879, Robert Green to Randall, Oct. 4, 1879, Randall Papers; Barlow to Marble, Dec. 30, 1879, Marble Papers.

50. *Evening Star*, Dec. 12, 1879; Barlow to Bayard, Jan. 12, May 7, 1880, Perry Belmont to Bayard, Mar. 1, 24, 1880, John Hunter to Bayard, Mar. 12, Apr. 17, May 10, 31, 1880, Bayard Papers; Randall to Marble, Feb. 22, 1880, Marble Papers; John Haskins to Randall, Apr. 17, 1880, Marvine Bovee to Randall, June 28, 1880, Randall Papers; Wood to Seymour, June 10, 1880, Seymour Papers, NYHS.

51. *Herald*, Dec. 4, 1879.

52. Ibid.

53. Sherman to Smith, Oct. 3, 1879, Smith Papers; *Times*, Nov. 26, Dec. 2, 7, 16, 31, 1879; *World*, Nov. 26, Dec. 3, 24, 31, 1879; *Herald*, Nov. 30, Dec. 4, 5, 6, 8, 12, 16, 27, 31, 1879; *Evening Star*, Jan. 5, 6, 1880; Sherman, *Recollections*, 2:758.

54. *Herald*, Jan. 8, 13, 19, Mar. 8, 10, 17, 24, 25, 26, Apr. 1, 6, 7, 14, 16, 23, 24, May 2, 5, 7, 9, 12, 15, 17, 25, 1880; *World*, Jan. 21, 27, 30, Feb. 6, 7, 24, Mar. 10, 13, 21, 25, 26, 31, Apr. 8, 10, 14, 16, May 14, 20, Sept. 1, 1880; Cox to Wells, Apr. 23, 1880, Wells Papers.

55. *World*, Jan. 4, 12, 14, 27, Feb. 3, 12, 14, 15, 17, 18, 25, 1880; *Evening Star*, Jan. 15, 25, Feb. 19, Mar. 22, 1880; *Herald*, Jan. 15, 16, 20, 25, 26, 28, Feb. 13, 18, 19, 1880; *Times*, Feb. 3, 11, 12, 13, 18, 25, Mar. 2, 1880.

56. McPherson, *Hand-Book. . .for 1880*, 148–49.

57. *Cong. Record*, 46th Cong., 2d sess., 1880, 10, pt. 2:1313–20.

58. *Times*, Mar. 5, 17, Apr. 5, 1880; *Herald*, Mar. 6, 1880; *Cong. Record*, 46th Cong., 2d sess., 1880, 10, pt. 2:1718–56.

59. *World*, Mar. 2, 3, 6, 9, 21, 26, Dec. 6, 1880; *Herald*, Mar. 31, 1880; *Times*, Apr. 19, 1880; *Evening Star*, May 13, June 2, 1880.

60. *Evening Star*, June 30, 1880.

61. McPherson, *Hand-Book...for 1880*, 195; Herbert J. Clancy, *The Presidential Election of 1880* (Chicago: Loyola Univ. Press, 1958), 122–50.

62. *World*, Sept. 3, 23, Oct. 1, 13, 27, Nov. 2, 1880; *Herald*, Sept. 20, 24, 26, Oct. 10, 13, 17, Nov. 1, 1880; *Evening Star*, Oct. 7, 16, 1880; *Times*, Oct. 22, 31, Nov. 1, 1880.

63. *Herald*, Oct. 31, Nov. 3, 1880; *Times*, Nov. 5, 7, 1880; *Evening Star*, Nov. 13, 1880.

64. *Herald*, Nov. 29, Dec. 2, 7, 8, 10, 23, 1880; *Times*, Nov. 29, Dec. 1, 14, 15, 16, 23, 24, 1880; *World*, Dec. 6, 9, 14, 15, 16, 19, 20, 21, 22, 1880; *Evening Star*, Dec. 10, 11, 21, 1880; *Daily Graphic*, Jan. 17, Feb. 14, 1880; *Cong. Record*, 46th Cong., 3d sess., 1881, 11, pt. 1:12, 18, 37, 39, 59, 61, 106, 109, 134–43, 159, 261, 274, 281, 293.

65. Wood to John Sherman, Dec. 13, 1879, John Sherman Papers, LC; *World*, Dec. 15, 23, 1880; *Times*, Dec. 15, 23, 1880; *Cong. Record*, 46th Cong., 3d sess., 1881, 11, pt. 1:294, 296–311; Fred E. Haynes, *James Baird Weaver* (Iowa City: State Historical Society of Iowa, 1919), 179–96.

66. *Herald*, Jan. 1, 4, 6, 8, 1881; *Times*, Jan. 5, 6, 7, 8, 1881; *Daily Graphic*, Jan. 5, 1881; *World*, Jan. 6, 7, 8, Feb. 14, 1881; Wood to Randall, Jan. 6, 8, 1881, Randall Papers.

67. *Times*, Jan. 7, 8, 13, 14, 19, 1881; *Herald*, Jan. 9, 10, 12, 13, 14, 15, 19, 1881; *World*, Jan. 9, 10, 13, 19, 1881; *Cong. Record*, 46th Cong., 3d sess., 1881, 11, pt. 1:456–74, 563–81, 658–67, 769.

68. *World*, Jan. 13, 19, 1881; *Herald*, Jan. 15, 19, 1881; *Times*, Jan.19, 1881; *Cong. Record*, 46th Cong., 3d sess., 1881, 11, pt. 1:606–15, 729–41, 770.

69. *Evening Post*, Jan. 19, 20, 1881; *Evening Star*, Jan. 18, 20, 1881; *Herald*, Jan. 20, 1881; *Cong. Record*, 46th Cong., 3d sess., 1881, 11, pt. 1:745–46, 771–72.

70. Belmont to Sherman, Jan. 14, 1880, Sherman Papers; *World*, Jan. 20, 1881; *Tribune*, Jan. 20, 1881; *Cong. Record*, 46th Cong., 3d sess., 1881, 11, pt. 1:773; Sherman, *Recollections*, 2:796–801.

71. Wood to Randall, Jan. 25, 26, n.d. [January], 1881, Randall Papers; *Evening Star*, Jan. 25, Feb. 10, 14, 1881.

72. McPherson, *Hand-Book...for 1882*, 10–37.

14. THE MAN AND HIS CAREER

1. *World*, Feb. 14, 15, 16, 17, 18, 20, 21, 1881; *Washington Evening Star*, Feb. 18, 1881; *Daily Graphic*, Feb. 18, 1881; *Cong. Record*, 46th Cong., 3d sess., 1881, 11, pt. 2:1579; ibid., pt. 3:1842, 1892, 2191, 2241–47.

2. *The Nation*, Feb. 17, 1881, 105; *Daily Graphic*, Feb. 15, 1881; *Times*, Feb. 15, 1881. For more on Godkin see Diana Kiebanow, "E. L. Godkin, the City, and Civic Responsibility," *NYHSQ* 50 (Jan. 1971): 52–75.

3. *Biographical Dictionary of American Mayors, 1820–1980*, ed. Melvin G. Holli and Peter d' A. Jones (Westport, Conn.: Greenwood Press, 1981).

4. *Times*, Jan. 15, 1878; Albert S. Bolles, *The Financial History of the United States from 1861 to 1885* (New York: D. Appleton & Company, 1886), 338–39; Sherman, *Recollections*, 2:839–41; Hepburn, *History of Coinage and Currency*, 242–43. On Dec. 5, 1881, Sherman, who was back in the Senate, introduced a refunding bill that was based on 3 percent interest bonds.

BIBLIOGRAPHY

GOVERNMENT DOCUMENTS,
PUBLISHED AND UNPUBLISHED

Congressional Globe. 46 vols. Washington, D.C., 1834–73.

Congressional Quarterly's Guide to the Congress of the United States: Origins, History and Procedures. Washington, D.C.: Congressional Quarterly Service, 1973.

Congressional Record. Washington, D.C., 1873–81.

District of Columbia. General Index Trusts & Leases, Liber D, Number 4, 1868–69. Records of Deeds, District of Columbia.

Hough, Franklin B. *Census of the State of New York for 1855.* Albany: Charles Van Benthuysen, 1857.

———. *Census of the State of New York for 1865.* Albany: Charles Van Benthyusen & Sons, 1867.

———. *Statistics of Population of the City and County of New York, as shown by the State Census of 1865, with the Comparative Results of This and Previous Enumerations, and Other Statistics Given by the State and Federal Census, From the Earliest Period.* New York: New York Printing Company, 1866.

Inter-University Consortium for Political and Social Research. University of Michigan.

Mills, Abby B. "Last Will and Testament." October 25, 1872. Record of Wills, Liber 189. Surrogate's Court, New York City Hall of Records.

Mills, C. Drake "Last Will and Testament." February 6, 1863. Record of Wills, Liber 151. Surrogate's Court, New York City Hall of Records.

New York County. Assessor's Property Evaluation, 22d Ward, 1860. New York City Municipal Archives and Record Center.

———. Mayor's Papers. New York City Municipal Archives and Record Center.

———. Municipal Real Estate Libers, 1848–81. Grantor's Index to Deeds. Grantee's Index to Deeds. Grantor's Index to Mortgages. Grantee's Index to Mortgages. County Recorder, New York City Hall of Records.

New York State. *Journal of the Assembly of the State of New York at their Eightieth Session, 1857.* Albany: Charles Van Benthyusen, 1857.

——. *Journal of the Senate of the State of New York at their Eightieth Session.* Albany: Charles Van Benthyusen, 1857.

Reports of the Industrial Commission on Immigration, including Testimony, with Review and Digest and Special Reports and on Education, including Testimony, with Review and Digest. Vol. 15. Washington, D.C.: GPO, 1901.

Richardson, James D., ed. *A Compilation of the Messages and Papers of the Presidents of the United States, 1789–1907.* 10 vols. New York: Bureau of National Literature and Art, 1908.

San Francisco Volume of Deeds, Old Series, Vol. 2, Book 483, May 28, 1851. San Francisco Hall of Records.

U.S. Bureau of Census. *Population Schedules of the Sixth Census of the United States, 1840. Population Schedules of the Seventh Census of the United States, 1850. Population Schedules of the Eighth Census of the United States, 1860. Population Schedules of the Ninth Census of the United States, 1870.* National Archives, 1959. Microfilm.

U.S. Congress. House. Select Committee on Alleged New York City Election Frauds. *Alleged New York City Election Frauds.* 40th Cong., 3d sess., 1869. Report no. 31.

U.S. Congress. House. *Use of the Army in Certain of the Southern States.* 44th Cong., 2d sess., 1877. Ex. Doc. no. 30.

Wood, Fernando. "Last Will and Testament." February 23, 1881. Record of Wills. Surrogate's Court, New York City Hall of Records.

——. Final Judicial Settlement of the Account of the Executors of the Will of Fernando Wood, February 8, 1884. Surrogate's Court, New York City Hall of Records.

Wood, Fernando v. Wood, Anna W.: New York County Court of Chancery. June 14, 1839. Index no. BW-W2127. Surrogate's Court, New York City Hall of Records.

NEWSPAPERS

Albany Argus 1840, 1850, 1856, 1860, 1864, 1866, 1868, 1874
Albany Evening Journal 1859–61, 1864
Buffalo Daily Courier 1850–54, 1864–73
The Man (New York) 1837
Morning Courier and New York Enquirer 1850–59
New York American 1837, 1840
New York Atlas 1850
New York Commercial Advertiser 1848–51, 1860–65, 1868
New York Daily Graphic 1874–81
New York Daily News 1855–71, 1874
New York Evening Post 1835–81
New York Herald 1835–81
New York Irish-American 1850–71
New York Irish Citizen 1868
New York Journal of Commerce 1850, 1854, 1860–62, 1866

New York Leader 1858–71
New York New Era 1837
New York Plaindealer 1837
New York Sun 1850–61, 1874–81
New York Sunday Times and Noah's Weekly Messenger 1849–50
New-York Times 1837
New York Times 1851–81
New York Tribune 1850–81
New York Weekly Tribune 1859
New York Workingman's Advocate 1835–37
New York World 1862–81
Richmond Examiner 1860–64
San Francisco Alta California 1849–52
Washington Evening Star 1864, 1867–81

MANUSCRIPT COLLECTIONS

Adams Family Papers. Massachusetts Historical Society, Boston.
Allen, Elisha H. Papers. Library of Congress, Washington, D.C.
Anderson, Martin B. Papers. Rush Rhees Library, University of Rochester, Rochester, N.Y.
Anderson, Robert. Papers. Library of Congress, Washington, D.C.
Badeau, Adam. Papers. Library of Congress, Washington, D.C.
Banks, Nathaniel P. Papers. Library of Congress, Washington, D.C.
Barlow, Samuel L. M. Papers. Henry E. Huntington Library, San Marino, Calif.
Bayard, Thomas F. Papers. Library of Congress, Washington, D.C.
Bennett, James G. Papers. Library of Congress, Washington, D.C.
Berry Family Papers. John M. Olin Library, Cornell University, Ithaca, N.Y.
Black, Jeremiah S. Papers. Library of Congress, Washington, D.C.
Blaine, James G. Papers. Library of Congress, Washington, D.C.
Blair Family Papers. Library of Congress, Washington, D.C.
Brock Collection. Henry E. Huntington Library, San Marino, Calif.
Buchanan, James. Papers. Historical Society of Pennsylvania, Philadelphia.
Burke, Edmund. Papers. Library of Congress, Washington, D.C.
Calhoun, John C. Papers. Clemson University Library, Clemson, S.C.
Campbell, Lewis A. Papers. Ohio Historical Society, Columbus.
Carroll, Anna Ella. Papers. Maryland Historical Society, Baltimore.
Comly, James R. Papers. Ohio Historical Society, Columbus.
Corning, Erastus. Papers. Albany Institute of History and Art, Albany, N.Y.
Cox, Samuel S. Papers. John Hay Library, Brown University, Providence, R.I.
Cushing, Caleb. Papers. Library of Congress, Washington, D.C.
Davis, David. Papers. Illinois State Historical Society, Springfield.
Dawes, Henry A. Papers. Library of Congress, Washington, D.C.

Dreer Collection. Historical Society of Pennsylvania, Philadelphia.

Dix, John A. Papers. Rare Book and Manuscript Library, Columbia University, New York, N.Y.

Douglas, Stephen A. Papers. Joseph Regenstein Library, University of Chicago, Chicago, Ill.

Drowne Collection. Henry E. Huntington Library, San Marino, Calif.

Fairchild Family Papers. New-York Historical Society, New York, N.Y.

Fish, Hamilton. Papers. Library of Congress, Washington, D.C.

Flagg, Azariah C. Papers. New York Public Library, New York, N.Y.

Garfield, James A. Papers. Library of Congress, Washington, D.C.

Gratz, Simon. Collection. Historical Society of Pennsylvania, Philadelphia.

Greeley, Horace. Papers. Library of Congress, Washington, D.C.

———. New York Public Library, New York, N.Y.

Halpine, Charles G. Papers. Henry Huntington Library, San Marino, Calif.

Hayes, Rutherford B. Papers. Presidential Center, Fremont, Ohio.

Historical Documents Collection. Queens College, Flushing, N.Y.

Howard, Oliver O. Papers. Bowdoin College Library, Brunswick, Maine.

Hunt, Washington. Papers. New York State Library, Albany, N.Y.

Johnson, Andrew. Papers. Library of Congress, Washington, D.C.

Kernan Family Papers. John M. Olin Library, Cornell University, Ithaca, N.Y.

King, Horatio. Papers. Library of Congress, Washington, D.C.

Larkin, Thomas O. Papers. Bancroft Library, University of California, Berkeley, Calif.

Letters of Application and Recommendation during the Administrations of John Tyler, James K. Polk, Zachary Taylor, and Millard Fillmore. National Archives, Washington, D.C.

Lincoln, Robert Todd. Papers. Library of Congress, Washington, D.C.

Long, Alexander. Papers. Cincinnati Historical Society, Cincinnati, Ohio.

McClellan, George B. Papers. Library of Congress, Washington, D.C.

Madigan Collection. Henry E. Huntington Library, San Marino, Calif.

Marble, Manton. Papers. Library of Congress, Washington, D.C.

Marcy, William L. Papers. Library of Congress, Washington, D.C.

Miller, Joseph T. Papers. Rush Rhees Library, University of Rochester, Rochester, N.Y.

Morgan, Edwin D. Papers. New York State Library, Albany, N.Y.

Paul, George H. Papers. Wisconsin Historical Society, Madison.

Pierce, Franklin. Papers. Library of Congress, Washington, D.C.

Polk, James K. Papers. Library of Congress, Washington, D.C.

Poore, Ben: Perley. Papers. Haverhill Public Library, Haverhill, Mass.

Pruyn, John V. L. Diary. Albany Institute of History and Art, Albany, N.Y.

Ramsey, Albert. Papers. New-York Historical Society, New York, N.Y.

Randall, Samuel J. Papers. Van Pelt Library, University of Pennsylvania, Philadelphia.

Rosecrans, William S. Papers. Bancroft Library, University of California, Berkeley, Calif.

Schell, Augustus. Papers. New-York Historical Society, New York, N.Y.

Schurz, Carl. Papers. Library of Congress, Washington, D.C.

Seward, William H. Papers. Rush Rhees Library, University of Rochester, Rochester, N.Y.

Seymour, Horatio. Papers. New York State Library, Albany, N.Y.

Sherman, John. Papers. Library of Congress, Washington, D.C.

Smith, William H. Papers. Ohio Historical Society, Columbus.

Stanton, Edwin M. Papers. Library of Congress, Washington, D.C.

Stephens, Alexander H. Papers. Library of Congress, Washington, D.C.

Thurman, Allen. Papers. Ohio Historical Society, Columbus.

Tilden, Samuel J. Papers. New York Public Library, New York, N.Y.

Trimble, John A. Papers. Ohio Historical Society, Columbus.

Van Buren, Martin. Papers. Library of Congress, Washington, D.C.

Wadsworth Family Papers. Rush Rhees Library, University of Rochester, Rochester, N.Y.

Washburne, Elihu B. Papers. Library of Congress, Washington, D.C.

Weed, Thurlow. Papers. New York State Library, Albany, N.Y.

——. Rush Rhees Library, University of Rochester, Rochester, N.Y.

Wells, David A. Papers. Library of Congress, Washington, D.C.

Wise, Henry A. Papers. Alderman Library, University of Virginia, Charlottesville.

——. Archives Branch, Virginia State Library, Richmond.

——. Virginia Historical Society, Richmond.

Wood, Fernando. Papers. New-York Historical Society, New York, N.Y.

——. New York Public Library, New York, N.Y.

CITY DIRECTORIES

Dawes, Edward. *The Philadelphia Directory for 1817.* Philadelphia, 1817.

Doggett, John Jr. *Doggett's City Business Directory for 1846–7.* New York: John Doggett, Jr., 1847.

——. *Doggett's New York City Street Directory, for 1851.* New York: John Doggett, Jr., 1851.

——. *Doggett's New York Directory.* New York: John Doggett, Jr., 1842–53.

——. *The New-York City Co-Partnership Directory for 1844–5.* New York: John Doggett, Jr., 1845.

Kite's Philadelphia Directory for 1814. Philadelphia: B. & T. Kite, 1814.

Longworth, Thomas. *Longworth's American Almanac, New-York Register, and City Directory.* New York: Thomas Longworth, 1832–43.

Moorehead, Thomas. *Mercantile Register for 1848–9.* New York: John P. Prall, 1848.

Paxton, John A. *Philadelphia Directory and Registry.* Philadelphia: B. & T. Kite, 1813, 1818, 1819.

Richards, T. P. *Commercial List Containing the Names & Occupations of the Principle Merchants in the City.* New York: William H. Rose, 1853.

Robinson, James. *The Philadelphia Directory*. Philadelphia: W. Woodhouse, 1807–11, 1816, 1817.

Wilson, Henry. *Wilson's Business Directory*. New York: John F. Trow, 1849–51.

CONTEMPORARY WORKS
AND PUBLISHED DIARIES, LETTERS, AND MEMOIRS

Adams, John Quincy. *Memoirs of John Quincy Adams, Comprising Portions of his Diary from 1795 to 1848*. Ed. Charles F. Adams. 12 vols. Philadelphia: J. B. Lippincott, 1877.

Ambler, Charles H., ed. "Correspondence of Robert M. T. Hunter" *American Historical Association, Annual Report for the Year 1916*. Washington: GPO, 1918.

Beach, Moses Y. *The Wealthy Citizens of New York*. 13th ed. New York, 1855.

Boyd, William H. *Boyd's New York City Tax-Book, Being a List of Persons, Corporations & Co-Partnerships, Resident and Non-Resident, Who were Taxed According to the Assessors' Book, 1856 and 1857*. New York: William H. Boyd, Publisher, 1857.

Brawley, James R. *A Brief Account of the Catholic Church on the Island of New York*. New York: E. Dunigan & Brothers, 1853.

Briggs, Emily E. *The Olivia Letters*. New York: Neal Publishing, 1906.

Brooks, Noah. *Washington, D.C. in Lincoln's Time*. Ed. Herbert Mitgang. New York: Collier Books, 1962.

Bryant, William Cullen. *The Letters of William Cullen Bryant*. Ed. William C. Bryant II and Thomas G. Viss. 4 vols. New York: Fordham Univ. Press, 1984.

Bryce, James. *The American Commonwealth*. 2 vols. New York: Macmillan, 1888.

Byrne, Stephen. *Irish Immigration to the United States*. New York: Catholic Publication Society, 1873.

Byrdsall, Fitzwilliam. *The History of the Loco-Foco, or Equal Rights Party*. New York: Clement and Packard, 1842.

Cox, Samuel S. *Union – Disunion – Reunion: Three Decades of Federal Legislation, 1855 to 1885*. 2 vols. Providence, R.I.: J. A. & R. A. Reid, 1886.

Darling, William A. *List of Persons, Co-partnerships & Corporations, who were Taxed on Seventeen Thousand Five Hundred Dollars, and Upwards in the City of New York in the Year 1850*. New York: John F. Whitney, 1851.

Davenport, John. *The Election and Naturalization Frauds in New York City, 1860–1870*. New York: Printed by the Author, 1894.

Dickinson, Daniel S. *The Speeches, Correspondence, Etc. of the Late Daniel S. Dickinson*. Ed. John Dickinson. 2 vols. New York: G. P. Putnam & Sons, 1867.

Dix, John Adams. *Memoirs of John Adams Dix*. Ed. Morgan Dix. 2 vols. New York: Harper & Brothers, 1883.

Documents Relative to the Withdrawal of Nelson J. Waterbury form the Canvass in the Eighth Congressional District. New York, 1862.

Durand, Edward D. *The Finances of New York City*. New York: Macmillan, 1898.

"The Ermine in the Ring: A History of the Wood Lease Case." *Putnam's Magazine Supplement* (Nov. 1868): 1–81.

Glentworth, James. *A Statement of the Frauds on the Elective Franchise in the City of New York.* New York, 1840.

"The Great Want of New-York City." *New-York Quarterly* 3 (Apr. 1854): 80–101.

Hammond, George P., ed. *The Larkin Papers: Personal, Business, and Official Correspondence of Thomas Oliver Larkin, Merchant and United States Consul in California.* 9 vols. Berkeley: Univ. of California Press, 1964.

Hardy, John. *Manual of the Corporation of the City of New York for 1870.* New York: New York Printing Company, 1870.

Haswell, Charles S. *Reminiscences of an Octogenarian of the City of New York (1816–1860).* New York: Harper & Brothers, 1897.

Headley, Joel T. *The Great Riots of New York, 1712–1873.* New York: E. B. Treat, 1873.

[Herrick, Anson]. *A Condensed Biography of Fernando Wood.* New York, 1866.

Hesseltine, William B., ed. *Three Against Lincoln: Murat Halstead Reports the Caucuses of 1860.* Baton Rouge: Louisiana State Univ. Press, 1960.

Hewitt, Abram S. *Selected Writings of Abram S. Hewitt.* Ed. Allan Nevins. New York: Columbia Univ. Press, 1937.

Hinsdale, Mary L., ed. *Garfield-Hinsdale Letters: Correspondence Between James Abram Garfield and Burke Aaron Hinsdale.* Ann Arbor: Univ. of Michigan Press, 1949.

Honeyman, A. Van Doren, ed. *Documents Relating to the Colonial History of New Jersey, First Series. Calendar of New Jersey Wills, Administration, Etc.* 11 vols. Somerville: The Unionist-Gazette Association, 1918.

Howard, Oliver O. *Autobiography of Oliver Otis Howard.* 2 vols. New York: The Baker & Taylor Company, 1907.

Hoyes, Stephen. *The Political Situation Resulting from the Late State Election. (Herald Interview with Peter B. Sweeny.)* New York: The Jackson Association, 1869.

Hunt's Merchant's Magazine and Commercial Review. 1849, 1850, 1854, 1856, 1860.

[Hutchinson, E. A.]. *A MODEL MAYOR: Early Life, Congressional Career, & Triumphant Municipal Administration of Hon. Fernando Wood, Mayor of New York City.* New York: American Family Publications, 1855.

Ingraham, Abijah. *A Biography of Fernando Wood. A History of the Forgeries, Perjuries and Other Crimes of Our "Model Mayor."* New York, 1856.

Johannsen, Robert W., ed. *The Letters of Stephen A. Douglas.* Urbana: Univ. of Illinois Press, 1961.

Kendall, Isaac C. *The Growth of New York.* New York, 1865.

King, Moses. *King's Handbook of New York City, 1893.* Boston: Moses King, Publisher, 1893.

Knapp, Friedrich. *Immigration and the Commissioners of Emigration of the State of New York.* New York, 1870.

McCabe, James D., Jr. *Behind the Scenes in Washington.* Philadelphia: National Publishing Company, 1873.

MacLeod, Donald. *Biography of the Honorable Fernando Wood, Mayor of the City of New York.* New York: O. F. Parsons, 1856.

McPherson, Edward. *Hand-Book of Politics.* Various editions, 1871–82. Washington, D.C.: Philips & Solomons, 1872–82.

——. *The Political History of the United States of America During the Period of Reconstruction: April 15, 1865–July 15, 1870.* Washington, D.C.: Philips & Solomons, 1871.

"New-York Government" *New-York Quarterly* 4 (Apr.–July 1855): 1–20.

New York Hards and Softs: Which is the True Democracy? New York, 1856.

Nicolay, John G., and John Hay. *Abraham Lincoln: A History.* 10 vols. New York: The Century Co., 1890.

Owen, Samuel. *The New-York Legal Observer.* New York: Samuel Owen, 1852.

Poore, Ben: Perley. *Perley's Reminiscences of Sixty Years in the National Metropolis.* 2 vols. Philadelphia: Hubbard Brothers, Publishers, 1884.

Proceedings of the Great Peace Conference Held in the City of New York June 3, 1863: Speeches, Addresses, Resolutions & Letters from Leading Men. New York, 1863.

Prowell, George R. *The History of Camden County, New Jersey.* Philadelphia: L. J. Richards and Co., 1886.

Rasmussen, Louis J. *San Francisco Ship Passenger Lists.* Colma, Calif.: San Francisco Historical Record and Geneological Bulletin, 1965.

Refutation of the Whig Slander Against Mr. Fernando Wood. New York, 1840.

[Scoville, Joseph A.] *The Old Merchants of New York City. By Walter Barrett, Clerk. First Series.* New York: Carleton, Publisher, 1863.

——. *The Old Merchants of New York City. By Walter Barrett, Clerk. Second Series.* 4 vols. New York: Carleton, Publisher, 1864.

Sherman, John. *John Sherman's Recollections of Forty Years in the House, Senate and Cabinet. An Autobiography.* 2 vols. New York: The Werner Company, 1895.

The Softs, the True Democracy of the State of New York. New York, 1856.

Statement of the Majority of the Grand Council of the Tammany Society, or Columbian Order, in Reply to a Protest of the Minority; Also the Addresses and Resolutions of the Grand Council Adopted February 14, 1857, Relative to the Political Use of Tammany Hall. New York, 1857.

Stevens, John A. *The Union Defense Committee of the City of New York.* New York: Published by the Committee, 1885.

Still, Bayrd. *Mirror for Gotham: New York as Seen by Contemporaries from Dutch Days to the Present.* New York: New York Univ. Press, 1956.

Storke, Elliott G. *History of Cayuga County, New York, 1789–1879.* Syracuse: D. Mason & Co., 1879.

Strong, George T. *The Diary of George Templeton Strong.* Ed. Allan Nevins and Milton H. Thomas. 4 vols. New York: Macmillan, 1952.

Sugar Frauds: Investigation of the Committee on Ways and Means at New York City Custom House, September 17 and 18, 1878. Boston: Henry A. Brown, 1878.

Turner, Justin G., and Linda L. Turner, eds. *Mary Todd Lincoln: Her Life and Letters.* New York: Alfred A. Knopf, 1972.

Valentine, David T. *The Manual of the Corporation of the City of New York.* Various years. 19 vols. New York, 1850–68.

Vose, Reuben. *The Rich Men of New York.* 2d ser. New York, 1861.

Weed, Harriet, ed. *Autobiography of Thurlow Weed.* 2 vols. Boston: Houghton Mifflin, 1883.

Williams, Charles R. *Diary and Letters of Rutherford B. Hayes.* 5 vols. Columbus: The F. J. Heer Printing Company, 1924.

Wilson, Clyde N. *The Papers of John C. Calhoun, 1841–1843.* Vol. 10. Columbia: Univ. of South Carolina Press, 1984.

Wood, Fernando. *Speech of Fernando Wood delivered Before the Meeting of the National Democratic Delegation to the Charleston Convention at Syracuse, February 7, 1860.* New York, 1860.

BOOKS

Adams, Henry C. *Public Debts: An Essay in the Science of Finance.* New York: D. Appleton and Company, 1898.

Alexander, DeAlva S. *A Political History of the State of New York.* 4 vols. New York: Henry Holt & Company, 1906–24.

Alexander, Thomas B. *Sectional Stress and Party Strength: A Study of Roll Call Voting Patterns in the United States House of Representatives 1836–1860.* Nashville: Vanderbilt Univ. Press, 1967.

Allswang, John M. *Bosses, Machines, and Urban Voters: An American Symbiosis.* Port Washington: Kennikat Press, 1977.

Baker, Jean H. *Affairs of Party: The Political Culture of Northern Democrats in the Mid-Nineteenth Century.* Ithaca, N.Y.: Cornell Univ. Press, 1983.

Barnard, Harry. *Rutherford B. Hayes and His America.* Indianapolis: Bobbs-Merrill, 1954.

Belz, Herman. *Emancipation and Equal Rights: Politics and Constitutionalism in the Civil War Era.* New York: W. W. Norton & Company, 1978.

——. *Reconstructing the Union: Theory and Policy During the Civil War.* Ithaca, N.Y.: Cornell Univ. Press, 1969.

Benedict, Michael Les. *A Compromise of Principle: Congressional Republicans and Reconstruction, 1863–1869.* New York: W. W. Norton & Company, 1973.

Berger, Mark L. *The Revolution in the New York Party System, 1840–1860.* Port Washington: Kennikat Press, 1973.

Bogue, Allan G. *The Congressman's Civil War.* New York: Cambridge Univ. Press, 1989.

Bolles, Albert S. *The Financial History of the United States from 1861 to 1885.* New York: D. Appleton & Company, 1886.

Booraem, Hendrik, V. *The Formation of the Republican Party in New York: Politics and Conscience in the Antebellum North.* New York: New York Univ. Press, 1983.

Bowen, Croswell. *The Elegant Oakey.* New York: Oxford Univ. Press, 1959.

Bridges, Amy B. *A City in the Republic: Antebellum New York and the Origins of Machine Politics.* New York: Cambridge Univ. Press, 1984.

Brock, William R. *An American Crisis: Congress and Reconstruction, 1865–1867.* New York: Harper & Row, 1963.

Brummer, Sidney D. *Political History of New York State During the Period of the Civil War.* New York: Columbia Univ. Press, 1911.

Callow, Alexander B., Jr. *The Tweed Ring*. New York: Oxford Univ. Press, 1965.

Carpenter, John A. *Sword and Olive Branch: Oliver Otis Howard*. Pittsburgh: Univ. of Pittsburgh Press, 1964.

Castel, Albert. *The Presidency of Andrew Johnson*. Lawrence: Regents Press of Kansas, 1979.

Clancy, Herbert J. *The Presidential Election of 1880*. Chicago: Loyola Univ. Press, 1958.

Cole, Donald C. *Martin Van Buren and the American Political System*. Princeton: Princeton Univ. Press, 1984.

Coleman, Charles H. *The Election of 1868: The Democratic Effort to Regain Control*. New York: Columbia Univ. Press, 1933.

Cook, Adrian. *The Armies of the Streets: The New York City Draft Riots of 1863*. Lexington: Univ. of Kentucky Press, 1974.

Cox, Lawanda, and John H. Cox. *Politics, Principles, and Prejudice 1865–1866: Dilemma of Reconstruction America*. New York: Atheneum, 1969.

Crouthamel, James L. *James Watson Webb: A Biography*. Middletown, Conn.: Wesleyan Univ. Press, 1969.

Dell, Christopher. *Lincoln and the War Democrats: The Erosion of Conservative Tradition*. Rutherford: Fairleigh Dickinson Press, 1975.

Dewey, David R. *Financial History of the United States*. New York: Longmans, Green and Co., 1928.

Donald, David. *Charles Sumner and the Rights of Man*. New York: Alfred A. Knopf, 1970.

Duffy, John R. *A History of Public Health in New York City, 1625–1886*. New York: Russell Sage Foundation, 1968.

Ernst, Robert. *Immigrant Life in New York City, 1825–1863*. New York: Columbia Univ. Press, 1949.

Feder, Leah H. *Unemployment Relief in Periods of Depression: A Study of Measures Adopted in Certain American Cities, 1851 through 1922*. New York: Russell Sage Foundation, 1936.

Fermer, Douglas. *James Gordon Bennett and the New York Herald: A Study of Editorial Opinion in the Civil War Era*. New York: St. Martin's Press, 1986.

Field, Phyllis F. *The Politics of Race in New York: The Struggle for Black Suffrage in the Civil War Era*. Ithaca, N.Y.: Cornell Univ. Press, 1982.

Flick, Alexander C. *Samuel Jones Tilden: A Study in Political Sagacity*. New York: Dodd, Mead & Company, 1939.

Foner, Philip S. *Business and Slavery: The New York Merchants and the Irrepressible Conflict*. Chapel Hill: Univ. of North Carolina Press, 1941.

———. *A History of Cuba and Its Relations with the United States*. 2 vols. New York: International Publishers, 1963.

Foord, John. *The Life and Public Service of Andrew Haskell Green*. Garden City: Doubleday, Page & Company, 1913.

Freeman, Andrew A. *Abraham Lincoln Goes to New York*. New York: Coward-McCann, 1960.

Fuess, Claude M. *The Life and Times of Caleb Cushing*. 2 vols. New York: Harcourt, Brace and Company, 1923.

Furer, Howard. *William Frederick Havemeyer: A Political Biography.* New York: American Press, 1965.

Galloway, George B. *History of the House of Representatives.* New York: Thomas Y. Crowell, 1976.

Gambill, Edward L. *Conservative Ordeal: Northern Democrats and Reconstruction, 1865–1869.* Ames: Iowa State Univ. Press, 1981.

Gibson, Florence E. *The Attitudes of the New York Irish toward State and National Affairs, 1848–1892.* New York: Columbia Univ. Press, 1951.

Gilje, Paul A. *The Road to Mobocracy: Popular Disorder in New York City, 1763–1834.* Chapel Hill: Univ. of North Carolina Press, 1987.

Gillette, William. *Retreat from Reconstruction, 1869–1879.* Baton Rouge: Louisiana State Univ. Press, 1979.

Grossman, Lawrence. *The Democratic Party and the Negro: Northern and National Politics, 1868–92.* Urbana: Univ. of Illinois Press, 1976.

Gunn, L. Ray. *The Decline of Authority: Public Economic Policy and Political Development in New York State, 1800–1860.* Ithaca, N.Y.: Cornell Univ. Press, 1988.

Hamilton, Holman. *Prologue to Conflict: The Crisis and Compromise of 1850.* New York: W. W. Norton & Company, 1966.

Hanchett, William G. *IRISH/Charles G. Halpine in Civil War America.* Syracuse: Syracuse Univ. Press, 1970.

Harrington, Fred H. *Fighting Politician: Major General N. P. Banks.* Westport, Conn.: Greenwood Press, 1970.

Hartog, Hendrik. *Public Property and Private Power: The Corporation of the City of New York in American Law, 1730–1870.* Chapel Hill: Univ. of North Carolina Press, 1983.

Haynes, Frederick E. *James Baird Weaver.* Iowa City: State Historical Society of Iowa, 1919.

Headley, Joel T. *The Great Riots of New York, 1712–1873.* New York: E. B. Treat, 1873.

Hepburn, A. Burton. *History of Coinage and Currency in the United States and the Perennial Contest for Sound Money.* New York: Macmillan, 1903.

Hershkowitz, Leo. *Tweed's New York: Another Look.* New York: Anchor Press, 1977.

Hoogenboom, Ari. *Outlawing the Spoils: A History of the Civil Service Reform Movement, 1865–1883.* Urbana: Univ. of Illinois Press, 1961.

——. *The Presidency of Rutherford B. Hayes.* Lawrence: Regents Press of Kansas, 1988.

Hyman, Harold A. *A More Perfect Union: The Impact of Civil War and Reconstruction on the Constitution.* Boston: Houghton-Mifflin, 1975.

Jenkins, Brian. *Fenians and Anglo-American Relations During Reconstruction.* Ithaca, N.Y.: Cornell Univ. Press, 1969.

Johannsen, Robert W. *Stephen Douglas.* New York: Oxford Univ. Press, 1973.

Jordan, David. *Roscoe Conkling of New York: Voice in the Senate.* Ithaca, N.Y.: Cornell Univ. Press, 1971.

Katz, Irving. *August Belmont: A Political Biography.* New York: Columbia Univ. Press, 1968.

Keller, Morton. *Affairs of State: Public Life in Late Nineteenth Century America.* Cambridge: Belknap Press, 1977.

Klement, Frank L. *The Copperheads in the Middle West*. Chicago: Univ. of Chicago Press, 1960.

——. *The Limits of Dissent: Clement L. Vallandigham and the Civil War*. Lexington: Univ. of Kentucky Press, 1970.

Klein, Philip S. *President James Buchanan*. University Park: Pennsylvania State Univ. Press, 1962.

Knox, John Jay. *A History of Banking in the United States*. New York: Bradford Rhodes & Company, 1900.

Laughlin, J. Laurence. *The History of Bimetallism in the United States*. New York: D. Appleton & Company, 1897.

Lee, Basil Leo. *Discontent in New York City, 1861–1865*. Washington, D.C.: Catholic Univ. Press, 1943.

Leech, Margaret. *Reveille in Washington 1860–1865*. New York: Harper & Brothers, 1941.

Leech, Margaret, and Harry J. Brown. *The Garfield Orbit*. New York: Harper & Row, 1978.

Lindsey, David. *"Sunset" Cox: Irrepressible Democrat*. Detroit: Wayne State Univ. Press, 1959.

Lotchin, Roger W. *San Francisco, 1846–1856: From Hamlet to City*. New York: Oxford Univ. Press, 1974.

Luthin, Reinhard H. *The First Lincoln Campaign*. Cambridge: Harvard Univ. Press, 1944.

Lynch, Dennis T. *"Boss" Tweed: The Story of a Grim Generation*. New York: Boni & Liveright, 1927.

McFeely, William S. *Grant: A Biography*. New York: W. W. Norton & Company, 1981.

McJimsey, George T. *Genteel Partisan: Manton Marble, 1843–1917*. Ames: Iowa State Univ. Press, 1971.

McKitrick, Eric L. *Andrew Johnson and Reconstruction*. Chicago: Univ. of Chicago Press, 1960.

McMahon, William H. *South Jersey Towns: History and Legend*. New Brunswick: Rutgers Univ. Press, 1973.

Mandelbaum, Seymour J. *Boss Tweed's New York*. New York: John Wiley & Sons, 1965.

Mantell, Martin E. *Johnson, Grant, and the Politics of Reconstruction*. New York: Columbia Univ. Press, 1973.

Miller, Wilber R., Jr. *Cops and Bobbies: Police Authority in New York and London, 1830–1879*. Chicago: Univ. of Chicago Press, 1977.

Mitchell, Stewart. *Horatio Seymour of New York*. Cambridge: Harvard Univ. Press, 1938.

Mohr, James C. *The Radical Republicans and Reform in New York during Reconstruction*. Ithaca, N.Y.: Cornell Univ. Press, 1973.

Montgomery, David. *Beyond Equality: Labor and the Radical Republicans, 1862–1872*. New York: Alfred A. Knopf, 1967.

Murphy, James B. *L. Q. C. Lamar: Pragmatic Patriot*. Baton Rouge: Louisiana State Univ. Press, 1983.

Mushkat, Jerome. *Tammany: The Evolution of a Political Machine, 1789–1865*. Syracuse: Syracuse Univ. Press, 1971.

Muzzey, David S. *James G. Blaine: A Political Idol of Other Days*. New York: Dodd, Mead & Company, 1934.

Myers, Gustavus. *The History of Tammany Hall*. New York: Boni & Liveright, 1917.

Myers, Margaret G. *The New York Money Market: Origins and Development*. New York: Columbia Univ. Press, 1931.

Myers, William S. *General George Brinton McClellan: A Study in Personality*. New York: D. Appleton-Century Company, 1934.

Nevins, Allan. *Hamilton Fish: The Inner History of the Grant Administration*. New York: Dodd, Mead & Company, 1936.

Nichols, Roy F. *The Democratic Machine, 1850–1854*. New York: Columbia Univ. Press, 1924.

——. *The Disruption of American Democracy*. New York: Macmillan, 1948.

——. *Franklin Pierce: Young Hickory of the Granite Hills*. Philadelphia: Univ. of Pennsylvania Press, 1931.

Niven, John. *Martin Van Buren: The Romantic Age of American Politics*. New York: Oxford Univ. Press, 1983.

Nugent, Walter T. K. *Money and American Society, 1865–1880*. New York: Free Press, 1968.

——. *The Money Question During Reconstruction*. New York: W. W. Norton & Company, 1967.

Parson, Stanley B., William W. Beach, and Dan Hermann. *United States Congressional Districts, 1788–1841*. Westport, Conn.: Greenwood Press, 1978.

Patterson, Robert T. *Federal-Debt Management Policies, 1865–1879*. Durham, N.C.: Duke Univ. Press, 1954.

Pessen, Edward. *Most Uncommon Jacksonians*. Albany: State Univ. of New York Press, 1961.

——. *Riches, Class, and Power Before the Civil War*. Lexington: D. C. Heath, 1973.

Pleasants, Samuel A. *Fernando Wood of New York*. New York: Columbia Univ. Press, 1948.

Polakoff, Keith I. *The Politics of Inertia: The Election of 1876 and the End of Reconstruction*. Baton Rouge: Louisiana State Univ. Press, 1973.

Pratt, Fletcher. *Stanton: Lincoln's Secretary of War*. New York: W. W. Norton & Company, 1953.

Pred, Allan R. *The Spatial Dynamics of U.S. Urban-Industrial Life*. Cambridge: MIT Press, 1966.

Randall, James. *Lincoln the President, Midstream*. New York: Dodd, Mead & Company, 1953.

Ravitch, Diana. *The Great School Wars: New York City, 1805–1973*. New York: Basic Books, 1974.

Rawley, James A. *The Politics of Union: Northern Politics during the Civil War*. Hinsdale: Dryden Press, 1973.

Rayback, Robert J. *Millard Fillmore: Biography of a President*. Buffalo: Henry Stewart, 1959.

Redlich, Fritz. *The Molding of American Banking: Men and Ideas*. 2 vols. New York: Hafner Publishing Company, 1951.

Richardson, James F. *The New York Police: Colonial Times to 1901*. New York: Oxford Univ. Press, 1970.

Roper, Laura W. *FLO: A Biography of Frederick Law Olmstead*. Baltimore: The Johns Hopkins Press, 1973.

Rosenwaike, Ira. *Population History of New York City*. Syracuse: Syracuse Univ. Press, 1972.

Ross, Earle D. *The Liberal Republican Movement*. New York: Henry Holt and Company, 1919.

Schlesinger, Arthur M., Jr. *The Age of Jackson*. Boston: Little, Brown and Company, 1950.

Scisco, Louis D. *Political Nativism in New York State*. New York: Columbia Univ. Press, 1901.

Sears, Stephen W. *George B. McClellan: The Young Napoleon*. New York: Ticknor & Fields, 1988.

Seip, Terry L. *The South Returns to Congress: Men, Economic Measures, and Intersectional Relationships, 1868–1879*. Baton Rouge: Louisiana State Univ. Press, 1983.

Sharkey, Robert P. *Money, Class, and Party: An Economic Study of Civil War and Reconstruction*. Baltimore: The Johns Hopkins Press, 1959.

Silbey, Joel H. *A Respectable Minority: The Democratic Party in the Civil War Era, 1860–1868*. New York: W. W. Norton & Company, 1977.

——. *The Shrine of Party: Congressional Voting Behavior, 1841–1852*. Pittsburgh: Univ. of Pittsburgh Press, 1967.

Simpson, Craig M. *A Good Southerner: A Life of Henry A. Wise of Virginia*. Chapel Hill: Univ. of North Carolina Press, 1985.

Simpson, John E. *Howell Cobb: The Politics of Ambition*. Chicago: Adams Press, 1973.

Spann, Edward K. *The New Metropolis: New York City, 1840–1857*. New York: Columbia Univ. Press, 1981.

Stansell, Cristine. *City of Women: Sex and Class in New York, 1789–1860*. New York: Alfred A. Knopf, 1986.

Stebbins, Homer A. *A Political History of the State of New York, 1865–1869*. New York: Columbia Univ. Press, 1913.

Stewart, Frank H. *Notes on Old Gloucester County, New Jersey*. Baltimore: Genealogical Publications Company, 1977.

Summers, Mark W. *The Plundering Generation: Corruption and the Crisis of the Union, 1849–1861*. New York: Oxford Univ. Press, 1987.

Swanburg, William A. *Sickles The Incredible*. New York: Charles Scribner's Sons, 1956.

Tate, Merze. *Hawaii: Reciprocity or Annexation*. East Lansing: Michigan State Univ. Press, 1968.

Taussig, Frank W. *The Tariff History of the United States*. New York: G. P. Putnam's Sons, 1931.

Taylor, Joe G. *Louisiana Reconstructed, 1863–1877*. Baton Rouge: Louisiana State Univ. Press, 1974.

Terrill, Tom E. *The Tariff, Politics, and American Foreign Policy, 1874–1901*. Westport, Conn.: Greenwood Press, 1973.

Thayer, William P. *The Life and Letters of John Hay*. 2 vols. Boston: Houghton-Mifflin, 1902.

Thompson, Margaret S. *The "Spider's Web": Congress and Lobbying in the Age of Grant*. Ithaca, N.Y.: Cornell Univ. Press, 1985.

Trefousse, Hans L. *Ben Butler: The South Called Him BEAST!* New York: Twayne Publishers, 1957.

Trelease, Allen W. *White Terror: The Ku Klux Klan Conspiracy and Southern Reconstruction*. New York: Harper & Row, 1971.

Toll, Robert C. *Blacking Up: The Minstrel Show in Nineteenth-Century America*. New York: Oxford Univ. Press, 1974.

Unger, Irwin. *The Greenback Era: A Social and Political History of American Finance, 1865–1879*. Princeton, N.J.: Princeton Univ. Press, 1964.

Van Dusen, Glyndon G. *Thurlow Weed: The Wizard of the Lobby*. Boston: Little, Brown and Company, 1947.

——. *William Henry Seward*. New York: Oxford Univ. Press, 1967.

Weinstein, Allen. *Prelude to Populism: Origins of the Silver Issue, 1867–1878*. New Haven, Conn.: Yale Univ. Press, 1970.

Wells, Damon. *Stephen Douglas: The Last Years, 1857–1861*. Austin: Univ. of Texas Press, 1971.

Wilentz, Sean. *Chants Democratic: New York City and the Rise of the American Working Class, 1788–1850*. New York: Oxford Univ. Press, 1984.

Wood, John S. *An Index of Wood Families in America*. Baltimore: Garrett & Massie, 1966.

Woodward, C. Vann. *Reunion and Reaction: The Compromise of 1877 and the End of Reconstruction*. New York: Doubleday & Company, 1956.

Zornow, William F. *Lincoln and the Party Divided*. Norman: Univ. of Oklahoma Press, 1954.

ARTICLES

Anbinder, Tyler G. "Fernando Wood and New York City's Secession from the Union: A Political Reappraisal." *New York History* 68 (Jan. 1987): 67–92.

Anderson, George L. "The South and Problems of Post–Civil War Finance." *Journal of Southern History* 9 (Aug. 1943): 181–95.

Auchampaugh, Philip G. "The Buchanan-Douglas Feud." *Journal of the Illinois Historical Society* 24 (Apr.–July 1932): 5–48.

Azbug, Robert. "The Copperheads: Historical Approaches to Civil War Dissent." *Indiana Magazine of History* 66 (Mar. 1970): 40–55.

Baker, Jean H. "A Loyal Opposition: Northern Democrats in the Thirty-seventh Congress." *Civil War History* 55 (June 1979): 139–55.

Baum, Dale, and Dale T. Knobel. "Anatomy of a Realignment: New York Presidential Politics, 1848–1860." *New York History* 65 (Jan. 1984): 61–81.

Benedict, Michael Les. "The Rout of Radicalism: Republicans and the Elections of 1867." *Civil War History* 18 (Dec. 1971): 334–44.

——. "Southern Democrats in the Crisis of 1876–1877: A Reconsideration of *Reunion and Reaction.*" *Journal of Southern History* 46 (Nov. 1980): 489–524.

Bonham, Milledge L., Jr. "New York and the Election of 1860." *New York History* 15 (Apr. 1934): 124–43.

Bridges, Amy B. "Plutocracy and Politics in New York City." *Political Science Quarterly* 97 (Spring 1982): 57–71.

Callow, Alexander B., Jr. "'What Are You Going To Do About It?' The Crusade Against the Tweed Ring." *New-York Historical Quarterly* 49 (Apr. 1965): 117–42.

Carleton, William G. "Civil War Dissidence in the North: The Perspective of a Century." *South Atlantic Quarterly* 55 (Summer 1966): 390–402.

Chalmers, Leonard. "Fernando Wood and Tammany Hall: The First Phase." *New-York Historical Society Quarterly* 52 (Oct. 1968): 379–402.

——. "Tammany Hall, Fernando Wood, and the Struggle to Control New York City, 1857–1860." *New-York Historical Society Quarterly* 53 (Jan. 1969): 7–33.

Coben, Stanley. "Northeastern Business and Radical Reconstruction: A Re-examination." *Mississippi Valley Historical Review* 46 (June 1959): 67–90.

Curran, Thomas J. "Seward and the Know-Nothings." *New-York Historical Society Quarterly* 51 (Apr. 1967): 141–59.

Curry, Leonard. "Congressional Democrats, 1861–1863." *Civil War History* 12 (Sept. 1966): 213–29.

Curry, Richard O. "'The Union As It Was': A Critique of Recent Interpretations of the Copperheads." *Civil War History* 13 (Mar. 1967): 23–39.

Degler, Carl. "The Locofocos: Urban 'Agrarians.'" *Journal of Economic History* 16 (Sept. 1956): 322–33.

Downey, Matthew T. "Horace Greeley and the Politicians: The Liberal Republican Convention in 1872." *Journal of American History* 43 (Mar. 1967): 727–50.

Dozer, Donald M. "Opposition to Hawaiian Reciprocity, 1876–1888." *The Pacific Historical Review* 14 (June 1945): 157–83.

Ellis, David. "'Upstate Hicks' Versus 'City Slickers.'" *New-York Historical Society Quarterly* 43 (Apr. 1954): 202–20.

Fitzsimons, Matthew A. "Calhoun's Bid for the Presidency, 1841–1844." *Mississippi Valley Historical Review* 28 (June 1951): 39–60.

Gilfoyle, Timothy, Jr. "Strumpets and Misogynists: 'Brothel Riots' and the Transformation of Prostitution in Antebellum New York City." *New York History* 68 (Jan. 1987): 45–65.

Ginsberg, Judah B. "Barnburners, Free Soilers, and the New York Republican Party." *New York History* 57 (Oct. 1976): 475–500.

Graebner, Norman A. "James K. Polk: A Study in Federal Patronage." *Mississippi Valley Historical Review* 38 (Mar. 1952): 613–32.

Hartman, William. "Custom House Patronage Under Lincoln." *New-York Historical Society Quarterly* 41 (Oct. 1957): 440–57.

——. "The New York City Custom House: The Seats of Spoils Politics." *New York History* 34 (Apr. 1953): 149–63.

Hershkowitz, Leo. "The Loco-Foco Party of New York: Its Origins and Career, 1835–1837." *New York Historical Society Quarterly* 46 (July 1962): 305–29.

Heslin, James. "'Peaceful Compromise' in New York City, 1860–1861." *New-York Historical Society Quarterly* 44 (Oct. 1960): 349–62.

Hirsch, Mark D. "More Light on Boss Tweed." *Political Science Quarterly* 60 (June 1945): 267–78.

——. "Samuel J. Tilden: The Story of a Lost Opportunity." *American Historical Review* 56 (July 1951): 788–802.

House, Albert V., Jr. "Northern Congressional Democrats as Defenders of the South During Reconstruction." *Journal of Southern History* 6 (Feb. 1940): 46–71.

——. "Republicans and Democrats Search for New Identities, 1870–1890." *Review of Politics* 31 (Oct. 1969): 466–76.

——. "The Speakership Contest of 1875: Democratic Response to Power." *Journal of American History* 42 (Sept. 1965): 252–74.

Hubbell, John T. "The Northern Democrats and Party Survival, 1860–1861." *Illinois Quarterly* 36 (Sept. 1973): 22–33.

Hugins, Walter B. "Ely Moore: The Case History of a Jacksonian Labor Leader." *Political Science Quarterly* 65 (Mar. 1950): 105–25.

Huston, James L. "A Political Response to Industrialism: The Republican Embrace of Protectionist Labor Doctrines." *Journal of American History* 70 (June 1983): 35–57.

James, John A. "Financial Underdevelopment in the Post Bellum South." *Journal of Interdisciplinary History* 11 (Winter 1981): 443–54.

Jentz, John B. "The Antislavery Constituency in Jacksonian New York City." *Civil War History* 27 (June 1981): 101–22.

Johnson, Ludwell. "Lincoln's Solution to the Problem of Peace Terms, 1864–1865." *Journal of Southern History* 34 (Nov. 1968): 576–86.

Kiebanow, Diana. "E. L. Godkin, the City, and Civic Responsibility." *New-York Historical Society Quarterly* 50 (Jan. 1971): 52–75.

Kindall, James K. "Economic Factors in Specie Resumption: The United States, 1869–79." *Journal of Political Economy* 69 (Feb. 1961): 30–48.

Klebaner, Benjamin J. "Poverty and Its Relief in American Thought, 1815–1861." *Social Service Review* 38 (Dec. 1964): 382–99.

Krout, John A. "The Maine Law in New York Politics." *New York History* 17 (July 1936): 260–72.

Leonard, Ira M. "The Politics of Charter Revision in New York City, 1845–1847." *New-York Historical Society Quarterly* 62 (Jan. 1978): 43–70.

——. "The Politics of Charter Revision in New York City, 1847–1849." *New-York Historical Society Quarterly* 63 (Jan. 1979): 7–23.

Lerche, Charles O., Jr. "Congressional Interpretations of the Guarantee of a Republican Form of Government during Reconstruction." *Journal of Southern History* 15 (May 1949): 192–211.

Linden, Glenn M. "'Radicals' and Economic Policies: The House of Representatives, 1861–1873." *Civil War History* 13 (Mar. 1967): 51–65.

Lofton, Williston. "Northern Labor and the Negro During the Civil War." *Journal of Negro History* 34 (Oct. 1949): 251–73.

Man, Albon P., Jr. "Labor Competition and the New York Draft Riots of 1863." *Journal of Negro History* 36 (Oct. 1951): 375–405.

Merrill, Louis T. "General Benjamin Franklin Butler in the Presidential Campaign of 1864." *Mississippi Valley Historical Review* 33 (Mar. 1948): 537–70.

Murdock, Eugene C. "Horatio Seymour and the 1863 Draft." *Civil War History* 11 (June 1965): 117–41.

Mushkat, Jerome. "Ben Wood's *Fort Lafayette:* A Source for Studying the Peace Democrats." *Civil War History* 21 (June 1975): 160–71.

Owsley, Harriet C. "Peace and the Presidential Election of 1864." *Tennessee Historical Quarterly* 17 (Mar. 1959): 3–19.

Perman, Michael. "The South and Congress's Reconstruction Policy, 1866–67." *Journal of American Studies* 4 (Feb. 1971): 181–200.

Peskin, Allan. "Was There a Compromise of 1877?" *Journal of American History* 60 (June 1973): 63–75.

Pessen, Edward. "The Egalitarian Myth and American Social Reality: Wealth, Mobility, and Equality in the 'Era of the Common Man.'" *American Historical Review* 76 (Oct. 1971): 989–1034.

——. "The Wealthiest New Yorkers of the Jacksonian Era." *New-York Historical Society Quarterly* 54 (Apr. 1970): 145–72.

——. "Who Governed the Nation's Cities in the 'Era of the Common Man'?" *Political Science Quarterly* 87 (Dec. 1972): 591–614.

——. "Who Has Power in the Democratic Capitalistic Community? Reflections on Antebellum New York City." *New York History* 58 (Apr. 1977): 129–54.

Rable, George C. "Southern Interests and the Election of 1876: A Reappraisal." *Civil War History* 26 (Dec. 1980): 347–61.

"Radicalism." *The United States Magazine and Democratic Review* 3 (Oct. 1839): 99–111.

Rezneck, Samuel. "The Influence of Depression Upon American Public Opinion." *Journal of Economic History* 2 (May 1942): 1–23.

Richardson, James F. "Mayor Fernando Wood and the New York Police Force, 1855–1857." *New-York Historical Society Quarterly* 50 (Jan. 1966): 5–40.

Rorabaugh, William J. "Rising Spirits: Immigrants, Temperance, and Tammany Hall." *Civil War History* 22 (June 1976): 139–57.

Ross, Earle D. "Samuel Jones Tilden and the Revival of the Democratic Party." *South Atlantic Quarterly* 19 (Jan. 1920): 43–54.

Russ, William, Jr. "Registration and Disfranchisement under Radical Reconstruction." *Mississippi Valley Historical Review* 21 (Sept. 1934): 163–80.

Saxton, Alexander. "George Wilkes: The Transformation of a Radical Ideology." *American Quarterly* 33 (Fall 1981): 437–58.

Schell, Herbert S. "Hugh McCulloch and the Treasury Department, 1865–1869." *Mississippi Valley Historical Review* 17 (Dec. 1930): 404–21.

Sears, Louis. "New York and the Fusion Movement of 1860." *Journal of the Illinois Historical Society* 16 (Apr.–July 1923): 58–62.

Shipley, Max L. "The Background and Legal Aspects of the Pendleton Plan." *Mississippi Valley Historical Review* 24 (Sept. 1937): 329–40.

Shofner, Jerrell H. "Florida Courts and the Disrupted Election of 1876." *Florida Historical Quarterly* 48 (July 1969): 24–46.

Spann, Edward K. "Gotham in Congress: New York's Representatives and the National Government, 1840–1854." *New York History* 57 (July 1986): 305–28.

Staudenraus, P. J. "The Popular Origins of the Thirteenth Amendment." *Mid-America* 50 (Apr. 1968): 108–15.

Stewart, Ian R. "Politics and the Park: The Fight for Central Park." *New-York Historical Society Quarterly* 61 (July–Oct. 1977): 124–55.

Summers, Mark W. "'A Band of Brigands': Albany Lawmakers and Republican National Politics, 1860." *Civil War History* 30 (June 1984): 101–19.

Swinney, Everette. "Enforcing the Fifteenth Amendment, 1870–1877." *Journal of Southern History* 28 (May 1962): 202–18.

Terrill, Tom E. "David A. Wells, The Democracy, and Tariff Reduction." *Journal of American History* 46 (Dec. 1969): 540–55.

Timberlake, Richard H., Jr. "Ideological Factors in Specie Resumption and Treasury Policy." *Journal of Economic History* 24 (Mar. 1964): 29–52.

Trimble, William. "Diverging Tendencies in the New York Democracy in the Period of the Locofocos." *American Historical Review* 24 (Apr. 1919): 396–421.

——. "The Social Philosophy of the Loco-Foco Democracy." *American Journal of Sociology* 26 (May 1921): 705–21.

Unger, Irwin. "Businessmen and Specie Resumption." *Political Science Quarterly* 74 (Mar. 1959): 46–70.

Wagstaff, Thomas. "The Arm-in-Arm Convention." *Civil War History* 14 (June 1968): 101–19.

Weinbaum, Paul O. "Temperance, Politics, and the New York City Riots of 1857." *New-York Historical Society Quarterly* 59 (July 1975): 246–70.

Wilson, Charles R. "McClellan's Changing Views on the Peace Plank of 1864." *American Historical Review* 38 (Apr. 1933): 498–505.

Winther, Oscar O. "The Soldier Vote in the Election of 1864." *NYH* 25 (Oct. 1944): 440–58.

Zornow, William F. "Clement L. Vallandigham and the Democratic Party in 1864." *Historical and Philosophic Society of Ohio* 29 (Jan. 1961): 21–37.

——. "McClellan and Seymour in the Chicago Convention." *Journal of the Illinois Historical Society* 43 (Winter 1950): 282–95.

UNPUBLISHED DISSERTATIONS

Hemmer, Joseph J., Jr. "The Democratic National Conventions of 1860: Discourse of Disruption in Rhetorical-Historical Perspective." Ph.D. diss., University of Wisconsin, 1969.

Long, David A. "*The New York Daily News,* 1855–1906: Spokesman for the Underprivileged." Ph.D. diss., Columbia University, 1950.

McCarthy, John L. "Reconstruction Legislation and Voting Alignments in the House of Representatives, 1863–1869." Ph.D. diss., Yale University, 1970.

INDEX

313

DATE DUE